# PROSECUTING SEXUAL AND GENDER-BASED CRIMES AT THE INTERNATIONAL CRIMINAL COURT

The 1998 Rome Statute, the treaty … minal Court (ICC), includes a longer l… es than any previous instrument of internationa…

The Statute's twentieth anniversary provides an opportunity to examine how successful the ICC has been in prosecuting gender-based crimes, what challenges it has faced and how its case law on these crimes might develop in future.

Taking up that opportunity, this book analyses the ICC's practice in prosecuting gender-based crimes across all war crimes cases, crimes against humanity and genocide in the ICC up until mid-2018. This analysis is based upon a detailed examination of court records and original interviews with prosecutors and gender experts at the Court.

This book covers topics of emerging interest to practitioners in this field, including wartime sexual violence against men and boys, persecution on the grounds of gender and sexual orientation and sexual violence against 'child soldiers'.

DR ROSEMARY GREY is a University of Sydney Postdoctoral Fellow, based in the Sydney Law School and Sydney Southeast Asia Centre. Her research focuses on gender and international criminal law. She has consulted and interned for Amnesty International, Women's Initiatives for Gender Justice, the International Bar Association and the International Criminal Court. From 2016 to 2018, she completed a postdoctoral fellowship at Melbourne Law School, where she co-taught the International Criminal Justice Clinic, and was a visiting scholar at the Grotius Centre for International Legal Studies (Leiden) and PluriCourts (Oslo).

CAMBRIDGE STUDIES IN INTERNATIONAL AND COMPARATIVE LAW: 143

Established in 1946, this series produces high quality, reflective and innovative scholarship in the field of public international law. It publishes works on international law that are of a theoretical, historical, cross-disciplinary or doctrinal nature. The series also welcomes books providing insights from private international law, comparative law and transnational studies which inform international legal thought and practice more generally.

The series seeks to publish views from diverse legal traditions and perspectives, and of any geographical origin. In this respect, it invites studies offering regional perspectives on core *problématiques* of international law, and in the same vein, it appreciates contrasts and debates between diverging approaches. Accordingly, books offering new or less orthodox perspectives are very much welcome. Works of a generalist character are greatly valued and the series is also open to studies on specific areas, institutions or problems. Translations of the most outstanding works published in other languages are also considered.

After seventy years, Cambridge Studies in International and Comparative Law sets the standard for international legal scholarship and will continue to define the discipline as it evolves in the years to come.



A list of books in the series can be found at the end of this volume.

# PROSECUTING SEXUAL AND GENDER-BASED CRIMES AT THE INTERNATIONAL CRIMINAL COURT

## Practice, Progress and Potential

ROSEMARY GREY

*University of Sydney*

**CAMBRIDGE**
**UNIVERSITY PRESS**

University Printing House, Cambridge CB2 8BS, United Kingdom

One Liberty Plaza, 20th Floor, New York, NY 10006, USA

477 Williamstown Road, Port Melbourne, VIC 3207, Australia

314-321, 3rd Floor, Plot 3, Splendor Forum, Jasola District Centre, New Delhi - 110025, India

79 Anson Road, #06-04/06, Singapore 079906

Cambridge University Press is part of the University of Cambridge.

It furthers the University's mission by disseminating knowledge in the pursuit of education, learning and research at the highest international levels of excellence.

www.cambridge.org
Information on this title: www.cambridge.org/9781108455985
DOI: 10.1017/9781108652346



First published 2019
First paperback edition 2020

*A catalogue record for this publication is available from the British Library*

ISBN 978-1-108-47043-8 Hardback
ISBN 978-1-108-45598-5 Paperback

To my grandparents, parents, sister, brothers
and brothers-in-law, and my love

Your support made this book possible

CONTENTS

# FIGURES

# TABLES

# ACKNOWLEDGEMENTS

I thank my hosts and colleagues at the places where I wrote this book: at Melbourne Law School and Sydney Law School, my two institutional 'homes'; at the Grotius Centre for International Legal Studies (Leiden) and at Pluricourts (Oslo), where I was welcomed as a visiting scholar; and at the Peace Palace library in The Hague, where I have enjoyed many writing spells over the years.

Among the many people whose input has enriched this book, there are several people to whom I owe particular thanks.

For their feedback, advice and inspirational scholarship, I thank my mentor at the University of Melbourne, Professor Hilary Charlesworth and my (then) PhD supervisors at the University of New South Wales, Professor Louise Chappell and Professor Sarah Williams. I also thank my PhD examiners, Professor Valerie Oosterveld at the University of Western Ontario and Professor Fiona Mackay at the University of Edinburgh, for their insightful comments on my thesis.

For their time and perspectives, I thank all of my interviewees at the International Criminal Court. I also thank staff of the Office of the Prosecutor who assisted with organising interviews and who engaged with my research, especially Hans Bevers, Helen Brady, Matthew Cross, Benjamin Gumpert and Annie O'Reilly.

For their input on draft sections of the book, I thank Professor Andreas Føllesdal and Professor Geir Ulfstein at the University of Oslo; Dr Maria Elander at La Trobe University; Dr Emma Irving at Leiden University; Dr Lucas Lixinski at the University of New South Wales; Dr Simon McKenzie at the University of Melbourne; Dr Emma Palmer at Griffith University; Professor Laurajane Smith at the Australian National Universit; Melinda Reed and Siobhan Hobbs of Women's Initiatives for Gender Justice; and Jonathan O'Donohue, Chiara Loiero and Dorine Llanta of Amnesty International.

For their guidance throughout the writing process, I thank Professor Michelle Foster, Professor Matthew Harding, Professor Tim McCormack,

Professor Jenny Morgan, Professor Anne Orford, Professor Bruce Oswald, Professor Dianne Otto and Professor Sundhya Pahuja at the University of Melbourne; Professor Emily Crawford at the University of Sydney; and Professor Andrea Durbach at the University of New South Wales.

For their professionalism and assistance, I thank my editors at Cambridge University Press.

For their collegiality and good humour, I thank Dr Ashley Barnwell, Dr Annie Blatchford, Dr Monique Cormier, Dr Kobi Leins, Dr Florence Seow, Dr Elizabeth Sheargold, Dr Christoph Sperfeldt and Dr Braidais York at the University of Melbourne; Dr Thea Coventry, Dr Kushtrim Istrefi and Dr Cale Davis at Leiden University; Dr Alexandra Grey at the University of Sydney; Dr Scott McBride at the University of New South Wales; and Dr Sophie Rigney at the University of Dundee.

For friendships made through a shared interest in international criminal law, I thank Dr Dieneke de Vos, Dr Amrita Kapur, Maria Radziejowska, Zane Ratniece, Isabel Robinson, Rens van der Werf and Nuria Vehils.

For the hospitality in their homes, which enabled me to conduct my research within available means, I thank Vid and Amel in Leiden; my parents, Sally, Alex, and Dave in Sydney; and Ed, Chad, Mechelle, Beckett, Ash, and Joe in Melbourne.

The opinions expressed in this book are, of course, my own.

This book contains descriptions of violence, including sexual violence.

# ABBREVIATIONS

| | |
|---|---|
| AQIM | Al Qaeda in the Maghreb |
| CAR | Central African Republic |
| DCC | Document Containing the Charges |
| DRC | Democratic Republic of Congo |
| ECCC | Extraordinary Chambers in the Courts of Cambodia |
| ECtHR | European Court of Human Rights |
| EoC | ICC Elements of Crimes |
| FDLR | Forces Démocratiques pour la Liberation du Rwanda |
| FIDH | Fédération Internationale des Ligues des Droits de l'Homme |
| FNI | Front des Nationalistes et Intégrationnistes |
| FRPI | Force de Résistance Patriotique en Ituri |
| IACtHR | Inter-American Court of Human Rights |
| ICC | International Criminal Court |
| ICCPR | International Covenant on Civil and Political Rights |
| ICTR | International Criminal Tribunal for Rwanda |
| ICTY | International Criminal Tribunal for the Former Yugoslavia |
| IDP | Internally Displaced Persons |
| IHL | International Humanitarian Law |
| ILC | International Law Commission |
| IWPR | Institute for War and Peace Reporting |
| LGBTIQ | Lesbian, gay, bisexual, transgender, intersex and/or queer |
| LRA | Lord's Resistance Army |
| MLC | Mouvement de Libération du Congo |
| NGO | Non-governmental organisation |
| OPCD | Office of Public Counsel for the Defence |
| OPCV | Office of Public Counsel for Victims |
| OTP | Office of the Prosecutor |
| RPE | ICC Rules of Procedure and Evidence |
| RS | Rome Statute |
| SCSL | Special Court for Sierra Leone |
| UK | United Kingdom |

| | |
|---|---|
| UN | United Nations |
| UNESCO | UN Educational, Scientific and Cultural Organization |
| UNICEF | UN Children's Fund |
| UPC | Union des Patriotes Congolais |
| US | United States of America |

# 1

# Seeing Gender amid 'Unimaginable Atrocities'

## 1.1 Introduction

As the first permanent international body with power to try individuals for war crimes, crimes against humanity, genocide and aggression, the International Criminal Court (ICC) has a unique place in the crowd of international courts and tribunals established since World War II. The preamble of its founding instrument, the 1998 Rome Statute, sets out the hopes and fears that led to the Court's creation. It recognises that the twentieth century was scarred by 'unimaginable atrocities that deeply shock the conscience of humanity', affirms that 'the most serious crimes of concern to the international community as a whole must not go unpunished' and vows to 'put an end to impunity for the perpetrators of these crimes and thus to contribute to [their] prevention'.[1]

Entering the ICC premises, now based in six gleaming towers near the flock of embassies and international institutions in The Hague, 'unimaginable atrocities' are not the first image that springs to mind. The immediate impression is of cosmopolitanism and order: flags of 123 nations in the foyer; staff of diverse nationalities; security checks at the doors. There is no sound of gunfire; no wailing infants or shouting soldiers; no obvious trace of conflict, terror and pain. Yet piece by piece, over the course of cases that can last over a decade, those are the scenes that emerge from witness testimony and documentary evidence, from the filings of the parties and participants and from the judgments of the Court.

In almost all of those cases, there is evidence of the commission of gender-based crimes, such as rape, sexual slavery, sexualised torture and sex-selective massacres, to name a few.[2] The same was true of ad hoc international criminal courts that preceded the ICC. Yet until recently,

[1] Preamble, Rome Statute of the International Criminal Court ('RS'), Rome, 17 July 1998, 2187 UNTS 90 (entered into force 1 July 2002) ('RS').

[2] The meaning of the term 'gender-based crime' is discussed further in Chapter 2.

gender-based crimes were almost entirely invisible in instruments of international criminal law and were seldom charged in international criminal courts. In particular, crimes of sexual violence – which in most conflicts are committed primarily against women and girls – were largely ignored. Reflecting on this fact in 2000, feminist scholar Rhonda Copelon stated:

> Before the 1990s, sexual violence in war was, with rare exception, largely invisible. If not invisible, it was trivialized; if not trivialized, it was considered a private matter or justified as an inevitable by-product of war, the necessary reward for the fighting men.[3]

To explain this critique, Copelon highlighted the inattention to gender-based crimes in early treaties on the laws of war, the silences around these crimes in trials before the Nuremberg and Tokyo Tribunals in the 1940s and the absence of charges for the rape of women in early cases before the International Criminal Tribunal for the former Yugoslavia (ICTY) and International Criminal Tribunal for Rwanda (ICTR) in the 1990s.[4] She was by no means alone in making this critique; in the late 1990s and early 2000s, numerous feminist scholars and activists lamented the historic marginalisation of gender-based crimes in international criminal law.[5]

Looking at this field today, particularly if one looks only at the statutes, rules and policies of international and semi-international criminal courts, it is tempting to think that these critiques belong to the past. After being overlooked or not taken seriously for centuries, gender-based crimes are now expressly criminalised in international instruments and frequently charged in international criminal courts. In particular, crimes of sexual violence are almost universally perceived as crimes of serious

[3] R. Copelon, 'Gender Crimes as War Crimes: Integrating Crimes against Women into International Criminal Law' (2000) 46 *McGill Law Journal* 217, 220.

[4] Ibid., 220–230.

[5] See K. Askin, *War Crimes Against Women: Prosecution in International War Crimes Tribunals* (Martinus Nijhoff, 1997); H. Charlesworth and C. Chinkin, *The Boundaries of International Law: A Feminist Analysis* (Manchester University Press, 2000) 10; S. Chesterman, 'Never Again ... and Again: Law, Order, and the Gender of War Crimes in Bosnia and Beyond' (1997) 22 *Yale Journal of International Law* 299; S. SáCouto and K. Cleary, 'The Importance of Effective Investigation of Sexual Violence and Gender Based Crimes at the International Criminal Court' (2009) 17(2) *American University Journal of Gender, Social Policy & the Law* 337; P.V. Sellers, 'Gender Strategy Is Not Luxury for International Courts' (2009) 17(2) *American University Journal of Gender, Social Policy & the Law* 301; B. Van Schaack, 'Obstacles on the Road to Gender Justice: The International Criminal Tribunal for Rwanda as Object Lesson' (2009) 17(2) *American University Journal of Gender, Social Policy & the Law* 362.

concern to the international community as a whole.[6] These changes, along with the increased number of women in roles previously dominated by men, the introduction of more gender-sensitive investigative strategies and related changes to rules of procedure and evidence, are the results of a decades-long process of making international criminal law more inclusive, less male oriented and more sensitive to socially constructed gender norms.

A turning point in this reform process was the adoption of the Rome Statute on 17 July 1998. It was a time when sexual violence was emerging as a key theme in cases before the ICTY and ICTR,[7] and feminist scholars were starting to elevate the concept of *gender*, as a social construct, in international criminal law.[8] In this climate, women's rights activists, working together with delegates from like-minded states, lobbied hard to create a gender-sensitive ICC. Their efforts met some resistance, because proposals to give the Court jurisdiction over certain crimes (most notably, forced pregnancy and gender-based persecution) clashed with widely held cultural and religious beliefs.[9] Nonetheless, efforts to create

[6] E.g. RS, Art. 7(1)(g), 8(2)(c)(xxii) and 8(2)(e)(vi); Statute of the Special Court for Sierra Leone ('SCSL Statute'), adopted 16 January 2002, 2178 UNTS 145 (entered into force 12 April 2002), Art. 2(g); 3(e); 'Crimes against Humanity: Texts and Titles of the Draft Preamble, the Draft Articles and the Draft Annex Provisionally Adopted by the Drafting Committee on First Reading, UN Doc A/CN.4/L.892' (26 May 2017) Art. 3(g), 3(h).

[7] See: K. Askin, 'Prosecuting Wartime Rape and Other Gender Related Crimes: Extraordinary Advances, Enduring Obstacles' (2003) 21(2) *Berkeley Journal of International Law* 288; S. Brammertz and M. Jarvis (eds), *Prosecuting Conflict-related Sexual Violence in the ICTY* (Oxford University Press, 2016); H. Brady, 'The Power of Precedents: Using the Case Law of the Ad Hoc International Criminal Tribunals and Hybrid Courts in Adjudicating Sexual and Gender-Based Crimes at the ICC' (2012) 18(2) *Australian Journal of Human Rights* 75; A. de Brouwer, *Supranational Criminal Prosecution of Sexual Violence: The ICC and the Practice of the ICTY and ICTR* (Intersentia, 2005).

[8] E.g. R. Copelon, 'Surfacing Gender: Re-Engraving Crimes against Women in Humanitarian Law' (1994) 5 *Hastings Women's Law Journal* 243; C. Niarchos, 'Women, War, and Rape: Challenges Facing the International Tribunal for the Former Yugoslavia' (1995) 17(4) *Human Rights Quarterly* 629.

[9] Copelon, see n. 3, 233–239; L. Chappell, *The Politics of Gender Justice at the International Criminal Court: Legacies and Legitimacy* (Oxford University Press, 2016) Ch. 4; V. Oosterveld, 'The Definition of Gender in the Rome Statute of the International Criminal Court: A Step Forward or Back for International Criminal Justice?' (2005) 18 *Harvard Human Rights Journal* 55; C. Steains, 'Gender Issues' in R.S. Lee (ed.), *The International Criminal Court: The Making of the Rome Statute* (Kluwer Law International, 1999) 357; P. Kirsch and J.T. Holmes, 'The Birth of the International Criminal Court: The 1998 Rome Conference' in O. Bekou and R. Cryer (eds), *The International Criminal Court* (Ashgate, 2004) 3, 15.

a gender-sensitive ICC were largely successful: the Rome Statute enumerates a wider range of gender-based crimes than any previous instrument of international criminal tribunal; requires that victims of these crimes be treated with sensitivity and respect; encourages a fair representation of male and female judges; affirms the value of gender expertise in the judiciary, the Office of the Prosecutor (OTP) and the Registry; and requires the Court to interpret and apply the law without adverse discrimination on gender grounds.[10]

Feminist scholars and activists who applauded these features of the Rome Statute were aware that there was still much work to be done. They knew that the inclusion of gender-based crimes in the ICC's legal framework did not *guarantee* that these crimes would be effectively investigated and prosecuted in practice.[11] Yet, because of the long-running silence around these crimes in international criminal law, many feminist scholars and activists viewed the Rome Statute as a 'step forward'. They were relieved that the Statute affirmed the seriousness of gender-based crimes, gave the ICC Prosecutor a clear mandate to investigate and prosecute those crimes and set standards for national jurisdictions to follow.[12] As argued by Barbara Bedont and Katherine Hall-Martinez, both of whom participated in the Rome Statute negotiations as part of the Women's Caucus for Gender Justice:

> No treaty or court judgment can remedy the suffering of wartime victims of rape, forced pregnancy, and other sexual violence, or undo society's gender constructs that so cruelly multiply their suffering to include shame and guilt. Yet the codification of a mandate to end impunity for these acts is a significant step in the right direction. It was high time that such crimes cease to be regarded as the 'inevitable by-products of war' and receive the serious attention that they deserve.[13]

[10] V. Oosterveld, 'The Making of a Gender-Sensitive International Criminal Court' (1999) 1(1) *International Law Forum du Droit International* 38, 41.

[11] E.g. Copelon, see n. 3, 329.

[12] Askin, 'Prosecuting Wartime Rape', see n. 7; Chappell, *The Politics of Gender Justice*, see n. 9, 1; Copelon, see n. 3; A. Facio, 'All Roads Lead to Rome, But Some Are Bumpier than Others' in S. Pickering and C. Lambert (eds), *Global Issues: Women and Justice* (Sydney Institute for Criminology, 2004) 308, 333; R. Lehr-Lehnardt, 'One Small Step for Women: Female-Friendly Provisions in the Rome Statute of the International Criminal Court' (2002) 16(2) *Brigham Young University Journal of Public Law* 317; Oosterveld, 'A Gender-Sensitive ICC', see n. 10.

[13] B. Bedont and K. Hall-Martinez, 'Ending Impunity for Gender Crimes Under the International Criminal Court' (1999) 6(1) *Brown Journal of World Affairs* 65, 80.

Following the Rome Statute's entry into force on 1 July 2002 and the start of its first Prosecutor's term in June 2003, the focus of feminist scholarship on the ICC has shifted from the 'law on the books' to the implementation of that law in specific cases before the Court. In particular, there has been a wealth of feminist scholarship on the ICC's first four trials, *Lubanga, Ngudjolo, Katanga* and *Bemba*, all of which involved allegations of sexual violence crimes, but none of which resulted in a final conviction for those crimes.[14] Non-government organisations (NGOs) have also closely monitored the ICC's investigations and prosecutions and have often called for greater attention to gender-based crimes. A particularly active group has been the Women's Initiatives for Gender Justice, with larger NGOs such as Amnesty International and Human Rights Watch also advocating on gender themes.

The twentieth anniversary of the Rome Statute presents an opportunity to enter into the discussion about the ICC's practice in prosecuting gender-based crimes, to reflect on how that practice has evolved during the terms of its first two Prosecutors and to consider how the Court might make full use of its progressive legal framework in future prosecutions for gender-based crimes. Those are the motivations for this book, which – based on an examination of court records, as well as interviews with officials and advisors of the ICC – analyses the ICC's practice in prosecuting gender-based crimes up until the date of the twentieth anniversary on

[14] E.g. Chappell, *The Politics of Gender Justice*, see n. 9, 4; L. Chappell, 'Conflicting Institutions and the Search for Gender Justice at the International Criminal Court' (2014) 67(1) *Political Research Quarterly* 183; L. Chappell, 'The Gender Injustice Cascade: "Transformative" Reparations for Victims of Sexual and Gender-Based Crimes in the Lubanga Case at the International Criminal Court' (2017) 21(9) *International Journal of Human Rights* 1223; M. D'Aoust, 'Sexual and Gender-Based Violence in International Criminal Law: A Feminist Assessment of the Bemba Case' (2017) 17(1) *International Criminal Law Review* 208; D. De Vos, 'A Day to Remember: Ongwen's Trial Starts on 6 December' on *Int Law Grrls* (5 December 2016); N. Hayes, 'Sisyphus Wept: Prosecuting Sexual Violence at the International Criminal Court' in W. Schabas, Y. McDermott and N. Hayes (eds), *The Ashgate Research Companion to International Criminal Law* (Ashgate, 2013) 7; N. Hayes, 'La Lutte Continue: Investigating and Prosecuting Sexual Violence at the ICC' in C. Stahn (ed.), *The Law and Practice of the International Criminal Court* (Oxford University Press, 2015) 801; K. O'Smith, 'Prosecutor v. Lubanga: How the International Criminal Court Failed the Women and Girls of the Congo' (2013) 54(2) *Howard Law Journal* 467; S. SáCouto, 'The Impact of the Appeals Chamber Decision in Bemba: Impunity for Sexual and Gender-Based Crimes?' on *International Justice Monitor* (22 June 2018).

17 July 2018.[15] The book is forward-looking, in the sense of contemplating new and untested interpretations of the Rome Statute. However, throughout the book, history is never far away. In particular, the history of international criminal law is used to understand how far the ICC has come in terms of prosecuting gender-based crimes and how habits of thinking and operating that impeded accountability for these crimes in the past – habits that Louise Chappell has called 'gender legacies' – linger in this new court.[16]

The ICC has been the focus of my research since 2010, when the Court sat in a former office block in The Hague's outer suburbs and was in the throes of its first trial, against Democratic Republic of Congo militia leader Thomas Lubanga Dyilo. Much has changed since that case, in which the (then) Prosecutor, Luis Moreno-Ocampo, was widely criticised for not bringing any charges of gender based crimes.[17] Final judgment has now been rendered in five cases: a small sample, but not too small to identify patterns, shifts and 'lessons learned'. The first Prosecutor completed his term in June 2012 and his successor, former Deputy Prosecutor Fatou Bensouda, has singled out accountability for gender-based crimes as a key priority during her term.[18] In 2014, her Office published its *Policy Paper on Sexual and Gender-Based Crimes ('Gender Policy')*, which commits to 'integrating a gender perspective and analysis into all of its work' and 'being innovative in the investigation and prosecution of these crimes'.[19] The Court has made some important contributions to the jurisprudence on gender-based crimes, particularly those committed against 'child soldiers'.[20] Most importantly, an

[15] These 24 cases are identified in §1.2.1.

[16] Chappell, *The Politics of Gender Justice*, see n. 9.

[17] See Chapter 4, §4.1.1.

[18] F. Bensouda, 'Statement' (at the ceremony for the solemn undertaking of the Prosecutor of the International Criminal Court, The Hague, 15 June 2012); ICC OTP, 'Strategic Plan June 2012–2015' (11 October 2013) 27; ICC OTP, 'Strategic Plan 2016–2018' (16 November 2015) 19–20.

[19] ICC OTP, 'Policy Paper on Sexual and Gender-Based Crimes' (June 2014), [5], [14], [21], [27], [37], [53], [103], [111].

[20] The term 'child soldier' is not used in the Rome Statute. Nonetheless, it is used widely in ICC filings and decisions to describe a person aged fifteen or younger who has allegedly been conscripted or enlisted into an armed force or group, or used to participate actively in hostilities. For brevity, the term 'child soldier' is adopted in this book. However, the quotation marks are retained to avoid normalising the idea of child combatants and to stress the fact that militarising a child in the way described above is illegal: it is prohibited under IHL and amounts to war crimes under the Rome Statute. The quotation marks are my way of acknowledging these points, without the need for lengthy caveats every time the term is used.

examination of gender-based crimes has now become routine: these crimes have been identified in numerous ICC preliminary examinations[21] and charged in multiple cases, including the three in trial when I returned to The Hague in 2017 and 2018 to conduct interviews for this book.

The first of those trials concerned Dominic Ongwen, a Ugandan ex-'child soldier' turned rebel commander, who has been charged (among other things) with forced pregnancy and forced marriage, neither of which has previously been tried in the ICC. In the next courtroom were former Côte d'Ivoire president Laurent Gbagbo and his ally Charles Blé Goudé, both on trial for rape and other crimes against humanity allegedly committed in the wake of Côte d'Ivoire's 2010 presidential election. In the third was Bosco Ntaganda, a former commander of the same armed group that was the focus of the *Lubanga* case. Yet, unlike his once co-accused Thomas Lubanga, Ntaganda has been charged with a range of gender-based crimes, including the rape of girls who were allegedly recruited for use as fighters, 'wives' and sex slaves by troops under his command. These cases show that gender-based crimes are on the radar of the OTP, and as a result, of the Court as a whole.

Yet, over the course of this study, there have also been some serious setbacks in the ICC's practice in prosecuting gender-based crimes. At times, the evidence to support these crimes has been weak, or has been introduced too late in the proceedings. In addition, the OTP appears to have missed some opportunities to prosecute gender-based crimes, including the newly codified crime of gender-based persecution and several documented examples of sexual violence crimes.[22] Criticism of this nature was directed at the first Prosecutor in particular,[23] including, in some instances, by judges of the Court.[24] At other times, the judges seem to have been part of the problem. On several occasions, they have underestimated the gravity of sexual violence crimes, misunderstood the sexual character of violence directed at men and boys or found – without clear reasons – that rape is more difficult to attribute to the leaders of armed groups than other common wartime offences.[25] The combined result is that, twenty years after the ICC was established, accountability

[21] E.g. ICC OTP, 'Report on Preliminary Examination Activities 2017' (4 December 2017).

[22] See Chapter 5.

[23] E.g. Chappell, *The Politics of Gender Justice*, see n. 9, 4; Hayes, 'Sisyphus Wept', see n. 14; O'Smith, see n. 14.

[24] E.g. *Lubanga* (ICC-01/04-01/06-2901), 10 July 2012, [60].

[25] See Chapter 5.

for gender-based crimes in this court remains elusive. To be sure, we have come a long way since the 1990s, when experts were still debating basic questions such as whether sexual violence could be a 'grave breach' of the Geneva Conventions[26] and/or an act of torture,[27] and whether it was accurate to describe rape as a 'a forgotten war crime'.[28] And yet, in ICC cases, gender-based crimes have less likely been established than other crimes at every stage of proceedings, culminating in a total of zero convictions for gender-based crimes as of 17 July 2018.[29] That figure suggests that, despite its progressive legal framework, the ICC is not insulated from the practices and misperceptions that contributed to impunity for gender-based crimes in the past.

Seeing how those practices and misperceptions continue to manifest in ICC cases can be difficult because the proceedings are long, complex and technical. Providing a clear and accessible commentary on the ICC's practice in prosecuting gender-based crimes, so that interested scholars, practitioners and observers can better understand this aspect of the Court's work, is therefore the first aim of this book. The second aim is to analyse this aspect of the ICC's practice from a 'feminist perspective', which as explained subsequently, means being interested in the experiences of marginalised groups, conscious of gender hierarchies, attentive to intersections between gender and other identities, and wary of the 'hidden gender' of the law. Third, the book explores avenues for advancing the ICC's jurisprudence on gender-based crimes in the decades to come. In this respect, the book seeks to contribute to emerging feminist jurisprudence in international law.[30]

The book's assessment of the ICC's practice in prosecuting gender-based crimes is not rose-tinted, but it is cautiously optimistic. This optimism is grounded in a detailed analysis of the ICC's case law, which shows

[26] See K. Askin, 'Katanga Judgment Underlines Need for Stronger ICC Focus on Sexual Violence' on *Open Society Foundations* (11 March 2014).

[27] Copelon, see n. 8, 248–257; M. Jarvis and N. Nabti, 'Policies and Institutional Strategies for Successful Sexual Violence Prosecutions' in S. Brammertz and M. Jarvis (eds), *Prosecuting Conflict-related Sexual Violence at the ICTY* (Oxford University Press, 2016) 73, 92–93.

[28] See R. Seifert, 'War and Rape: A Preliminary Analysis' in A. Stiglmayer (ed.), *Mass Rape: The War Against Women in Bosnia-Herzegovina* (University of Nebraska Press, 1994) 54, 69.

[29] See Chapter 5.

[30] The concept of 'feminist jurisprudence' is explored further in Chapter 6. For examples in international law, see Y. Brunger et al., 'Prosecutor v. Thomas Lubanga Dyilo: International Criminal Court' in L. Hodson and T. Lavers (eds), *Feminist Judgments in International Law* (Hart Publishing, forthcoming).

that despite the startling 'zero convictions' figure, progress is being made: the OTP has become more effective at prosecuting these crimes, charges are starting to reflect a wide variety of gender-based crimes against males and females, and the Court has made some positive contributions to the international jurisprudence on gender-based crimes. Of course, prosecuting gender-based crimes in conflict or post-conflict settings is an inherently challenging task, and it will continue to be so. Yet, slowly, through the hard work of people within and around the Court, these challenges are being overcome. As a result, the ICC is starting to reach its potential as a tool for strengthening accountability for gender-based crimes and showing the gendered face of conflict to the world.

That said, there are limits to the Court's potential in this regard that cannot be resolved by the implementation of new policies or by shifts in practice alone. While this book does not focus on these limits, I want to acknowledge them here at the start. One major limit relates to the bodies of law most relevant to the ICC: international criminal law, international humanitarian law, use of force law and international human rights law. These are, to use Hilary Charlesworth's words, 'disciplines of crisis'.[31] They have emerged chiefly in response to atypical situations such as war and genocide, rather than the structural inequalities and associated violence of 'everyday life'. Thus, they do not challenge broad patterns of gender inequality; address ubiquitous gender-based crimes such as child marriage, domestic violence and spousal rape; or tackle the political, economic and cultural factors that enable gender-based violence in wartime and peacetime alike. As a result of this limitation in its legal framework, the ICC can only prosecute a small fraction of gender-based violence that actually occurs worldwide. The violence must satisfy certain contextual or *chapeau* requirements: it must be committed with an intent to destroy a national, ethnic, racial or religious group (genocide); or occur as part of a widespread or systematic attack directed against any civilian population (crimes against humanity); or take place in the context of and associated with an armed conflict (war crimes).

There are also other constraints on the ICC's capacity generally, which apply across all categories of crimes. First, as a criminal court, the ICC's version of 'justice' is narrower than what victims may desire: the Court is not a truth commission or a forum for seeking damages, and its

[31] H. Charlesworth, 'International Law: A Discipline of Crisis' (2002) 65(3) *Modern Law Review* 377.

judgments do not necessarily help the affected community to heal.[32] In addition, because of its criminal justice function, the ICC must show 'full respect' for the rights of the accused.[33] This emphasis on the rights of the accused is essential to the ICC's fairness and its legitimacy, but it means that the interests of the victims will not always prevail. Second, like most international criminal tribunals, the ICC generally only prosecutes military and political leaders. This focus on high-level perpetrators can leave victims unsatisfied. As explained by one interviewee from the OTP:

> There are some [victims] at the end of the day who are not as happy as we would expect. Yes, they're happy that you're coming to hear their story and collect evidence, but at the end of the day, they want to hear that the person who raped them, the direct perpetrator, has been caught and put behind bars.[34]

Third, investigating and prosecuting the kinds of crimes enumerated in the Rome Statute is an extremely costly endeavour, and the Court's resources are limited.[35] For this reason, the Prosecutor cannot investigate or prosecute *all* crimes that theoretically fall within the jurisdiction of the Court. Indeed, in the absence of sufficient support from states and the United Nations (UN) Security Council, her Office is already struggling to secure adequate resources to do its job.[36] Fourth, the ICC depends on states to conduct tasks of great importance, such as arresting and surrendering suspects or facilitating in-country investigations.[37] This dependence on states, coupled with the enormity and complexity of ICC cases, makes for slow justice: in Yassin Brunger's words, it means that 'international justice lags woefully behind the atrocities themselves'.[38] Fifth, the ICC's deterrent capacity is limited: its

[32] R. Nickson and J. Braithwaite, 'Deeper, Broader, Longer Transitional Justice' (2014) 11(4) *European Journal of Criminology* 445.

[33] RS, Art. 64(2). See also Art. 67.

[34] Interview H, ICC OTP, 2017. See also Nickson and Braithwaite, see n. 32.

[35] The ICC's approved program budget for 2018 was €147,431,500, €45,991,800 of which was allocated to the OTP. 'Resolution of the Assembly of States Parties on the Proposed Programme Budget for 2018, ICC-ASP/16/Res.1' (14 December 2017), [1].

[36] See, e.g. ICC OTP, 'Twenty-Seventh Report of the Prosecutor of the International Criminal Court to the United Nations Security Council Pursuant to UNSCR 1593 (2005)' (20 June 2018) 23–24.

[37] See A. Cassese, 'On the Current Trends towards Criminal Prosecution and Punishment of Breaches of International Humanitarian Law' (1998) 9(1) *European Journal of International Law* 2.

[38] Y. Brunger, 'ICC's Bemba Ruling Is a Landmark, but Falls Short of a Big Leap' on *The Conversation* (25 March 2016).

influence is felt most strongly by governments and rebel groups who *want* to be perceived as legitimate by international or domestic consistencies and who expect to lose out in that respect if their leaders become the subject of proceedings in the ICC. By contrast, the ICC poses little threat to governments and non-state groups who reject the authority or judgment of the international community represented by the Court.[39] Sixth, the issue of witness corruption looms large: it has been alleged in relation to several ICC cases[40] and proven beyond a reasonable doubt in the *Bemba et al.* case, concerning Democratic Republic of Congo politician Jean-Pierre Bemba Gombo and certain members of his former Defence team.[41]

Yet despite those constraints and challenges, the ICC can potentially make a unique contribution to broader efforts to recognise and strengthen accountability for gender-based crimes. As an international court with a mandate to investigate and prosecute crimes of the 'most serious concern to the international community as a whole',[42] it has strong expressive power: that is, the power to express and instill values, to act as a 'normative megaphone'.[43] At a general level, the value expressed by the Court is a respect for the rule of law. More specifically, by prosecuting and punishing particular conduct, the Court can express the shared disavowal of that conduct by state parties.[44] For example, by prosecuting wartime rape, a crime that has historically received little attention, the ICC can send a message that the international community abhors this conduct and

[39] J. Ho and B. Simmons, 'Can the International Criminal Court Deter Atrocity?' (2016) 70(3) *International Organization* 443.

[40] See *Ntaganda* (ICC-01/04-02/06-1817-Red), 8 March 2017; *Barasa* (ICC-01/09-01/13-1-Red2), 2 August 2013; *Gicheru & Bett* (ICC-01/09-01/15-1-Red), 15 March 2015.

[41] *Bemba et al.* (ICC-01/05-01/13-1989-Red), 19 October 2016; *Bemba et al.* (ICC-01/05-01/13-2275-Red), 8 March 2018.

[42] RS, preamble, [4].

[43] I thank Professor Andreas Føllesdal at the University of Oslo for suggesting this term.

[44] See R. Sloane, 'The Expressive Capacity of International Punishment' (39–94) 43(1) *Stanford Journal of International Law* 2007; M. Drumbl, *Atrocity, Punishment, and International Law* (Cambridge University Press, 2007) 173–174; S. Song, 'From Punishment to Prevention Reflections on the Future of International Criminal Justice' (at the 'Justice for All' Conference, University of New South Wales, 14 February 2012).

For a more critical view on the 'expressive' capacity of international criminal courts, see J. Ramji-Nogales, 'Designing Bespoke Transitional Justice: A Pluralist Process Approach' (2010) 32(1) *Michigan Journal of International Law* 1; M. Elander, 'The Victim's Address: Expressivism and the Victim at the Extraordinary Chambers in the Courts of Cambodia' (2013) 7 *International Journal of Transitional Justice* 95.

regards it as one of the 'most serious crimes of international concern'.[45] The audience for this message can include civil society, the media and the general public, as well as domestic lawmakers and law enforcement bodies, who may be influenced to take steps to ensure accountability for gender-based crimes under national law.[46]

In addition, like other international criminal tribunals, the ICC has a history-making role. It performs this role through the presentation of evidence by the parties, the findings of fact by the judges and the dissemination of those findings in public judgments – all of which can affect what the public 'knows' (or 'believes') about the nature and causes of violence in a particular war[47] and who was the 'victim' and a 'perpetrator' in that war.[48] Whether or not a criminal court *should* strive to write history is the subject of debate.[49] But as many feminist legal scholars have acknowledged, for better or worse, international criminal tribunals *do* perform both functions: they adjudicate cases *and* promote a 'collective memory' of war.[50] Importantly, a feminist perspective suggests that the historical record produced by an international criminal tribunal is not 'an impartial and objective record of events' as has previously been claimed.[51] Rather, it is a record that affirms some forms of victimhood

[45] RS, Art. 1; M. deGuzman, 'An Expressive Rationale for the Thematic Prosecution of Sex Crimes' in M. Bergsmo (ed.), *Thematic Prosecution of International Sex Crimes* (Torkal Opsahl Academic EPublisher, 2012) 11.

[46] D. De Vos, Complementarity's Gender Justice Prospects and Limitations: Examining Normative Interactions between the Rome Statute and National Accountability Processes for Sexual Violence Crimes in Colombia and the Democratic Republic of Congo (PhD Thesis, European University Institute, 2017); A. Kapur, 'Complementarity as a Catalyst for Gender Justice in National Prosecutions' in F. Ní Aoláin et al. (eds), *The Oxford Handbook of Gender and Conflict* (Oxford University Press, 2018) 226.

[47] D. Buss, 'Knowing Women: Translating Patriarchy in International Criminal Law' (2014) 23(1) *Social & Legal Studies* 73; Drumbl, see n. 44, 174–76.

[48] Elander, see n. 44.

[49] H. Arendt, *Eichmann in Jerusalem: A Report on the Banality of Evil* (Viking, 1963), 233. C.f. L. Douglas, *The Memory of Judgment: Making Law and History in the Trials of the Holocaust* (Yale University Press, 2001); G. Simpson, *Law, War & Crime: War Crimes Trials and the Reinvention of International Law* (Polity Press, 2007) Ch. 4.

[50] N. Henry, 'Silence as Collective Memory: Sexual Violence and the Tokyo Trial' in Y. Tanaka, T. McCormack and G. Simpson (eds), *Beyond Victor's Justice? The Tokyo War Crimes Trial Revisited* (Brill/Nijhoff, 2010) 263, 279. See also Buss, 'Knowing Women', see n. 47; N. Henry, 'The Fixation on Wartime Rape: Feminist Critique and International Criminal Law' (2014) 23(1) *Social & Legal Studies* 93; C. Mibenge, *Sex and International Tribunals: The Erasure of Gender from the War Narrative* (University of Pennsylvania Press, 2013).

[51] See Cassese, see n. 37, 9.

while leaving others unrecognised,[52] often reinforces gender stereotypes[53] and tends to overlook the significance of gender norms and hierarchies when explaining both the causes and consequences of crimes.[54] The ICC, as one of numerous international and semi-international criminal tribunals currently in existence, cannot on its own ensure a more nuanced and gender-sensitive history of war. However, by engaging with arguments about the significance of gender – intersecting with variables such as race and ethnicity – it can contribute to a more accurate and more inclusive historical record than its predecessors managed to do.[55]

Incorporating principles of 'restorative justice', the ICC also offers some participatory rights and material redress to victims, including victims of gender-based crimes.[56] This is a response to concerns about the limited role of victims in previous war crimes trials, including concerns raised by feminist scholars.[57] For example, the Court can order a convicted person to pay reparations to victims,[58] a remedy that is not specific to victims of gender-based violence, but that reflects an increased focus on victims' interests more broadly and received strong support from women's rights activists at the Rome Conference.[59] In addition, the Statute gives victims a right to express their views and concerns during proceedings – which,

[52] See Buss, 'Knowing Women', see n. 47; Simpson, see n. 49, Ch. 4; Douglas, see n. 49; Elander, see n. 44.

[53] K. Engle, 'Feminism and Its (Dis)Contents: Criminalizing Wartime Rape in Bosnia and Herzegovina' (2005) 99(4) *American Journal of International Law* 778; J. Gardam, 'A New Frontline for Feminism and International Humanitarian Law' in M. Davies and V. Munro (eds), *The Ashgate Research Companion to Feminist Legal Theory* (Ashgate, 2013) 217.

[54] Mibenge, see n. 50. See also Copelon, see n. 8; Niarchos, see n. 8; D. Buss, 'The Curious Visibility of Wartime Rape: Gender and Ethnicity in International Criminal Law' (2007) 25 *Windsor Yearbook of Access to Justice* 3.

[55] For a similar perspective, see C. MacKinnon, 'Creating International Law: Gender as Leading Edge' (2013) 36(1) *Harvard Journal of Law & Gender* 105.

[56] See B. Schiff, *Building the International Criminal Court* (Cambridge University Press, 2008) 32–34.

[57] E.g. J. Mertus, 'Shouting from the Bottom of the Well' 6(1) *International Feminist Journal of Politics* 110.

[58] RS, Art. 75. See also: A. Durbach and L. Chappell, 'Leaving Behind the Age of Impunity: Victims of Gender Violence and the Promise of Reparations' (2014) 16(4) *International Feminist Journal of Politics* 543.

[59] Women's Caucus for Gender Justice, 'Gender Justice and the ICC' (at the United Nations Diplomatic Conference of Plenipotentiaries on the Establishment of an International Criminal Court, Rome, 15 July 1998) 51–53 (on file); C. McCarthy, *Reparation and Victim Support in the International Criminal Court* (Cambridge University Press, 2012) 52–53; P. Spees, 'Women's Advocacy in the Creation of the International Criminal Court: Changing the Landscapes of Justice and Power' (2003) 28(4) *Signs* 1233, 1238.

in practice, usually means a handful of victims' counsel representing hundreds of victims collectively.[60] The Statute has also been interpreted as allowing victims to present evidence, if the Chamber permits.[61]

For all of these reasons, although the ICC is by no means a panacea to gender-based violence, it has the potential to make a positive contribution in this regard. Returning to the words of Rhonda Copelon, whose remarks about the historic sidelining of gender-based crimes in international criminal law began this chapter:

> The Court is not only a potentially important concrete mechanism of accountability; it also establishes basic norms of gender justice that operate as an inspiration and model for political advocacy and domestic systems. … The Rome Statute's codification [of sexual and gender violence crimes] will not avert the danger of exclusion or impunity in the ICC, or in the accountability processes – national and international – to which it should give rise. But it provides a *critical new tool*.[62]

## 1.2 The Book at a Glance

### *1.2.1 Scope of Analysis*

This book analyses the ICC's emerging practice in prosecuting gender-based crimes up until the Rome Statute's twentieth anniversary on 17 July 2018. It considers the 24 cases that were initiated in this period,

[60] RS, Art. 68(3). For a range of views on the ICC's victim participation scheme, see: S. SáCouto, 'Victim Participation at the International Criminal Court and the Extraordinary Chambers in the Courts of Cambodia: A Feminist Project' (2012) 18(2) *Michigan Journal of Gender and Law* 297; C. Van den Wyngaert, 'Victims before International Criminal Courts: Some Views and Concerns of an ICC Trial Judge' (2011) 44(1) *Case Western Review of International Law* 475; M. Pena and G. Carayon, 'Is the ICC Making the Most of Victim Participation' (2013) 7(3) *International Journal of Transitional Justice* 518; S. Kendall and S. Nouwen, 'Representational Practices at the International Criminal Court: The Gap between Juridified and Abstract Victimhood' (2013) 24/2013 *University of Cambridge Faculty of Law Research Paper*; L. Smith-van Lin, 'Victims' Participation at the International Criminal Court: Benefit or Burden' in W. Schabas, Y. McDermott and N. Hayes (eds), *The Ashgate Research Companion to International Criminal Law* (Ashgate, 2013) 181.

[61] *Lubanga* (ICC-01/04-01/06-1432), 11 July 2008, [86]–[105]. See also S. Vasiliev, 'Victim Participation Revisited: What the ICC Is Learning About Itself' in C. Stahn (ed.), *The Law and Practice of the International Criminal Court* (Oxford University Press, 2015) 1133, 1168–77.

[62] Copelon, see n. 3, 329.

namely: six from the Democratic Republic of Congo (*Lubanga, Ntaganda, Ngudjolo, Katanga, Mbarushimana* and *Mudacumura*), two from Uganda (*Kony et al.* and *Ongwen*), five from Sudan (*Ahmad Harun & Ali Kushayb, Al-Bashir, Abu Garda, Banda* and *Hussein*), one from the Central African Republic (*Bemba*), two from Kenya (*Muthaura et al.* and *Ruto et al.*), four from Libya (*Gaddafi, Al-Senussi, Al-Tuhamy* and *Al-Werfalli*), two from Côte d'Ivoire (*Gbagbo & Blé Goudé* and *Gbagbo*) and two from Mali (*Al Mahdi* and *Al Hassan*). Several of these cases were joined and/or severed during the period under analysis. To manage this issue, this book's 'case count' is based on the status of proceedings as of 17 July 2018. The book does not analyse prosecutions for offences against the administration of justice, e.g. bribing witnesses, which comprise a second set of cases before the ICC.

The book's focus is on developments in ICC proceedings, as opposed to the Courts' impact beyond The Hague. Throughout the book, I pay particular attention to the work of the OTP, the unit that investigates and prosecutes crimes within the jurisdiction of the ICC. As others have observed, the ICC Prosecutor plays a key role in setting the agenda of the Court.[63] He or she can initiate proceedings *proprio motu*, i.e. without a referral from a state party or the UN Security Council,[64] and is responsible for deciding whether the statutory criteria for opening an investigation are satisfied.[65] The ICC Prosecutor also determines, once an investigation is opened, how long it should extend and what its focus should be. There is now an extensive literature, including publications by ICC staff, on how best to investigate gender-based crimes.[66] It is the job

[63] E.g. Sellers, 'Gender Strategy Is Not Luxury', see n. 5; SáCouto and Cleary, see n. 5; Van Schaack, see n. 5; Chappell, 'Conflicting Institutions', see n. 14; Hayes, 'Sisyphus Wept', see n. 14.

[64] RS, Art. 15. See: R. Grey and S. Wharton, 'Lifting the Curtain: Opening a Preliminary Examination at the International Criminal Court' (2018) 16(3) *Journal of International Criminal Justice* 593.

[65] RS, Art. 53(1).

[66] E.g. Jarvis and Nabti, see n. 27; D. Luping, 'Investigation and Prosecution of Sexual and Gender-Based Crimes Before the International Criminal Court' (2009) 17(2) *American University Journal of Gender, Social Policy and the Law* 433; X. Agirre Aranburu, 'Sexual Violence beyond Reasonable Doubt: Using Pattern Evidence and Analysis for International Cases' (2000) 23(3) *Leiden Journal of International Law* 609; M. Marcus, 'Investigation of Crimes of Sexual and Gender-Based Violence under International Criminal Law' in A. de Brouwer et al. (eds), *Sexual Violence as an International Crime: Interdisciplinary Approaches* (Intersentia, 2013) 211; B. Nowrojee, 'Shattered Lives: Sexual Violence During the Rwandan Genocide and Its Aftermath' (Human Rights Watch/FIDH, 1996) 25–26, 91–93.

of OTP's investigations division, and ultimately, the Prosecutor, to ensure that best practices are followed. On the basis of these investigations, the Prosecutor, supported by high-level staff of the Office, makes decisions about prosecutorial strategy. This includes deciding which individuals (if any) to charge, what conduct to charge them for, how to legally characterise that conduct, which witnesses to call, what questions to put to those witnesses and how to 'frame' the case in opening and closing statements. Many of these decisions are structured by the Rome Statute and are subject to a degree of judicial authorisation or review.[67] However, they decisions fall at first instance to the OTP, hence the OTP's central place in this book.

Having said that, this book does not *only* consider the decisions taken by the OTP. It recognises that the Office faces numerous external challenges,[68] and that it cannot be effective without support from other actors in and around the ICC. These actors include each panel of judges (in ICC parlance, each 'Chamber'), who must ensure that proceedings are conducted fairly and expeditiously,[69] that the rights and dignity of victims and witnesses are respected[70] and that the law is interpreted and applied in accordance with 'internationally recognized human rights' and without adverse distinction on certain grounds, including gender.[71] It also includes the ICC Registry, which is responsible for providing protection for victims and witnesses[72] and organising victim participation in ICC proceedings, among other things.[73] As noted previously, the cooperation of state officials (including government officials, bureaucrats and national police forces) is also crucial. Without such support, suspects will not be arrested and surrendered to the ICC, investigations will not be adequately resourced and certain evidence will remain out of reach. This book considers all of these actors, especially where their conduct undermines

[67] To cite a few illustrative examples, the charges must be confirmed by the Pre-Trial Chamber in order to proceed to trial (RS, Art. 61), and the Trial Chamber has the power to modify the legal characterisation of facts within certain limits, which can lead to a change to a charge or mode of liability (Regulations of the Court, Reg. 55).

[68] See: See ICC OTP, 'Strategic Plan 2016–2018', see n. 18, 3.

[69] E.g. RS, Art. 64(2); 64(8)(b); 67; 68(1), (3), and (5); 69(4); 82(1)(d); 83(2).

[70] E.g. RS, Art. 57(3)(c); 64(2) and (6)(e); 68.

[71] RS, Art. 21(3). See also R. Grey and L. Chappell, '"Gender Just Judging" in International Criminal Courts: New Directions for Research' in S. Harris-Rimmer and K. Ogg (eds), *Research Handbook on The Future of Feminist Engagement with International Law* (Edward Elgar, forthcoming).

[72] RS, Art. 43(6) and 68(4).

[73] RS, Art. 68(3).

accountability for gender-based crimes. It also recognises the role of civil society and journalists, who raise the alarm about gender-based crimes before ICC investigators come onto the scene,[74] and of victims, whose testimony reveals the personal impact of the crimes and helps to prove the charges in Court.

### *1.2.2 Source Material*

This is not only a study of the ICC's 'law on the books', but of how that law is interpreted and applied in practice. To understand that phenomenon, a detailed study of court records was required. These records included filings (written submissions of the parties and participants), decisions (determinations by the judges) and transcripts (written records of the words spoken in court). It was necessary to be selective about *which* court records to examine because some cases have been underway for over a decade and comprise thousands of documents, with the result that reviewing every available document would not be feasible. To give a recent example, by the time the Trial Chamber in the *Ntaganda* case retired to deliberate, it had held 248 hearings, heard 80 witnesses, rendered 604 decisions and received over 2,300 filings from the prosecution, victims' counsel and defence.[75] Those numbers do not include the 290-odd records from the pre-trial stage, the forthcoming trial judgment, or any appeals that may ensue. To manage the challenge of working with such a large data set across 24 cases, I began with a common set of significant records from each case[76] and added other materials where necessary to make sense of that common set of records.

Confidential information was excluded from the source material, which is a limiting factor, but one that could not be overcome: 'outsiders'

[74] The same was true of previous international criminal tribunals. See, e.g. G. Harbour, 'International Concern Regarding Conflict-Related Sexual Violence in the Lead-up to the ICTY's Establishment' in S. Brammertz and M. Jarvis (eds), *Prosecuting Conflict-related Sexual Violence at the ICTY* (Oxford University Press, 2016) 19.

[75] ICC, 'ICC Trial Chamber VI to Deliberate on the Case against Bosco Ntaganda' (30 August 2018).

[76] Where available, these records included: the application for an arrest warrant or summons to appear; the decision on that application; the warrant/summons itself; the document containing the charges and amendments thereto; the transcript of the confirmation hearing; the confirmation of charges decision; the pre-trial brief; the transcript of opening and closing statements; the closing briefs; the judgment, sentence and reparations order; and any appeal briefs or appeal decisions against the judgment, sentence or reparations order.

are not privy to such information, and 'insiders' have a duty not to disclose confidential information to the public. Nonetheless, the vast collection of court records on the ICC's website provide a good sense of the daily workings of the Court. In addition, numerous hearings that occurred in closed session have now been reclassified as public, which allows for a more accurate understanding of the evidence and arguments presented in court. Commentary by other observers was also useful – not as evidence of the Court's practice (it is no substitute for reviewing the official records oneself), but because it allowed reactions to ongoing cases to be gauged, and issues for further research to be identified.

To complement my analysis of court records, I interviewed a sample of ICC officials and relevant experts, including Patricia Viseur Sellers, a veteran prosecutor of international crimes, and since December 2017, the ICC Prosecutor's Special Advisor on Gender; Fabricio Guariglia, head of the OTP's Prosecution Division; Helen Brady, head of the OTP's Appeal Division; Paolina Massidda, Principal Counsel in the Office of the Public Counsel for Victims (OPCV) and, at the time of our interview, counsel for over 600 victims in the *Ongwen* case; Xavier-Jean Keïta, Principal Counsel in the Office of Public Counsel for Defence (OPCD); his colleague Marie O'Leary, OPCD Counsel; Niamh Hayes of UN Women, who in 2017 was seconded as a gender expert to the OTP; and trial lawyers (mostly senior trial lawyers) who at the time were working on the *Bemba, Ongwen, Ntaganda* and *Gbagbo & Blé Goudé* cases, several of whom had also worked on prior cases including *Lubanga, Katanga* and *Kony et al.*[77] In the NGO world, I had the privilege to exchange ideas with colleagues at Amnesty International and Women's Initiatives for Gender Justice, whose executive director, Melinda Reed, was interviewed for this book.

These interviews provide a range of perspectives on how the concept of 'gender-based crimes' is understood in the ICC, what counts as a 'successful' practice in prosecuting these crimes, and how the Court's practice in prosecuting these crimes can and should evolve. Importantly, I did not only seek the views of known 'gender experts', bearing in mind Charli Carpenter's observation that 'the litmus test for gender sensitivity in any institution is not whether there are a few gender experts on staff who "get it" but whether anyone else does'.[78] Rather, I sought

[77] In accordance with my university's requirements, ethics approval was obtained before these interviews took place. All interviewees were invited to review the interview transcript and make necessary changes within a specified timeframe, if they chose.

[78] C. Carpenter, *Forgetting Children Born of War: Setting the Human Rights Agenda in Bosnia and Beyond* (Columbia University Press, 2010) 100.

interviews with all past and present ICC judges, as well as prosecutors, legal representatives for victims (henceforth, 'victims' counsel') and Defence counsel. As is expected, some people did not respond, some were unavailable and some declined.[79] However, the final sample, while not necessarily representative of the Court as a whole, provided a valuable cross-section of views.

For the most part, the interview responses are anonymised throughout the book in accordance with the interviewees' preferences.[80] However, readers may be interested to know that there was no discernible difference in the pattern of responses from male versus female interviewees.

## 1.3 Feminist Approaches to Research

The analysis presented in this book is indebted to generations of feminist thought. Feminism, defined broadly, is a movement aimed at exposing and challenging inequality. More specifically, it seeks to expose and challenge inequality between men and women, although that is by no means the only issue of concern. As explained by feminist academic and peace activist Cynthia Cockburn:

> Different feminisms have different slants. But there is one constant in a feminist gender analysis, whoever makes it: the differentiation and relative positioning of women and men is seen as an important ordering principle that pervades the system of power and is sometimes its very embodiment. Gender does not necessarily have primacy in this respect. Economic class and ethnic differentiation can also be important relational hierarchies, structuring a regime and shaping its mode of ruling. But these other differentiations are always also gendered, and in turn they help construct what is a man or a woman in any given circumstance.[81]

79 In response to my request to interview ICC judges, the Head of Chambers replied: 'Unfortunately, I think there would be great difficulty for sitting Judges to be able to respond regarding offences which may be before them in future. It doesn't seem appropriate for Judges, in their disinterested role, to be speaking about what constitutes a successful prosecution practice, or about changing prosecution practices. Those are largely matters for others, such as officers of the OTP, and I note you are seeking to interview such people. I am not in a position to contact former judges'. (on file).

80 Not all interviewees indicated a preference for anonymity. However, as the sample was fairly small, I decided to anonymise responses generally in order to protect the anonymity of those who requested it.

81 C. Cockburn, 'The Continuum of Violence: A Gender Perspective on War and Peace' in W. Giles and J. Hyndman (eds), *Sites of Violence: Gender and Conflict Zones* (University of California Press, 2004) 24, 28.

Feminist research methods have a long history in the disciplines in which I work, namely law and the social sciences. Before explaining those research methods, it is useful to pause to explain a concept which is central to feminist thought: the concept of gender.

### *1.3.1 Feminist Perspectives on 'Gender'*

For most feminist thinkers, myself included, gender is a social construct: it is 'the social meaning attached to the shape of our bodies'.[82] More specifically, it is the social meaning associated with 'sex' (where 'sex' refers to our classification as 'male' or 'female' or other, depending on our physiology and hormone levels).[83] Not all societies draw a sharp line between 'male' and 'female' or attribute much significance to those categories.[84] However, in many societies around the world, those categories play a major part in shaping expectations about how we should act, when we should speak, where we should work, what we should aspire to, and who should be our leaders, our heroes, our partners, our protectors, and so forth.

In Western philosophy, one of the first scholars to articulate the idea of gender as a social construct was Simone de Beauvoir, who in *The Second Sex* (1949), argued 'one is not born, but rather becomes, woman'.[85]

[82] L. Shepherd, 'Sex or Gender? Bodies in Global Politics and Why Gender Matters' in L. Shepherd (ed.), *Gender Matters in Global Politics: A Feminist Introduction to International Relations* (Routledge, 2nd edn, 2015) 24, 26.

[83] S. Cowan, '"What a Long and Strange Trip It's Been": Feminist and Queer Travels with Sex, Gender, and Sexuality' in M. Davies and V. Munro (eds) (*The Ashgate Research Companion to Feminist Legal Theory*, 2016) 105, 106. Note: when discussing the relationship between 'sex' and 'gender', some feminist scholars present 'sex' as a trait which is biologically-determined and 'gender' as an identity which is culturally produced. E.g. R. Cook, 'Human Rights and Reproductive Self-Determination' (1995) 44(4) *American University Law Review* 975, 982 ('Sex is determined as a matter of biology, but gender is a product of social construction, culture, and psychology'); H. Charlesworth, 'Feminist Methods in International Law' (1999) 93(2) *American Journal of International Law* 379, 379 ('The term "gender" refers to the social construction of differences between women and men and ideas of "femininity" and "masculinity" – the excess cultural baggage associated with biological sex'). For other feminist scholars, sex and gender are both culturally constructed: we assign a sex to individuals *because* we have a preconceived idea of gender. E.g. J. Butler, *Gender Trouble* (Routledge, 1990); Shepherd, see n. 82. There is not space here to do justice to either of these positions. Instead, it will suffice to say that most feminists agree that gender is socially constructed and set aside the question of whether the same holds true for sex.

[84] See: N. Menon, *Seeing Like a Feminist* (Zubaan/Penguin Books, 2012) 2.

[85] S. de Beauvoir, *The Second Sex (1949)* (Vintage, 2011) 293.

De Beauvoir's work remains an important reference for feminist scholars, although ideas about gender have developed since her time. In particular, it is increasingly understood that gender does not only concern *women* or define concepts of *womanhood*: rather, in most societies, *everyone* is socialised to be feminine or masculine, roles that are interpreted differently across cultures, but which are almost universally defined in relation to one another.[86] Some people find meaning in their assigned role or are reassured that a template exists. In addition, those who play their role 'correctly' tend to receive positive feedback from others, and those who do not face social (and sometimes, legal) penalties. As a result of these positive and negative experiences, many people internalise, perform or aspire to the characteristics associated with their sex.[87]

A second development is the turn to 'intersectionality', which means considering how gender intersects with factors such as race, class and caste. The term was coined by race theorist Kimberlé Crenshaw in 1989, who argued that black women in America did not simply face 'sex discrimination' *and* 'race discrimination' as two isolated challenges; they faced a *sui generis* form of cumulative discrimination on multiple, intersecting grounds.[88] An awareness of intersectionality has made feminist thinkers attentive to the differences *among* women and *among* men. For instance, Rebecca Solnit states that 'the category of *women* is a long boulevard that intersects with many other avenues, including class, race, poverty, and wealth',[89] Hilary Charlesworth warns against 'generating grand theories of women's oppression'[90] and Sharon Cowan has argued that the future for feminists lies in articulating the way that gender and other hierarchies 'are profoundly interconnected'.[91]

[86] E.g. Cockburn, see n. 81; R. Grey and L. Shepherd, '"Stop Rape Now?" Masculinity, Responsibility, and Conflict-Related Sexual Violence' (2013) 16(1) *Men and Masculinities* 115; F. Ní Aoláin et al., 'Introduction' in F. Ní Aoláin et al. (eds), *The Oxford Handbook of Gender and Conflict* (Oxford University Press, 2017) xxxv, xxxvi; Menon, see n. 84, 87–90.

[87] Butler, see n. 83; R. Connell and R. Pearce, *Gender in World Perspectives* (Polity Press, 3rd edn, 2015) 15; R. Connell, *Masculinities* (Allen & Unwin, 2000); C. Ngozi Adichie, *We Should All Be Feminists* (Vintage, 2014).

[88] K. Crenshaw, 'Demarginalizing the Intersection of Race and Sex' (1989) 140 *University of Chicago Legal Forum* 139.

[89] R. Solnit, *The Mother of All Questions: Future Feminisms* (Granta, 2017) 24 (emphasis original).

[90] Charlesworth, 'Feminist Methods in International Law', see n. 84, 384.

[91] Cowan, see n. 83, 119.

The issue of power is central to feminist conceptions of gender. In feminist thought, it is widely understood that the categories of 'masculinity' and 'femininity' operate as a hierarchy. One manifestation of this hierarchy is the differential social, economic and/or legal status of people associated with the categories of 'masculinity' and 'femininity' (i.e. men and women, respectively). One need only look at who walks the halls of power, who can vote and hold office in more electorates, and who receives an education when poverty precludes all children from accessing this right, to know which group is on top. The resultant injustices have been called out at various points in history, long before the language of 'feminism', 'sexism' or 'gender' came into use.[92] However, since the 1960s, we have seen the proliferation of scholarship, activism and art which uses these terms.

Within this post-1960s feminist movement, an influential voice has been Catharine MacKinnon, singled out here because, from 2008 to 2012, she served as the inaugural Special Advisor on Gender to the ICC Prosecutor. In her book *Feminist Unmodified* (1987), MacKinnon condemned 'the hierarchy that is gender'[93] and argued: 'gender is an inequality of power, a social status based on who is permitted to do what to whom'.[94] This conception of gender as an axis of power is central to feminist scholarship and activism. For example, Cockburn has argued that 'while formulations of gender show rich diversity from culture to culture, a dominance of men and masculinity is pervasive'.[95] Similarly, Nivedita Menon has argued that:

> A feminist perspective recognizes that the hierarchical organizing of the world around gender is key to maintaining social order; that to live lives marked 'male' and 'female' is to live different realities.[96]

As Menon has observed, the existence of this hierarchy is often seen as 'natural' and therefore unproblematic or even legitimate.[97] A similar observation has been made by Margaret Urban-Walker, who states that

[92] E.g. J. de la Cruz, Answer by the Poet to the Most Illustrious Sister Filotea de La Cruz (1691) (2008); O. de Gouges, Declaration of the Rights of Woman and of the Female Citizen (1791); M. Wollstonecraft, A Vindication of the Rights of Woman (1792).

[93] C. MacKinnon, *Feminism Unmodified: Discourses on Life and Law* (Harvard University Press, 1987) 5.

[94] Ibid., 8. For critiques of MacKinnon's scholarship, see Cowan, see n. 83, 107–109; V. Kesic, 'A Response to Catharine MacKinnon's Article "Turning Rape into Pornography: Postmodern Genocide"' (1994) 5(2) *Hastings Women's Law Journal* 267.

[95] E.g. Cockburn, see n. 81, 28.

[96] Menon, see n. 84, viii.

[97] Ibid., 61.

gender inequality is often presented as 'proper, divinely ordained, socially functional, natural, inevitable, innate, or biologically determined or predisposed'.[98] In short, because of its ubiquity, gender inequality often hides in plain sight. This can impede people's ability to recognise gender as a basis on which people are victimised, as I argue later in the book.[99]

### 1.3.2 *Feminist Methods in Law*

As Judith Gardam has observed, feminism came 'somewhat late' to international law, with the turning point being the late 1980s and early 1990s.[100] It is therefore necessary to go back further in time to explain feminist methods in law before turning to critiques of international criminal law specifically.

Feminist legal scholarship is a vast field which brings together diverse voices and views. Yet there is a common thread in this scholarship, namely an interest in the links between gender, power and law. Moreover, there is a shared understanding that the historic exclusion of women from forums where law is made and enforced has *ongoing* consequences for the content, application and interpretation of law. The problem is not solved by diversifying the profession; as Simon Chesterman has observed, 'bound up with the "sea of male faces" are power relations which, although gendered, go beyond the *sex* of those in power'.[101] An early proponent of this argument was seventeenth-century philosopher François Poulain de la Barre, who observed: 'those who made and compiled the laws, being men, favoured their own sex'.[102] Making the same point several centuries later, Rebecca Cook has argued that:

> Law-making and law enforcement have evolved as male-gendered activities ... The interests of women have, accordingly, been identified by, and represented in, law through the instrumentality of men, and have centered around men's perceptions and interpretations of women's needs.[103]

[98] M. Urban-Walker, 'Gender and Violence in Focus: A Background for Gender Justice in Reparations' in R. Rubio Marín (ed.), *The Gender of Reparations: Unsettling Sexual Hierarchies while Redressing Human Rights Violations* (Cambridge University Press, 2009) 1, 24.

[99] Chapter 5, §5.3.2.

[100] Gardam, see n. 53, 220.

[101] Chesterman, see n. 5, 332 (emphasis original).

[102] Cited in: de Beauvoir, see n. 85, 11.

[103] Cook, see n. 83, 985.

There are a number of questions that, generally speaking, feminist scholars in law tend to ask.[104] These include: 'Whose interests does the law protect?', 'Whose experiences does it recognise?', 'What values does it express?' and 'How can it be used to challenge inequality between and among gender groups?'. The answers to these questions vary depending on which laws are analysed, and the researcher's sensitivity to issues of race, culture, colonisation and class. However, these questions, or variations of them, are a hallmark of feminist scholarship in law. An attention to gaps in legal frameworks is another hallmark of feminist scholarship, because these gaps help us to understand whose experiences are seen as most important and whose are forgotten or overlooked. For this reason, Charlesworth and Chinkin have described 'searching for the silences' as an important part of feminist research in law.[105]

By applying these research techniques, feminist scholars have exposed the 'gender' of the law. This does not only mean pointing out obvious examples of gender bias, such as the under-representation of women in judicial positions, or use of the term 'men' to mean 'people' in legal texts.[106] It also means revealing the '*hidden* gender of law',[107] which requires 'looking beneath the surface of the law to identify the gender implications of rules and the assumptions underlying them'.[108] In most cases, this deeper mode of enquiry shows that: (a) laws that do not discriminate on their face can often have that effect in practice; and (b) the people who generally benefit from such discrimination are (white, educated, heterosexual) men.[109] One way in which this gender discrimination occurs is through the disparate treatment of violence in the 'public' and 'private' spheres in legal frameworks.[110] For example, feminist scholars have shown that

[104] E.g. H. Barnett, *Introduction to Feminist Jurisprudence* (Cavendish Publishing, 1998); K. Bartlett, 'Feminist Legal Methods' (1989) 103(4) *Harvard Law Review* 829; Charlesworth and Chinkin, see n. 5; J. Morgan and R. Graycar, *The Hidden Gender of Law* (Federation Press, 2002); P. Kotiswaran, 'Feminist Approaches to Criminal Law' in M. Dubber and T. Hörnle (eds), *The Oxford Handbook of Criminal Law* (Oxford University Press, 2014) 59.

[105] Charlesworth and Chinkin, see n. 5, 60.

[106] E.g. International Law Commission, 'Draft Code of Crimes against the Peace and Security of Mankind, UN Doc. A/CN.4/L.532 + Corr.1–3' ('1996 Draft Code of Crimes') (17 July 1996).

[107] See Morgan and Graycar, see n. 104.

[108] Bartlett, see n. 104, 834.

[109] Ibid., 837.

[110] For a detailed feminist analysis of the 'public/private dichotomy' in criminal law, see Morgan and Graycar, see n. 104, 2.

criminal law in many states is 'deeply imbued with masculinity'.[111] A concrete example is the exclusion of spousal rape – a form of violence occurring in the 'private' sphere – from criminal codes. Even when framed in terms that do not discriminate on the basis of sex, this exclusion works to women's disadvantage. That is because, due to their subordinate social and economic position, women are more likely to be raped in a marriage, and unable to leave that marriage, than men.[112]

The process of revealing the law's hidden gender is sometimes described as 'asking the woman question'[113] – a rather unsuitable shorthand, which does not tell the full story. To be sure, early feminist thinkers tended to focus on the subordination of 'women' collectively, with little regard for the vastly different positions of women of different races, education levels and wealth. However, most contemporary feminist thinkers are more nuanced in their approach: some have argued that the categories of 'woman' and 'man' are themselves social constructs,[114] and there has been an increased attention to differences *among* women and *among* men. This shift been driven by feminists of colour, queer feminists and feminists from the 'developing world', whose experience of 'womanhood' differs markedly from the philosophers, authors and suffragettes associated with early feminist thought.[115] Acknowledging this point in her seminal 1989 article, Katharine Bartlett argued that feminist scholars must ask 'a set of far-reaching questions that go beyond issues of gender bias to seek out other bases of exclusion', such as race and class.[116] That same

[111] Barnett, see n. 104, 22. See also Kotiswaran, see n. 104; H. Douglas et al., 'Reflections on Rewriting the Law' in H. Douglas et al. (eds), *Australian Feminist Judgments* (Hart, 2014) 28.

[112] Kotiswaran, see n. 104, 61. For a historic example of the exclusion of marital rape from the criminal code, see: Australian Law Reform Commission, *Family Violence: A National Legal Response* (2010), [24.59]–[24.60]. For a contemporary example, see: *Indian Penal Code* 1860, s 375 (exception 2).

[113] Bartlett, see n. 104, 837; Cook, see n. 83, 986; Douglas et al., see n. 111, 28.

[114] Butler, see n. 84; Shepherd, see n. 83.

[115] E.g. b. hooks, *Ain't I a Woman?: Black Women and Feminism* (South End Press, 1981); A. Lorde, 'The Master's Tools Will Never Dismantle The Master's House' in C. Moraga and G. Anzaldúa (eds), *This Bridge Called My Back: Writings by Radical Women of Color* (Kitchen Table Press, 1981) 94; C. Mohanty, 'Under Western Eyes: Feminist Scholarship and Colonial Discourses' (1984) 12(3) *Boundary 2* 333; A. Rich et al., 'Compulsory Heterosexuality and Lesbian Experiences' in *Powers of Desire: The Politics of Sexuality* (Virago, 1983) 177; Combahee River Collective, '1977 Combahee River Collective Statement' in B. Smith (ed.), *Home Girls: A Black Feminist Anthology* (Kitchen Table Press, 1983) 264.

[116] Bartlett, see n. 104, 848.

year, Crenshaw published her seminal article on 'intersectionality', which was mentioned previously. The concept of 'intersectionality' has since become central to feminist scholarship, literature and art.[117]

One of the earliest works to bring these ideas to international law was Charlesworth, Chinkin and Wright's 1991 article 'Feminist Approaches to International Law'.[118] The authors argued that because of the dearth of women in forums where international law has been developed and enforced, 'international law is a thoroughly gendered system'.[119] In other words, the 'long-time domination' of men in the field of international law has meant that:

> Issues traditionally of concern to men become seen as general human concerns, while 'women's concerns' are relegated to a special, limited category. Because men generally are not the victims of sex discrimination, domestic violence, and sexual degradation and violence, for example, these matters can be consigned to a separate sphere and tend to be ignored. The orthodox face of international law and politics would change dramatically if their institutions were truly human in composition: their horizons would widen to include issues previously regarded as domestic – in the two senses of the word.[120]

In the years since that article was published, we have seen flourishing feminist scholarship in international law.[121] In relation to international criminal law specifically, three main feminist critiques can be identified. One is that international criminal law's focus on situations of war and

[117] E.g. Buss, 'Curious Visibility', see n. 54; D. Buss, 'Sexual Violence, Ethnicity, and Intersectionality in International Criminal Law' in E. Grabham et al. (eds), *Intersectionality and Beyond* (Routledge, 2009) 105; Mibenge, see n. 50; V. Oosterveld, 'Prosecuting Gender-Based Persecution as an International Crime' in A. de Brouwer et al. (eds), *Sexual Violence as an International Crime: Interdisciplinary Approaches* (Intersentia, 2013) 57.

[118] H. Charlesworth, C. Chinkin and S. Wright, 'Feminist Approaches to International Law' (1991) 85(4) *American Journal of International Law* 613. For other early examples, see C. Bunch, 'Women's Rights as Human Rights: Toward a Re-Vision of Human Rights' (1990) 12(4) *Human Rights Quarterly* 486; A. Byrnes, 'Women, Feminism, and International Human Rights Law' (1989) 12 *Australian Year Book of International Law* 205; J. Gardam, 'A Feminist Analysis of Certain Aspects of International Humanitarian Law' (1989) 12 *Australian Yearbook of International Law* 265.

[119] Charlesworth, Chinkin and Wright, see n. 118, 614–615.

[120] Ibid., 625.

[121] E.g. H. Charlesworth, 'The Hidden Gender of International Law' (2002) 16(1) *Temple International and Comparative Law Journal* 93; A. Manji and D. Buss (eds), *International Law: Modern Feminist Approaches* (Hart, 2005); D. Otto, 'Feminist Approaches to International Law' in A. Orford and F. Hoffmann (eds), *The Oxford Handbook of the Theory of International Law* (Oxford University Press, 2016) 489.

genocide makes it unresponsive to the violence, poverty and oppression that women face in times of peace. This critique is concerned with the 'crisis' mentality of international law, as discussed previously.[122] A second critique focuses on the *application* of international criminal law, arguing that even where this legal framework permits the prosecution of gender-based crimes in theory, such crimes have been poorly investigated and prosecuted in practice, in part because they are considered less serious, and more difficult to prove, than other crimes of international concern.[123] A third critique focuses on the histories that international criminal tribunals produce – specifically, on the lack of attention to gender.[124] For example, feminist scholars have shown that in the ICTY and ICTR, the rape of women was often explained by reference to the victim's religion or ethnicity, with no acknowledgment of the significance of gender norms and hierarchies to the commission of the crimes.[125] As a result, those tribunals have perpetuated the 'degendering of sexual violence',[126] and have been complicit in the 'erasure of gender from the war narrative'.[127]

These critiques – particularly the second and third – are the 'jumping off' point for the analysis in this book. They underpin the design of this book, including its attention to forms of gender-based violence beyond rape, its focus on the application of the legal framework and its interest in the representation of gender in trial narratives. Picking up on Charlesworth and Chinkin's point about the importance of silences, the book sifts carefully through transcripts, filings and judgments to uncover stories of gender-based violence that were discussed in passing but did not emerge as a key theme in a particular case. Informed by the idea of intersectionality, the book considers examples of persecution on multiple grounds (gender *and* ethnicity, for example). As a close study of the ICC's practice, this book does not focus on 'big picture' critiques about

[122] E.g. Charlesworth and Chinkin, see n. 5, 335; Chesterman, see n. 5; K. Grewal, 'Rape in Conflict, Rape in Peace: Questioning the Revolutionary Potential of International Criminal Justice for Women's Human Rights' (2010) 33 *Australian Feminist Law Journal* 57; R. Kapur, 'Gender, Sovereignty and the Rise of a Sexual Security Regime in International Law and Postcolonial India' (2013) 14(2) *Melbourne Journal of International Law* 317, 337–38; C. MacKinnon, 'Women's September 11th: Rethinking the International Law of Conflict' (2006) 47(1) *Harvard International Law Journal* 1.

[123] E.g. Askin, *War Crimes Against Women*, see n. 5; Chappell, *The Politics of Gender Justice*, see n. 9; Hayes, 'Sisyphus Wept', see n. 14; Hayes, 'La Lutte Continue', see n. 14.

[124] E.g. Niarchos, see n. 8.

[125] E.g. Buss, 'Curious Visibility', see n. 54; Mibenge, see n. 50.

[126] Engle, see n. 53, 814.

[127] Mibenge, see n. 50.

the limitations of international criminal law. Yet those critiques influence the tone of the book. They explain why, even as I chart a story of progress in the ICC's jurisprudence, the tone of the book is subdued: I remain conscious that this court alone will never have the capacity to 'end' impunity for gender-based crimes, much less end the crimes themselves.

### *1.3.3 Feminist Institutionalism*

Complementing the use of feminist legal methods, the book also applies a 'feminist institutionalist' approach. This approach first developed in the field of political science, with some recent crossover into international criminal law.[128] Broadly speaking, institutionalist scholars argue that the behaviour of individuals in an institutional setting is shaped by the 'formal rules' (such as the institution's charter) as well as by inherited ways of thinking and operating, which institutionalists would describe as 'informal rules' or 'rules in use'.[129] Those informal rules are not written down in official documents; they are the standard ways of thinking and operating that one learns on the ground. Often, those ways of thinking and operating have a long history, which predates the establishment of the institution in question. For that reason, newly created institutions can never make a clean break from the past: they are populated with people whose ideas are shaped by past experience, leading to history repeating itself in unexpected ways. This does not mean that, in an institutional environment, values and practices will *never* change. However, it indicates that lasting change takes place through 'a culmination of seemingly small adjustments' in an institution's culture and practices, rather than by simply enacting new 'formal rules'.[130]

Feminist institutionalists share these views about continuity and change in an institutional setting and also bring a gender lens to their

[128] E.g. Chappell, *The Politics of Gender Justice*, see n. 9; Chappell, 'Conflicting Institutions', see n. 14; E. Palmer and S. Williams, 'A "Shift in Attitude"? Institutional Change and Sexual and Gender-Based Crimes at the Extraordinary Chambers in the Courts of Cambodia' (2017) 19(1) *International Feminist Journal of Politics* 22; L. McLeod et al., 'Gendering Processes of Institutional Design: Activists at the Negotiating Table' (2014) 16(2) *International Feminist Journal of Politics* 54.

[129] E. Ostrom, 'Institutional Rational Choice' in P. Sabatier (ed.), *Theories of the Policy Process* (Westview Press, 1999) 21; V. Lowndes and M. Roberts, *Why Institutions Matter: The New Institutionalism in Political Science* (Palgrave Macmillan, 2013).

[130] K. Thelen, cited in Chappell, *The Politics of Gender Justice*, see n. 9, 9.

analysis.[131] In particular, they are interested in how actors behave in institutions whose 'formal rules' have been designed to rectify past problems of gender bias, or which prohibit discrimination between women and men. Placing these institutions in their historical and political context, feminist institutionalists contend, helps to explain why 'even the most well-designed formal gender equality rules [...] often fail to produce their intended effects'.[132] Applying this approach to a range of case studies, feminist institutionalists have shown that gendered ideas about how women and men should behave, and whose interests should take precedence, have proven to be especially 'sticky'. That is because such ideas often continue to enjoy support in the outside world, even if they are at odds with the new institution's 'formal rules'.

For example, Fiona Mackay has applied this theory in her study of the Scottish Parliament, a legislature created in the 1990s through constitutional reforms in the United Kingdom. Mackay explains that the designers of the new parliament 'had self-conscious aspirations to create a new set of institutions that would depart from the Westminster model and that would promote a different political culture'.[133] Reflecting these aspirations, the new Parliament's rules promote the values of equality, power-sharing and consensus. On paper, these rules create 'conducive conditions for the successful integration of women as actors and new ideas about more inclusive politics'.[134] Despite that, Mackay observed that many Scottish parliamentarians reverted to the aggressive, partisan style of politics derived from Westminster 'in order to be politically effective'.[135] She concludes that 'as a higher-order institution and a powerful legacy, the institutions and norms of the Westminster model exert a considerable drag. In so doing, it constrains the potential for new paths and limits reform'.[136] Using that case study as an illustrative example, Mackay rejects the idea that feminist actors can set an

[131] E.g. F. Mackay, M. Kenny and L. Chappell, 'New Institutionalism Through a Gender Lens: Towards a Feminist Institutionalism?' (2010) 31(5) *International Political Science Review* 573; M. Krook and F. Mackay (eds), *Gender, Politics and Institutions: Towards a Feminist Institutionalism* (Palgrave Macmillan, 2010).

[132] L. Chappell and G. Waylen, 'Gender and The Hidden Life of Institutions' (2013) 91(3) *Public Administration* 599, 612.

[133] F. Mackay, 'Nested Newness, Institutional Innovation, and the Gendered Limits of Change' (2014) 10(4) *Politics & Gender* 549, 558.

[134] Ibid., 557.

[135] Ibid., 559.

[136] Ibid., 561.

institution on the right course by 'locking in' principles of inclusion and equality in its formal rules. She argues:

> New formal institutions, even those that seem to represent a break with the *status quo* that went before, are neither blank slates nor free floating. Rather, they are the carriers of multiple – sometimes contradictory – interests and ideas; they are marked by past institutional legacies and are shaped by initial and ongoing interactions with already existing institutions (formal structures and rules, informal rules, practices and norms) within which they are 'nested' and interconnected.[137]

In the field of international criminal law, Chappell has used a feminist institutionalist approach to analyse 'gender justice' outcomes at the ICC, including its early practice in prosecuting gender-based crimes. In Chappell's view, several of the assumptions and operating procedures that contributed to the under-prosecution of gender-based crimes in the past, such as a tendency to view these crimes as less serious than other wartime offences, have seeped into the ICC.[138] Following Chappell's lead, this book also applies feminist institutionalist theory to interpret the practice of the Court. The influence of this theory is most apparent in Chapter 5, which considers whether, and in what ways, the attitudes that contributed to impunity for gender-based crimes in the past have continued to influence outcomes at the ICC. More broadly, this theory has shaped my interest in the daily practices of the Court, because an institutionalist approach suggests that it is here – rather than in the grand moments of institutional design – that one would expect to see signs of the gradual, day-by-day process of 'gendering' international criminal law.

## 1.4 'Success' in Prosecuting Gender-based Crimes

It is worth reflecting on what a 'successful' practice in prosecuting gender-based crimes might look like at the ICC, so that we have something to compare the actuality to. Conceptions of 'success' in this respect vary, as people have different expectations of the Court, and some view convictions as the metric of 'success'. For my part, I take the view that success cannot be measured by convictions alone. Indeed, it is problematic to judge any court by the number of convictions; a court's first duty is to ensure fair and impartial proceedings, and it *should* render an acquittal

[137] Ibid., 555.
[138] Chappell, *The Politics of Gender Justice*, see n. 9.

if there is insufficient evidence to establish the charges or if a successful defence has been made. As expressed by Mr Keïta, Principal Counsel of the OPDC, 'we ought to fight for justice. A court or tribunal is not here to condemn but to give justice'.[139] At the same time, the ICC cannot deliver meaningful justice if gender-based crimes are not investigated or prostituted effectively: that is in itself an injustice which has taken decades of activism to recognise, as detailed in Chapter 3.

Within the ICC, the responsibility for avoiding that injustice lies first with the OTP. If the ICC is to be successful in prosecuting gender-based crimes, it is necessary that the OTP conducts thorough investigations of these crimes; brings charges of these crimes where possible, making full use of the opportunities provided by the Rome Statute; and constructs cases that are strong enough, in terms of legal argument and evidence, to result in convictions at the end of a fair trial. It is equally important that the judges adjudicate charges of gender-based crimes fairly, without requiring more evidence to establish that these crimes were committed, or that the accused was responsible for them, than would be required for any other category of crime. These are pre-requisites to ending impunity for gender-based crimes under international law.

However, from a feminist perspective, curbing impunity for gender-based crimes – by bringing strong charges and building a jurisprudence that expands rather than curtails options for accountability – is not the only outcome that matters. As discussed further in Chapter 3, the *representation* of gender-based crimes in high-profile war crimes trials matters also. That is, there is value in bringing charges that reflect a broad spectrum of gender-based crimes against male *and* female victims, and in producing trial records that recognise the relevance of gender norms to the commission of these crimes and challenge narrow and inaccurate gender stereotypes, such as the stereotype of women as passive victims, for example.

A similarly far-reaching concept of 'success' is articulated in the OTP's 2014 *Gender Policy*. Among other things, it states that the OTP will: 'ensure that charges for sexual and gender-based crimes are brought wherever there is sufficient evidence',[140] 'bring charges for sexual and gender-based crimes explicitly as crimes *per se*, in addition to charging these acts as forms of other violence within the Court's subject-matter jurisdiction',[141]

[139] Interview, 17 July 2018.
[140] ICC OTP, 'Gender Policy', see n. 19, [71].
[141] Ibid., [72].

'seek to highlight the gender-related aspects of sexual and other crimes within [the ICC's] jurisdiction',[142] utilise the newly recognised crime of gender-based persecution 'to the fullest extent possible',[143] 'consider not only acts of violence and discrimination based on sex, but also those related to socially constructed gender roles'[144] and 'positively advocate for the inclusion of sexual and gender-based crimes and a gender perspective in litigation before the Chambers'.[145] Importantly, the *Gender Policy* also sets out goals with regard to the representation of gender-based crimes. For example, it states that the OTP will apply a 'gender analysis' to all crimes within the ICC's jurisdiction, which involves:

> An examination of the underlying differences and inequalities between women and men, and girls and boys, and the power relationships and other dynamics which determine and shape gender roles in a society, and give rise to assumptions and stereotypes. In the context of the work of the Office, it requires a consideration of whether, and in what ways, crimes, including sexual and gender-based crimes, are related to gender norms and inequalities.[146]

In line with the *Gender Policy,* all OTP staff interviewed for this book presented a broad conception of their role in prosecuting gender-based crimes. When asked what a 'successful' practice in prosecuting these crimes would look like, not one person focused solely on convictions; they also spoke about developing the jurisprudence, telling a meaningful story and other qualitative indicators of success. For example, one interviewee stated: 'the ultimate measure of success is definitely a conviction. But what also can be a measure of success, if a victim, when capable and strong enough and willing, to tell his or her story in front of the world stage, with or without protective measures, can also be seen in the long future history of this court as the beginning of success'.[147] Another stated: 'obviously, we want to see convictions for each and every one of our charges for sexual crimes. But I think it's important also to see how does the Chamber deal with the underlying acts.

[142] Ibid., [74].
[143] Ibid., [68].
[144] Ibid., [27].
[145] Ibid..
[146] Ibid., [20] (emphasis added).
[147] Interview L, ICC OTP, 2017.

I think another indicator of success would be how will crimes against males be dealt with in the future'.[148] A third replied:

> I'm reluctant to distinguish between one crime and another. I think it's absolutely true that gender-based [crimes] have been distressingly little-prosecuted, and therefore, a successful practice for an institution whose job is to prosecute is to ensure that that previous failure stops. But I wouldn't single out gender-based crimes. We just need to do it all, vigorously, and not in a mealy-mouthed way. [However], there is an interest in the early stages of this institution to have some case law [on gender-based crimes]. It would be a mistake to give too much prominence to that 'developmental' approach, but at this early stage, you can tilt the balance a little more towards the desirability of having some judge-made law on the necessary evidence and the necessary elements for the crimes.[149]

The most detailed responses to this question came from Fabricio Guariglia, Director of the Prosecution Division, and Helen Brady, Senior Appeals Counsel and Head of the Appeals Section. Guariglia stated:

> Conviction rate is one performance indicator [of 'success']. I do not belong to the school of prosecutions that thinks that basically the higher the conviction rate, necessarily the better job you're doing. I mean you could be doing a horrible job, and if the justice system is failing, you may be getting a very high conviction rate. Now that's not right. But, in any event, conversely, I think that if all your cases are falling apart at trial and you're not getting convictions then you're not doing your job properly. So obviously, the rate of convictions, in relation to gender crimes, is critical. Bringing a solid cluster of gender charges that survives confirmation and then basically lead to a conviction is a clear indicator of success. [Next], how meaningful the stories are. We can't bring every single instance of gender criminality and gender victimisation to the courtroom. This was a discussion in the *Bemba* case. It was sexual violence on an industrial fashion in Bangui [in the Central African Republic]. It was unusual – you had an enormous amount of cases documented, which normally doesn't happen that way. So what we decided was that we can't bring 1,000 counts of sexual violence; we need to present a representative sample. So we have to choose stories that are meaningful enough that those victims that have not appeared can relate to the stories, and the narrative that comes from the judgment is a comprehensive narrative. It had men and women, for example. And then one thing we had to do in the sentencing hearing was to really portray the impact of the crimes in the community, in the affected women and the affected men. So, if at the end of the day, if what you're bringing is a marginal story that is told in a fragmented

[148] Interview K, ICC OTP, 2017.
[149] Interview I, ICC OTP, 2017.

> fashion, and what you get is a conviction for one charge of sexual violence, it doesn't really tell the story, and it does not really contribute to portraying what has happened in its full dimension, then you may not be doing exactly what you want.[150]

Brady stated:

> We have performance indicators in the OTP. We do track, for example, how many charges we bring for sexual and gender-based crimes, how many cases have an element of SGBC [sexual and gender-based crimes] involved, how many SGBC charges are confirmed and convictions rendered, etc. Numbers are great, and we track those. They're going to be more end-result driven, though. So what we need to do, and we've developed a plan or checklist for teams to use, is to make sure that from the earliest phases of the investigation, indeed even at the preliminary examination stage and in particular at the investigation stage, that we are making all appropriate efforts to ensure that we cover these crimes. We have to make sure that we bring the evidence out, and we have to make sure that we conduct our investigations and our prosecutions in a way that victims are comfortable to speak about these matters. That could involve, for example, utilising various procedures we have in the Court's procedural framework. We have certain tools within the Statute and the Rules that could assist us. Of course, you have to balance such procedures and make sure all the protections are there for the rights of the accused, that they can properly test the evidence, etc. So, when I consider if we have had 'success' in our SGBC investigations and prosecutions, this can be indicated by certain markers, quantitative and qualitative markers. But I think that 'success' is really about making sure that at all phases of the process, from the earliest investigative steps right through to the trial, even to the appeal and beyond (if there are post-appeal proceedings), that sexual and gender-based crimes are firmly on our radar and are pro-actively considered.[151]

Paolina Massidda, Principal Counsel of the OPCV, put even less emphasis on convictions than the OTP interviewees. When I asked her whether convictions were the best indicator of 'success' in prosecuting gender-based crimes, she replied:

> I think that it's important to have justice for the crimes, but the way in which you arrive at having justice may have some importance. Victims of these types of crimes are often satisfied when they see that their suffering is brought before the judges. So, there is already a 'successful' factor in this sense, that the case is *brought before the judges* … Another factor is the repetitive pattern of incriminating someone for these types of crimes. If you systematically charge these types of crimes, I think this could also

[150] Interview, ICC OTP, 2017 (ellipses omitted).
[151] Interview, ICC OTP, 2017 (ellipses omitted).

> be a 'success' in the sense that it launches a signal in situations of crisis. In addition, it could also have repercussions in fighting impunity, and also on the conscience of women or men who have suffered these crimes to come forward, because it will not be perceived any more as a shame.[152]

As one might expect, the responses from the OPCD - the office supporting Defence counsel - were different again. For these interviewees, my question about what makes a 'successful' practice in prosecuting gender-based crimes seemed misplaced, or better suited to the OTP. From their perspective, the priority was to ensure that the accused had adequate notice of the charges, that the trial was fair and that the Court respected the principle of *sécurité juridique,* which requires that decisions are made in accordance with known and certain laws.[153] It would be interesting to hear more about the role of the Defence in cases involving gender-based crimes, such as how they might adapt their cross-examination style for traumatised or disempowered witnesses, or how the Court can ensure legal certainty given that some gender-based crimes, such as the newly codified crime of 'other forms of sexual violence', are by definition flexible.

Some interviewees also defined 'success' in terms of the ICC's impact beyond The Hague. For example, in addition to 'convictions', one OTP interviewee cited four indicators of 'success'. First, how much effort the staff, especially the investigators, 'put into proactively investigating [sexual and gender-based crimes].' Second, 'how the Office is perceived by the outside world, particularly by NGOs, but more so, by victims [for example], remarks that some of them make during the investigation, of people coming out to listen to their stories, they have an opportunity to explain themselves, of having their victimisation recognised'. Third, 'the effect or influence the Court has on this particular topic on national jurisdictions. Do they borrow from the Rome Statute, do they domesticate it? Do they look at the Court for training?' Fourth, 'a decrease of sexual crimes in conflicts. The deterrent aspect of it'.[154] Another OTP lawyer stated:

> Achieving success would not be just to arrive at something completely isolated, a trial, which happened in The Hague, where we do our few years in Court, we got the result on the paper, and everybody says 'great!' and we're done. We need to make sure that the case is about them, that the victims, those for whom justice is made, get their part there. By 'their part', I don't mean only money, but they recognise that it was about their suffering. That they understand the meaning of the judgment, good or bad, I mean

[152] Interview, June 2017 (ellipses omitted).
[153] Interview, July 2018.
[154] Interview H, ICC OTP, 2017.

> acquittal or not, few years or long period of sentence. Making that link and making sure that they went through the process and they're getting something at the end of that in terms of understanding the process, feeling themselves the relief, got a sense of the trial and a personal meaning for them. And not something like that 'oh, there was something far away, there were these people, these Europeans, they did a trial about what I suffered'.[155]

These responses, which focus on the ICC's impact beyond The Hague, reinforce the value of empirical research into how the ICC is viewed by victimised communities.[156] However, the type of 'success' described by these respondents is not the focus of this book as it would require an altogether different research method.

## 1.5 The Chapters Ahead

The book is divided into six chapters, including this introductory one. Chapter 2 defines the concept of 'gender-based crimes', taking into account the analysis of feminist scholars, the negotiating history around the Rome Statute and interviews with officials and advisors of the ICC. This definition of gender-based crimes is deliberately broad, extending to both sexual and non-sexual crimes. Chapter 3 considers how gender-based crimes have moved from the margins to the centre of international criminal law in recent decades, including during the negotiations for the Rome Statute and ICC Elements of Crimes. This historical overview provides a context for understanding what has occurred since those legal texts entered force. Chapter 4 provides a concise analysis of each case that has come before the ICC as of 17 July 2018, paying particular attention to the inclusion or exclusion of gender-based crimes. This case-by-case analysis can be read collectively, or readers may be more selective if their interest lies in one particular case. Based on those case studies, Chapter 5 assesses how successful ICC prosecutors have been in prosecuting gender-based crimes so far and seeks to explain developments in this area of practice with reference to feminist institutionalism. Looking forward, Chapter 6 explores the possibilities for developing the ICC's jurisprudence of gender-based crimes.

[155] Interview J, ICC OTP, 2017.

[156] E.g. C. Tenove, 'International Justice for Victims? Assessing the International Criminal Court from Victims' Perspectives in Kenya and Uganda' (Africa Initiative Research Papers, September 2013).

# 2

# Gender-based Crimes

The terms 'gender-based crimes', 'gender crimes' and 'gender-based violence' have been used by feminist scholars in international criminal law since the 1990s,[1] but feminists have been joining the dots between gender and violence for several decades more.[2] In my interviews, and when pouring over court records, I have been struck by how often these same terms are now used at the International Criminal Court (ICC). In particular, the term 'sexual and gender-based crimes', sometimes abbreviated to 'SGBC', is now part of the daily jargon of the Office of the Prosecutor (OTP) and is increasingly used by ICC judges,[3] victims' counsel[4] and Defence counsel[5] as well. But what do these actors mean when they speak of 'gender-based crimes', a term that is neither defined, nor used, in the Rome Statute? Do they mean the same thing as each other? Do they mean the same thing as feminist scholars do, when they use the term? Are there multiple meanings in the feminist scholarship, too? And how, if at all, is the term 'gender-based crimes' relevant to the work of the Court?

I did not initially identify these definitional quandaries as key research questions when I began writing this book. However, the more I spoke with

[1] E.g. K. Askin, *War Crimes Against Women: Prosecution in International War Crimes Tribunals* (Martinus Nijhoff, 1997); B. Bedont and K. Hall-Martinez, 'Ending Impunity for Gender Crimes Under the International Criminal Court' (1999) 6(1) *Brown Journal of World Affairs* 65; R. Copelon, 'Gender Crimes as War Crimes: Integrating Crimes against Women into International Criminal Law' (2000) 46 *McGill Law Journal* 217; C. Niarchos, 'Women, War, and Rape: Challenges Facing the International Tribunal for the Former Yugoslavia' (1995) 17(4) *Human Rights Quarterly* 629.

[2] E.g. S. Brownmiller, *Against Our Will: Men, Women and Rape* (Simon & Schuster, 1975); Combahee River Collective, '1977 Combahee River Collective Statement' in B. Smith (ed.), *Home Girls: A Black Feminist Anthology* (Kitchen Table Press, 1983) 264; C. MacKinnon, *Sexual Harassment of Working Women: A Case of Sex Discrimination* (Yale University Press, 1979).

[3] E.g. *Ongwen* (ICC-02/04-01/15-422-Red), 23 March 2016, [86], [102], [136].

[4] E.g. *Ongwen* (ICC-02/04-01/15-40318 January 2016), [48].

[5] E.g. *Ongwen* (ICC-02/04-01/15-404-Red3), 25 May 2016, [8], [131], [135].

people in and around the ICC, the more unsettled the meanings of the term 'gender-based crimes' became. Hence the emergence of this chapter, which grapples with the multiple interpretations of that term and defines it for the purposes of this book. This definition may, I hope, be useful for future research and discussion on prosecuting gender-based crimes. More immediately, its purpose is to enable readers to make sense of the findings of this book. That is because, when reading the court records, I coded all charges as either 'gender-based crimes' or 'other crimes' (in social science research, 'coding' simply means sorting one's data into relevant categories, in order to reveal patterns and trends).[6] This coding system allowed me to draw meaningful comparisons, such as by comparing the outcomes for gender-based crimes with the outcomes for other crimes within the jurisdiction of the Court. The classification was based on the known facts underpinning the charges, rather than the legal characterisation used by the Prosecutor or the Bench.[7] For example, charges of forced sexual penetration were always coded as 'gender-based crimes', regardless of whether the prosecutors and judges characterised the conduct as 'rape', 'torture', 'persecution' or any other crime enumerated in the Rome Statute.

Section 2.1 of the chapter considers how the term 'gender based crimes' is understood in the ICC, taking into account relevant provisions of the Rome Statute, my interviews with ICC staff and advisors and the OTP's June 2014 *Policy Paper on Sexual and Gender-Based Crimes* ('*Gender Policy*').[8] Building on that discussion, and taking into account decades of feminist literature on this topic, Section 2.2 puts forward a three-dimensional definition of this term. Finally, Section 2.3 considers a contested issue, namely, whether sexual violence is *always,* or only *sometimes,* a 'gender-based crime'. The chapter refers to relevant provisions of the Rome Statute, most obviously, the definition of 'gender' found in Article 7(3). However, as that definition does not do justice to generations of thought, art and activism about the meaning of gender and its relationship to violence, the Statute is not central to in this chapter, while feminist scholarship comes to the fore.

[6] See B. Ackerly and J. True, *Doing Feminist Research in Political and Social Science* (Palgrave Macmillan, 2010) 180, 221.

[7] Where the facts were not disclosed in the public records, the label of 'other crimes' was applied.

[8] ICC OTP, 'Policy Paper on Sexual and Gender-Based Crimes' (June 2014).

## 2.1 Views from the ICC

### 2.1.1 'Gender' in the Rome Statute

In the previous chapter, gender was explained as a social construct – a set of ideas about what it means to be male or female in a given society – and the associated power inequalities that emerge. This notion of gender emerged from the margins, from people who questioned so-called truths about the differences between 'women' and 'men', as well as the stability of those two categories. It has since been embraced, at least nominally, by numerous international institutions including that with the highest number of States Parties: the United Nations (UN).[9] For example, the World Health Organization (WHO), the UN's agency for public health, defines 'gender' as 'the socially constructed characteristics of women and men – such as norms, roles and relationships of and between groups of women and men',[10] and UN Women states that:

> Gender refers to the social attributes and opportunities associated with being male and female and the relationships between women and men and girls and boys, as well as the relations between women and those between men. These attributes, opportunities and relationships are socially constructed and are learned through socialization processes. They are context/time-specific and changeable. Gender determines what is expected, allowed and valued in a woman or a man in a given context. In most societies there are differences and inequalities between women and men in responsibilities assigned, activities undertaken, access to and control over resources, as well as decision-making opportunities.[11]

The ICC's definition is briefer, and according to some commentators, 'bizarre', 'peculiar' and 'stunningly narrow'.[12] This definition is found in Article 7(3) of the Rome Statute, which states:

> For the purposes of this Statute, it is understood that the term 'gender' refers to the two sexes, male and female, within the context of society. The term 'gender' does not indicate any meaning different from the above.

[9] V. Oosterveld, 'The Definition of Gender in the Rome Statute of the International Criminal Court: A Step Forward or Back for International Criminal Justice?' (2005) 18 *Harvard Human Rights Journal* 55, 67.

[10] World Health Organization, *Gender* (undated, accessed 23 April 2018): www.who.int/gender-equity-rights/understanding/gender-definition/en/.

[11] UN Women, *Concepts and Definitions* (undated, accessed 23 April 2018): www.un.org/womenwatch/osagi/conceptsandefinitions.htm.

[12] See citations in: Oosterveld, 'The Definition of Gender', see n. 9, 55–56.

Interpretations of this definition differ, in part because the text points in two directions at once: it refers to 'the two sexes, male and female', implying a binary, biologically determined notion of gender. At the same time, these two sexes are located 'within the context of society', implying that social conceptions of 'maleness' and 'femaleness' also matter.[13] For some commentators, it is clear that this definition 'presents gender primarily as an issue of biology rather than one of social construction'.[14] Others argue against that interpretation,[15] and some are simply unsure.[16] Accounts of the Statute's drafting history help to explain how this confusing definition came about.[17]

In the lead-up to the Rome Conference, the term 'gender' first appeared in a 1996 report by the ICC Preparatory Committee, which noted a recommendation that 'the Court's composition should ensure gender balance'.[18] Further references to 'gender' were included in subsequent draft ICC Statutes, including in a provision referring to persecution on 'gender' grounds, a provision directing the Court to interpret and apply the law without adverse distinction on 'gender' grounds, and several provisions aimed at protecting and empowering victims of 'gender violence' in ICC investigations and prosecutions.[19] At the 1998 Rome

[13] Ibid., 284.

[14] H. Charlesworth and C. Chinkin, *The Boundaries of International Law: A Feminist Analysis* (Manchester University Press, 2000) 335.

[15] E.g. B. Bedont, 'Gender Specific Provisions in the Statute of the International Criminal Court' in F. Lattanzi and W. Schabas (eds), *Essays on the Rome Statute of the International Criminal Court* (Il Sirente, 1999) 183, 187; Oosterveld, 'The Definition of Gender', see n. 9, 72–73; V. Oosterveld, 'Prosecuting Gender-Based Persecution as an International Crime' in A. de Brouwer et al. (eds), *Sexual Violence as an International Crime: Interdisciplinary Approaches* (Intersentia, 2013) 57, 67.

[16] B. Cossman, 'Gender Performance, Sexual Subjects and International Law' (2002) 15(2) *Canadian Journal of Law & Jurisprudence* 281, 284.

[17] Bedont, see n. 15; Bedont and Hall-Martinez, see n. 1; L. Chappell, *The Politics of Gender Justice at the International Criminal Court: Legacies and Legitimacy* (Oxford University Press, 2016) 44–47; Copelon, see n. 1; Oosterveld, 'The Definition of Gender', see n. 9; V. Oosterveld, 'Constructive Ambiguity and the Meaning of "Gender" for the International Criminal Court' 16(4) *International Feminist Journal of Politics* 563; C. Steains, 'Gender Issues' in R.S. Lee (ed.), *The International Criminal Court: The Making of the Rome Statute* (Kluwer Law International, 1999) 357; A. Facio, 'All Roads Lead to Rome, But Some Are Bumpier than Others' in S. Pickering and C. Lambert (eds), *Global Issues: Women and Justice* (Sydney Institute for Criminology, 2004) 308.

[18] Oosterveld, 'The Definition of Gender', see n. 9, 59 citing: 'Report of the Preparatory Committee on the Establishment of an International Criminal Court: Volume I, UN Doc. A/51/22' (13 September 1996), [36].

[19] Oosterveld, 'The Definition of Gender', see n. 9, 59.

Conference, these references to 'gender' received strong support from non-government organisations (NGOs) including the Women's Caucus for Gender Justice[20] and the Asian Centre for Women's Human Rights,[21] as well as like-minded states.[22] This 'pro-gender' bloc argued that the term 'gender' was necessary 'to capture sociological aspects rather than mere biological distinctions' and argued that the Rome Statute should use this term to keep pace with the UN, which had already used it for over a decade.[23]

They faced opposition from the Holy See and several primarily Catholic and primarily Muslim states, most of whom had likewise opposed the use of the word 'gender' three years earlier at the 1995 World Conference on Women in Beijing.[24] Many states and NGOs in this bloc feared that the criminalisation of gender-based persecution might compel them to recognise rights based on sexual orientation or to desist from discriminating against homosexual people and/or women under domestic law.[25] For example, the delegate from Azerbaijan stated that his delegation was 'concerned' about the use of the word 'gender' in the persecution crime and asked 'did that provision imply that a conviction by a national court for homosexual acts might be regarded as persecution and thus fall within the jurisdiction of the Court as a crime against humanity?'[26] That bloc was supported by the conservative NGOs, some of which spread the myth that homosexuality is itself a gender, rather than a sexual orientation that defies

[20] Women's Caucus for Gender Justice, 'Gender Justice and the ICC' (at the United Nations Diplomatic Conference of Plenipotentiaries on the Establishment of an International Criminal Court, Rome, 15 July 1998) (on file).

[21] Official Records: United Nations Diplomatic Conference of Plenipotentiaries on the Establishment of an International Criminal Court, Rome, 15 June–17 July 1998, Vol. II ('Rome Conference Official Records, Vol II') 120, [83].

[22] These states included Australia, Belgium, Canada, Chile, Colombia, Costa Rica, Finland, France, Greece, Italy, Kenya, Mexico, Mozambique, Netherlands, New Zealand, Norway, Samoa, Senegal, Slovenia, South Africa and the US. See Oosterveld, 'The Definition of Gender', see n. 9, 63. For examples of 'pro-gender' statements made by state delegates during the recorded sessions at Rome, see Rome Conference Official Records, Vol. II, 163, [153]; 154, [169]; 157, [26].

[23] Bedont, see n. 15, 186–187; Steains, see n. 17, 372–373.

[24] These states included Bahrain, Brunei, Egypt, Guatemala, Iran, Kuwait, Libya, Oman, Qatar, Saudi Arabia, Sudan, Syria, Turkey, the United Arab Emirates, the Vatican, Venezuela and Yemen. Oosterveld, 'The Definition of Gender', see n. 9, 63.

[25] Oosterveld, 'The Definition of Gender', see n. 9, 63; P. Spees, 'Women's Advocacy in the Creation of the International Criminal Court: Changing the Landscapes of Justice and Power' (2003) 28(4) *Signs* 1233, 1244; Copelon, see n. 1, 236–237; Steains, see n. 17, 372.

[26] Rome Conference Official Records, Vol. II, 272, [61].

deeply entrenched, heterosexist gender norms. For example, the Center for Family & Human Rights (C-FAM) argued that including the term 'gender' in the Rome Statute 'could be interpreted as criminalizing any national laws or policies that favor heterosexual marriage over homosexual couplings, on the grounds that homosexuality is a recognized "gender"'.[27]

There was also an argument that the term 'gender' was confusing or could not be translated into all official UN languages and should therefore be omitted from the Rome Statute or substituted for the word 'sex'.[28] The fact that this translation problem could be easily solved by including a definition in the Rome Statute, and that it was not raised in respect of other potentially confusing grounds of persecution such as 'ethnic' and 'cultural' grounds,[29] suggests that this concern was either disingenuous or poorly thought out. The debate over whether to criminalise persecution on 'gender' grounds merged with a debate as to whether the ICC judges should be required to interpret the law without discrimination on the basis of 'gender'.[30] After extensive debate, the delegates agreed to include the term 'gender' in the Statute, subject to the definition found in Article 7(3). Valerie Oosterveld recalls that the sub-committee that drafted the definition *deliberately* chose terms vague enough to appease both sides, a negotiating tactic known as 'constructive ambiguity'.[31] Thus, they made the definition 'as skeletal as possible', leaving it to the judges to interpret it at a later stage.[32]

As of the Rome Statute's twentieth anniversary, the judges are yet to take up that challenge. However, the OTP has clarified its interpretation of the definition in its June 2014 *Gender Policy*, as advised by several groups who gave comments on the draft policy released earlier

[27] A. Ruse, 'Feminists Refuse to Define Their "Gender Agenda" for the International Criminal Court' on *C-Fam* (26 June 1998): c-fam.org/feminists-refuse-to-define-their-gender-agenda-for-the-international-criminal-court/. See also M. Glasius, *The International Criminal Court: A Global Civil Society Achievement* (Routledge, 2006) 86; Oosterveld, 'Constructive Ambiguity', see n. 17, 565.

[28] Facio, see n. 17, 327–328; Oosterveld, 'The Definition of Gender', see n. 9, 63; Oosterveld, 'Constructive Ambiguity', see n. 17, 566; Spees, see n. 23, 1244; Steains, see n. 17, 373.

[29] 'Report of the Preparatory Committee on the Establishment of an International Criminal Court: Addendum 1 (Draft Statute of the International Criminal Court), UN Doc. A/CONF.183/2/Add'. (14 April 1998) 26.

[30] Oosterveld, 'The Definition of Gender', see n. 9, 58–66; Oosterveld, 'Constructive Ambiguity', see n. 17, 564–568; Steains, see n. 17, 371–375.

[31] Oosterveld, 'The Definition of Gender', see n. 9, 57; Oosterveld, 'Constructive Ambiguity', see n. 17.

[32] Oosterveld, 'Prosecuting Gender-Based Persecution as an International Crime', see n. 15, 67.

that year.[33] According to the *Gender Policy*, the ICC's definition of 'gender' 'acknowledges the *social construction of gender*, and the accompanying roles, behaviours, activities, and attributes assigned to women and men, and to girls and boys'.[34] All OTP staff that I interviewed in 2017 and 2018 acknowledged this *Policy* definition of 'gender'. However, even among my small sample of interviewees, it was apparent that views on the utility of the term 'gender' varied. For example, one interviewee noted that although it was appropriate to cite the definition when representing the Office,

> I think the word gender has come into use because people are a bit afraid of saying 'sex'. They think it's slightly embarrassing. I don't think it is, when it describes the unique characteristics of 50 per cent of the human race. I think we should be prepared to call a spade a spade, to use words in their plain meaning, and not alter the usage of the language because we may feel a bit embarrassed about it. ... Certainty of the law is absolutely crucial.[35]

### *2.1.2 From 'Gender' to 'Gender-Based Crimes'*

Taking up that point about the importance of 'certainty of the law', it is remarkable that term 'gender-based crimes' is now widely used in the ICC, given that is not used or defined in the Rome Statute or other relevant instruments (e.g. the 1948 Genocide Convention, the 1949 Geneva Conventions or their 1977 Additional Protocols). However, the Rome Statute include several references to 'gender violence',[36] signalling that its drafters contemplated the links between gender and violence and intended the Court to do the same. During the Statute negotiations, some delegates questioned the necessity of the term 'gender violence', given that the term 'sexual violence' already appeared in numerous provisions.[37] However, other delegates defended the reference to 'gender violence' on the grounds that it 'encompassed violence directed at a person *because of his or her gender*, and therefore was not necessarily covered by the term

[33] E.g. Refugee Law Project, 'Comments on the ICC Draft Policy Paper on Sexual and Gender Based Crimes' (23 February 2014), [11]. See also ICC OTP, 'Draft Policy Paper on Sexual and Gender Based Crimes' (February 2014), [13].

[34] ICC OTP, 'Gender Policy', see n. 8, 3.

[35] Interview I, ICC OTP, 2017.

[36] Articles 42(9); 54(1)(b); 68(1).

[37] Steains, see n. 17, 388.

"sexual violence"'.[38] For example, referencing the (then) recent events in Srebrenica, the Canadian delegates referred to civilian men being rounded up and killed because they were seen as being capable of waging war – 'an ability imputed to them on the basis of their sex, their age and their sociological role as potential soldiers' – as an example of 'gender violence' that would not fall within the narrower category of 'sexual violence'.[39] A similar understanding of the term 'gender violence' was advanced by women's rights activists who took part in the negotiations at the Women's Caucus for Gender Justice. They argued:

> Gender violence is violence that is targeted at women or men because of their sex and/or their socially constructed gender roles. Gender violence disproportionately affects the members of one sex more than another. The recent conflicts in the former Yugoslavia and Rwanda have seen many examples of gender violence. Examples include: the forcible recruitment of young boys into the army who are put through violent indoctrination, and then made to perform suicidal missions in order to prove their masculinity; and the killing of pregnant women by the slashing of their wombs and removal of their fetuses.[40]

In several early cases, the OTP evoked this idea of 'gender violence', albeit in slightly different terms. For example, in November 2009, in his opening statements in the *Katanga & Ngudjolo* trial, Prosecutor Moreno-Ocampo described the alleged rape and abduction of women and girls during an attack on a village in Ituri, Democratic Republic of Congo. He argued: 'these women were victimised *on the basis of their gender.* They were attacked in particular *because they were women*'.[41] Twelve months later, on the first day of the *Bemba* trial, the Prosecutor argued that the 'massive rapes' allegedly committed by Bemba's troops in the Central African Republic 'were not just sexually motivated; as *gender crimes*, they were crimes of domination and humiliation directed against women, but also directed against men with authority'.[42] He continued: '[w]omen were raped systematically to assert dominance and to shatter resistance. Men were raped in public to destroy their authority, their capacity to lead'.[43]

[38] Ibid., 388 (emphasis added).

[39] Ibid., n. 99.

[40] Women's Caucus for Gender Justice, 'Clarification of Term "Gender"' (undated): www.iccwomen.org/wigjdraft1/Archives/oldWCGJ/resources/gender.html.

[41] ICC-01/04-01/07-T-80-ENG, 24 November 2009, page 25, lines 19–25.

[42] ICC-01/05-01/08-T-32-ENG, 22 November 2010, page 10, lines 14–16 (emphasis added).

[43] Ibid., lines 18–19.

This language coincided with the term of Professor Catharine Mackinnon, who from November 2008 to August 2012 served as the ICC Prosecutor's Special Advisor on Gender.[44] In a 2013 article, Mackinnon explained that the idea of 'gender crimes' began as a way to re-conceive of sexual violence crimes as crimes that happen 'because of the *social meaning* of sex'.[45] She continued:

> What had been thought of as a crime without social particularity, considered a crime against an individual victim, when understood as a gender-biased violation became reconfigured as a crime against groups being inflicted on its members. Women in this view are raped or otherwise sexually violated as women, men as men who are specifically marked for the humiliation, denigration, and conquest of feminization, typically based as well on their physical stature, age, ethnicity or religion or race, or perceived sexuality or gender.[46]

In the intervening years, the OTP has settled on a different phrase to communicate this idea, namely 'gender-based crimes'. The term has been used in countless press releases, filings and oral arguments, most often, within the expression 'sexual and gender-based crimes'.[47] A brief definition can be found in the 2014 *Gender Policy*, which states:

> 'Gender-based crimes' are those committed against persons, whether male or female, *because of their sex and/or socially constructed gender roles*. Gender-based crimes are not always manifested as a form of sexual violence. They may include non-sexual attacks on women and girls, and men and boys, because of their gender.[48]

My interviews suggest that this definition is understood widely, albeit not universally, within the OTP. When asked how they would explain the term 'gender-based crimes', all OTP interviewees noted that these crimes could be committed against men and women, and *most* referred to crimes directed at people because of their socially constructed gender identity, as opposed only to sexual violence crimes. Several people elaborated on the

[44] The OTP did not refer to 'gender' in its opening statements in the *Lubanga* case, delivered before MacKinnon's appointment. See: ICC-01/04-01/06-T-107-ENG, 26 January 2009, 4(10)-36(4).

[45] C. MacKinnon, 'Creating International Law: Gender as Leading Edge' (2013) 36(1) *Harvard Journal of Law & Gender* 105, 105.

[46] Ibid., 106.

[47] E.g. *Ongwen* (ICC-02/04-01/15-533), 6 September 2015; ICC OTP, 'Statement of ICC Prosecutor, Fatou Bensouda, on International Day for the Elimination of Violence against Women' (25 November 2017).

[48] ICC OTP, 'Gender Policy', see n. 8, 3 (emphasis added).

*Gender Policy's* definition, indicating that those two sentences had not just been rote-learned. For example, one person stated: 'for me, gender-based crimes would really be considering the gender of the victims and for that reason, adopt[ing] a certain attitude or behaviour to the victim, who could be female, or male'.[49] Another stated that the term 'gender-based crime' applies where:

> The victim is targeted for that particular conduct because of the person's gender. Because of the particular role that the perpetrators expect the victims of that particular gender to play. So, that is the operative thing in the minds of the perpetrators when they target a specific individual or individuals for certain crimes ... It's what the perpetrator wants out of the person that makes it a gender crime – how that fits within the cultural/social context and expected roles/behaviour etc. in a given society.[50]

A third person stated:

> The concept of a 'gender-based crime' is a crime which has been committed against a person on the grounds of their gender, the most obvious being male and female genders, i.e. the physical 'two sexes, male and female'. However, I would not restrict it to simply those categories. I think it encompasses a wider set of criteria which could define people. That is, I think sexual orientation would be encompassed by that concept, people of intersex gender, transgender and a variety of other people. In fact, I would say that it is a crime that occurs based on those attributes of a person's gender, not necessarily defined by their physical attributes, but also defined in sociological or social ways ... A classic gender-based crime could be persecution based on someone's gender. Obviously, women could be persecuted based on them performing a female role in that society, let's say a mothering role, or they could be persecuted to the extent that they were not allowed to be educated past a certain age, or discriminated against in other ways, or certain practices carried out upon them which could be considered discrimination on the grounds of gender. You could also have situations where men or boys were discriminated against.[51]

Departing from this pattern, one OTP interviewee defined a 'gender-based crime' as 'an attack on the physical integrity of a person, with a sexual connotation, meaning that any breach of the physical integrity of a person has to relate to usually sexual body parts'.[52] However, that was the only person to narrow the definition to sexual violence crimes. Indeed,

[49] Interview J, ICC OTP, 2017.
[50] Interview H, ICC OTP, 2017 (ellipses omitted).
[51] Interview B, ICC OTP, 2017.
[52] Interview L, ICC OTP, 2017.

the idea that gender-based crimes *necessarily* involve sexual violence was refuted expressly – and without prompting – by several OTP interviewees. For example, one person observed:

> Some people understand gender-based crimes as being sexual crimes solely, which I believe is not the case. For me, sexual crimes could be gender-based crimes, but gender-based crimes are not automatically sexual violence crimes.[53]

Another stated:

> A lot of people confuse gender-based crimes and sexual crimes and most of them have the idea that gender-based crimes are limited to crimes like rape. Most of the time, rape is the first crime that comes to mind. And sometimes the only crime that comes to mind. But gender-based crimes are distinct from sexual crimes because they do not *always* have a sexual component to it.[54]

Moreover, when I asked for some examples of 'gender-based crimes', several OTP interviewees offered a non-sexual example *first.* For instance, one person led with the example of 'the specific targeting of boys for use as child soldiers on the frontline', explaining:

> In the Uganda case, there was very much a targeting of children for abduction and enslavement for specific uses. Girls were also used and continue to be used for the frontline, but it was predominantly the boys that were seen as being targeted for abduction and enslavement specifically for the purpose of frontline use. So that's an example to me of a gender-based crime. Other examples include mutilation of both females and males, genital mutilation, that would be a gender-based crime. The very obvious gender-based crimes – sexual violence related crimes, whether it's rape, sexual slavery, forced marriage, forced sterilisation, forced pregnancy, those are clearly gender-based crimes.[55]

To give another example:

> The classic example which can be given is the men and boys who were rounded up in the Srebrenica killing. It was a gender-based crime because they were rounded up and killed because the men, and the boys in future, could be seen as performing a soldier role, or a male soldier role. So that would also be an example of a gender crime. If you're just killing women, or just killing men, that can become a gendered crime. Genocide can also be gendered, because of the means by which genocide can be carried out. For example, genocide by preventing marriages within a group,

[53] Interview J, ICC OTP, 2017.
[54] Interview H, ICC OTP, 2017 (emphasis added).
[55] Interview K, ICC OTP, 2017.

> sterilization to prevent births within a group, etc. The crime of deportation does not in its elements have any gender aspect. But factually, these crimes could have gender aspects.[56]

Similar responses to the question 'what is a gender-based crime' were provided by Xavier-Jean Keïta, Principal Counsel of the Office of Public Counsel for Defence (OPCD), and Paolina Massidda, Principal Counsel of the Office of Public Counsel for Victims (OPCV). Specifically, Keïta stated: 'gender-based crimes are not only limited to sexual acts but also extend to non-sexual acts against men and women respectively', adding, 'it is often forgotten that men may be humiliated on par with women in peacetime or/and in times of an armed conflict. It is unfortunate that these types of crimes are alleged to have been committed'.[57] For her part, Massidda defined a 'gender-based crimes' as:

> Any crime which is based on gender, being against female or male (because of course it can be on both sides) because of the gender of that person and also because of the social standing of that person. Not necessarily limited to sexual violence, because you can have an attack against a male or female which is not necessarily a sexual assault, but which has an implication of gender-based crimes because of the motivation of the crime.[58]

These interview responses are not necessarily representative of the ICC, due to the small sample size and the fact that all interviewees were in senior roles, being heads of sections and/or very seasoned prosecutors. There is reason to think that this group may be more well-versed in gender theory than some of their colleagues: according to gender expert Niamh Hayes, who in late 2018 commenced a role in the OTP, but at the time of our interview was there on secondment from UN Women, 'if you ask "is there a gender aspect in your case"?, they sometimes say "no, there's no rape"'.[59] Yet it is significant that even in the small group that I interviewed, there was some variation in views: everyone agreed that 'gender-based crimes' could be committed against women and men, but they did not all agree on whether the category included anything *other* than sexual violence crimes, or why sexual violence crimes are necessarily 'gender-based'.

In terms of gaps and silences, it is interesting that all interviewees focused on the gender identity of the victim(s), without paying equal

[56] Interview B, ICC OTP, 2017 (ellipses omitted).
[57] Interview, July 2018.
[58] Interview, June 2017.
[59] Interview, July 2017.

attention to the gender identity of the perpetrator. In addition, crimes targeted at lesbian, gay, bisexual, transgender, intersex and/or queer (LGBTIQ) people were seldom discussed, although these can arguably be prosecuted as 'gender-based persecution' in the ICC, as I argue in Chapter 6.[60] One OTP interview described 'the victimisation of gay and lesbian and transsexual people' as 'one area we have to at some point have a closer look [at].',[61] and another stated that 'sexual orientation would be encompassed by that concept [of gender]'.[62] Beyond that, the topic was not broached by the ICC interviewees. This was not surprising, given that the OTP's *Gender Policy* confirms neither that 'gender' includes sexual orientation, nor that violence on the basis of sexual orientation or gender identity is a 'gender-based crime'.[63] By contrast, Hayes's position on this issue was clear. In her words:

> I can't think of a scenario where the intentional targeting of sexual minorities *wouldn't* be based on the understanding in that society of the role of men and the role of women. They've gone outside of socially accepted gender norms, or they've transgressed gender boundaries. Such as 'corrective rape' of lesbian women in Uganda because of the social belief that you're not a 'real woman' unless you've been with a man.[64]

## 2.2 A Broader Approach

Having outlined in broad terms how the term 'gender-based crimes' is understood in the ICC, this section of the chapter explains how it is understood in this book. In the scholarship on international criminal law, commentators often refer to crimes such as rape, sexual slavery, enforced prostitution, forced pregnancy, enforced sterilisation, sexual mutilation, all-male or all-female killings and forced marriage as 'gender-based

[60] See §6.2.1.

[61] Interview A, ICC OTP, 2017.

[62] Interview B, ICC OTP, 2017.

[63] The *Policy* moves towards this interpretation of 'gender' and 'gender-based crimes'. It acknowledges, in a footnote, 'the efforts of the UN Human Rights Council and the Office of the High Commissioner for Human Rights (OHCHR) to put an end to violence and discrimination on the basis of sexual orientation or gender identity'. However, the *Policy* does not confirm such violence constitutes a 'gender-based crime', as defined by the OTP. Nor does it confirm that by June 2014, when the *Policy* was published, the statutory definition of 'gender', when interpreted in accordance with internationally recognised human rights in accordance with Article 21(3) of the Rome Statute, necessarily includes sexual orientation. See ICC OTP, 'Gender Policy', see n. 8, [26], n. 23.

[64] Interview, July 2017.

crimes' or simply 'gender crimes'.[65] Searching for a common denominator in this list, one might infer that crimes are 'gender-based' if they involve acts of sexual violence and/or sex-based discrimination, whether as a legal requirement or on the facts of a particular case. But what is gained by lumping these offences together and describing them collectively as 'gender-based crimes'? Why is this a *meaningful* description? What does it add to our ability to narrate violence in conflict settings?

I venture that there are three main answers to this question: the term 'gender-based crimes' is a meaningful label if victims are targeted because of their gender identity; if the perpetrator is seeking to affirm their own gender identity; or if the crime is intended as punishment for defying gender norms (or any combination of the three). These three options are explained in more detail below. Importantly, this interpretation is not inconsistent with the Rome Statute's definition of 'gender': it does not assert the existence of more than 'two sexes, male and female'; it just takes seriously the instruction to consider both sexes 'within the context of society'. In this respect, I agree fully with Hayes, who argues that the statutory definition is 'a lot broader than people realise'. In her view:

> When they see 'the two sexes, male and female', that's because of certain states during the drafting and negotiation process for the Rome Statute being frightened of what they saw as a feminist conspiracy to recognise multiple genders, and trying to shut it down to just the two biological sexes. But the inclusion of the additional reference to how those two sexes are understood 'in the context of society', that kicks the door wide open.[66]

### 2.2.1 *Targeting Based on the Victim's Gender*

First, and picking up on the definition found in the OTP's *Gender Policy*, it is meaningful to describe crimes as 'gender-based' when the victims are targeted 'because' of their gender. I use quotation marks here to signify that a person's gender does not *on its own* invite or cause violence; rather, ideas about their gender influence the perpetrator's

[65] E.g. Bedont and Hall-Martinez, see n. 1; Copelon, see n. 1; Chappell, see n. 17; V. Oosterveld and P.V. Sellers, 'Issues of Sexual and Gender-Based Violence at the ECCC' in S. Meisenberg and I. Stegmiller (eds), *The Extraordinary Chambers in the Courts of Cambodia: Assessing Their Contribution to International Criminal Law* (Springer, 2016) 321; K. Natale, 'I Could Feel My Soul Flying away from My Body: A Study on Gender-Based Violence during Democratic Kampuchea in Battambang and Svay Rieng Provinces' (Cambodian Defenders Project, November 2011).

[66] Interview, July 2018.

conscious or unconscious decision-making about whom to target, and what kind(s) of violence to inflict.

This understanding of gender-based crimes has its roots in feminist scholarship on conflict-related sexual violence, particularly responses to reports of 'mass rape' and 'genocidal rape' in the wars that led to the creation of the ad hoc tribunals for the former Yugoslavia and Rwanda. As argued by feminist scholars at that time, a concept of gender was necessary to understand the reports of widespread rape during these and prior wars. Without a concept of gender, one cannot explain why such rapes disproportionately affected *women and girls* from targeted ethnic or national groups, or why rape is so damaging to men's sense of authority within their communities.[67] As emphasised by many of those scholars, this reconception of conflict-related rape did not only shed light on patterns of violence in the context of genocide, 'ethnic cleansing' and war. It also made visible the connections between conflict-related sexual violence, on the one hand, and the objectification and subordination of women in times of peace. In others words, it allows us to see that these forms of violence exist on a continuum of violence against women and girls.[68] In other words, 'the innocuous makes space for the horrific. And women have to live with the effects of both and everything in between'.[69]

Even in that early scholarship on wartime rape, there was an understanding that gender was not the *sole* factor at play. It was understood that gender intersects with other variables to make certain people more vulnerable to sexual violence than others, and that the risk of sexual violence is heightened by grievances over unequal access to land and resources, a breakdown of law enforcement, a separation of families and communities, an increased accessibility of weapons, a desensitisation to violence and an intensification of hate-filled and incendiary rhetoric.[70] For example,

[67] See R. Copelon, 'Surfacing Gender: Re-Engraving Crimes against Women in Humanitarian Law' (1994) 5 *Hastings Women's Law Journal* 243; S. Chesterman, 'Never Again ... and Again: Law, Order, and the Gender of War Crimes in Bosnia and Beyond' (1997) 22 *Yale Journal of International Law* 299, 329; R. Chowdhury, 'Kadic v. Karadzic: Rape as a Crime against Women as a Class' (2002) 20(1) *Law & Inequality: A Journal of Theory and Practice* 91; Niarchos, see n. 1.

[68] C. Cockburn, 'The Continuum of Violence: A Gender Perspective on War and Peace' in W. Giles and J. Hyndman (eds), *Sites of Violence: Gender and Conflict Zones* (University of California Press, 2004) 24; Charlesworth and Chinkin, see n. 14, 334.

[69] T. Ross, 'A Woman's Fury Holds Lifetimes of Wisdom' (at the TED Conference, April 2018): www.ted.com/talks/tracee_ellis_ross_a_woman_s_fury_holds_lifetimes_of_wisdom.

[70] Cockburn, see n. 68; S. Davies and J. True, 'The Pandemic of Conflict-Related Sexual Violence and the Political Economy of Gender Inequality' in A. Powell, N. Henry and A. Flynn (eds), *Rape Justice Beyond the Criminal Law* (Palgrave Macmillan, 2015) 160.

writing in 1994, Copelon observed that 'the mass rape in Bosnia has captured world attention largely because of its association with "ethnic cleansing" or genocide'.[71] Concerned about the simplistic explanations of this sexual violence in media reports of the time, Copelon urged readers to 'avoid dualistic thinking', meaning we need not explain these rapes in terms of sexism *or* ethnic hatred; instead, we should recognise that *both* ideologies contributed to the crimes.[72]

In the intervening years, the scholarship on conflict-related gender crimes has expanded beyond its initial focus on sexual violence against women, to include a wider range of violations, and a more diverse group of victims. There have also been numerous empirical studies which explore how local conceptions of gender contribute to violence in particular wars. While it is impossible to summarise this broad field of research here, some case studies will help to bring out the key ideas.

The first case study is the 'second Congo war', which took place in the Democratic Republic of Congo from 1998 to 2003 and which is the backdrop to six ICC cases to date.[73] Numerous studies indicate that the rampant sexual violence in this conflict was attributable, among other things, to a widespread belief that men have a 'need' for sex and are entitled to abuse women to satisfy that 'need'.[74] For example, based on their interviews with 226 soldiers and officers from armed groups in Kinshasa, Kitona and the Kivus, Maria Eriksson Baaz and Maria Stern found that 'the Congolese military celebrates certain ideals of macho heterosexual masculinity. A (male) soldier's libido is understood as a formidable natural force, which ultimately demands sexual satisfaction from women'.[75] In the words of one their respondents,

> If [a soldier] has nothing in his pocket, he cannot eat or drink his coke, he has nothing to give to a woman – he will take her by force … Physically, men have needs. He cannot go a long time without being with a woman.[76]

[71] Copelon, see n. 67, 245–246.

[72] Ibid., 247.

[73] See Chapter 4.

[74] For an overview, see: S. Meger, 'Rape of the Congo: Understanding Sexual Violence in the Conflict in the Democratic Republic of Congo' (2010) 28(2) *Journal of Contemporary African Studies* 119.

[75] M. Eriksson Baaz and M. Stern, 'The Complexity of Violence: A Critical Analysis of Sexual Violence in the Democratic Republic of Congo' (SIDA/Nordiska Afrikainstitutet, 2010) 47.

[76] Ibid., 31.

Eriksson Baaz and Stern conclude that 'according to this line of reasoning, it is as "somewhat unavoidable" that a man – who in any way is "denied sex" through lack of financial or other means – will eventually rape'.[77] Very similar views emerge from the 2013 study by Thomas Elbert et al., based on interviews with 213 ex-combatants in North and South Kivus.[78] In that study, one respondent stated: 'we rape women. How can you stay for two weeks without sex?! Every soldier needs sex', another stated: 'no man can stay five years without sex. If they are not allowed to see their wives, they have to take another woman by force', and a third explained:

> Soldiers rape when they have had too many days without sex. They just need it. They are not allowed to bring their wives to the bush. So they need other women. But if you ask a woman who does not know you to have sex with you, she refuses. Then you have to force her. Even commanders rape.[79]

While both of those studies from the Democratic Republic of Congo focused on sexual violence crimes and their link to masculine entitlement, it would be wrong to assume that this was the *only* gender-based crime suffered by women and girls during the succession of wars in that state. For example, in the ICC's first trial (*Lubanga*), which concerned the recruitment and use of 'child soldiers' by one of the militias involved in this conflict, an insider witness recalled that female 'child soldiers' were forced to cook and clean for the commanders: labour described by the witness as 'feminine tasks'.[80] Further evidence of female 'child soldiers' being forced to perform domestic work can be found in the *Ntaganda* case, which focuses on the same group as the *Lubanga* case.[81]

A second case study, chosen in order to illustrate the intersections between gender and other markers of identity, is the abuse of so-called 'comfort women' (慰安婦) by the Japanese military during World War II. The term 'comfort women' is a misnomer: it refers to the estimated 80,000–200,000 women who were enslaved in military-operated facilities, where they faced a life of 'unmitigated misery'.[82] They were beaten,

[77] Ibid., 47.

[78] T. Elbert et al., 'Sexual and Gender-Based Violence in the Kivu Provinces of the Democratic Republic of Congo: Insights from Former Combatants' (World Bank, September 2013).

[79] Ibid., 47.

[80] ICC-01/04-01/06-T-178-ENG, 26 May 2009, 78(1–5).

[81] *Ntaganda* (ICC-01/04-02/06-503-AnxA-Red2), 1 September 2015, [345], [449], [452], [454].

[82] U. Dolgopol and S. Paranjape, 'Comfort Women: An Unfinished Ordeal: Report of a Mission' (International Commission of Jurists, 1994) 15.

underfed, denied medical treatment, subjected to forced abortions and raped by an average of ten to 30 soldiers a day. Many died from these conditions, and those who survived faced ongoing stigmatisation as well as serious physical and psychological harm.[83] This system was established in response to the international condemnation directed at Japan for the mass rapes at Nanking and elsewhere. As explained by Iris Chang,

> The plan was straightforward. By luring, purchasing, or kidnapping between eighty thousand and two hundred thousand women – most of them from the Japanese colony of Korea but many also from China, Taiwan, the Philippines and Indonesia – the Japanese military hoped to reduce the incidence of random rape of local women (thereby diminishing the opportunity for international criticism), to contain sexually transmitted diseases through the use of condoms, and to reward soldiers for fighting on the battle front for long stretches of time.[84]

The fact that the victims were all women and were forced to perform what was regarded as women's work provides strong circumstantial evidence that gender played a part in their selection. Yet these victims were not selected due to their gender alone. The fact that they came chiefly from states under Japan's colonial rule or occupation, including Korea, Taiwan, the Philippines, Indonesia, China and various Pacific islands – in other words, their status as 'foreign' – also played a part. As explained by Japanese historian Yuki Tanaka, the 'comfort women' system was based on 'two ideological structures that are fundamental to the Japanese nationalist mentality', namely 'xenophobia' and 'the contempt with which women are held in Japanese society and the exploitation of their sexuality by Japanese men'.[85] The same point was made by the Tokyo Women's War Crimes Tribunal, a 'people's tribunal' established in 2000 to symbolically prosecute these crimes in response to 50 years of inaction by states. As its judgment observed,

> The Japanese military targeted women and girls primarily of subjugated populations viewed as inferior by Japanese Imperial culture, for the provision of forced sexual services because they were female and

[83] Ibid. See also Y. Tanaka, *Hidden Horrors: Japanese War Crimes in World War II* (Rowman & Littlefield, 2nd edn, 2018) Ch. 3; J. Ruff-O'Herne, 'Fifty Years of Silence: Cry of the Raped' in H. Durham and T. Gurd (eds), *Listening to the Silences: Women and War* (Martinus Nijhoff, 2005) 3; 'Report on the Mission to the Democratic People's Republic of Korea, the Republic of Korea and Japan on the Issue of Military Sexual Slavery in Wartime, UN Doc. E/CN.4/1996/53/Add.1' (4 January 1996).

[84] I. Chang, *The Rape of Nanking: The Forgotten Holocaust of World War II* (Penguin Books, 1997) 52–53. See also Dolgopol and Paranjape, see n. 82, 30–31; Copelon, see n. 1, 222–223.

[85] Tanaka, see n. 83, 88.

> thus seen as disposable ... The creation of the 'comfort women' system reflects the intersection of discrimination based on both gender and race/ethnicity.[86]

These case studies from the Democratic Republic of Congo and Japan are somewhat similar, in that they both concern crimes directed at women and girls. Yet as noted by all of my ICC interviewees, men and boys (and, I would add, people who are not male *or* female) can also be victims of gender-based crimes. This point is well illustrated by the third case study, namely the 1995 Srebrenica massacre, in which approximately 8,000 Bosnian Muslim men were marched out of a UN 'safe area' in the town of Srebrenica and then killed by the Bosnian Serb Army, while the women, infants and elderly men were forcibly removed.[87] Ethnicity was clearly relevant here, as the people in Srebrenica were targeted in the context of 'ethnic cleansing' because they were non-Serbs. However, gender and age also played a crucial role: the younger men were murdered because they were perceived as potential combatants, whereas the remaining victims were not seen to pose that same threat.[88] For this reason, Srebrenica has been described by Patricia Sellers, current Gender Advisor to the ICC Prosecutor, as a 'gendered genocide'.[89]

In many cases, violence is also directed at men in order to *undermine* their masculinity, that is, to diminish their cultural status as a 'real man'. In particular, men may be targeted for sexual violence in order to make them feel 'emasculated', 'feminised' or 'homosexualised'. Reflecting on this point, feminist political scientist Cynthia Cockburn has argued 'when men too are raped or sexually humiliated, or their genitalia mutilated, the act is no less gendered: it is their masculinity that enemy men are deriding'.[90] An example can be seen in the ICC's *Bemba* case, in which a male rape victim from the Central African Republic told the Court that

[86] Women's International War Crimes Tribunal for the Trial of Japan's Military Sexual Slavery, 'Judgment, The Prosecutors and the Peoples of the Asia-Pacific Region v. Hirohito Emperor Showa et al.' (4 December 2001), [929].

[87] See: Appeal Judgment, *Krstić* (IT-98-33-A), 19 April 2004, [2].

[88] M. Jarvis, 'Overview: The Challenge of Accountability for Conflict-Related Sexual Violence Crimes' in S. Brammertz and M. Jarvis (eds), *Prosecuting Conflict-Related Sexual Violence at the ICTY* (Oxford University Press, 2016) 1, 11, 14–15; C. Carpenter, '"Women and Children First": Gender, Norms, and Humanitarian Evacuation in the Balkans 1991–95' (2003) 57(4) *International Organization* 661.

[89] P.V. Sellers, 'Genocide Gendered: The Srebrenica Cases' (at the *9th Annual International Humanitarian Law Dialogs*, Chautauqua Institution, 31 August 2015).

[90] Cockburn, see n. 82, 36.

Bemba's soldiers 'sodomised me. They treated me as if I were a woman and – as even if I were a woman'.[91] The same witness explained:

> I considered myself to be dead because a man cannot sleep with another man. With what they did to me, I knew that I was dead. I could no longer feel like a human being. And after that, my second wife refused me because she considered that I was a woman like her.[92]

From a feminist perspective, being made to feel feminine or homosexual is not in itself negative and should not be uncritically accepted as such. However, one might acknowledge that for people of any sex or sexual orientation, being made to feel feminine or homosexual may be *experienced* as a harm if it denies that person access to the power and privilege associated with masculinity in many cultural contexts.[93] That is, being 'emasculated' can be regarded as a harm because of its negative social consequences, in the same way that a forced loss of 'virginity' can be regarded as a harm, even if one does not see 'virginity' as a virtue in its own right.

Sometimes, gender-based targeting works in an indirect way, such as where a woman is raped in order to 'emasculate' the man who, according to cultural norms, is 'meant' to be her protector.[94] As argued by Susan Brownmiller in her seminal 1975 book *Against Our Will*, 'the body of a raped woman becomes a ceremonial battlefield, a parade ground for the victor's trooping of the colors. The act that is played out upon her is a message passed between men—vivid proof of victory for one and loss and defeat for the other'.[95] Or by Ruth Seifert in Stiglmayer's 1994 collection *Mass Rape*:

> In the context of war, … the rape of women carries an additional message: it communicates from man to man, so to speak, that the men around the woman in question are not able to protect 'their' women. They are thus wounded in their masculinity and marked as incompetent.[96]

[91] ICC-01/05-01/08-T-51-Red2-ENG, 21 January 2011, 35(4–5).

[92] Ibid., 35(8–11).

[93] R. Connell and J. Messerschmidt, 'Hegemonic Masculinity: Rethinking the Concept' (2005) 19(6) *Gender & Society* 829; C. Dolan, 'Victims Who Are Men' in F. Ní Aoláin et al. (eds), *The Oxford Handbook of Gender and Conflict* (Oxford University Press, 2018) 86; Eriksson Baaz and Stern, see n. 75, 44; S. Sivakumaran, 'Sexual Violence against Men in Armed Conflict' (2007) 18(2) *European Journal of International Law* 253, 267–275.

[94] M. Urban-Walker, 'Gender and Violence in Focus: A Background for Gender Justice in Reparations' in R. Rubio Marín (ed.), *The Gender of Reparations: Unsettling Sexual Hierarchies while Redressing Human Rights Violations* (Cambridge University Press, 2009) 1, 35; Eriksson Baaz and Stern, see n. 75, 41; Elbert et al., see n. 78, 58.

[95] Brownmiller, see n. 2, 38.

[96] R. Seifert, 'War and Rape: A Preliminary Analysis' in A. Stiglmayer (ed.), *Mass Rape: The War Against Women in Bosnia-Herzegovina* (University of Nebraska Press, 1994) 54, 59.

### 2.2.2 *Violence to Affirm the Gender Identity of the Perpetrator*

The previous discussion of gender-based crimes focused on the gender of the victim. However, that is only part of the story: often, the perpetrator's own gender identity is relevant too. The concept of masculinity is again relevant here. In many cultures, masculinity is not a fixed status: it must continuously be 'earned' and affirmed.[97] Violence can be an effective currency in this context.[98] As explained by gender scholar Raewyn Connell, 'violence often arises in the construction of masculinities, as part of the practice by which particular men or groups of men claim respect, intimidate rivals, or try to gain material advantages'.[99] Thus, in cultures where the masculinity is equated with might, a man (or anyone who wants to claim the privilege that comes with being seen as 'like a man') might use violence to prove that masculine identity to others.[100]

This often occurs in military cultures where the idea of being a 'real soldier' requires the performance of macho, misogynistic masculinity. An example of this way of thinking can be seen in the aforementioned study by Elbert et al. into sexual violence in the Democratic Republic of Congo, in which 'around one-third of the participants (32 per cent) agreed raping women was necessary to prove manhood or strength'.[101] Similarly, in a 1994 study by the International Commission of Jurists into Japan's use of 'comfort women' during World War II, the researchers spoke to several former Japanese soldiers who explained 'you would often hear statements in the military that you were not really a soldier unless you could rape a woman'.[102]

Another common ideal of masculinity involves protecting and providing for one's family. This too can push men towards violence, as a response to the shame and anger experienced by men who cannot achieve those goals. For example, in Erikkson Baaz and Stern's study in the Democratic Republic of Congo, rape was widely viewed as a way to

97 Ibid. See also: J. Vandello et al., 'Precarious Manhood' (2008) 95(6) *Journal of Personality and Social Psychology* 1325.

98 For a similar analysis, see Meger, see n. 74.

99 R. Connell, 'On Hegemonic Masculinity and Violence: Response to Jefferson and Hall' (2002) 6(6) *Theoretical Criminology* 89, 95.

100 Urban-Walker, see n. 94, 27.

101 Elbert et al., see n. 78, 47.

102 Dolgopol and Paranjape, see n. 82, 25.

reclaim a sense of 'manhood' by soldiers who, due to war and poverty, could not live up to the cultural ideal of earning a decent living and attracting a wife.[103] Erikkson Baaz and Stern conclude that in this setting, 'feelings of "failed masculinity" can be seen to contribute to sexual violence in that it becomes a way to try to perform and try to regain masculinity and power'.[104] This finding rings true with research in the field of psychology, which indicates that men tend to use violence as a 'manhood-restoring strategy', particularly where they feel that their masculinity is in doubt.[105]

It is less common to see violence used to claim or affirm a *feminine* identity, most likely because idealised 'feminine' qualities tend to include being peaceful, nurturing and non-violent[106] (of course, this does not mean that women always live up to those ideals in reality: like men, we are violent for many reasons, some of them more defensible than others). However, in settings where women are in the minority, and where an aggressive, domineering form of masculinity is privileged, women may use violence in order to claim their place as an 'insider' in the group. For example, based on their review of empirical research and reporting across numerous late twentieth century and early twenty-first century conflicts, Dara Kay Cohen et al. found that:

> Women combatants may seek to conform to norms of strength and masculinity within their armed groups, and performing acts of sexual violence is one means of fitting in. Other possible reasons may include the desire to redirect sexual violence against other victims or to humiliate an ethnic opponent or enemy.[107]

[103] Eriksson Baaz and Stern, see n. 75, 49–50; M. Eriksson Baaz and M. Stern, 'Knowing Masculinities in Armed Conflict?: Reflections from Research in the Democratic Republic of Congo' in F. Ní Aoláin et al. (eds), *The Oxford Handbook of Gender and Conflict* (Oxford University Press, 2018) 533, 538–539.

[104] Eriksson Baaz and Stern, 'Knowing Masculinities', see n. 103, 541.

[105] Vandello et al., see n. 97, 1327. See also J Bosson et al., 'Precarious Manhood and Displays of Physical Aggression' (2009) 35(5) *Personality and Social Psychology Bulletin* 623.

[106] C. Gentry and L. Sjoberg, *Mothers, Monsters, Whores: Women's Violence in Global Politics* (Zed Books, 2015); N. Hodgson, 'Gender Justice or Gendered Justice? Female Defendants in International Criminal' (2017) 25(3) *Feminist Legal Studies* 337.

[107] D.K. Cohen, A.H. Green and E.J. Wood, 'Wartime Sexual Violence: Misconceptions, Implications, and Ways Forward' (United States Institute of Peace, February 2013) 5.

### 2.2.3 Punishment of 'Gender Traitors'

A third way that crimes can be 'gender-based' is that they can be committed in order to punish a person for failing to conform to gender norms – that is, to punish perceived 'gender traitors'.[108] As philosopher Judith Butler has argued, 'those who fail to do their gender right are regularly punished'.[109] Similarly, political scientist Nivedita Menon has observed that:

> Societies generally value 'masculine' characteristics more highly than 'feminine' ones and at the same time, ensure that men and women who do not conform to these characteristics are continuously disciplined into the appropriate behaviour. For instance, a man who expresses sorrow publicly by crying would be humiliated by the taunt, '*Auraton jaise ro rahe ho*?' (Why are you crying like a woman? [in Hindi]).[110]

Punishment of this nature, when it takes the form of murder, torture, sexual violence or comparably grave offences, comprises a third category of gender-based crimes. Violence directed at people who are homosexual, or are perceived as homosexual, is a prime example. It is a long-running phenomenon, which continues in many parts of the world.[111] Current examples include the persecution of homosexuals by militant Islamist groups[112] and the 'corrective rape' of lesbian women,[113] to name a few. But it is not only perpetrated by non-state actors: states are complicit too. An example is the criminalisation of consensual sex between men in 77 states, 45 of which also criminalise consensual sex between women, which empowers state authorities to imprison and/or kill people who

[108] This term is inspired by Margaret Atwood's 1985 dystopia *The Handmaid's Tale*, in which the Christian fundamentalist regime running America enforces strict gender norms, and refers to homosexual people using this term. See Chapter XII ('Jezebel's').

[109] J. Butler, 'Performative Acts and Gender Constitution: Essay in Phenomenology and Feminist Theory' (1988) 40(4) *Theatre Journal* 519, 522.

[110] N. Menon, *Seeing Like a Feminist* (Zubaan/Penguin Books, 2012) 62.

[111] Regarding the persecution of homosexuals under Nazi rule, see Chapter 3, §3.1.6. For recent examples, see 'Discriminatory Laws and Practices and Acts of Violence against Individuals Based on Their Sexual Orientation and Gender Identity: Report of the United Nations High Commissioner for Human Rights, UN Doc. A/HRC/29/23' (4 May 2015), [21].

[112] E.g. CUNY Law School, MADRE, and Organization of Women's Freedom in Iraq, 'Communication to the ICC Prosecutor Pursuant to Article 15 of the Rome Statute Requesting a Preliminary Examination into the Situation of: Gender-Based Persecution and Torture as Crimes against Humanity and War Crimes Committed by the Islamic State of Iraq and the Levant (ISIL) in Iraq' (8 November 2017).

[113] 'Discriminatory Laws and Practices and Acts of Violence against Individuals Based on Their Sexual Orientation and Gender Identity: Report of the United Nations High Commissioner for Human Rights, UN Doc. A/HRC/19/41' (17 November 2011), [29].

are convicted of such acts.[114] This violence is premised on narrow ideas about how a man, or how a woman, should behave in the sexual realm. Men should be with women and vice versa, in other words. Hence, the UN High Commissioner for Human Rights has described homophobic attacks as 'a form of gender-based violence, driven by a desire to punish those seen as defying gender norms'.[115]

Importantly, the notion of punishing 'gender traitors' does not only refer to attacks against people who are homosexual (or perceived as such): it includes any punishment for behaviour that the perpetrators deem improper for a person of the victim's sex. Examples include the abduction of schoolgirls by Boko Haram in Nigeria, the oppression of women by the Taliban in Afghanistan and the denial of women's rights by Islamist groups in Mali – all of which have come to the attention of the Prosecutor of the ICC.[116] It also includes attacks on people who do not fit into rigid ideas of what it means to be a 'man' or a 'woman', including people who are transgender, androgynous or intersex. Attacks of this nature are also defined as 'gender-based violence' by the UN High Commissioner for Human Rights[117] and are starting to receive more attention in the fields of conflict studies and international criminal law.[118]

Thus, when I refer to 'gender-based crimes' in this book, I mean crimes that are committed because of the victim and/or perpetrator's gender identity, as well as crimes that are committed to punish deviation from gender norms. I note that gender may also be relevant *after* a crime is committed, because it can magnify or alter the effects of the crime.[119] For example, in the Democratic Republic of Congo, many women who

[114] A. Carroll and L. Mendos, 'State Sponsored Homophobia 2017: A World Survey of Sexual Orientation Laws' (International Lesbian, Gay, Bisexual, Trans and Intersex Association, 2017) 8.

[115] 'Discriminatory Laws and Practices and Acts of Violence against Individuals Based on Their Sexual Orientation and Gender Identity: Report of the United Nations High Commissioner for Human Rights, UN Doc. A/HRC/29/23', see n. 111, [20].

[116] Regarding Boko Haram, see ICC OTP, 'Report on Preliminary Examination Activities 2016' (14 November 2016), [293]. Regarding the Taliban, see *Situation in Afghanistan* (ICC-02/17-7-Red 20-11-2017), 20 November 2017, [115]–[121]. Regarding Islamist groups in Mali, see *Al Hassan* (ICC-01/12-01/18-1-Red), 31 March 2018.

[117] 'Discriminatory Laws and Practices and Acts of Violence against Individuals Based on Their Sexual Orientation and Gender Identity: Report of the United Nations High Commissioner for Human Rights, UN Doc. A/HRC/19/41', see n. 113, [20].

[118] E.g. F. Ní Aoláin et al., 'Introduction' in F. Ní Aoláin et al. (eds), *The Oxford Handbook of Gender and Conflict* (Oxford University Press, 2017) xxxv, xi.

[119] Urban-Walker, see n. 94.

were raped during the conflict were rejected by their husbands or deemed unmarriageable by their communities, and therefore left as sole carers for children born as a result of rape. These harms do not happen simply because some people are capable of childbirth and others are not. Rather, they happen due to deeply ingrained ideas about gender, such as a belief that a woman is dishonoured or sullied when she is raped, and a belief that women, preferably, the woman who delivered the child, should take primary responsibility for his or her care.[120] In this book, crimes whose harms are magnified by socially constructed gender norms are referred to as crimes causing 'gendered harms', but not necessarily as 'gender-based crimes'.

## 2.3 Sexual Violence: *Always* a Gender-based Crime?

I will close by addressing a somewhat under-examined question about the relationship between 'sexual violence crimes' and 'gender-based crimes'. Some people take the view that the former category always falls within the latter. For example, in our 2017 interview, Hayes stated: 'all sexual violence crimes will necessarily be gender-based. But not all gender-based crimes are sexual'.[121] By contrast, during the Rome Statute negotiating process, the Women's Caucus for Gender Justice took a more equivocal view. They argued:

> Sexual violence, whether directed to women or men, is *usually* a form of gender violence, since it is an attack on one's gender identity, whether masculine or feminine. That is, women are raped, for example, to control and destroy them as women and to signal male ownership over them as property; men are raped to humiliate them through forcing them in the position of women and, thereby, rendering them, according to the prevailing stereotypes, weak and inferior.[122]

The view that sexual violence is not *always* gender-based continues to enjoy some support. For example, Gloria Gaggioli, Professor of Law at the

[120] Eriksson Baaz and Stern, see n. 75, 41; Réseau des Femmes pour un Développement Associatif, Réseau des Femmes pour la Défense des Droits et la Paix, International Alert, 'Women's Bodies as a Battleground: Sexual Violence against Women and Girls during the War in the Democratic Republic of Congo South Kivu (1996–2003)' (2005) 42–44.

[121] Interview, July 2017.

[122] Women's Caucus for Gender Justice, 'Recommendations and Commentary for December 1997 PrepCom on The Establishment of An International Criminal Court' (1 December 1997) 33: (emphasis added) www.iccnow.org/documents/5PrepComRecommWomensC.pdf.

University of Geneva, argues that 'sexual violence can be seen as sometimes broader than gender-based violence. A detainee may be raped in detention – as a method of torture – independently of his/her gender or socially ascribed role in society'.[123] More recently, in a seminar hosted by Women's Initiatives for Gender Justice in 2018, a participant described unlawful body-cavity searches of the kind documented in North Korea as a crime which was 'sexual' but *not* 'gender-based'.[124] In my interviews, only one person in the OTP seemed to share that view. That person stated that if sexual violence was directed systematically against both women *and* men, 'then we would have a sexual crime but *not* a gender-based crime'.[125] All other interviewees took the view that sexual violence crimes were *necessarily* gender-based crimes. However, they did not all explain *why* they took that view. Rather, for some people, the answer was self-evident. For example, when asked for an example of 'gender-based crimes', one person began: 'sure, we have the obvious ones, right. Like sexual crimes are clearly gendered in nature'.[126] In the second interview where this occurred, I asked a follow-up question. The discussion proceeded as follows:

AUTHOR: Where does 'gender' come into it for you? Would it be right to just call them 'sexual violence' crimes, or does it have something to do with gender?

INTERVIEWEE: The word 'gender'?

AUTHOR: Yes.

INTERVIEWEE: Well I've been prosecuting these crimes in my national system and then it was just simply sexual violence. The crime of rape doesn't exist in [interviewee's state], so it's sexual violence cases. So for me, the use of the word 'gender' as a lawyer is not needed. But in order to put an emphasis and highlight the specificity of these crimes, by using the word gender, you really zoom in. For me, gender is very neutral. We're not focusing on women, we're not focusing on men, we're not focusing on children. It could be anyone. So I can understand from an outreach perspective, the need to emphasise the crime by associating it with the word 'gender', but as a prosecutor, it's not necessary for me.

123 G. Gaggioli, 'Sexual Violence in Armed Conflicts: A Violation of International Humanitarian Law and Human Rights Law' (2014) 96(984) *International Review of the Red Cross* 503, 510.

124 See 'Report of the Detailed Findings of the Commission of Inquiry on Human Rights in the Democratic People's Republic of Korea, UN Doc. A/HRC/25/CRP.1' (7 February 2014), [416]–[422].

125 Interview J, June 2017 (emphasis added).

126 Interview A, ICC OTP, 2017 (emphasis added).

By contrast, several interviewees gave detailed reasons for describing sexual violence crimes as 'gender-based crimes', indicating for them, this description was not only a difference in vocabulary, but in meaning. For example, one person stated:

> If you are using women for the purpose of sex, and for having babies, and for domestic labour, it's a very gender-specific crime. [The perpetrator's logic is that] 'I'm raping that woman or I'm enslaving her in the role that I perceive for her. My slave is carrying out the roles or the functions as a slave in a role that I see females as having'. With males, it's possibly even easier for some people to view it as a very gender-specific crime. If you're raping a male, and you're targeting that male for rape, it's a sense of targeting their masculinity. It's a very gendered way of targeting your victim: you're trying to perhaps belittle and show the power.[127]

Referring to the aforementioned *Bemba* case, another interviewee explained:

> We didn't find the evidence of the *explicit* intention of the authors that it was specifically from the angle of gender, if I may say. What is for sure is the systematic raping of women show that females were the primary target. Regardless of the age, the conditions, the situation. Females were the primary target for rape. If we have to give some figures, I would say something like in a town like Bangui, we easily find more than 1,000 women being raped, and when it comes to men – we called two to testify, and from the information we have, probably we heard about eight or ten instances where rape of men happened.[128]

The interviewee explained that the rapes of those eight to ten men were also 'gender-based crimes', because 'there was a specific purpose of raping men in the conditions they raped these men, being men in authority, being raped in public to diminish their authority in the whole community'.[129] Outside the OTP, there was also consensus that sexual violence crimes are 'gender-based crimes'. When asked why, the responses were quite specific and detailed. For example, Massidda explained:

> It could be that you are raped because you are a member of a certain group, and therefore the rape can be used to humiliate you, which could also be the same reason for committing these types of crimes against male victims. In the Central African Republic for instance, there was really this component of raping men in front of their wife because of this idea of humiliating the person.[130]

[127] Interview K, ICC OTP, 2017 (ellipses omitted).
[128] Interview J, ICC OTP, 2017(ellipses omitted; emphasis added).
[129] Ibid.
[130] Interview, 15 June 2017 (ellipses omitted).

Or in the words of Melinda Reed, Executive Director of Women's Initiatives for Gender Justice:

> Typically, the instances we've seen are designed for the purposes of humiliation or the destruction of societal norms and cultures associated with each gender. When it is an act of sexual violence perpetrated by a male against a female, it is designed to 'tarnish' the female or to make her 'dirty' to the men in her community, and that is specifically about her role as a female in that society. When it's male on male, again it can be typically designed to humiliate the male victim in a culture where homosexuality is considered taboo. These crimes are generally targeting victims based on their gender in order to denigrate, humiliate, and undermine them within their societies. With the Yazidis (in Iraq) for example, who are not supposed to have relations outside the Yazidi community, any sexual relations with a non-Yazidi would result in them being considered outcasts by their community.[131]

Determining the relationship between sexual violence crimes and gender-based crimes is complex, not least because there is no agreed definition of 'gender-based crimes' *or* 'sexual violence crimes'. Within the OTP, there appears to be no 'official' position on this question: the *Gender Policy* notes that the category of 'gender-based crimes' is broader than the category of 'sexual violence'[132] but is silent on whether 'sexual violence' is always a 'gender-based crime'. However, in light of decades of scholarship and empirical research showing that sexual violence is almost always fuelled by socially constructed gender norms, I treat sexual violence crimes as presumptively 'gender-based' in this book.

By 'sexual violence crimes', I mean acts that violate a person's sexual (and often, reproductive) autonomy, including forced penetration of the victim's vagina or anus with any part of the perpetrator's body or an object; severing, mutilating, electrifying or applying poisonous chemicals to the victim's breasts or genitals; forcing the victim to simulate masturbation; forcing the victim to undress or remain undressed against their will; forcing the victim to participate in any of the aforementioned acts with another person or animal; forcing a second victim to witness any of the aforementioned acts; recording the victim in any of the aforementioned acts without their consent; distributing such recordings within the victim's consent; forcibly making the victim pregnant; preventing the victim from accessing safe abortion which was otherwise available to

[131] Interview, 9 July 2018.
[132] OTP 2014, 3.

them; forcibly sterilising the victim or forcing them to use contraception; or forcing the victim to lose a pregnancy through abortion, miscarriage or otherwise removing the foetus from the victim's body. This list is deliberately broad, given that the meaning of the term 'sexual violence' has been contested in ICC case law.[133]

## 2.4 Conclusion

Due to the diversity of backgrounds in international criminal justice, the concept of 'gender' is not familiar to everyone in this field. Nor is it easy for everyone to acquire that familiarity: the daily pressures of reviewing evidence, constructing arguments, effecting disclosure and checking transcripts leave little time for much else. Hence, as observed by Hayes, 'when you try to explain the idea of a "gender lens", sometimes you can see peoples' souls leave their bodies because they just think "oh God, this sounds like sociology and it's bullshit and I'm out"'.[134] Yet without understanding gender, in a sociological sense, we cannot appreciate why certain crimes are committed, or why they have certain effects. To paraphrase feminist scholar Catherine Niarchos, just as the Holocaust would be inexplicable without reference to racism and anti-Semitism, many acts of violence are inexplicable without thinking about sexism, heteronormativity and misogyny.[135] Or as Hayes continued, a gender analysis 'brings into light relevant patterns; you're less likely to miss something important. It's the difference between viewing something in black and white or in colour'.[136]

It is therefore positive to see that in the twenty years since the Rome Statute was adopted, the prevailing view of what constitutes 'gender-based crimes' has evolved. Reflecting on this point during our interview, Patricia Sellers explained:

> We've gone from a very classical use of gender, looking at sexual assault jurisprudence, where gender is often a code word for females, often for young female adults (not necessarily female children, although there's slight expansions there). During the past twenty years, I think we've given gender much broader connotations. We're starting to reflect more on

[133] See Chapter 5, §5.3.5.
[134] Interview, July 2017.
[135] Niarchos, see n. 1, 679.
[136] Interview, July 2017.

> what are the *cluster of ideas around gender*; to look at males and females, however they may identify themselves on the spectrum, and we're looking at adults and children, boys and girls, men and women.[137]

This observation is borne out by OTP's *Gender Policy,* the language used in court records and the interviews discussed previously. It is clear that people are thinking broadly about gender, although not paying equal attention to the gender of the victims *and perpetrators,* and not always articulating the gender dimension of sexual violence crimes.

[137] Interview, February 2018.

# 3

# The Road to Rome

As a foundation for the forthcoming analysis of the International Criminal Court's (ICC's) practice in prosecuting gender-based crimes, this chapter goes back in history. It considers developments from the late nineteenth century, when the treaties that form the basis of modern international criminal law were adopted, through to the adoption of the Rome Statute on 17 July 1998 and the adoption of the Elements of Crimes at the first meeting of States Parties in September 2002. As the chapter will show, efforts to give the ICC a clear mandate to investigate and prosecute gender-based crimes generally received broad support at Rome. However, certain proposals which potentially diminished the right of states to regulate women's reproductive lives and to discriminate on the grounds of sex and sexual orientation met fierce opposition from the Holy See (i.e. the Vatican, a United Nations [UN] observer state since 1964), certain majority-Catholic and majority-Muslim states and self-titled 'pro-life' and 'pro-family' non-government organisations (NGOs).

This chapter is part literature review and part original research: it sets out existing critiques of international criminal law, particularly critiques of feminist scholars, but it also incorporates my own analysis of court records and legal instruments to illustrate the arguments made and to provide references for interested scholars and practitioners to follow up.

The historical analysis presented in this chapter serves several purposes. One purpose is to show how progressive the Rome Statute is in terms of gender-based crimes: it expressly enumerates a range of sexual violence crimes as war crimes[1] and crimes against humanity,[2] and is the first international instrument to criminalise persecution on 'gender' grounds.[3] For women's rights activists who participated in the Rome

[1] RS, Art. 8(2)(b)(xxii) and 8(2)(e)(vi).
[2] RS, Art. 7(1)(g).
[3] RS, Art. 7(1)(h).

Conference, the inclusion of these crimes was seen as an 'historic development' and an 'important breakthrough'.[4] In particular, the reference to gender-based persecution was seen as an 'exciting, and potentially revolutionary, development'.[5] To understand these responses, it is necessary to have an awareness of what international criminal law looked like before.

A second purpose is to assist interested lawyers, scholars and commentators in the interpretation of the Rome Statute. This is because in international law, reviewing the preparatory work of a treaty is a valid method for interpreting the terms of that treaty when the meaning is ambiguous or obscure.[6] At the same time, a review of the drafting history can draw attention to latent conflicts that are written into the Statute, waiting to flare up in cases before the Court.

A third purpose is to make visible the 'gender of international criminal justice'. By this, I do not simply mean the ratio of men and women in treaty negotiations and judicial forums. Rather, I mean the gendered assumptions and values that are written into legal texts and reinforced through legal practices: assumptions and values that Louise Chappell describes as the 'gender legacies of international law'.[7] In particular, I am interested in the 'gender legacies' that impact on the prosecution of gender-based crimes. As a feminist institutionalist scholar, I take the view that an appreciation of these legacies is not simply interesting; it is analytically useful, because it can help to explain some of the more regressive steps that have been taken in cases before the ICC. This is because, as Chappell has argued, 'the influences of these legacies did not end with the creation of the Rome Statute; it has been carried forward into the practice of the ICC'.[8]

The chapter is divided into two sections. Section 3.1 identifies some recurring tendencies, or 'gender legacies', that have contributed to silences around gender-based crimes in international war crimes trials. Section 3.2 focuses on the preparation of the ICC's legal framework, beginning with the

[4] B. Bedont and K. Hall-Martinez, 'Ending Impunity for Gender Crimes Under the International Criminal Court' (1999) 6(1) *Brown Journal of World Affairs* 65, 70; R. Copelon, 'Gender Crimes as War Crimes: Integrating Crimes against Women into International Criminal Law' (2000) 46 *McGill Law Journal* 217, 237.

[5] V. Oosterveld, 'Prosecuting Gender-Based Persecution as an International Crime' in A. de Brouwer et al. (eds), *Sexual Violence as an International Crime: Interdisciplinary Approaches* (Intersentia, 2013) 57, 77.

[6] *Vienna Convention on the Law of Treaties*, 23 May 1969, 1155 UNTS 331 (entered into force 27 January 1980), Art. 32.

[7] L. Chappell, The Politics of Gender Justice at the International Criminal Court: Legacies and Legitimacy (Oxford University Press, 2016) 36–39.

[8] Ibid., 3.

work of the Preparatory Committee in 1995 and ending with the adoption of the Elements of Crimes in 2002. The focus of this section is on women's rights activism in the drafting of the Rome Statute and Elements of Crimes. It also refers to contemporaneous developments in the International Criminal Tribunal for the former Yugoslavia (ICTY) and International Criminal Tribunal for Rwanda (ICTR) that influenced the ICC's legal texts.

## 3.1 Recurring Tendencies

There are several tendencies in the field of international criminal law that have impeded the prosecution and recognition of gender-based crimes. These include a tendency to underestimate the seriousness of sexual violence, to over-estimate the challenges to investigating it, to make assumptions about who can be a victim of a gender-based crime, and to ignore the ways that gender norms contribute to the commission of war crimes, crimes against humanity and genocide. Each of these tendencies are discussed in more detail in Sections 3.1.1–3.1.6.

### *3.1.1 Silences around Sexual Violence in Legal Instruments*

Sexual violence, including rape within marriage, sexual harassment and forced prostitution, is an everyday occurrence for many people in times of peace – especially for women and girls. But sexual violence is also rife in the situations where international criminal law applies, such as during armed conflict, genocide, 'ethnic cleansing', rebellions, and post-election violence. Sexual violence is common in these situations of conflict for many reasons: because it shatters communities and breaks the spirit of individuals; because it is a cheap and effective form of retaliation against a perceived enemy; because misogyny takes new forms when accompanied by access to weapons, a desensitisation to violence and a rise in rhetoric that dehumanises an ethnic, political or national 'other'; and because by committing sexual and gender-based crimes, perpetrators can perform the macho, dominating masculinity that is idealised in many armed groups.[9]

[9] M. Eriksson Baaz and M. Stern, 'The Complexity of Violence: A Critical Analysis of Sexual Violence in the Democratic Republic of Congo' (SIDA/Nordiska Afrikainstitutet, 2010) 47–50; S. Brownmiller, *Against Our Will: Men, Women and Rape* (Simon & Schuster, 1975); C. MacKinnon, 'Creating International Law: Gender as Leading Edge' (2013) 36(1) *Harvard Journal of Law & Gender* 105, 111–112; R. Seifert, 'War and Rape: A Preliminary Analysis' in A. Stiglmayer (ed.), *Mass Rape: The War Against Women in Bosnia-Herzegovina* (University of Nebraska Press, 1994) 54.

The effects of such violence are extremely serious. As explained by Patricia Viseur Sellers, former Special Advisor on Gender to the ICTY Prosecutor and current Special Advisor on Gender to the ICC Prosecutor, sexual violence 'goes to the very psyche of the person, it goes to the physical sense of the person, it goes to the social sense of the person … the person somehow feels that they have experienced a death, and yet are condemned to live'.[10] The testimony of survivors echoes these sentiments. For example, in the ICTY's *Čelebići camp* case, a female witness stated that as a result of repeated rape by male soldiers in that notorious prison camp, 'psychologically and physically I was completely worn out. They kill you psychologically'.[11] Similarly, in the ICC's *Bemba* case, a male witness recalled that as a result of being gang-raped by armed men in front of his family, 'I knew that I was dead. I could no longer feel like a human being'.[12] In addition to these psychological and emotional harms, sexual violence can cause physical injuries including damage to reproductive organs and transmission of HIV. On top of all this, women and girls who become pregnant through sexual violence often face further injuries as a result of miscarriage or childbirth, not to mention economic hardship, social stigmatisation and/or interruption of education if a child is born.[13]

Yet despite its prevalence in conflict settings, and its serious consequences, sexual violence has historically been overlooked in instruments of international criminal law and its legal forerunner, international humanitarian law (IHL). This point has been emphasised by many feminist scholars, most of whom link the silences around sexual violence in these legal instruments to a dismissive attitude toward violence against women on the part of generations of male lawmakers. For example, Kelly Askin, whose scholarship in this field has spanned over 30 years, has observed:

> Women and girls have habitually been sexually violated during wartime, yet even in the twenty-first century, the documents regulating armed conflict either minimally incorporate, inappropriately characterize, or wholly fail to mention these crimes. Until the 1990s, men did the drafting and enforcing of humanitarian law provisions; thus, it was primarily men who neglected to enumerate, condemn, and prosecute these crimes.[14]

[10] R. Barsony, Sexual Violence and the Triumph of Justice (ICTY, 2012) 00:09:30.

[11] See testimony cited in: Judgment, *Mucić et al.* (IT-96-21-T), 16 November 1998, [938].

[12] *Bemba*, ICC-01/05-01/08-T-51-Red2-ENG, 21 January 2011, 32(9–10).

[13] See, e.g. B. Nowrojee, 'Shattered Lives: Sexual Violence During the Rwandan Genocide and Its Aftermath' (Human Rights Watch/FIDH, 1996) 67–80.

[14] K. Askin, 'Prosecuting Wartime Rape and Other Gender Related Crimes: Extraordinary Advances, Enduring Obstacles' (2003) 21(2) *Berkeley Journal of International Law* 288, 295.

This is not to imply that before the 1990s, wartime rape was always *permitted*. To the contrary, well before the nineteenth century, scholars argued that rape was forbidden in war, or at least, forbidden except in certain circumstances (such as during a siege, or when at war with 'infidels', or when women took up arms).[15] Moreover, rape was expressly prohibited in the 1863 Lieber Code, a set of instructions to the Union forces during America's Civil War, which was based on customary international law.[16] Yet when it came to codifying the laws of war in binding international conventions, sexual violence was sidelined: the drafters of these conventions routinely declined to expressly prohibit this crime. For example, sexual violence is not mentioned in the 1864 Geneva Convention, which aims to ameliorate the suffering of wounded combatants on the battlefield.[17] It is somewhat circular to argue that the convention does not mention sexual violence because the impetus for the convention was Swiss humanitarian Henri Dunant's report of the suffering of soldiers following the 1859 battle of Solferino;[18] the point is that it was the plight of soldiers on bloodied battlefields, and not the equally heinous phenomenon of wartime rape, that prompted the European powers to develop what is widely regarded as the first instrument of IHL.

As IHL continued to be codified, the marginalisation of sexual violence continued also. For example, sexual violence was not expressly prohibited in the 1899 or 1907 Hague Conventions on the laws of war on land,[19] although the latter treaty required warring parties to show respect for 'family honour', which was apparently a euphemistic prohibition on rape.[20] World War II did

[15] K. Askin, *War Crimes Against Women: Prosecution in International War Crimes Tribunals* (Martinus Nijhoff, 1997) 22–35; P.V. Sellers, 'The Context of Sexual Violence: Sexual Violence as Violations of International Humanitarian Law' in G. Kirk MacDonald and O. Swaak-Goldman (eds), *Substantive and Procedural Aspects of International Criminal Law: Vol 1* (Kluwer Law International, 2000) 263, 265–270.

[16] *Instructions for the Government of Armies of the United States in the Field* ('Lieber Code'), promulgated as General Orders No. 100 by President Lincoln, 24 April 1863, Art. 44 and 47; Askin, *War Crimes Against Women*, see n. 15, 36; Sellers, see n. 15, 271–273.

[17] Convention for the Amelioration of the Condition of the Wounded in Armies in the Field, Geneva, 22 August 1864 (entered into force 22 June 1865).

[18] Regarding the history of the 1864 Geneva Convention, see: Askin, *War Crimes Against Women*, see n. 15, 37; R. Cryer et al., *An Introduction to International Criminal Law and Procedure* (Cambridge University Press, 3rd edn, 2014) 264–265.

[19] Convention (II) with Respect to the Laws and Customs of War on Land and Its Annex: Regulations Concerning the Laws and Customs of War on Land, The Hague, 29 July 1899 (entered into force 4 September 1900); Convention (IV) Respecting the Laws and Customs of War on Land, The Hague, 18 October 1907 (entered into force 26 January 1910).

[20] Askin, 'Prosecuting Wartime Rape', see n. 14, 295, 300; M. Bassiouni, *Crimes Against Humanity* (Cambridge University Press, 2011) 428.

not prompt any major developments in IHL or international criminal law, although there was talk of establishing an international tribunal to prosecute the German Kaiser and other high officials from the defeated powers (the tribunal was never established, in part because the Netherlands declined to extradite the Kaiser).[21] Nor was sexual violence referenced in the first instruments of international criminal law, namely the Charter of the International Military Tribunal (the 'Nuremberg Tribunal'), drafted by jurists from the United States of America (USA), United Kingdom (UK), France and Soviet Union in August 1945,[22] or the Charter of the International Military Tribunal for the Far East (the 'Tokyo Tribunal'), which was promulgated in January 1946 by General Douglas MacArthur in his role as Supreme Commander for the Allied Powers.[23] It bears noting that rape *was* enumerated as a crime against humanity in Control Council Law 10, the law adopted by the US, UK, France and Soviet Union in December 1945 to enable the prosecution of alleged German war criminals after the closure of the Nuremberg Tribunal. And yet, the war crimes provisions in that instrument made no reference to rape or any other sexual violence crime.[24]

The silence on sexual violence in the Nuremberg and Tokyo Tribunal Charters was not legally necessary; as noted previously, rape was already prohibited under IHL before World War II and could therefore have been expressly listed as a war crime in these charters. Moreover, rape and enforced prostitution had been identified as war crimes in 1919 by the international commission established by the Allies after World War II,[25] and in 1943 by the UN War Crimes Commission.[26] However,

[21] Cryer et al., see n. 18, 115–116.

[22] *Agreement for the Prosecution and Punishment of the Major War Criminals of the European Axis*, London, 8 August 1945, 82 UNTC 280 (Annex 1: Charter of the International Military Tribunal).

[23] Charter of the International Military Tribunal for the Far East, Tokyo, 19 January 1946.

[24] Control Council Law No. 10, Punishment of Persons Guilty of War Crimes, Crimes Against Peace and Against Humanity, Berlin, 20 December 1945 (entered into force 20 December 1945), Art. 2(1)(b) and (c).

[25] Commission on the Responsibility of the Authors of the War and on Enforcement of Penalties, 'Report Presented to the Preliminary Peace Conference, 29 March 1919' (1920) 14(1) *American Journal of International Law* 95, 114.

[26] In a list of 32 war crimes, the crimes of rape and enforced prostitution came in at number five and six, respectively. *Annex 1: War Crimes Committee: Report of the Subcommittee* (2 December 1943) www.legal-tools.org/doc/3e7e05/. For a discussion, see D. Plesch, S. SáCouto and C. Lasco, 'The Relevance of the United Nations War Crimes Commission to the Prosecution of Sexual and Gender-Based Crimes Today' (2014) 25(1) *Criminal Law Forum* 349.

the jurists and politicians responsible for the Nuremberg and Tokyo Charters took the view that unlike other widely reported crimes such as murder and deportation, sexual violence did not need to be recognised as a war crime in its own right. This double standard has been rightly described as 'discriminatory' because of the disproportionate impact of sexual violence on women and girls.[27]

No international criminal tribunals were established during the Cold War, but the development of international criminal law chugged along. One important development was the Genocide Convention, adopted by the UN General Assembly in 1948.[28] The definition of genocide in this convention, which was later replicated in the ICTY, ICTR and ICC Statutes, sets out five acts that can constitute genocide when committed with an intent to destroy a national, ethnic, racial or religious group. Sexual violence is not specifically mentioned among these acts.[29]

Another major development during the Cold War was the adoption of the four Geneva Conventions of 1949. These conventions are concerned primarily with *state responsibility* for violations of the laws of war. However, certain violations (called 'grave breaches') also attract *individual criminal responsibility*, meaning that individuals can be prosecuted for these violations as war crimes. Sexual violence is not expressly listed as a 'grave breach', unlike murder, torture, biological experiments, unlawful deportation or transfer, hostage-taking and extensive destruction of property.[30] The only mention of sexual violence is in Article 27 of

[27] Bedont and Hall-Martinez, see n. 4, 71.

[28] *Convention on the Prevention and Punishment of the Crime of Genocide*, New York, 9 December 1948, 78 UNTS 277 (entered into force 12 January 1951).

[29] Article 2 of the convention defines genocide to mean: 'any of the following acts committed with intent to destroy, in whole or in part, a national, ethnical, racial or religious group, as such: (a) Killing members of the group; (b) Causing serious bodily or mental harm to members of the group; (c) Deliberately inflicting on the group conditions of life calculated to bring about its physical destruction in whole or in part; (d) Imposing measures intended to prevent births within the group; (e) Forcibly transferring children of the group to another group.'

[30] Convention (I) for the Amelioration of the Condition of the Wounded and Sick in Armed Forces in the Field, Geneva, 12 August 1949, 75 UNTS 31 (entered into force 21 October 1950), Art. 49 and 50; Convention (II) for the Amelioration of the Condition of Wounded, Sick and Shipwrecked Members of Armed Forces at Sea, Geneva, 12 August 2919, 75 UNTS 85 (entered into force 21 October 1950), Art. 50 and 51; Convention (III) relative to the Treatment of Prisoners of War, Geneva, 12 August 1949, 75 UNTS 135 (entered into force 21 October 1950), Art. 129 and 130; Convention (IV) relative to the Protection of Civilian Persons in Time of War, Geneva, 12 August 2012, 75 UNTS 287 (entered into force 21 October 2013), Art. 146 and 147.

Convention IV, which states: 'women shall be especially protected against any attack on their honour, in particular against rape, enforced prostitution, or any form of indecent assault'. While this prohibition is at least explicit, it is of limited use. It also applies only to *civilians*, specifically, civilian women, and not civilian men. Moreover, it is not a 'grave breach' provision, it does not present sexual violence as conduct causing severe physical and psychological harm, and it depicts women as people needing protection, rather than rights bearers who are entitled to bodily integrity and sexual autonomy.[31] Similar critiques have been made of the two 1977 Additional Protocols to the Geneva Conventions, which prohibit certain forms of sexual violence in international and non-international armed conflicts, respectively.[32]

Sexual violence was fractionally more visible in the ICTY Statute, drafted in 1993. The Security Council resolution that established the ICTY referred to reports of 'widespread and flagrant violations of international humanitarian law' in the former Yugoslavia, including the 'rape of women',[33] suggesting that an awareness of this crime was 'imbedded in the very foundations of the Tribunal'.[34] Despite that, the ICTY Statute did not expressly list any sexual violence crimes as war crimes, and it

[31] B. Bedont, 'Gender Specific Provisions in the Statute of the International Criminal Court' in F. Lattanzi and W. Schabas (eds), *Essays on the Rome Statute of the International Criminal Court* (Il Sirente, 1999) 183, 190; Bedont and Hall-Martinez, see n. 4, 70–71; H. Charlesworth and C. Chinkin, *The Boundaries of International Law: A Feminist Analysis* (Manchester University Press, 2000) 314; R. Copelon, 'Surfacing Gender: Re-Engraving Crimes against Women in Humanitarian Law' (1994) 5 *Hastings Women's Law Journal* 243, 248–250; Copelon, see n. 4, 220–221; C. Niarchos, 'Women, War, and Rape: Challenges Facing the International Tribunal for the Former Yugoslavia' (1995) 17(4) *Human Rights Quarterly* 629, 671–675; F. Ní Aoláin, D. Haynes and N. Cahn, 'International and Local Criminal Accountability for Gendered Violence' in F. Ní Aoláin, D. Haynes and N. Cahn (eds), *On The Frontlines: Gender, War and the Post-Conflict Process* (Oxford University Press, 2011) 153, 157.

[32] Protocol Additional to the Geneva Conventions of 12 August 1949, and Relating to the Protection of Victims of International Armed Conflicts (Protocol I), Geneva, 8 June 1977, 1125 UNTS 3 (entered into force 7 December 1978), Art. 75(2)(b), 76(1), 77(1); Protocol Additional to the Geneva Conventions of 12 August 1949, and Relating to the Protection of Victims of Non-International Armed Conflicts (Protocol II), Geneva, 8 June 1977, 1125 UNTS 609 (entered into force 7 December 1978), Art. 4(2)(e). For critiques, see Bedont, see n. 31, 191; Bedont and Hall-Martinez, see n. 4, 71; Askin, 'Prosecuting Wartime Rape', see n. 14, 304; Niarchos, see n. 31, 675–676.

[33] S/RES/827 (1993), 25 May 1993, [3].

[34] P. Kuo, 'Prosecuting Crimes of Sexual Violence in an International Tribunal' (2002) 34(3) *Case Western Reserve Journal of International Law* 305, 309. See also G. Harbour, 'International Concern Regarding Conflict-Related Sexual Violence in the Lead-up to the ICTY's Establishment' in S. Brammertz and M. Jarvis (eds), *Prosecuting Conflict-Related Sexual Violence at the ICTY* (Oxford University Press, 2016) 19, 26–28.

listed just one (rape) as a crime against humanity.[35] That was the most that could be achieved by the numerous 'female academics, women's groups, and individual women' who urged the UN Secretary-General and the US legal team which drafted the Statute to expressly recognise sexual violence crimes as war crimes and crimes against humanity within the jurisdiction of the ICTY.[36] The ICTR Statute, adopted in 1994, went slightly further. In addition to listing rape a crime against humanity,[37] it also listed 'outrages upon personal dignity, in particular humiliating and degrading treatment, rape, enforced prostitution and any form of indecent assault' as war crimes within the jurisdiction of the ICTR.[38] This was the first international instrument to expressly recognise that acts of sexual violence could constitute war crimes.

### *3.1.2 Under-Prosecution of Sexual Violence Crimes*

Compounding the silences in legal frameworks, a related problem has been the weak enforcement of international prohibitions on sexual violence crimes in the *practice* of international courts. This pattern can be traced back to the 1940s, when the allied victors of World War II created the Nuremberg and Tokyo Tribunals to prosecute alleged war criminals from Germany and Japan. It is only fair to acknowledge that even in this fledging period of international criminal justice, impunity for sexual violence was not absolute. For example, rape was prosecuted in several war crimes trials under domestic law, including the trial of General Yamashita by an American military commission, the British '*Belsen camp*' trial, and several Australian and Chinese prosecutions of lower-level Japanese soldiers.[39] However, in prosecutions conducted under *international* law, the record was far from satisfactory.

[35] ICTY Statute, Art. 5(g).

[36] P.V. Sellers, 'Gender Strategy Is Not Luxury for International Courts' (2009) 17(2) *American University Journal of Gender, Social Policy & the Law* 301, 306. See also: D. Scheffer, *All the Missing Souls: A Personal History of the War Crimes Tribunals* (Princeton University Press, 2012) 25; J. Green et al., 'Affecting the Rules for the Prosecution of Rape and Other Gender-Based Violence Before the International Criminal Tribunal for the Former Yugoslavia: A Feminist Proposal and Critique' (1994) 5(2) *Hastings Women's Law Journal* 171.

[37] ICTR Statute, Art. 3(g).

[38] Ibid., Art. 4(e).

[39] See: Plesch, SáCouto and Lasco, see n. 26; Askin, 'Prosecuting Wartime Rape', see n. 14, 302–303; D. Dunne and H. Durham, 'The Prosecution of Crimes against Civilians' in F. Fitzpatrick, T. McCormack and N. Morris (eds), *Australia's War Crimes Trials 1945–51* (Brill/Nijhoff, 2016) 196, 213–216; I. Chang, *The Rape of Nanking: The Forgotten Holocaust of World War II* (Penguin Books, 1997) 170.

At Nuremberg, the French and Soviet prosecutors brought extensive evidence of the rape of civilian women by invading German forces, and there was also some evidence of the sexual abuse of women in Nazi concentration camps.[40] These allegations came within the tribunal's jurisdiction, because although rape was not expressly mentioned in the Nuremberg Charter, it was implicitly covered by the crime against humanity of 'other inhumane acts' and the war crime of 'ill treatment'.[41] Despite hearing that evidence, the tribunal did not refer to rape or sexual violence once in a judgment exceeding 200 pages, with the result that these crimes were rendered invisible once again.[42] As to the trials conducted under Control Council Law, not one of the 177 accused was charged with rape.[43]

The situation in the Tokyo Tribunal was marginally better. There, the prosecutors charged rapes committed by Japanese soldiers under Article 5(b) of the Charter ('conventional war crimes'), by reference to the prohibitions on 'inhumane treatment', 'ill-treatment' and disrespect for 'family honour', as defined in previous international instruments.[44] The Tribunal referred specifically to several such rapes in its 1948 judgment, including 'approximately 20,000 cases of rape' within the first month of the Japanese occupation of Nanking in 1937,[45] as well as an unspecified number of rapes by Japanese soldiers elsewhere in China,[46] Manila[47] and Hong Kong,[48] among other sites. As several feminist scholars have

[40] E.g. Trial of the Major War Criminals Before the International Military Tribunal, Nuremberg, 14 November 1945–1 October 1946 ('Blue Series') (William S. Hein & Co, 1951), Vol. VI, 25 January 1946, 178, 28 January 1946, 213–214, 31 January 1946, 404–407; Vol. VII, 14 February 1946, 456–457. See also K. Askin, 'A Treatment of Sexual Violence in Armed Conflicts: A Historical Perspective and The Way Forward' in A. de Brouwer et al. (eds), *Sexual Violence as an International Crime: Interdisciplinary Approaches* (Intersentia, 2013) 19, 34–45; Niarchos, see n. 31, 663–665; G. Kirk MacDonald, 'Crimes of Sexual Violence: The Experience of the International Criminal Tribunal' (2010) 39 *Columbia Journal of Transnational Law* 1, 10.

[41] Askin, 'A Treatment of Sexual Violence in Armed Conflict', see n. 40, 33; Bassiouni, see n. 20, 428.

[42] 'International Military Tribunal: Judgment and Sentence, October 1, 1946' (1947) 41 *American Journal of International Law* 172.

[43] Askin, 'A Treatment of Sexual Violence in Armed Conflict', see n. 40, 37–38; Copelon, see n. 4, 221; Kirk MacDonald, see n. 40, 10; Niarchos, see n. 31, 677.

[44] Askin, 'A Treatment of Sexual Violence in Armed Conflicts', see n. 40, 39; N. Boister and R. Cryer, *Documents on the Tokyo International Military Tribunal: Charter, Indictment and Judgments* (Oxford University Press, 2008) 60, 62; Sellers, see n. 15, 287–288.

[45] Boister and Cryer, see n. 44, 536.

[46] Ibid., 540.

[47] Ibid., 548, 549.

[48] Ibid., 548.

acknowledged, this was a welcome departure from the pattern of impunity for wartime rape.[49] Yet it is concerning that this rare instance of accountability occurred without one victim being called to testify about their experience of rape,[50] and that one judge (Judge Pal) described the relevant conduct as 'misbehaviour on the part of the Japanese soldiers with the Chinese women' rather than as rape.[51]

The Tokyo Tribunal's most glaring omission, however, was its ignorance of the systematic sexual enslavement of approximately 80,000–200,000 'comfort women' in facilities operated by the Japanese military (see Chapter 2, §2.2.1). These crimes were not charged in the indictment[52] and were referenced in the most fleeting terms in the judgment, with no acknowledgment of the scale or institutionalised nature of this sexual violence.[53] In 2000, survivors, human rights activists, judges and prosecutors formed a people's tribunal to symbolically prosecute the crimes committed against the 'comfort women'. This people's tribunal, known as the Women's International War Crimes Tribunal on Japan's Military Sexual Slavery, relied on the initiative of the survivors and their supporters, who were committed to addressing an issue that states had ignored.[54]

Numerous explanations for these silences around sexual violence have been advanced, some more persuasive than others. In regards to the lack of charges for crimes against 'comfort women', it has been suggested that Japan's destruction of documentary evidence at the end of the war may have prevented prosecution of these crimes.[55] That argument now seems

[49] E.g. Brownmiller, see n. 9, 61–62; Niarchos, see n. 31, 666; Askin, *War Crimes against Women*, see n. 15, 202–203; N. Henry, 'Silence as Collective Memory: Sexual Violence and the Tokyo Trial' in Y. Tanaka, T. McCormack and G. Simpson (eds), *Beyond Victor's Justice? The Tokyo War Crimes Trial Revisited* (Brill/Nijhoff, 2010) 263, 266.

[50] Henry, see n. 49, 273.

[51] Askin, *War Crimes Against Women*, see n. 15, 181–185.

[52] Boister and Cryer, see n. 44, 16–69. For a discussion of this gap in the charges, see Copelon, see n. 4, 221–223; Kirk MacDonald, see n. 40, 10; Ní Aoláin, Haynes and Cahn, see n. 31, 157.

[53] E.g. The judgment notes: 'During the period of Japanese occupation of Kweilin, they committed all kinds of atrocities such as rape and plunder. They recruited women labour [sic] on the pretext of establishing factories. They forced the women thus recruited into prostitution with Japanese troops'. Boister and Cryer, see n. 44, 540.

[54] I. Sajor, 'Challenging International Law: The Quest for Justice of the Former "Comfort Women"' in S. Pickering and C. Lambert (eds), *Global Issues: Women and Justice* (Sydney Institute for Criminology, 2004) 288; U. Dolgopol, 'The Tokyo Women's Tribunal' in A. Byrnes and G. Simm (eds), *People's Tribunals and International Law* (Cambridge University Press, 2018) 84.

[55] Ní Aoláin, Haynes and Cahn, see n. 31, 157.

unsustainable due to research showing that the allies had documentary evidence of the 'comfort women' system in their own archives,[56] that although many Japanese documents were destroyed, some survived[57] and that the Tribunal itself possessed many official documents of this nature.[58] It has also been suggested that the 'comfort women' system was not prosecuted in the Tokyo Tribunal because of 'the reality that until relatively recently, few survivors of the comfort stations were willing to come forward to discuss their ordeals'.[59] However, absent any evidence that the tribunal investigators actually *tried* to collect testimony using appropriate techniques, but were unsuccessful in those efforts, this seems to unfairly lay blame on the traumatised survivors, rather than on professional investigators. Another explanation is that sexual violence received little attention in 1940s international war crimes trials because it was not widely viewed as a serious crime at the time.[60] This reason seems more plausible. It would make sense if investigators, prosecutors and judges held that view, given the silence on sexual violence crimes in the tribunal charters, not to mention the fact that women, who are disproportionately affected by sexual violence in peacetime and in war, were absent from the Bench in both tribunals and almost entirely absent from the prosecution teams.[61]

It has also been suggested that the Allies may have abstained from prosecuting sexual violence crimes committed by their wartime enemies because their own forces had also committed such crimes.[62] This explanation is also credible, given the reports of extensive sexual violence crimes committed by Allied forces and aligned mercenaries during the war.[63] Yet as Nicola Henry has argued, it is only a 'partial explanation' because the Allies tried *certain* wartime sexual violence crimes under domestic law.[64] In Henry's view, a more complete explanation is that wartime rape

[56] U. Dolgopol and S. Paranjape, 'Comfort Women: An Unfinished Ordeal: Report of a Mission' (International Commission of Jurists, 1994) 16.

[57] Women's International War Crimes Tribunal for the Trial of Japan's Military Sexual Slavery, 'Judgment, The Prosecutors and the Peoples of the Asia-Pacific Region v. Hirohito Emperor Showa et al.' (4 December 2001), [948].

[58] Henry, see n. 49, 271.

[59] Ní Aoláin, Haynes and Cahn, see n. 31, 157.

[60] Copelon, see n. 4, 221.

[61] There were three female assistant prosecutors in the Tokyo Tribunal, and no female prosecutors (of any level) in the Nuremberg Tribunal. See Askin, *War Crimes Against Women*, see n. 15, 103, 167.

[62] Ibid., 163; Copelon, see n. 4, 222.

[63] For examples, see Copelon, see n. 4, 52, 59, 60.

[64] Henry, see n. 49, 269.

was poorly prosecuted in the post-war period as a result of sexism, racism and vested political interests combined. This helps to explain the Tokyo Tribunal's willingness to condemn the mass rape in Nanking (China was involved in the creation of the tribunal and was represented there by a judge and a lead prosecutor) versus its silence on the abuse of 'comfort women' (most of whom hailed from different states than the tribunal judges and prosecutors).[65] It also helps to explain why the crimes against the 'comfort women' were not prosecuted in any Allied state after the war, except for one Dutch prosecution for forced prostitution in Batavia (now Jakarta), which only addressed the experience of Dutch women, and not the local women who suffered similar abuse.[66]

Whatever the reason for the under-prosecution of wartime rape in the 1940s, the effect of this pattern is clear: it prevented the production of an accurate and inclusive narrative of World War II; it enabled ignorance and denialism of the extent of sexual violence during the war, such as revisionist histories in Japan which dispute the existence and/or scale of the 'comfort women' system;[67] and it also reinforced a perception that sexual violence is not serious enough, or perhaps, 'not *political* enough',[68] to be thoroughly investigated, charged and adjudicated as a crime under international law.

Even in the 1990s, the under-prosecution of sexual violence crimes remained a significant risk. Peggy Kuo, a former ICTY trial attorney, recalls that although Prosecutor Richard Goldstone was committed to prosecuting sexual crimes, some investigators in the tribunal's early years made comments such as 'I've got ten dead bodies, how do I have time for rape? That's not as important' and 'so a bunch of guys got riled up after a day of war, what's the big deal?'.[69] A trace of those views can be seen in the Prosecution's first filing in the *Tadić* case, dated 11 October 1994.[70] The filing alleged that in context of 'ethnic cleansing' in Bosnia and Herzegovina, women were raped at Serbian military bases[71] and were gang-raped in the Trnopolje detention camp as a 'regular occurrence',[72]

[65] Ibid., 269.
[66] Ibid., 270.
[67] See Chang, see n. 59, 209; BBC News, 'Osaka Cuts San Francisco Ties Over "Comfort Women" Statue' (4 October 2018).
[68] Henry, see n. 49, 268 (emphasis added).
[69] Kuo, see n. 34, 310–311.
[70] Application for Deferral by the Federal Republic of Germany, *Tadić* (IT-94-1), 11 October 1994.
[71] Ibid., [4.2].
[72] Ibid., [5.7].

and that Tadić personally participated in those rapes at Trnopolje 'on multiple occasions'.[73] And yet, in the Prosecution's words, 'it was at the Omarska camp, however, that Tadić's actions were *most serious*'.[74] At that camp, he allegedly killed and abused male prisoners, including one incident in which a prisoner was forced to drink motor oil and then bite off the testicles of three other male prisoners, who died as a result.[75]

Concerned that the ICTY prosecutors would continue to present the repeated gang-rape of female prisoner as less serious than the similarly heinous treatment of male prisoners, three American legal scholars filed an *amicus curiae* brief which 'emphasized the failure to treat rape as an indictable offence'.[76] These scholars included Rhonda Copelon, who as detailed in Section 3.2, would also play a lead role in women's rights activism during the Rome Statute negotiations. The same concern was raised at the first hearing, in which Judge Elizabeth Odio Benito reminded the Prosecutor of the gravity of rape and informed him: 'there will be no justice unless women are part of that justice'.[77] The Prosecutor subsequently added charges for the alleged rape of women in the Trnopolje and Omaraska camps, but later withdrew three counts relating the alleged rape of Witness F in Omarska camp because she became too frightened to testify[78] (according to one report, she lost trust in the tribunal's protective measures after her identity was leaked and publicised).[79]

Despite this inauspicious beginning, the ICTY went on to prosecute a wide range of conflict-related sexual violence crimes. This was achieved through the work of dedicated individuals in the ICTY OTP and Chambers, an openness to learning lessons from unsuccessful prosecutions and what former ICTY Deputy Prosecutor Michelle Jarvis describes

[73] Ibid., [6.6].

[74] Ibid., [6.7] (emphasis added).

[75] Ibid., [6.7].

[76] Copelon, see n. 4, 229. See also M. Jarvis and K. Vigneswaran, 'Challenges to Successful Outcomes in Sexual Violence Cases' in S. Brammertz and M. Jarvis (eds), *Prosecuting Conflict-related Sexual Violence at the ICTY* (Oxford University Press, 2016) 33, 56–57.

[77] Transcript, *Tadić* (IT-94-1), 8 November 1994 (a.m. session), 27(10)–28(3).

[78] K. Vigneswaran, 'Charging and Outcomes in ICTY Cases Involving Sexual Violence' in *Prosecuting Conflict-related Sexual Violence at the ICTY* (Oxford University Press, 2016) 429, 477–478; K. Askin, 'Sexual Violence in Decisions and Indictments of the Yugoslav and Rwandan Tribunals: Current Status' (1999) 93(1) *American Journal of International Law* 97, 101.

[79] G. Mischkowski and G. Mlinarevic, 'The Trouble with Rape Trials: Views of Witnesses, Prosecutors and Judges on Prosecuting Sexualised Violence during the War in the Former Yugoslavia [Sic]' (Media Mondiale, 2009) 35.

as a willingness to 'take on "risky" cases', meaning cases in which accountability for conflict-related sexual violence was achieved by interpreting and applying crimes in innovative ways.[80] A case that exemplified that innovative approach was the *Kunarac et al.* case, which concerned crimes committed in Foča, Bosnia and Herzegovina.[81] The indictment, filed by Prosecutor Goldstone in June 1996, alleged that male Serb forces committed numerous sexual violence crimes against Muslim and Croat women, including raping them vaginally, orally and anally; ejaculating on them; biting their breasts; and forcing them to dance naked on a table. Making full use of the ICTY Statute, the Prosecutor characterised those acts as crimes against humanity (rape, torture and persecution on political, racial and/or religious grounds) and war crimes (torture, willfully causing great suffering, inhumane treatment and outrages on personal dignity).[82] In 2002, the Trial Chamber accepted that interpretation of the ICTY Statute, and that result was upheld on appeal.[83]

Yet even in this progressive tribunal, inherited ways of thinking and operating sometimes posed a challenge to the prosecution of sexual violence crimes. For example, Jarvis and her colleague Najwa Nabti recall that within the ICTY OTP, there was a debate as to whether sexual violence could be charged as torture. The Office ultimately decided it *could* be done, however, 'this view required fundamentally challenging the prevailing view of the crime, which most dominantly reflected the experiences of male victims, such as the historical focus on interrogation within the crime'.[84] Moreover, writing with her colleague Kate Vigneswaran, Jarvis recalls that even in the ICTY OTP, it was necessary

[80] M. Jarvis, 'Overview: The Challenge of Accountability for Conflict-Related Sexual Violence Crimes' in S. Brammertz and M. Jarvis (eds), *Prosecuting Conflict-Related Sexual Violence at the ICTY* (Oxford University Press, 2016) 1, 9.

[81] Vigneswaran, see n. 78, 447–450.

[82] Indictment, *Kunarac et al.* ('Foča' case), IT-96-23 & 23/1, 18 June 1996.

[83] Judgment, *Kunarac et al.* ('Foča' case), (IT-96-23-T & IT-96-23/1-T), 22 February 2002; Appeal Judgment (*Kunarac et al.* ('Foča' case), (IT-96-23 & IT-96-23/1-A,) 12 June 2002. For a discussion of other legally groundbreaking ICTY sexual violence cases, see Askin, 'Prosecuting Wartime Rape', see n. 15; H. Brady, 'The Power of Precedents: Using the Case Law of the Ad Hoc International Criminal Tribunals and Hybrid Courts in Adjudicating Sexual and Gender-Based Crimes at the ICC' (2012) 18(2) *Australian Journal of Human Rights* 75; Sellers, see n. 36, 312–313.

[84] M. Jarvis and N. Nabti, 'Policies and Institutional Strategies for Successful Sexual Violence Prosecutions' in S. Brammertz and M. Jarvis (eds), *Prosecuting Conflict-Related Sexual Violence at the ICTY* (Oxford University Press, 2016) 73, 91.

to grapple with the misconception that sexual violence is less serious than other crimes. In their words,

> The instinctive approach, as in many prosecution offices around the world, was to create a hierarchy of crimes, with murder at the pinnacle. Generally, the number of killings became a measure of the seriousness of the 'crime base'. Sexual violence was, at times, regarded as well down the hierarchy. Consistent with this, when the question of charging sexual violence as an underlying act of genocide was first raised strong views were express that this would water down the gravity of the crime.[85]

Yet over time, through strong leadership, including that of Jarvis in her role as Deputy Prosecutor and Sellers in her role as Gender Advisor, these attitudes and misconceptions were overcome.[86] As of September 2016, a total of 78 individuals (or 48 per cent of all ICTY accused) had been charged with sexual violence crimes, 32 of whom were convicted of those crimes, and 14 of whom were acquitted for those crimes (the remaining cases include ongoing proceedings, cases in which the charges were withdrawn or the accused died before trial and cases referred to national jurisdictions).[87]

The ICTR also got off to a poor start in prosecuting sexual violence crimes. Such crimes were rife during the 1994 conflict that prompted the establishment of the ICTR. According to a 1996 report on the conflict by the UN Special Rapporteur of the Commission on Human Rights, 'rape was the rule and its absence the exception'.[88] The majority of reported rape victims were women and girls, many of whom became pregnant as a result of this crime.[89] There is some evidence that men and boys were subjected to sexual violence during the Rwanda conflict also.[90] Despite that, none of the early cases before the ICTR included charges of sexual violence crimes.

[85] Jarvis and Vigneswaran, see n. 76, 36–37.

[86] See Sellers, see n. 36.

[87] ICTY, 'Sexual Violence: In Numbers' (undated): www.icty.org/en/features/crimes-sexual-violence/in-numbers.

[88] 'Report on the Situation of Human Rights in Rwanda Submitted by Mr. René Degni-Ségui, Special Rapporteur of the Commission on Human Rights, under Paragraph 20 of Resolution S-3/1 of 25 May 1994, UN Doc. E/CN.4/1996/68' (29 January 1996), [16]. See also Nowrojee, see n. 13, 41–44, 78–79.

[89] 'Report on the Situation of Human Rights in Rwanda Submitted by Mr. René Degni-Ségui, Special Rapporteur of the Commission on Human Rights, under Paragraph 20 of Resolution S-3/1 of 25 May 1994, UN Doc. E/CN.4/1996/68', see n. 88, [16]–[17], [23]–[24]; Nowrojee, see n. 13, 76–80.

[90] 'Report on the Situation of Human Rights in Rwanda Submitted by Mr. René Degni-Ségui, Special Rapporteur of the Commission on Human Rights, under Paragraph 20 of Resolution S-3/1 of 25 May 1994, UN Doc. E/CN.4/1996/68', see n. 88, [18].

The *Shattered Lives* report, published in September 1996 by Human Rights Watch and FIDH, cited three reasons for that pattern. First, there was a lack of political will to investigate sexual violence crimes due to 'a widespread perception among the Tribunal investigators that rape is somehow a "lesser" or "incidental" crime not worth investigating'.[91] Second, there was a 'mistaken assertion by staff members of the Tribunal that they do not need to devote scarce resources to investigating rape because Rwandan women will not come forward to talk'.[92] In the words of the (then) ICTR Deputy Prosecutor Honoré Rakotomanana, who was later forced to resign following reports of his incompetence,[93] 'African women don't want to talk about rape'.[94] This assertion showed little insight into the need to adjust investigative techniques for crimes that are culturally sensitive and was contradicted by the *Shattered Lives* report, which included numerous rape testimonies of Rwandan women. Third, where the Tribunal investigators had tried to collect rape testimony, inappropriate techniques had been used. For example, investigators and interpreters were mostly male, whereas most women who spoke with the *Shattered Lives* research team expressed a preference for discussing their experiences of rape with other women.[95]

Similar concerns were expressed in a report issued two years later by the UN Special Rapporteur on Violence Against Women, Radhika Coomaraswamy, following her mission in Rwanda.[96] According to this report, 'the [ICTR] OTP is not pro-active. The Sexual Assault Team does not go out and investigate or search for cases of sexual violence; rather, women victims or potential witnesses must approach the OTP'.[97] In addition, the report noted concerns that the investigators were 'culturally insensitive' and until recently, were all male, and that women did not have confidence in the ICTR's witness protection scheme.[98] Commenting on the ITCR's performance overall, Coomaraswamy stated that she was 'absolutely appalled that the first indictment on the grounds of sexual

[91] Nowrojee, see n. 13, 92.

[92] Ibid.

[93] 'Report of the Office of Internal Oversight Services on the Audit and Investigation of the International Criminal Tribunal for Rwanda, A/51/789' (6 February 1997), [91]; J. Goshko, 'U.N. Chief Fires Top Officials of Rwanda War Crimes Tribunal' (Washington Post, 27 February 1997).

[94] Nowrojee, see n. 13, 92.

[95] Ibid., 92–93.

[96] 'Report of the Mission to Rwanda on the Issues of Violence against Women in Situations of Armed Conflict, E/CN.4/1998/54/Add.1' (4 February 1998), [25]–[37].

[97] Ibid., [48].

[98] Ibid., [49]–[51].

violence at the [ICTR] was issued only in August 1997, and then only after heavy international pressure from women's groups'.[99]

That pressure was applied in the *Akayesu* case, which concerned Jean-Paul Akayesu, former mayor of Rwanda's Taba *commune*, where many women and girls were reportedly raped by Hutu militia during the genocide.[100] There were no sexual violence charges in the initial *Akayesu* indictment, submitted by Prosecutor Goldstone on 13 February 1996.[101] However, sexual violence emerged as a key theme after two prosecution witnesses raised this issue during trial, provoking questions from all three trial judges.[102] In response to these developments, a coalition of women's rights activities – again including Copelon – filed an *amicus curiae* brief which observed that despite reports of widespread sexual violence during the conflict, the ICTR Prosecutor was yet to charge a *single person* with rape.[103] Two weeks later, the Prosecutor requested permission to add sexual violence crimes to Akayesu's indictment, a request that the Chamber allowed.[104] The Prosecution then called additional witnesses to give evidence of these crimes, and the case ultimately led to the first conviction, by any court, for rape as an act of genocide.[105]

After *Akayesu*, the ICTR prosecutors became more vigilant about charging sexual violence crimes.[106] However, this trend did not last,

[99] Ibid., [38].

[100] Nowrojee, see n. 13, 41–44, 78–79.

[101] Askin, 'Prosecuting Wartime Rape', see n. 15, 318; Copelon, see n. 4, 224–225.

[102] Transcript, *Akayesu*, 27 January 1997, 101(20)–103(8); 104(17–24); 108(4–10); 136(21)–138(10) (thanks to Beth Van Schaack for sharing this transcript); Transcript, *Akayesu*, 6 March 1997, 106(25)–107(2); 7 March 1997, 26(1)–39(4).

[103] '*Amicus curiae* Brief Respecting Amendment of the Indictment and Supplementation of the Evidence to Ensure the Prosecution of Rape and Other Sexual Violence within the Competence of the Tribunal' (27 May 1997): www1.essex.ac.uk/armedcon/story_id/000053.pdf. See also B. Van Schaack, 'Engendering Genocide: The Akayesu Case before the International Criminal Tribunal for Rwanda' (Santa Clara Law School Digital Commons, 2008) 8–9.

[104] Amended Indictment, *Akayesu* (ICTR-96-4-T), 17 June 1997, Counts 13–16.

[105] Judgment, *Akayesu* (ICTR-96-4-T), 2 September 1998, [731]–[734]. For a discussion, see Askin, 'Prosecuting Wartime Rape', see n. 15, 318–319; Copelon, see n. 4, 224–226; Van Schaack, see n. 103, 6–11; S. SáCouto and K. Cleary, 'The Importance of Effective Investigation of Sexual Violence and Gender Based Crimes at the International Criminal Court' (2009) 17(2) *American University Journal of Gender, Social Policy & the Law* 337, 349–350.

[106] F. De Londras, 'Prosecuting Sexual Violence in the Ad Hoc International Criminal Tribunals for Rwanda and the Former Yugoslavia' in M. Albertson Fineman (ed.), *Transcending the Boundaries of Law: Generations of Feminism and Legal Theory* (Routledge, 2011) 290, 301.

following the appointment of Carla Del Ponte as ICTR Prosecutor in 1999. Del Ponte dismantled the team responsible for investigating sexual violence crimes, as she did not consider the investigation of these crimes as a key priority.[107] According to Beth Van Schaack, the ICTR OTP subsequently 'neglected, de-emphasized, or at times botched' the prosecution of sexual violence crimes until the end of Del Ponte's term in 2003.[108] In 2005, more than a decade after the ICTR's establishment, the lead author on the *Shattered Lives* report offered the following remarks on the tribunal's track record:

> Implicit in the mandate to prosecute persons responsible for serious violations of international humanitarian law in Rwanda is the need to establish an accurate public record of the events of 1994. The court's interpretation of those events, through its judgments, will colour how generations to come will view what happened in Rwanda and who bears responsibility. If the current trend continues, when the doors of the ICTR close, the judgments from this court will not tell the full story of what happened during the Rwandan genocide. They will not correctly reflect responsibility for the shocking rapes, sexual slavery and sexual mutilations that tens of thousands of Rwandan women suffered … The record of this tribunal in history will not only minimize responsibility for the crimes against women, but will actually deny that these crimes occurred. *A reader of the ICTR jurisprudence will be left mistakenly believing that the mass rapes had little or nothing to do with the genocidal policies of their leaders. This is indeed a serious miscarriage of justice.*[109]

The ICTR was closed in December 2015, 21 years since its establishment. Its final record on prosecuting sexual violence crimes was not strong: it indicted a total of 93 people, 52 of whom were charged with sexual violence crimes, but only twelve of whom were convicted of those crimes.[110]

Concerns about accountability for sexual violence crimes also arose in the Special Court for Sierra Leone (SCSL), a court established by the

[107] Ibid.

[108] B. Van Schaack, 'Obstacles on the Road to Gender Justice: The International Criminal Tribunal for Rwanda as Object Lesson' (2009) 17(2) *American University Journal of Gender, Social Policy & the Law* 362, 367. For similar critiques, see SáCouto and Cleary, see n. 105, 350; B. Nowrojee, '"Your Justice Is Too Slow" Will the ICTR Fail Rwanda's Rape Victims?' (UN Research Institute for Social Development, 2005) 10–17.

[109] Nowrojee, see n. 108, 6–7 (emphasis added).

[110] ICTR OTP, 'Best Practices Manual for the Investigation and Prosecution of Sexual Violence Crimes in Post-Conflict Regions: Lessons Learned from the Office of the Prosecutor for the International Criminal Tribunal for Rwanda' (30 January 2014) 5–6. Note: This manual refers to thirteen convictions, some of which had appeals pending

UN in agreement with the government of Sierra Leone to prosecute crimes committed in that country's civil war since 30 November 1996. The creation of the SCSL actually post-dates the ICC: the agreement for its establishment was signed on 16 January 2002 and entered force on 12 April 2002.[111] However, I refer to the SCSL here because it started prosecuting crimes before the ICC: the SCSL's first Prosecutor commenced his term in April 2002 and its first indictments were issued in March 2003,[112] whereas the ICC's first Prosecutor, Luis Moreno-Ocampo, commenced his term in June 2003 and its first indictments were issued in July 2005.[113] As Valerie Oosterveld has explained in detail, sexual violence crimes were successfully prosecuted in several SCSL cases, alongside other non-sexual gender-based violence such as forced domestic labour in the context of 'forced marriages' between abducted civilian women and male soldiers.[114] However, in the *'Civil Defence Forces (CDF) case'* the SCSL Prosecutor was barred from adding charges of sexual violence against women and girls based on evidence that became available after the indictment was issued, and from admitting that evidence in relation to the existing charges of cruel treatment and inhumane acts at trial, on the basis that this would be unfair to the accused. The Appeals Chamber found that the Trial Chamber had been wrong to exclude the Prosecutor's request to lead evidence of sexual violence in relation to the existing charges at trial, but it did not re-open the trial on that basis. As Oosterveld observes, the result was that 'the history of rape and other forms of sexual violence committed by the CDF against women and girls will never be recorded by the SCSL'.[115]

at the time that it was published. As of 23 September 2018, convictions of sexual violence crimes have been finalised for twelve individuals (Akayesu Bagosora, Bizimungu, Gacumbitsi, Hategekimana, Karemera, Muhimana, Ngirampatse, Niyitegeka, Ntahobali, Nyiramasuhuko, and Semanza). A thirteenth case including sexual violence charges has been referred to the MICT, and the judgment is pending (Ngirabatware).

[111] UN Audiovisual Library of International Law, 'Statute of the Special Court for Sierra Leone: Procedural History' (undated).

[112] Ibid.

[113] ICC-02/04-01/05-53, 28 September 2005.

[114] V. Oosterveld, 'Evaluating the Special Court for Sierra Leone's Gender Jurisprudence' in C. Jalloh (ed.), *The Sierra Leone Special Court and its Legacy: The Impact for Africa and International Criminal Law* (Cambridge University Press, 2014) 234.

[115] Ibid., 258.

### 3.1.3 Stereotyping Women

While efforts to break the silence on the rape of women in war have been viewed positively in feminist scholarship, some feminists have expressed concerns about the unintended consequences of this shift in practice. For example, Karan Engle observes that feminist activists in the 1990s succeeded in drawing international attention to the rape of women during the conflict in the former Yugoslavia. Yet in her view, the portrayal of these women in feminist scholarship tends to affirm a stereotype of women as passive victims, lacking in sexual or political agency.[116] Engle cautions against this trend, arguing that 'perpetuating images of women as powerless victims of war might unwittingly function to strip women of many types of power including the power to resolve or prevent conflict'.[117] A related concern about stereotyping has been raised by Judith Gardam, who argues that an over-emphasis on women's experiences of sexual violence in international criminal law and IHL 'reinforces the limited vision of women … as someone who only becomes visible through their sexual identity' and also 'deflects attention from the myriad of other pressing issues that women face during and after armed conflict'.[118] Gardam does not advocate for a return to the days when wartime sexual violence was largely ignored. Rather, her argument is that women should not appear *only* in the law and practice of international criminal courts as victims of sexual violence; a more accurate and nuanced presentation of women's experiences of war is warranted.

More recently, Erin Baines has problematised the stereotyping of women subjected to wartime rape. Baines argues that because international prosecutors are focused on proving that a crime occurred, 'victim's testimonies are often curated to focus on harm to the sexed body, and the person is portrayed as devoid of voice or subjectivity'.[119] Based on her empirical research with women who were forced into marriage and motherhood by the Lord's Resistance Army in Uganda, Baines also identified a second layer of stereotyping in affected communities. In that setting, the

[116] E.g. K. Engle, 'Feminism and Its (Dis)Contents: Criminalizing Wartime Rape in Bosnia and Herzegovina' (2005) 99(4) *American Journal of International Law* 778.

[117] Ibid., 812.

[118] J. Gardam, 'A New Frontline for Feminism and International Humanitarian Law' in M. Davies and V. Munro (eds), *The Ashgate Research Companion to Feminist Legal Theory* (Ashgate, 2013) 217, 218.

[119] E. Baines, *Buried in the Heart Women, Complex Victimhood and the War in Northern Uganda* (Cambridge University Press, 2017) 4–5.

figure of the abducted woman appears not as a helpless or fragile victim, but as 'a terrorist', 'a rebel' or 'a rebel's wife'.[120] Baine's findings suggest that in international justice processes as well as local settings, women's wartime experiences are often appropriated and re-packaged in service of other goals. As Baines explains:

> In these multiple, conflicting and contradictory stories about the sexually violated woman, she rarely appears as a subject. Instead, her body and her experience are the object of contending political projections, quests for justice and justifications for war.[121]

These concerns about the representation of women as victims pose a challenge for ICC, and for the OTP in particular. The OTP cannot tackle impunity for gender-based crimes, or demonstrate the gravity of these crimes, without presenting evidence of the victimisation of women and girls. Yet there is some scope for the OTP to challenge reductive stereotypes of women and girls. It can, for example, recognise that testifying about violent ordeals is itself a form of agency, it can be responsive to the views and concerns expressed by victims of gender-based crimes or their lawyers and it can ensure that female stories of courage, resistance and/or perpetration of violence are part of the narrative of the case.

### 3.1.4 *Inattention to Male Experiences of Sexual Violence*

In 2018, in an interview with International Justice Monitor, one of the victims' counsel in the ICC's *Ongwen* case stated: 'normally, of course, the perception is that it is only women that suffer these sexual and gender-based crimes. But for this conflict it turns out that there are many men that suffered this type of violence and many of them spoke to us openly about this'.[122] The conflict referred to by this lawyer, namely the 2002–2004 conflict in Uganda, is not unique in this respect. Rather, men and boys are frequently sexually abused in conflict situations, especially while in detention, including rape, sexual mutilation, forced nudity and being forced to participate in sexual acts with others.[123] For example, in 1994, the

[120] Ibid., 4.

[121] Baines, see n. 119, 4.

[122] T. Maliti, 'Manoba and Cox: There Is a Conspiracy of Silence About Male Victims of Sex Crimes' on *International Justice Monitor* (14 September 2018).

[123] See C. Dolan, 'Victims Who Are Men' in F. Ní Aoláin et al. (eds), *The Oxford Handbook of Gender and Conflict* (Oxford University Press, 2018) 86; Eriksson Baaz and Stern, see n. 9, 44; S. Sivakumaran, 'Sexual Violence Against Men in Armed Conflict' (2007) 18(2) *European Journal of International Law* 253.

UN Commission of Experts on violations of IHL in the former Yugoslavia reported that in addition to sexual violence against women,[124] 'men are also subject to sexual assault. They are forced to rape women and to perform sex acts on guards or each other. They have also been subjected to castration, circumcision or other sexual mutilation'.[125] In 1996, the UN Special Rapporteur on Human Rights reported during the Rwandan genocide, 'militiamen forced fathers or sons to have sexual relations with their own daughters or mothers and vice versa'.[126]

In light of these reports, the scholarship on international criminal law is increasingly engaging with the issue of sexual violence against men and boys. For the most part, this scholarship is critical of responses to this violence in international criminal tribunals.[127] For example, Sandesh Sivakumaran has argued that 'much of the time, male sexual violence is simply not prosecuted before the international criminal tribunals'.[128] He further argues that even when it *is* prosecuted, it is often 'mentioned but not characterized as sexual violence' or 'mentioned but without any consequences' for the accused.[129] In a similar vein, Oosterveld has observed that conflict-related sexual violence against men and boys 'has rarely been prosecuted in international courts and tribunals',[130] and that although this is beginning to change, 'the tribunals have been unpredictable in terms of whether and how they explain the sexual nature of the act'.[131]

These critiques are more warranted in relation to some tribunals than others. For example, the ICTY may have missed some opportunities to

[124] 'Final Report of the Commission of Experts Established Pursuant to Security Council Resolution 780 (1992), UN Doc. S/1994/674 (Annex 1)' (27 May 1994), [241]–[253].

[125] Ibid., [235].

[126] 'Report on the Situation of Human Rights in Rwanda Submitted by Mr. René Degni-Ségui, Special Rapporteur of the Commission on Human Rights, under Paragraph 20 of Resolution S-3/1 of 25 May 1994, UN Doc. E/CN.4/1996/68', see n. 88, [18].

[127] E.g. R. Grey and L. Shepherd, '"Stop Rape Now?" Masculinity, Responsibility, and Conflict-Related Sexual Violence' (2013) 16(1) *Men and Masculinities* 115; N. Hayes, 'The Bemba Trial judgment: A Memorable Day for the Prosecution of Sexual Violence by the ICC' on *PhD Studies in Human Rights* (21 March 2016); D. Lewis, 'Unrecognized Victims: Sexual Violence Against Men in Conflict Settings Under International Law' (2009) 27(1) *Wisconsin International Law Journal* 1.

[128] S. Sivakumaran, 'Lost in Translation: UN Responses to Sexual Violence against Men and Boys in Situations of Armed Conflict' (2010) 92(877) *International Review of the Red Cross* 259, 272.

[129] Ibid., 273–274.

[130] V. Oosterveld, 'Sexual Violence Directed against Men and Boys in Armed Conflict or Mass Atrocity' (2014) 10 *Journal of International Law and International Relations* 107, 110.

[131] Ibid., 113.

prosecute sexual violence against men,[132] but its record in this regard was fairly strong.[133] Charges were brought for forcing two brothers to have oral sex with one another in a detention facility (*Češić*),[134] placing a burning fuse cord around a male prisoner's genitals (*Mucić et al.*),[135] beating a prisoner in the genital area and forcing him to take a soldier's penis in his mouth (*Naletilić & Martinović*),[136] forcing five male prisoners to have oral sex with one another (*Prlić et al.*),[137] raping male prisoners and forcing them to engage in sexual acts with one another,[138] and forcing a prisoner to 'spread his legs so that they could beat him in the crotch' and telling him that 'Muslims should not propagate' (*Simić et al.*),[139] forcing male prisoners to simulate sexual acts with one another (*Stakić*),[140] forcing male prisoners to perform sexual acts with each other and with female prisoners (*Stanišić & Župljanin*)[141] and forcing a male prisoner to suck and mutilate another male prisoner's genitals (*Tadić*).[142]

These acts were charged using the war crime of torture or inhuman treatment;[143] the war crime of willfully causing great suffering or serious injury to body and health;[144] the war crime of cruel treatment;[145] the war crime of humiliating and degrading treatment;[146] and the crime against humanity of rape,[147] the crime against humanity of persecution (through

[132] See Oosterveld, 'Sexual Violence Directed against Men and Boys', see n. 130, 111–112.
[133] See S. Verrall, 'The Picture of Sexual Violence in the Former Yugoslavia Conflicts as Reflected in ICTY Judgments' in S. Brammertz and M. Jarvis (eds), *Prosecuting Conflict-Related Sexual Violence at the ICTY* (Oxford University Press, 2016) 299, 313–315.
[134] Third Amended Indictment, *Češić* (IT-95-10/1), 26 November 2002, [15].
[135] Indictment, *Mucić et al.* (IT-96-21), 19 March 1996, [31].
[136] Judgment, *Naletilić & Martinović* (IT-98-34), 31 March 2003, [462], [464].
[137] Second Amended Indictment, *Prlić et al.* (IT-04-74), 11 June 2008, [55]; Judgment, *Prlić et al.* (IT-04-74), 29 May 2013, Vol. II, [169] and Vol. III, [770], [1695].
[138] Judgment, *Simić et al.* (IT-95-9-T), 17 October 2003, [728].
[139] Ibid., [697], [771].
[140] Judgment, *Stakić* (IT-97-24), 31 July 2003, [241], read together with [806].
[141] Corrigendum and Prosecution's submission of second amended consolidated indictment, *Stanišić & Župljanin* (IT-08-91), 23 November 2009, [26(d)]; Judgment, *Stanišić & Župljanin* (IT-08-91), 27 March 2013, Vol. I, [404], [475], [1599].
[142] Second Amended Indictment, *Tadić* (IT-94-1), 14 December 1995, [6].
[143] Ibid.
[144] Ibid.
[145] Ibid.
[146] Third Amended Indictment, *Češić* (IT-95-10/1), 26 November 2002, [15].
[147] Ibid.

torture);[148] and the crime against humanity of other inhumane acts.[149] In all of those cases, those acts were acknowledged in the judgment,[150] and in most cases, were described in the judgment as 'sexual' crimes.[151]

However, in the ICTR, sexual violence against men was virtually invisible. There were no charges for the reported forced sexual intercourse between male and female family members, and although other forms of sexual violence against men were alleged, they received minimal attention in the judgment. Sivakumaran refers to two cases to illustrate this point: *Bagosora* and *Muhimana*. In both cases, Trial Chamber acknowledged having heard evidence of the mutilation of men's genitals, but did not describe the mutilations as 'sexual', although it used that term to describe the mutilation of a women's genitals.[152] While not cited by Sivakumaran, a third example is the *Niyitegeka* case, in which the Trial Chamber found that Hutu militia killed and sexually mutilated two Tutsi people: a man named Kabanda (the same man described in the *Muhimana* case), and an unnamed woman.[153] The Chamber convicted Niyitegeka for encouraging and ordering these crimes, but it referred only to the mutilation of the *woman's* body as 'sexual violence'.[154] In its 2014 'best practices' manual, the ICTR OTP stated that its

[148] Corrigendum and Prosecution's submission of second amended consolidated indictment, *Stanišić & Župljanin* (IT-08-91), 23 November 2009, [26(d)].

[149] Second Amended Indictment, *Tadić* (IT-94-1), 14 December 1995, [6].

[150] Plea Decision, *Češić* (IT-95-10/1), 8 October 2003, page 66, line 7 to page 67, line 19 and line 81, page 2 to page 86, line 3; Sentencing Decision, *Češić* (IT-95-10/1), 11 March 2014, [13]–[14], [17], [35]; Judgment, *Mucić et al.* (IT-96-21), 16 November 1998, [1035]–[1040]; Judgment, *Naletilić & Martinović* (IT-98-34), 31 March 2003, [462], [464]; Judgment, *Prlić et al.* (IT-04-74), 29 May 2013, Vol. II, [169]–[170], Vol. III, [770], [1695] and Vol. IV, [70]; Judgment, *Simić et al.* (IT-95-9-T), 17 October 2003, [697], [771], [728]; Judgment, *Stakić* (IT-97-24), 31 July 2003, [241] read together with [806]; Judgment, *Stanišić & Župljanin* (IT-08-91), 27 March 2013, Vol. I, [404], [475], [1599]; Judgment, *Tadić* (IT-94-1), 7 May 1997, [198], [206], [237].

[151] The exceptions are incident with the burning fuse cord charged in *Mucić et al.*, the genital beatings and forced oral sex charged in *Naletilić & Martinović*, and the genital beatings charged in *Simić et al.* See: Judgment, *Mucić et al.* (IT-96-21), 16 November 1998, [1035]–[1040]; Judgment, *Naletilić & Martinović* (IT-98-34), 31 March 2003, [462], [464]; Judgment, *Simić et al.* (IT-95-9-T), 17 October 2003, [697], [771].

[152] Sivakumaran, see n. 128, 273–274, citing Judgment, *Bagosora* (ICTR-98-41), 18 December 2008, [1908] c.f. [2224], [2266]; Judgment, *Muhimana* (ICTR-95-1B), 28 April 2005, [441]–[444], [448]–[450].

[153] Judgment, *Niyitegeka* (ICTR-96-14), 16 May 2003, Ch. III, [462]–[463] (noting that the attackers severed Kabanda's genitals and displayed them on a spike, and that they thrust a sharpened piece of wood into the woman's genitals after shooting her).

[154] Ibid., [465]–[467].

investigators discovered just *two* incidents of sexual violence against men in all of their investigations in Rwanda. The first concerned the killing of Kabanda, as described previously. The second 'involved a male victim in Kigali who was forced to live and have sexual intercourse with a female in exchange for his life'.[155] According to the manual, 'challenges encountered during the investigation prevented this incident from being prosecuted, and no evidence relating to this incident was presented in court'.[156] The manual does not describe those challenges or explain what steps, if any, the investigators took to try to overcome them.

The SCSL's record in prosecuting sexual violence against men also left much to be desired.[157] There were no charges of sexual violence against male victims in any case, although the indictments in the *Taylor*, *AFRC* and *RUF* cases all referred to sexual violence against 'women and girls'.[158] The flaw in that approach became apparent during trial, when witnesses in all three cases testified about sexual violence against males, including genital mutilation, forced nudity and forced sex between male and female victims.[159] In *Taylor*, the Trial Chamber declined to make any findings about the evidence of sexual violence against male victims because the Prosecutor had not given adequate notice of the allegations to the Defence.[160] The *AFRC* Trial Chamber took a similar approach, choosing to only acknowledge the evidence of sexual violence against females while making no mention of the alleged sexual violence against males.[161] By contrast, the RUF Trial Chamber found that the Defence had been given sufficient notice, and it made numerous factual findings about sexual violence crimes against boys and men.[162] That was the only

155 ICTR OTP, see n. 110, [40]–[41].

156 Ibid., [41].

157 V. Oosterveld, 'Gender and the Charles Taylor Case at the Special Court for Sierra Leone' (7–33) 19(1) *William & Mary Journal of Women and the Law* 2012, 14; V. Oosterveld, 'The ICC Policy Paper on Sexual and Gender-Based Crimes: A Crucial Step for International Criminal Law' (2018) 24(3) *William & Mary Journal of Women and the Law* 443, 447–448; Oosterveld, 'Sexual Violence Directed against Men and Boys', see n. 131, 113.

158 Prosecutor's memorandum and indictment, *Taylor* (SCSL-01-03-T), 7 March 2003, [39]; Amended consolidated indictment, *Brima et al.* (SCSL-04-16-T), 13 May 2004, [51]; Amended consolidated indictment, *Sesay et al.* (SCSL-04-15-T), 13 May 2004, [54].

159 See Prosecution Final Brief, *Taylor* (SCSL-01-03-T), 8 May 2011, [855] (including n. 2457), [861], [889], [931], [935], [936], [938]; Prosecution Final Brief, *Brima et al.* (SCSL-04-16-T), 6 December 2006, [1005], [1323]; Prosecution Final Brief, *Sesay et al.* (SCSL-04-15-T), 7 August 2008, [583], [586], [587].

160 Judgment, *Taylor* (SCSL-01-03-T), 18 May 2012, [132]–[134].

161 Judgment, *Brima et al.* (SCSL-04-16-T), 20 June 2007, [966]–[1188].

162 Judgment, *Sesay et al.* (SCSL-04-15-T), 2 March 2009, [1302]–[1309].

SCSL judgment to recognise the experiences of male victims of sexual violence during the war.

As these examples illustrate, sexual violence against men and boys has not been *uniformly* ignored in recent decades. However, it has remained vulnerable to being poorly investigated, and left off indictments, even in an era of increased attention to sexual violence against women and girls.

### *3.1.5 Presumptions against Criminal Responsibility for Sexual Violence Crimes*

After some initial stumbles, sexual violence crimes were charged in numerous cases before the ICTY and ICTR. The ICTY developed a particularly strong practice in this regard. Yet it should be noted that in that tribunal, most of the sexual violence cases concerned direct perpetrators (i.e. the individuals who physically committed the crimes) or others physically close to the scene of the crime.[163] By contrast, establishing that a military or political leader was responsible for sexual violence crimes committed by their subordinates has been more difficult, especially when that leader was not physically present for the crime. As observed by Susana SáCouto and Katherine Cleary, this difficulty has arisen in several ICTY and ICTR cases in which the Prosecution relied on circumstantial evidence to establish the criminal responsibility of the accused.[164]

Among the many examples referred to by SáCouto and Cleary is the *Gacumbitsi* case, from the ICTR. In that case, the Prosecution alleged that Gacumbitsi, former mayor of the Rusumo *commune*, instigated several of the rapes and sexual mutilations perpetrated by Hutu militia in that area.[165] Specifically, it alleged that in the first weeks of the genocide, he drove around the *commune* inciting violence through a megaphone, including telling Hutu men to rape Tutsi women and kill them if they refused to submit to rape.[166] The Trial Chamber accepted

[163] M. Jarvis and E. Martin Saldago, 'Future Challenges to Prosecuting Sexual Violence under International Law: Insights from ICTY Practice' in A. de Brouwer et al. (eds), *Sexual Violence as an International Crime: Interdisciplinary Approaches* (Intersentia, 2013) 101, 103, 106.

[164] SáCouto and Cleary, see n. 105, 353–354.

[165] Indictment, *Gacumbitsi* (ICTR-01-64), 20 June 2011, Count 5.

[166] Ibid., [21], [39].

that the accused acted in this manner.[167] It also accepted that numerous women were raped by Hutu militia in the relevant area in April 1994.[168] However, for several of those rapes, the Trial Chamber found that there was insufficient evidence that the sexual violence was causally related to Gacumbitsi's actions.[169] That included the rapes committed against Witness TAS, who testified that her attackers stated they were following Gacumbitsi's instructions.[170] The Trial Chamber's findings were upheld on appeal.[171] SáCouto and Cleary draw a comparison with the ICTY's *Brđanin* case, in which the accused was convicted, among other things, of instigating the deportation and forcible transfer of non-Serbs from the Autonomous Region of Krajina (now part of Bosnia and Herzegovina).[172] The Trial Chamber held that Brđanin instigated those crimes because in his role of head of Crisis Staff of the Autonomous Region of Krajina, he made statements advocating the resettlement of the non-Serb population.[173] Moreover, it held that those statements 'prompted the municipal authorities and the police, who implemented them, to commit the crimes of deportation and forcible transfer after those dates'.[174] As SáCouto and Cleary observe,

> The [ICTY] Trial Chamber did not require proof that the municipal authorities followed ARK staff decisions in direct response to Brđanin's inflammatory statements about non-Serbs or that they were even aware of such statements. Rather, the causal link between Brđanin's statements and the deportation and forcible transfer of non-Serbs appears to have rested entirely on the accused's position of authority in the ARK and his influence over municipal authorities.[175]

For SáCouto and Cleary, this comparison suggests that Chambers may be less willing to infer a causal relationship between the statements of the accused and the conduct of the direct perpetrators for sexual violence crimes compared to other crimes. Based on this comparison and an

[167] Judgment, *Gacumbitsi* (ICTR-01-64), 17 June 2004, [215], [224]. At para. 215, the Trial Chamber identified the relevant date as 16 April 1994. However, at para. 224, it identified the relevant date as 17 April 1994. The Appeals Chamber clarified that the correct date was 17 April 1994. See: Appeal Judgment, *Gacumbitsi* (ICTR-01-64-A), 7 July 2006, n. 318.

[168] Judgment, *Gacumbitsi* (ICTR-01-64), 17 June 2004, [226].

[169] Ibid., [227], [329].

[170] Ibid., [227].

[171] Appeal Judgment, *Gacumbitsi* (ICTR-01-64), 7 July 2006, [126]–[139].

[172] Judgment, *Brđanin* (IT-99-36) 1 September 2004, [577].

[173] Ibid., [572].

[174] Ibid., [574].

[175] SáCouto and Cleary, see n. 105, 355.

analysis of ICTY and ICTR cases in which other modes of liability were charged, SáCouto and Cleary argue that there is a 'tendency of chambers to require a higher level of proof [of the guilt of the accused] in cases of sexual and gender-based violence than in other types of cases'.[176] A similar tendency has been identified by Kelly Askin,[177] and Brigid Inder, former Executive Director of Women's Initiatives for Gender Justice and from August 2012 to August 2016, the ICC Prosecutor's Special Advisor on Gender.[178] Reflections by former ICTY prosecutors Michelle Jarvis and Kate Vigneswaran suggest that the tendency to see sexual violence crimes as opportunistic crimes, which are disconnected from a high-level official's orders, incitement to violence or provision of weapons, does not only affect judicial decision making. Rather, it can also affect decisions by investigators and prosecutors. As they explain:

> The failure to accurately see the connection between sexual violence and other violence crimes can cause significant problems when trying to link crimes to senior political or military leaders who are not direct perpetrators. The success of these cases, leadership cases, often depends on accurately seeing sexual violence in context and understanding the role it played in the violent campaign unleashed by the senior official … Like any other crime, it is possible that sexual violence can be an isolated act that does not form part of a broader pattern. However, based on our experience, *there is a disproportionate tendency to assume that sexual violence is an isolated act when compared to other crimes.*[179]

### 3.1.6 *Gender-Blindness*

Thus far, the chapter has focused on factors which impede the recognition and prosecution of sexual violence crimes in international criminal law. But as emphasised in Chapter 2, sexual violence is only one type of gender-based violence; there are also gendered forms of forced labour, gendered forms of killing, gendered forms of persecution through deprivation of civil and political rights, etc. For the most part, the gendered nature of these crimes – both sexual and non-sexual – has also

[176] Ibid., 353.

[177] K. Askin, 'Katanga Judgment Underlines Need for Stronger ICC Focus on Sexual Violence' on *Open Society Foundations* (11 March 2014).

[178] B. Inder, 'A Critique of the Katanga Judgment' (at the Global Summit to End Sexual Violence in Conflict, London, 11 June 2014): www.iccwomen.org/documents/Global-Summit-Speech.pdf.

[179] Jarvis and Vigneswaran, see n. 76, 38–39 (emphasis added).

gone unrecognised in international criminal law. This is not to say that the conduct has never been *charged*; but there has been little attempt to reckon with the links between the conduct and socially constructed ideas about femininity and masculinity. Or as Copelon more simply expressed this point in 1994, 'historically, gender has not been viewed as a relevant category of victimization'.[180]

This gender-blindness can be seen in the letter of the law, as well as in legal practice. To begin with law, it is striking that until the 1998 Rome Statute, persecution in the grounds of gender had never been defined as a crime against humanity under international law. By contrast, persecution on political, racial and religious grounds has been a crime against humanity since the 1940s: it is recognised in the Nuremberg Tribunal Charter, the Tokyo Tribunal Charter and in Control Council Law 10.[181] Consistent with the post-World War II legal framework, gender-based persecution was not listed as a crime against humanity in the ICTY, ICTR or SCSL Statutes either.

The silence on gender-based persecution in the post-World War II legal frameworks did not happen solely because 'the law was made to fit the facts', as has been suggested elsewhere.[182] Rather, the law was made to fit the facts *that the law-makers deemed relevant.* Had the law truly fit the facts, it would have recognised persecution on a broader range of grounds, including gender. To understand this point, one need only look at the evidence presented in the Nuremberg and Tokyo Tribunals through a gender lens. At Nuremberg, the prosecutors presented evidence of widespread sexual violence crimes against women and girls, as discussed in Section 3.1.2. Several prosecution witnesses also referred to the detention of homosexual men in concentration camps, where they were subjected to pseudo-scientific experiments involving sex hormones.[183] All of these crimes were gender-based crimes, in the sense of being based on ideas about the role of men and women, respectively. How else to explain

[180] Copelon, see n. 31, 262.

[181] Note: The Tokyo Tribunal Charter referred to persecution on political or racial grounds only.

[182] Bassiouni, see n. 20, 132.

[183] Trial of the Major War Criminals Before the International Military Tribunal, Nuremberg, 14 November 1945–1 October 1946 ('Blue Series'), see n. 40, Vol. IV, 8 January 1948, 507; Vol. V, 11 January 1946, 176; Vol. VI, 29 January 1946, 310. See also H. Heger, *The Men with the Pink Triangle* (Merlin-Verlag, 1972); M. Bureleigh and W. Wipperman, *The Racial State: Germany 1933–1945* (Cambridge University Press, 1991) 182–196.

why women and girls were raped, but men and boys from the same towns were not? And how else to explain the Nazis' prejudice against homosexual men as distinct from heterosexual men, except by reference to a deeply ingrained idea that men 'should' be sexually attracted only to women? Socially-constructed gender norms also appear relevant to the crimes prosecuted at the Tokyo Tribunal. For example, the prosecutors led extensive evidence of rapes committed by Japanese soldiers against civilian women and girls in Nanking.[184] They also presented evidence of crimes committed solely against men, such as the torture and murder of male prisoners working on the Thai-Burma railway.[185] Yet despite these and many other examples from the war, gender was not seen as a ground on which people could be persecuted.

The gender-blindness of international criminal law has not only resulted in gaps in legal frameworks; it has also led to gaps in the narratives produced by courts and tribunals enforcing international criminal law. For example, in the Nuremberg Tribunal, neither the prosecutors nor the judges offered any analysis of the gendered ideology that would explain the crimes described previously. By contrast, the prosecutors devoted considerable time to explaining the racist, fascist and anti-Semitic ideology that fuelled the Nazis' crimes,[186] and such ideologies also received attention in the judgment.[187] Reflecting on this omission, Catharine Niarchos observed:

> It may be anachronistic to expect the Nuremberg tribunals to have grasped this concept [of gender-based violence]; after all, it is still considered novel today. By analogy, however, it now would be unthinkable to cast the Holocaust as persecution of civilians, without taking into account the ethnic and religious aspects of the crime ... In the same way, it now would be insensible to fail to recognize rape, in war or in peace, as an extreme form of gender discrimination and as gynocide.[188]

[184] Sellers, see n. 15, 288–289. For examples, see UN War Crimes Commission, *Transcripts of Proceedings and Documents of the IMTFE*, 26 July 1946, 2,569(5)– 2,572(23); 29 July 1946, 2,640(15–25); 2,633(8)–2,634(25); 15 August 1946, 3,909(2)–3,909(10); 16 August 1946, 3,918(24)–3,918,(23); 3,929(11–24); 29 August 1946, 4464(15)–4465(22); 4,474(10–20); 30 August 1946, 4537(3–21); 4615(23–24); 2647(14–24).

[185] Boister and Cryer, see n. 44, 553–557.

[186] E.g. Trial of the Major War Criminals Before the International Military Tribunal, Nuremberg, 14 November 1945–1 October 1946 ('Blue Series'), see n. 40, Vol. II, 21 November 1945, 99–100, 118–127; Vol. VII, 8 February 1946, 151–154.

[187] 'International Military Tribunal: Judgment and Sentence, October 1, 1946', see n. 42, 243–247.

[188] Niarchos, see n. 31, 679.

In 1994, a time when the ICTY was beginning its work, Copelon implored states, jurists, academics and commentators to remedy this historic gender-blindness by 'surfacing gender' in their analysis.[189] Yet even after that call was made, there continued to be very little discussion of gender in cases before the ICTY and ICTR. A clear example can be seen in the aforementioned *Gacumbitsi* case, where the Trial Chamber held that the victims of rape 'were chosen because of their Tutsi ethnic origin, or because of their relationship with a person of the Tutsi ethnic group'.[190] In so finding, the Chamber showed no awareness that these rape victims were *all female*, which would strongly suggest that their status as *women* was equally relevant to their Tutsi identity or (in one woman's case) marriage to a Tutsi man. As argued by Doris Buss and Chiseche Salome Mibenge, the *Gacumbitsi* case is not an isolated example; rather, its over-emphasis on ethnic identity and simultaneous under-emphasis on gender identity is typical of the ICTY and ICTR's approach.[191] As a result, these tribunals have been complicit in what Mibenge calls 'the erasure of gender from the war narrative'.

## 3.2 Course Correction? Women's Rights Activism in the Creation of the ICC

The negotiations for the ICC's core legal texts took place at a time of heightened sensitivity to gender issues in the field of international criminal justice. Women's rights activists and feminist scholars had begun to diagnose the aforementioned problems in the law and practice of international criminal courts and had begun to propose some solutions. In addition, reports of mass rape during the conflicts in the former Yugoslavia and Rwanda, which had begun to be investigated and prosecuted in the ICTY and ICTR, made it increasingly difficult for the international community to minimise the scale and gravity of conflict-related sexual violence as it had previously done. Seizing this opportunity to influence the development of international criminal law, women's rights activists began

[189] Ibid.

[190] Judgment, *Gacumbitsi* (ICTR-01-64), 17 June 2004, [324].

[191] D. Buss, 'The Curious Visibility of Wartime Rape: Gender and Ethnicity in International Criminal Law' (2007) 25 *Windsor Yearbook of Access to Justice* 3; D. Buss, 'Sexual Violence, Ethnicity, and Intersectionality in International Criminal Law' in E. Grabham et al. (eds), *Intersectionality and Beyond* (Routledge, 2009) 105; C Mibenge, *Sex and International Tribunals: The Erasure of Gender from the War Narrative* (University of Pennsylvania Press, 2013).

to organise and lobby state representatives to give the ICC a clear mandate to investigate and prosecute sexual and gender-based crimes. This second half of the chapter looks in detail at these lobbying efforts leading up to, during, and after the negotiations for the ICC's core legal text, the Rome Statute.

### 3.2.1 *Negotiating the Rome Statute*

As a multilateral treaty, the Rome Statute was drafted by and on behalf of states. However, human rights groups and other NGOs also played an active role in the drafting process. Although NGOs did not have standing to vote at the 1998 Conference in Rome where the Statute was adopted, they were influential participants in the proceedings. As recalled by Philippe Kirsch and John Holmes, both members of the Canadian delegation at the Rome Conference, 'NGOs lobbied extensively and provided substantial expert advice to virtually all delegations on the full range of complex legal issues contained in the statute'.[192] These lobbying efforts did not begin at the Rome Conference; they began in 1995, when the UN General Assembly created a Preparatory Committee on the ICC, which would meet in New York six times before the diplomatic conference in Rome in June–July 1998.[193] In response to the creation of the Preparatory Committee, numerous NGOs started to work collectively as Coalition for the International Criminal Court (CICC), with a view to influencing the Committee's work.[194] By the time of the Rome Conference, the CICC included some 800 NGOs and was a 'formidable, disciplined, and omnipresent' participant in the proceedings.[195]

The CICC initially included no women's rights groups, as those groups were busy preparing for the 1995 UN World Conference on Women in Beijing. Realising this was a problem, the CICC secretariat contacted women's rights activists in the New York area to inform them of the situation. At that early point in the ICC negotiations, a small group of women's

[192] P. Kirsch and J.T. Holmes, 'The Birth of the International Criminal Court: The 1998 Rome Conference' in O. Bekou and R. Cryer (eds), *The International Criminal Court* (Ashgate, 2004) 3, 36.

[193] A/RES/50/46, 11 December 1995.

[194] M. Glasius, *The International Criminal Court: A Global Civil Society Achievement* (Routledge, 2006) 26–28.

[195] F. Benedetti and J. Washburn, 'Drafting the International Criminal Court Treaty: Two Years to Rome and an Afterword on the Rome Diplomatic Conference' (1999) 5(1) *Global Governance* 1, 22, 33.

rights activists began to participate in the meetings of the Preparatory Committee starting in February 1997.[196] They realised that to be effective, a more diverse and organised women's advocacy group was needed. In May 1997, two of these activists (Rhonda Copelon and Dorothy Thomas) reached out to a veteran of women's rights activism in Latin America, Alda Facio, to establish such a body in New York.[197] Facio took up the offer and began work in June 1997. She began by consulting with partners around the world, many of whom expressed doubts about what an ICC could actually achieve. They asked: 'if national courts have done so little for women, why would an international court be different?'[198] Facio shared these reservations. In her words,

> Although I too was not totally convicted that this new institution would bring justice to women, I thought that women from all over the world should have a voice in these negotiations ... we needed to make sure that if the ICC were established, it reflected at least some of our concerns.[199]

By August 1997, the group had chosen a name for itself: the Women's Caucus for Gender Justice. The Caucus was inspired by efforts of women's rights activists to influence the work of the ICTY and ICTR, such as the *amicus curiae* briefs in the *Akayesu* and *Tadić* cases, and by women's caucuses in other UN forums in the 1990s, including the 1993 World Conference on Human Rights in Vienna and the 1995 Beijing conference.[200] Its members were alive to the challenges of speaking for 'women' as a group, without diminishing the importance of differences among women based on their race, nationality, sexual orientation and so forth. Facio in particular hoped that the Caucus would not ignore these differences but would provide an opportunity to discuss strategies for effective and inclusive women's rights activism going forward.[201] But as a more immediate goal, the Caucus's

[196] A. Facio, 'All Roads Lead to Rome, But Some Are Bumpier than Others' in S. Pickering and C. Lambert (eds), *Global Issues: Women and Justice* (Sydney Institute for Criminology, 2004) 308, 308–310.

[197] Ibid., 311.

[198] Ibid.

[199] Ibid.

[200] Chappell, see n. 7, 36; Copelon, see n. 4, 219; Facio, see n. 196, 311; P. Spees, 'Women's Advocacy in the Creation of the International Criminal Court: Changing the Landscapes of Justice and Power' (2003) 28(4) *Signs* 1233, 1237.

[201] Facio, see n. 196, 319–320.

priority was to give women a voice in the process of designing the ICC. As their website explained:

> The Women's Caucus grew out of the work of a last minute organizing effort of a small group of women human rights activists at the February 1997 Preparatory Committee for the Establishment of an International Criminal Court at the UN. These women realized that without an organized caucus, women's concerns would not be appropriately defended and promoted ... Along with our focus on women's concerns, the Caucus consistently made our views known on issues which are generally not recognized as gendered, such as jurisdiction, independence of the prosecutor, complementarity, cooperation, financing, etc. Nevertheless, due to our limited human and financial resources and because *nobody else was doing it*, we had to prioritize those issues which were more directly of concern to women.[202]

The Women's Caucus had good reason to think that without an intervention, women's views would be poorly represented in the process of creating the ICC. By the time the Caucus formed, that process was already well underway. The International Law Commission (ICL) had produced two texts to serve as a starting point: the 1994 *Draft Statute of the International Criminal Court* ('1994 Draft ICC Statute'), and the 1996 *Draft Code of Crimes against the Peace and Security of Mankind* ('1996 Draft Code of Crimes'). Neither text was written with women's input (the ICL comprised 34 men and no women) and neither showed a sensitivity to gender concerns. For example, although the 1994 text contained provisions aimed at ensuring *national* diversity in the judiciary,[203] there was nothing to prevent an all-male judiciary of the kind seen in the Nuremberg or Tokyo Tribunals, or a majority-male judiciary like the ICTY had at the time.[204] The 1994 text also showed little awareness of gender-based crimes. It identified five categories of crimes that the ICC could prosecute: genocide, aggression, war crimes, crimes against humanity and certain treaty-based crimes.[205] The attached commentary, which the ICL provided to guide the interpretation of those categories, made no reference to sexual

[202] Women's Caucus for Gender Justice, 'About the Women's Caucus' (undated): www.iccwomen.org/wigjdraft1/Archives/oldWCGJ/aboutcaucus.html.

[203] International Law Commission, 'Draft Statute for an International Criminal Court with Commentaries ("1994 Draft ICC Statute")' (22 July 1994) 29.

[204] Of the eleven judges serving in the ICTY in 1994, two were women (Judge Elizabeth Odio Benito and Judge Gabrielle Kirk Macdonald). The other nine judges were men.

[205] 1994 Draft ICC Statute, 38.

violence as a war crime,[206] listed just one sexual violence crime as a crime against humanity (rape) and made no mention of persecution on gender grounds.[207]

The 1996 Draft Code of Crimes was somewhat more gender sensitive. It listed 'rape, enforced prostitution and any form of indecent assault' as war crimes, although it described these crimes as 'outrages upon personal dignity' rather than as crimes causing serious bodily and mental harm.[208] It also listed 'rape, enforced prostitution and other forms of sexual abuse' as crimes against humanity.[209] However, as with previous instruments, the 1996 Draft Code of Crimes did not list persecution on 'gender' grounds as a crime against humanity; only 'political, racial, religious or ethnic' persecution were recognised. The omission of 'gender' from that list was not simply negligent; it was deliberate. As the ILC noted, 'while noting that persecution on gender grounds *could* also constitute a crime against humanity … the Commission decided to limit the possible grounds for persecution to those contained in existing legal instruments'.[210] The ICL did not explain why it favoured that conservative approach, or why, having adopted that approach, it nonetheless broke with tradition by including persecution on 'ethnic' grounds as a crime against humanity and by defining a *new* offence of 'institutionalized discrimination on racial, ethnic or religious grounds'.[211] Clearly, the ICL was willing to break new ground in order to criminalise victimisation on *some* grounds, not including gender. It is also no small matter that the full title of the 1996 Code equated 'humanity' with 'mankind': such language normalises a form of sexism in which men are deemed to be normal people, while women are regarded as 'the Other', a deviation from the norm.[212]

Both of these ILC instruments were submitted to the ICC Preparatory Committee to guide its work. In April 1998, the Preparatory Committee

[206] Ibid., 39.
[207] Ibid., 40.
[208] Ibid., 54.
[209] Ibid., 47.
[210] Ibid., 50 (emphasis added).
[211] Ibid., 47. The Commission did not explain why 'institutionalized discrimination' on those grounds, and not others, should be listed as a crime against humanity. It simply stated that this new crime 'is in fact the crime of apartheid [as defined in the 1973 Convention] under a more general denomination. Institutionalized discrimination was not included as a crime against humanity in the previous instruments. For this reason, the Commission decided to limit this crime to racial, ethnic or religious discrimination'.
[212] For a similar view, see Charlesworth and Chinkin, see n. 31, 232; S. de Beauvoir, *The Second Sex (1949)* (Vintage, 2011) 5–6.

produced a final Draft ICC Statute, which formed the basis for the Conference in Rome.[213] This 1998 Draft Statute included roughly 1,400 bracketed terms, meaning terms which were contentious and needed to be resolved by delegates at Rome.[214] The Women's Caucus was influential in this final stage of negotiations. By the time that the delegates from 120 states assembled in Rome, the Women's Caucus was a highly organised group which was co-directed by Facio (Costa Rica) and Eleanor Condor (the Philippines) and a legal secretariat led by Rhonda Copelon (USA). The Caucus made recommendations on almost every aspect of the draft statute, including: the criteria for judicial appointments; the inclusion of gender expertise in the OTP; the role of victims and witnesses; the non-applicability of the death penalty; the ICC's reparations mandate; the principle of complementarity; the *chapeau* (or contextual) elements for genocide, crimes against humanity, war crimes and aggression; and the enumerated acts within each category of crime.[215] For the sake of brevity, this book only makes note of their submission on the latter issue.

Before delving into the details, three general points stand out. First, although the Caucus's stated aim was to represent the interests of *women,* its proposals were inclusive of other marginalised groups such as male victims of sexual violence, homosexual men and people who are intersex. This turned out to be fortunate, given that those other groups did not form a similarly active lobby at Rome. Second, while accountability for sexual violence crimes was high on the Caucus's agenda, the Caucus also sought accountability for *non-sexual* gender-based crimes. Third, the Caucus was adamant that the Statute should *expressly* enumerate a wide range of sexual violence crimes. In making this argument, the Caucus was aware that sexual violence could already be read into existing crimes: indeed, Copelon had actively encouraged prosecutors to use this technique at the ICTY and ICTR.[216] She and other Caucus members hoped that the ICC

[213] 'Report of the Preparatory Committee on the Establishment of an International Criminal Court: Addendum 1, UN Doc. A/CONF.183/2/Add.1 ("1998 Draft ICC Statute")' (14 April 1998).

[214] Kirsch and Holmes, see n. 192, 6.

[215] Women's Caucus for Gender Justice, 'Gender Justice and the ICC' (at the United Nations Diplomatic Conference of Plenipotentiaries on the Establishment of an International Criminal Court, Rome, 15 July 1998) (on file), 'Introduction'.

See also Chappell, see n. 7, Chapters 3–6; Facio, see n. 196, 324; Spees, see n. 200, 1233–1234.

[216] '*Amicus curiae* Brief Respecting Amendment of the Indictment and Supplementation of the Evidence to Ensure the Prosecution of Rape and Other Sexual Violence within the Competence of the Tribunal', see n. 104; Copelon, see n. 4, 225–225, 229.

prosecutors would continue to use that technique, which the Women's Caucus called the 'gender integration principle'.[217] However, they also wanted sexual violence crimes to be named explicitly in the Rome Statute, so that these crimes were 'always on the checklist and always understood as crimes in themselves'.[218]

Following the formation of the Women's Caucus, several NGOs with a commitment to conservative social values decided to enter the negotiations also.[219] These groups included REAL Women of Canada, the Campaign Life Coalition (also from Canada), the Catholic Family and Human Rights Institute (now 'C-FAM') and International Right to Life Federation (now 'Life Issues Institute') from the USA, all of which describe themselves as 'pro-family' and 'pro-life' groups. While their philosophies were not uniform, they shared a generalised objection to abortion and a tendency to view efforts to dismantle discrimination on the grounds of sex and sexual orientation with suspicion. For example, C-Fam described the Women's Caucus and its supporters as 'anti-lifers',[220] and the Campaign Life Coalition expressed 'fears' that the ICC would become 'a powerful instrument of forced social change by feminist, homosexual, and other radical groups', making it an 'extremely powerful weapon in the hands of the international anti-life, anti-family movement'.[221] Together with the Holy See and several majority-Catholic and majority-Muslim states, these groups opposed many of the proposals made by the Women's Caucus and like-minded states.[222] For example, this bloc was successful in blunting several of the Caucus's proposals in relation to the definition

[217] Women's Caucus for Gender Justice, 'Recommendations and Commentary for the Elements of Crimes and Rules of Procedure and Evidence, Submitted to the Preparatory Commission for the International Criminal Court' (12 June 2000) 6–8: www.iccnow.org/documents/WCGJElementsofCrimeMay2000.pdf.

[218] Copelon, see n. 4, 324.

[219] Glasius, see n. 194, 82.

[220] A. Ruse, 'Catholic, Muslim Nations Unite Against "Enforced Pregnancy" and "Gender Justice"' (C-Fam, 10 June 1998): https://c-fam.org/friday_fax/catholic-muslim-nations-unite-against-enforced-pregnancy-and-gender-justice/.

[221] 'ICC: Promise of Justice or Threat of Tyranny?' (The Interim: Canada's Life and Family Newspaper, 12 August 1998).

[222] Bedont and Hall-Martinez, see n. 4, 67; Glasius, see n. 194, Chapter 5; L. Chappell, 'Women's Rights and Religious Opposition: The Politics of Gender at the International Criminal Court' in Y. Abu-Laban (ed.), *Gendering the Nation State: Canadian Comparative Perspectives* (University of British Columbia Press, 2008) 139; V. Oosterveld, 'Constructive Ambiguity and the Meaning of "Gender" for the International Criminal Court' 16(4) *International Feminist Journal of Politics* 563, 565.

of crimes. This tousle between women's rights advocates and conservative forces was not unique to Rome; during the 1990s, women's rights activists faced similar push-back at other UN forums, which limited their ability to affect change.[223]

The following sections explain how these conflicts played out in the negotiations over the Rome Statute's list of crimes.

#### 3.2.1.1 Genocide

Since 1995, the Preparatory Committee favoured the idea of giving the ICC jurisdiction over the crime of genocide, as proposed in the ILC's 1994 Draft ICC Statute.[224] The Committee's 1998 Draft Statute therefore included the same definition as the 1948 Genocide Convention.[225] The definition was not bracketed, however; a footnote stated that the Committee 'took note of the suggestion to examine the possibility of addressing "social and political" groups in the context of crimes against humanity'.[226] The Women's Caucus sought to build on that suggestion by urging states to extend the definition to also include 'political, gender-based or other social groups including those based on age, health status or disability'.[227] However, there was virtually no appetite for this proposal at the Rome Conference: states were reluctant to depart from the definition found in the 1948 Convention, which had been regarded as the authoritative definition under customary international law since 1951.[228]

#### 3.2.1.2 War Crimes

At the February 1997 meeting of the Preparatory Committee, the delegates agreed to a proposal by New Zealand and Switzerland to enumerate 'rape, enforced prostitution and other sexual violence of comparable gravity'

[223] Chappell, see n. 7, 42–43; V. Oosterveld, 'The Definition of Gender in the Rome Statute of the International Criminal Court: A Step Forward or Back for International Criminal Justice?' (2005) 18 *Harvard Human Rights Journal* 55; D. Otto, 'Feminist Approaches to International Law' in A. Orford and F. Hoffmann (eds), *The Oxford Handbook of the Theory of International Law* (Oxford University Press, 2016) 489.

[224] H. von Hebel and D. Robinson, 'Crimes within the Jurisdiction of the Court' in R.S. Lee (ed.), *The International Criminal Court: The Making of the Rome Statute* (Kluwer Law International, 1999) 79, 89.

[225] 1998 Draft Statute, 11–12.

[226] Ibid.

[227] Women's Caucus for Gender Justice, 'Gender Justice and the ICC', see n. 215, 2.

[228] C. Steains, 'Gender Issues' in R.S. Lee (ed.), *The International Criminal Court: The Making of the Rome Statute* (Kluwer Law International, 1999) 357, 363; von Hebel and Robinson, see n. 224, 89.

as war crimes in both international and non-international armed conflicts, albeit in bracketed text.[229] This development gave the Women's Caucus a foundation to build upon. At the Committee's next meeting in December 1997, it urged states to expand that list to include 'rape, sexual slavery, forced prostitution, forced pregnancy, forced sterilization and other sexual or gender violence or abuse'.[230] A similar list had been considered in the first meeting of the Preparatory Committee in May 1996, albeit with no reference to 'gender violence',[231] and in the (then) recent 1993 *Vienna Declaration*, in which 171 states agreed that:

> Violations of the human rights of women in situations of armed conflict are violations of the fundamental principles of international human rights and humanitarian law. All violations of this kind, including in particular murder, systematic rape, sexual slavery, and forced pregnancy, require a particularly effective response.[232]

Against that backdrop, the proposal to expand the list of sexual violence crimes was widely supported at the August 1997 meeting: the Committee agreed to include 'rape, sexual slavery, enforced prostitution, enforced pregnancy, enforced sterilization, and any other form of sexual violence also constituting a grave breach of the Geneva Conventions' as war crimes in an international armed conflict and the same offences as war crimes in a non-international armed conflict (with the final clause adjusted to refer to 'serious violations of Common Article 3 of the Geneva Conventions', rather than 'grave breaches').[233] Christopher Hall recalls that delegates 'overwhelmingly' supported the inclusion of these crimes, and the references to the Geneva Conventions were meant to show that the Prosecutor could *also* prosecute acts of sexual violence under other headings, such

[229] 'Decisions Taken by the Preparatory Committee at Its Session Held from 11 to 21 February 1997, UN Doc. A/AC.249/1997/L.5' (12 March 1997) 5, 9–10.

[230] Women's Caucus for Gender Justice, 'Recommendations and Commentary for December 1997 PrepCom on The Establishment of an International Criminal Court' (1 December 1997) 32: www.iccnow.org/documents/5PrepComRecommWomensC.pdf.

[231] 'Summary of the Proceedings of the Preparatory Committee during the Period 25 March–12 April 1996, UN Doc. A/AC.249/1' (7 May 1996) [58]. ('There were proposals to refer to rape committed on national or religious grounds; rape, other serious assaults of a sexual nature, such as forced impregnation; or outrages upon person dignity, in particular humiliating and degrading treatment, rape or enforced prostitution, with attention being drawn to recent acts committed as part of a campaign of ethnic cleansing').

[232] Vienna Declaration and Programme of Action, A/CONF.157/23, 12 July 1993, [38].

[233] 'Decisions Taken by the Preparatory Committee at Its Session Held from 1 to 12 December 1997, UN Doc. A/AC.249/1997/L.9/Rev.1' (18 December 1997) 9, 12.

as torture.[234] The Committee also agreed to the Women's Caucus's plea that these sexual violence crimes were not described as 'humiliating or degrading treatment', as several past legal instruments had done.[235]

The same list of war crimes was included in the 1998 Draft ICC Statute produced by the Preparatory Committee at its final meeting in March–April 1998. The list was not bracketed, but it was one of two alternative options (the other option used the terms 'outrages upon personal dignity, in particular humiliating and degrading treatment').[236] However, the reference to 'forced pregnancy' was opposed by conservative NGOs and by the Holy See, which preferred the term 'forced impregnation', which would describe only the forced *instigation* of a pregnancy, and could not be interpreted as encompassing the subsequent denial of abortion services by Catholic healthcare providers.[237] The Women's Caucus urged states to resist the Vatican's proposal, which in its view, was too restrictive. Barbara Bedont, a member of the Women's Caucus, recalls:

> [The Holy See] wanted to restrict the definition to the Bosnian case. What about the examples of the Jewish women made pregnant by the Nazis to perform experiments on their fetuses? Or what about the kidnapping of pregnant women to sell their babies on the black market? We asked: Wasn't the Holy See interested in ending these types of crimes? Apparently not. Because of their preoccupation with controlling women's reproductive capacities, the Holy See was willing to thwart attempts to have these crimes punished.[238]

Bosnia and Herzegovina also lobbied against the Holy See's proposal. It argued that the Rome Statute *should* recognise forced pregnancy, in order to capture the 'distinct' form of sexual abuse suffered by women during the recent war in that state.[239] Bosnia and Herzegovina claimed that these

[234] C. Hall, 'The Fifth Session of the UN Preparatory Committee on the Establishment of an International Criminal Court' (1998) 92(2) *American Journal of International Law* 331, 333–336.

[235] Women's Caucus for Gender Justice, 'Recommendations and Commentary for December 1997 PrepCom on The Establishment of an International Criminal Court', see n. 230, 31, 41–42. See also Hall, see n. 234, 334; Copelon, see n. 4, 234.

[236] 1998 Draft ICC Statute, 20, 23.

[237] 'Proposal by the Holy See, UN Doc A/AC.249/1998/DP.13' (1 April 1998). See also Bedont, see n. 31, 197; Steains, see n. 228, 366.

[238] B. Bedont and D. Matas, 'Negotiating for an International Criminal Court' (1999) 14(5) *Peace Magazine* 21.

[239] 'Discussion Paper: Delegation of Bosnia and Herzegovina' (14 April 1998): www.legal-tools.org/doc/dd58b8/pdf/. See also Glasius, see n. 194, 90; V. Oosterveld, 'The Making of a Gender-Sensitive International Criminal Court' (1999) 1(1) *International Law Forum du Droit International* 38, 39.

forced pregnancies were 'distinct' due to their 'particular purpose', but did not specify what that purpose *was*. However, accounts of the negotiations suggest that Bosnia and Herzegovina was referring to reports of Serbian forces raping and detaining non-Serbian women in order to force them to give birth to 'Serbian babies' in the context of 'ethnic cleansing'.[240]

At the 1998 Rome Conference, the proposal to include the full list of sexual violence crimes received general support in the first few days.[241] According to Cate Steains, an Australian diplomat who participated in the negotiations, most delegates took the view that this list simply codified existing customary international law.[242] However, the crime of 'forced pregnancy' continued to be highly controversial at Rome.[243] Joining the Holy See, several states with large Catholic and Muslim populations opposed this crime based on concerns about its relationship to abortion.[244] For some of these states, the concern was that a *failure to provide abortion* would be an ICC crime, while others were worried that the *criminalisation of abortion* would be an ICC crime. For example, the delegate for Libya argued that the reference to 'forced pregnancy' 'warranted further consideration' because 'under Libyan legislation, abortion, too, was a crime.'[245] The delegate for the United Arab Emirates 'shared the Libyan delegation's reservations about the inclusion of enforced pregnancy'.[246] The delegate for Saudi Arabia argued that the 'forced pregnancy' crime 'should be deleted because the

[240] Steains, see n. 228, 366. For examples of such reports, see 'Report on the Situation of Human Rights in the Territory of the Former Yugoslavia Submitted by Mr. Tadeusz Mazowiecki, Special Rapporteur of the Commission on Human Rights, Pursuant to Commission Resolution 1992/S-1/1 of 14 August 1992, UN Doc. E/CN.4/1993/50' (10 February 1993) 69, [41]; 'Final Report of the Commission of Experts Established Pursuant to Security Council Resolution 780 (1992), UN Doc. S/1994/674 (Annex 1)', see n. 124, [248]; R. Fisk, 'Bosnia War Crimes: "The Rapes Went on Day and Night"' (Independent, 8 February 1993).

[241] T. Graditzky, 'War Crimes Issues Before the Rome Diplomatic Conference on the Establishment of and International Criminal Court' in O. Bekou and R. Cryer (eds), *The International Criminal Court* (Ashgate, 2004) 199, 205.

[242] Steains, see n. 228, 365.

[243] Kirsch and Holmes, see n. 192, 15; M. Cottier and S. Mzee, 'Paragraph 2(b)(Xxii)' in O. Triffterer and K. Amobs (eds), *The Rome Statute of the International Criminal Court: A Commentary* (CH Beck, Hart, Nomos, 3rd edn, 2016) 477, 498.

[244] M. Boot, 'Article 7(1) (G' in O. Triffterer (ed.), *Commentary on the Rome Statute of the International Criminal Court* (Nomos Verlagsgesellschaft, 1999) 139, 144; Facio, see n. 196, 327–329; Graditzky, see n. 241, 205; Steains, see n. 228, 366–369.

[245] Rome Conference Official Records, Vol. II, 160, [63].

[246] Ibid., 160, [66].

law in his country did not allow abortion'.[247] The delegate for Iran 'associated himself with previous speakers who considered that inclusion of the wording "enforced pregnancy" might be used as an argument against the prohibition of abortion and should therefore be dropped'.[248] For the so-called 'pro-life' NGOs, this increased opposition to the crime of 'forced pregnancy' was a welcome development. For example, C-Fam reported:

> Catholic and Muslim nations demonstrated a stiffening resolve over the last three days at the International Criminal Court (ICC) negotiations here in Rome … The religiously-based countries have made it increasingly clear that they will not accept an ICC that is ideologically skewed in favour of the radical-feminist agenda.[249]

However, the proposed reference to 'forced pregnancy' was not opposed by all states with large Muslim and Catholic populations; several such states supported this proposal. Examples included Bosnia and Herzegovina, which continued to press for the inclusion of this crime at Rome,[250] and Lebanon, which argued: 'in view of reports on crimes committed in Bosnia and Herzegovina … it might be better to refer to forcible pregnancies the purpose of which was to change the identity of a population group.'[251] Steains recalls that as the negotiations progressed, this issue of intent proved to be the main point of debate. In her words, 'the Catholic and Arab countries were committed to a high-threshold "ethnic cleansing" kind of intent; the other group of countries considered this approach too restrictive on the grounds that ethnic cleansing was only one of many situations in which this crime might occur'.[252] The Women's Caucus concurred with this second group. In a statement issued ten days into the conference, it highlighted a range of historical examples of what it considered to be 'forced pregnancy', including several with no link to 'ethnic cleaning'. In the Caucus's words:

> The most recent and publicized example of forced pregnancy occurred in Bosnia and Herzegovina, where soldiers raped women until they became pregnant and then continued to imprison them. Although not well publicized, forced pregnancy occurred in Rwanda where thousands of women were raped and then bore children as a result of those rapes.

[247] Ibid., 163, [21]. See also 148, [32].
[248] Ibid., 166, [72].
[249] Ruse, see n. 220.
[250] Graditzky, see n. 241, 205.
[251] Rome Conference Official Records, Vol. II, 163, [16].
[252] Steains, see n. 229, 368.

> This has caused terrible pain and social upheaval for the women and children affected. Forced pregnancy also took place during the period of African-American slavery. Women held as slaves were forced to bear children and were subjected to torture, beatings and other forms of coercion and deprivation if they did not. Some but not all of these pregnancies were the result of rape.[253]

The same statement sought to extricate the debate over 'forced pregnancy' from the politics of abortion, arguing:

> The effort to link the crime of forced pregnancy to the issue of abortion ignores that forced pregnancy is a violent crime committed with a violent intent, and it causes extreme suffering for the victims. It is clearly a crime of commission, not of omission ... *The issue of abortion has no place in the current discussions about the crime of forced pregnancy* (emphasis original) ... It is crucial that this conference recognize, punish and deter the future commission of this terrible crime against women. Therefore, the crime of 'forced pregnancy' should be listed as both a war crime and a crime against humanity. This will not affect national abortion laws or the omission to provide abortion.

On the second-last day of the conference, the delegates reached a compromise.[254] The crime of 'forced pregnancy' would be included as a war crime and a crime against humanity, with a definition stating:

> 'Forced pregnancy' means the unlawful confinement of a woman forcibly made pregnant, with the intent of affecting the ethnic composition of any population or carrying out other grave violations of international law. This definition shall not in any way be interpreted as affecting national laws relating to pregnancy.[255]

This definition was more restrictive than the Women's Caucus had hoped: it requires that the pregnancy was instigated by force *and* that the victim is unlawfully confined, which excludes some of the examples described by the Caucus as 'forced pregnancy'. However, the Caucus and like-minded states succeeded in ensuring that the crime is not limited to settings of 'ethnic cleansing'. This was achieved through the inclusion of two alternative intents: the perpetrator must seek *either* to change the ethnic composition of a population, *or* to carry out other grave violations of international law.[256]

[253] Women's Caucus for Gender Justice, 'Justice for Women: The Crime of Forced Pregnancy' (26 June 1998) (on file).
[254] Cottier and Mzee, see n. 243, 499; Steains, see n. 228, 367–368.
[255] RS, Art. 7(2)(f).
[256] Facio, see n. 196, 329.

As the previous discussion shows, and has been confirmed elsewhere, the crime of 'forced pregnancy' was drafted primarily with the Bosnian example in mind.[257] Looking at this debate twenty years later, the emphasis on the Bosnian experience raises a concern. The gravity of sexual violence in Bosnia, including the forced pregnancies in that context, is not in doubt. Yet there is something troubling about the readiness of states to condemn acts of rape, impregnation and detention of women reportedly committed as a means of 'ethnic cleansing' compared with the muted response to other situations in which women are forcibly impregnated and/or forced to proceed with an extant pregnancy – including through the threat of criminal sanctions for those accessing or providing abortion, or through the exclusion of abortion from publicly funded healthcare. The heightened response to forced pregnancy in the context of 'ethnic cleansing' as distinct from in 'everyday life' is part of a pattern, in which the violation of sexual and reproductive autonomy is not denounced as a crime when the harm is 'only' to women, rather than to the national, racial, ethnic or religious group to which those women 'belong'.[258] The centrality of this example can be traced back to the first meeting of the Preparatory Committee in 1996, in which:

> There were proposals to refer to rape committed *on national or religious grounds*; rape, other serious assaults of a sexual nature, such as forced impregnation; or outrages upon person dignity [sic], in particular humiliating and degrading treatment, rape or enforced prostitution, *with attention being drawn to recent acts committed as part of a campaign of ethnic cleansing.*[259]

#### 3.2.1.3 Crimes against Humanity

The 1998 Draft Statute defined the following acts as crimes against humanity when committed as part of a widespread and/or systematic attack on a civilian population:

a) murder;
b) extermination;
c) enslavement;
d) deportation or forcible transfer of population;

[257] E. La Haye, 'Article 8(2)(b)(Xxii)' in R.S. Lee (ed.), *The International Criminal Court: Elements of Crimes and Rules of Procedure and Evidence* (Transnational Publishers, 2001) 184, 194.

[258] See R. Grey, 'The ICC's First "Forced Pregnancy" Case in Historical Perspective' (2017) 15(5) *Journal of International Criminal Justice* 905.

[259] 'Summary of the Proceedings of the Preparatory Committee during the Period 25 March–12 April 1996, UN Doc. A/AC.249/1', see n. 231, [58] (emphasis added).

e) [detention or] [imprisonment] [deprivation of liberty] [in flagrant violation of international law] [in violation of fundamental legal norms];
f) torture;
g) rape or other sexual abuse [of comparable gravity,] or enforced prostitution;
h) persecution against any identifiable group or collectivity on political, racial, national, ethnic, cultural or religious [or gender] [or other similar] grounds [and in connection with other crimes within the jurisdiction of the Court];
i) enforced disappearance of persons;
j) other inhumane acts [of a similar character] [intentionally] causing [great suffering,] or serious injury to body or to mental or physical health.[260]

The Women's Caucus's made numerous proposals in relation to this list. Some of these proposals concerned sub-section (g), i.e. crimes of sexual violence. The Caucus urged states to expand this provision to include all types of sexual violence listed as war crimes in the 1998 Draft Statute and to delete the 'comparable gravity' test in case the comparison to rape was interpreted to require some degree of penetration.[261] The delegates at Rome generally supported the proposal to expand the list as they regarded this as codifying existing law.[262] However, the 'comparable gravity' test was retained, hence, the Rome Statute defines 'rape, sexual slavery, enforced prostitution, forced pregnancy, enforced sterilization, or any other form of sexual violence of comparable gravity' as crimes against humanity when committed as part of a widespread or systematic attack against a civilian population.[263] The inclusion of 'forced pregnancy' in this list was controversial, as it was in the war crimes provision, but the debate was eventually resolved by including the definition discussed in Section 3.2.1.2.[264]

The Women's Caucus also lobbied states to maintain the reference to persecution on 'gender' grounds.[265] In explaining this crime, the Caucus stressed that gender-based persecution can intersect with persecution on other grounds.[266] It also made it clear that gender-based persecution was

[260] 1998 Draft ICC Statute, 25–26. This text included numerous options for the *chapeau* elements for crimes against humanity.
[261] Women's Caucus for Gender Justice, 'Gender Justice and the ICC', see n. 215, 17.
[262] Steains, see n. 228, 365.
[263] RS, Art. 7(1)(g).
[264] Facio, see n. 196, 327–329; Kirsch and Holmes, see n. 192, 15; Steains, see n. 228, 365; von Hebel and Robinson, see n. 224, 100.
[265] Women's Caucus for Gender Justice, 'Gender Justice and the ICC', see n. 215, 18; Bedont, see n. 31, 186–187; Bedont and Hall-Martinez, see n. 4, 68–69; Oosterveld, 'The Definition of Gender', see n. 223, 58 (n. 21).
[266] Women's Caucus for Gender Justice, 'Gender Justice and the ICC', see n. 215, 18 ('Gender persecution may stand alone or be intertwined with other kinds of animus.').

not limited to sexual violence or to the victimisation of women, stating: 'gender-based persecution is involved, for example, when young boys are either killed to prevent their becoming soldiers or coerced and humiliated into becoming killers'.[267] The proposal to include this ground was first made in the February 1997 meeting of the Preparatory Committee, the first meeting attended by women's rights activists.[268] It has been suggested that this reference to 'gender' grounds was drawn from the ICTR Statute's definition of crimes against humanity.[269] It was not; the proposal was unprecedented: the term 'gender' had never before been used in an instrument of international criminal law.[270] The proposed reference to gender-based persecution led to a 'polarized' debate at Rome, as detailed in Chapter 2.[271] For states opposed to this crime, the primary concern was that the criminalisation of persecution on 'gender' grounds might require them to treat LGBTIQ and heterosexual people as equals.[272] After a long and difficult debate, 'gender' was retained as a ground of persecution, subject to a definition stating:

> For the purpose of this Statute, it is understood that the term 'gender' refers to the two sexes, male and female, within the context of society. The term 'gender' does not indicate any meaning different from the above.[273]

Third, the Caucus lobbied to retain or expand crimes against humanity of particular interest to women and girls. For example, it urged states to retain the crime against humanity of 'enforced disappearance', given that women, particularly in Argentina, 'led the fight for the recognition of forced disappearance as a distinct crime'.[274] It petitioned states to expand the crime against humanity of 'enslavement' to include slavery-like

[267] Ibid., 18.

[268] 'Decisions Taken by the Preparatory Committee at Its Session Held from 11 to 21 February 1997, UN Doc. A/AC.249/1997/L.5', see n. 229, 3; Oosterveld, 'The Definition of Gender', see n. 223, 59 (n. 24).

[269] D. Robinson, 'Defining "Crimes Against Humanity" at the Rome Conference' (1999) 93(1) *American Journal of International Law* 43, 54.

[270] Art. 3 of the ICTR Statute gives the tribunal the authority to prosecute crimes against humanity, defined to mean: 'the following crimes when committed as part of a widespread or attack against any civilian population on *national, political, ethnic, racial or religious* grounds [including] Persecutions *on political, racial and religious grounds*'.

[271] Oosterveld, 'The Definition of Gender', see n. 223, 63. See also Chappell, see n. 7, 44–47.

[272] Oosterveld, 'The Definition of Gender', see n. 223, 63; Steains, see n. 228, 372; Copelon, see n. 4, 236; Spees, see n. 200, 1244.

[273] RS, Article 7(3).

[274] Women's Caucus for Gender Justice, 'Gender Justice and the ICC', see n. 215, 19.

practices, including 'debt-bondage, serfdom, and forced marriage or the transfer of women for value or of children for exploitation or labour, including sexual slavery'.[275] It argued that the crime against humanity of 'imprisonment' and/or 'deprivation of liberty' should be defined to include 'situations where people are not *physically* restrained, but are in effective custody or under the control of another', such as when 'women are held in makeshift camps, in "forced temporary marriage", coerced under occupation, confined to the home, or otherwise deprive of their liberty through fear or assault'.[276] It also lobbied states to include a crime against humanity of 'institutionalized discrimination' as found in the 1996 Draft of Code of Crimes, but without limiting this offence to discrimination on 'racial, ethnic or religious grounds' as in that 1996 text.[277]

These proposals enjoyed mixed success. The Rome Statute refers to the crime against humanity of enforced disappearance[278] and expressly lists sexual slavery as a crime against humanity as well.[279] Moreover, it specifies that 'enslavement' means 'the exercise of any or all of the powers attaching to the right of ownership over a person and includes the exercise of such power in the course of trafficking in persons, in particular women and children'.[280] This definition seems broad enough to include debt-bondage, serfdom, and forced marriage as prohibited by the 1956 *Supplementary Convention on the Abolition of Slavery, the Slave Trade, and Institutions and Practices Similar to Slavery* (a contention which is confirmed by the Elements of Crimes).[281] The Statute also includes a crime against humanity of 'imprisonment or other severe deprivation of physical liberty in violation of fundamental rules of international law', which does not require physical confinement and could therefore potentially be applied to the scenarios listed by the Women's Caucus.[282] However, the suggestion to include a general crime against humanity of 'institutionalized discrimination' was not embraced. Rather, the Statute only refers to racial discrimination of that kind, in the crime against humanity of 'apartheid'.[283]

[275] Ibid., 16.

[276] Ibid., 17 (emphasis added).

[277] Ibid., 20.

[278] RS, Art. 7(1)(i).

[279] RS, Art. 7(1)(g)-2.

[280] RS, Art. 7(2)(c).

[281] EoC, Art. 7(1)(c); Supplementary Convention on the Abolition of Slavery, the Slave Trade, and Institutions and Practices Similar to Slavery, Geneva, 7 September 1956, 266 UNTS 3 (entered into force 30 April 1957), Art. 1.

[282] RS, Art. 7(1)(e).

[283] RS, Art. 7(1)(j).

### 3.2.2 *Negotiating the Elements of Crimes*

After the Rome Conference, the Women's Caucus participated in the negotiations for the Elements of Crimes. Put simply, the Elements of Crimes is a legal guideline. Its purpose is to 'assist the Court in the interpretation and application' of the Rome Statute provisions on genocide, crimes against humanity and war crimes, by listing the legal tests (or 'elements') for each specific crime.[284] It was prepared by the ICC Preparatory Commission (PrepComm), a forum of state representatives established by the Final Act of the Rome Conference. The PrepComm first met in February 1999 and finished its work on the Elements of Crimes at the fifth session in June 2000, resulting in the 2000 Draft Elements of Crimes.[285] That text entered force when it was adopted by the ICC Assembly of States Parties in September 2002.[286]

As recalled by Eve La Haye, the negotiations over the elements for the sexual violence crimes 'often touched raw nerves and generally aroused great emotion'.[287] There is not space to analyse the Elements of Crimes negotiations in depth. Yet some points about the negotiations over gender-based crimes stand out for discussion, both to illustrate the controversies that continued after Rome and to show where the Women's Caucus stood in these debates. The Elements of Crimes negotiations have been analysed in more depth by Louise Chappell and Marlies Glasius, both of whom discuss the tension between the Women's Caucus and conservative NGOs in this forum.[288]

In relation to genocide, at the first meeting of the PrepComm, the coordinator proposed the inclusion of a note stating that: 'the term "serious bodily or mental harm" in article 6(b) may include, but is not necessarily restricted to, acts of torture, rape, sexual violence or inhuman or degrading treatment', and another stating: 'rape and sexual violence may constitute genocide in the same way as any other act, provided that the criteria

[284] RS, Art. 9(1).

[285] K. Dörmann, *Elements of War Crimes under the Rome Statute of the International Criminal Court Sources and Commentary* (Cambridge University Press, 2003) 3; 'Report of the Preparatory Commission for the International Criminal Court: Addendum Part II Finalized Draft Text of the Elements of Crimes, PCNICC/2000/1/Add.2 ("Draft ICC Elements of Crimes")' (2 November 2000).

[286] 'Assembly of States Parties to the Rome Statute of the International Criminal Court: First Session, Official Records, ICC-ASP/1/3' (3 September 2002), [22].

[287] La Haye, see n. 257, 186.

[288] Glasius, see n. 194, Chapter 5; Chappell, see n. 222.

of the crime of genocide are met'.[289] Those proposed notes were consistent with the ICTR's *Akayesu* judgment (handed down three months after the Rome Statute was finalised), which was discussed by many states during the drafting of the Elements of Crimes.[290] That judgment held that sexual violence could amount to genocide through 'causing serious bodily or mental harm to members of the group'[291] and through 'imposing measures intended to prevent births within the group'.[292] These comments were strongly supported by several NGOs, especially the Women's Caucus.[293] Ultimately, only the first comment, relating to genocide through 'causing serious bodily or mental harm', was included.[294] The Women's Caucus endeavoured to have the more general comment included also,[295] but it did not succeed on that front. However, there is nothing to stop the ICC from reading sexual violence into *any* act of genocide in future cases, even without a comment in the Elements of Crimes to that effect.

In relation to the crime of 'forced pregnancy', the controversy continued into the negotiations for the Elements of Crimes. Following its December 1999 meeting, the PreComm's position was that the Elements of Crimes should specify that 'the accused intended to *keep the woman or women pregnant in order to* affect the ethnic composition of a population or to carry out another grave violation of international law'.[296] The Holy See and United Arab Emirates opposed that reference to keeping the woman pregnant.[297] Other states opposed the italicised text because it seemed applicable to the 'ethnic cleaning'-type intent, but not the intent

[289] C. Byron and D. Turns, 'The Preparatory Commission for the International Criminal Court' (2001) 50(2) *International and Comparative Law Quarterly* 420, 421. Citing: 'Proceedings of the Preparatory Commission at Its First Session (16–26 February 1999): Annex III, PCNICC/1999/L.3/Rev.1' (2 March 1999) 23.

[290] V. Oosterveld, 'The Elements of Genocide' in R.S. Lee (ed.), *The International Criminal Court: Elements of Crimes and Rules of Procedure and Evidence* (Transnational Publishers, 2001) 41, 43.

[291] Judgment, *Akayesu* (ICTR-96-4-T), 2 September 1998, [731]–[734].

[292] Ibid., [507]–[508].

[293] Byron and Turns, see n. 283, 421–422; Copelon, see n. 4, 235 (n. 57).

[294] EoC, n. 3.

[295] Women's Caucus for Gender Justice, 'Recommendations and Commentary for the Elements of Crimes and Rules of Procedure and Evidence, Submitted to the Preparatory Commission for the International Criminal Court', see n. 217, 6–7.

[296] 'Proceedings of the Preparatory Commission at Its First, Second and Third Sessions (16–26 February, 26 July–13 August and 29 November–17 December 1999): Annex III: Elements of Crimes, UN Doc. PCNICC/1999/L.5/Rev.1/Add.2' (22 December 1999) 11, 27, 34.

[297] La Haye, see n. 257, 194–195.

of carrying out other grave violations of international law.[298] Ultimately, the added words were discarded due to the 'strong opposition' of a small number of delegates who argued that this text 'would unduly restrict the scope of the crime'.[299] Those delegates were correct: the added words would have added two requirements that have no basis in the Rome Statute: first, that the purpose of the confinement was to keep the victim pregnant; second, that the purpose of keeping the victim pregnant was to affect the ethnic population or to carry out another grave violation of international law.

The efforts to change the definition of the crime do not seem to have been made in bad faith; rather, it seems that several delegates did not understand the compromise that had been reached at Rome. For example, Knut Dörmann states that some delegations 'seemed to see the essence of the crime as *making* the woman pregnant', and other states took the view that without the additional text, 'the aim of the crime would be changed' because 'in their view, the crime was meant to cover the conduct that occurred in Bosnia and Herzegovina, where women of one ethnicity were raped and detained in order to force them to bear basis of another ethnicity'.[300] Ultimately, because no agreement on how to elaborate on the definition could be reached, the PrepComm settled on a definition of 'forced pregnancy' that follows the compromise reached at Rome.[301] The EoC states that for this crime, the Prosecutor must show that:

> The perpetrator confined one or more women forcibly made pregnant, with the intent of affecting the ethnic composition of any population or carrying out other grave violations of international law.[302]

The definition of rape in the Elements of Crimes is another point of interest. Whether charged as a crime against humanity or as a war crime, rape was defined by the PrepComm to mean:

(1) The perpetrator invaded the body of a person by conduct resulting in penetration, however slight, of any part of the body of the victim or of the perpetrator with a sexual organ, or of the anal or genital opening of the victim with any object or any other part of the body.

[298] Ibid.

[299] Dörmann, see n. 279, 330, n. 5.

[300] Ibid., 330.

[301] La Haye, see n. 257, 195.

[302] EoC, Art. 7(1)(g)-4, 8(2)(b)(xxii)-4 and 8(2)(e)(vi)-4.

(2) The invasion was committed by force, or by threat of force or coercion, such as that caused by fear of violence, duress, detention, psychological oppression or abuse of power, against such person or another person, or by taking advantage of a coercive environment, or the invasion was committed against a person incapable of giving genuine consent.[303]

This definition was developed at a time when the ICTY and ICTR's jurisprudence on rape was still in flux. In September 1998, in the *Akayesu* case, the ICTR Trial Chamber had rejected a definition of rape based on 'a mechanical description of objects and body parts', and instead defined rape as 'a physical invasion of a sexual nature, committed on a person under circumstances which are coercive'.[304] The ICTY Trial Chamber followed that approach in November 1998, in the '*Čelebići camp*' case.[305] However, a month later, in the *Furundžija* case, a different ICTY Trial Chamber defined rape as vaginal or anal penetration, or oral penetration with the perpetrator's penis, obtained by 'coercion or force or threat of force against the victim or a third person'.[306] As noted previously, the ICC PrepComm presented its Draft Elements of Crimes in June 2000. The definition of rape in that text is close to the *Furundžija* approach: it requires penetration of specific body parts but does not require proof of the victim's non-consent. After that, the ICTY and ICTR jurisprudence continued to develop. In February 2001, in the *Kunarac et al.* case, the ICTY Trial Chamber held that rape means vaginal or anal penetration, or oral penetration with the perpetrator's penis, 'where such sexual penetration occurs *without the consent of the victim*'.[307] The Trial Chamber further noted: 'consent for this purpose must be consent given voluntarily, as a result of the victim's free will, assessed in the context of the surrounding circumstances'.[308] That definition was upheld by the joint ICTY/ICTR Appeals Chamber in June 2002.[309] Thus, the ad hoc tribunals ended up with a different definition of rape to the ICC: both definitions are based on 'a mechanical description of objects and body parts', but in the ICC, proof of the victims' non-consent is not a prerequisite.

[303] EoC, Art. 7(1)(g)-1, 8(2)(b)(xxii)-1 and 8(2)(e)(vi)-1.
[304] Judgment, *Akayesu* (ICTR-96-4-T), 2 September 1998, [597]–[598].
[305] Judgment, *Mucić et al.* (IT-96-21), 16 November 1998, [478]–[479].
[306] Judgment, *Furundžija* (IT-95-17/1-T), 10 December 1998, [185].
[307] Judgment, *Kunarac et al.* (IT-96-23-T&IT-96-23/1-T), 22 February 2001, [460] (emphasis added).
[308] Ibid.
[309] Appeal Judgment, *Kunarac et al.* (IT-96-23&IT-96-23/1-A), 12 June 2002, [128].

The ICC's definition of rape largely achieves the main aims of the Women's Caucus. The Caucus wanted a definition that: focused on the conduct and state of mind of the perpetrator, not the victim; did not require proof of *physical* force; was 'gender-neutral'; and was not 'unwieldy' or overly specific.[310] The final definition achieves the first three aims, even if in the view of some Caucus members, it does not achieve the last.[311] Importantly, the language adopted by the PrepComm is not only sex-neutral in relation to the victims but also to the perpetrators.[312] Admittedly, the definition is narrower than some delegates had sought. For example, Colombia had pressed for a definition which required only that the perpetrator 'had sexual access to the victim', without requiring penetration, in order to give effect to 'the legally protected right of sexual freedom or freedom to exercise control over one's body'.[313] Although that proposal was not accepted, the right to which Colombia referred is still protected by the crime of 'other forms of sexual violence'.[314]

It bears noting that in the ICC's definition, there is no requirement that the penetration occurred *for the purpose of sexual gratification*. Such a requirement has never been part of international criminal law, but it is sometimes assumed to exist. For example, in the ICTY's *Češić* case, the Defence argued that an incident in which prison guards forced two male detainees to have oral sex with each other could not be charged using the crime against humanity of rape because there was no evidence that the guards had sought to 'to satisfy a sexual impulse'. The Trial Chamber dismissed that argument, stating: 'the intent is needed to effect the sexual penetration for whatever motive. So it's not necessary that it is intended in order to satisfy any sexual feelings of the perpetrator'.[315] From an accountability perspective, it is positive that no 'sexual gratification' element was included in the Elements of Crimes. That element would have created strife for the Prosecutor, who would have to lead proof of the perpetrator's sexual desires, and would have excluded rapes committed for non-sexual reasons, such as to assert dominance over the victim, or for the perpetrator to ingratiate himself or herself with his or her peers.

[310] Spees, see n. 200, 1240.

[311] Ibid.

[312] Dörmann, see n. 285, 327.

[313] 'Comments by Colombia on Document PCNICC/1999/WGEC/RT.6, PCNICC/1999/WGEC/DP.30' (10 November 1999).

[314] RS, Art. 7(1)(g)-6, 8(2)(b)(xxii)-6 and 8(2)(e)(vi)-6.

[315] Oral Decision, *Češić* (IT-95-10/1), 8 October 2003, 83(18)–84(19).

Perhaps the most important contribution of the Women's Caucus during the Elements of Crimes negotiations was to expose the 'hidden gender' of a joint proposal by eleven states, mostly members of the Arab League, in December 1999.[316] The proposal sought to introduce a new *chapeau* element, i.e. a new contextual requirement, that would apply to every crime against humanity in the Rome Statute. This new *chapeau* element would stipulate that the inclusion of an act as a crime against humanity in the Statute 'do[es] not affect family matters recognized by different national laws of the State Parties'.[317] The proposal also sought restrictions on specific crimes. For example, it sought a caveat stating that the ICC's definition of rape does not affect 'natural and legal marital sexual relations in accordance with religious principles or cultural norms in different national laws', that the crime of sexual slavery does not include the 'rights, duties and obligations incident to marriage between a man and a woman', and that the crime of forced pregnancy excludes 'acts related to natural marital sexual relations or the bearing of children in different national laws in accordance with religious principles or cultural norms'.[318]

The Women's Caucus urged states to reject this proposal, as its adoption would 'clearly affect the ability of the Court to prosecute violations of women's human rights, particularly crimes of gender and sexual violence as these often take place within the realm of family'.[319] The Caucus argued that the proposed new *chapeau* element 'discriminates against women' by 'trying to exclude from the jurisdiction of the Court crimes which affect women disproportionately'.[320] It further observed that the proposal conflicted with the UN General Assembly's 1993 *Declaration on the Elimination of Violence Against Women*, which provides that 'states should condemn violence against women and should not invoke any custom, tradition or religious consideration to avoid their obligations with respect to its elimination'.[321] A majority of

[316] Regarding the 'hidden gender of the law' argument, see Chapter 1, §1.3.2.

[317] 'Proposal Submitted by Bahrain, Iraq, Kuwait, Lebanon, the Libyan Arab Jamahiriya, Oman, Qatar, Saudi Arabia, the Sudan, the Syrian Arab Republic and United Arab Emirates Concerning the Elements of Crimes against Humanity, PCNICC/1999/WGEC/DP.39' (3 December 1999) 1.

[318] Ibid., 3.

[319] Women's Caucus for Gender Justice, 'ICC: Urgent Action Alert' (1 December 1999): www.jca.apc.org/fem/news/women2000/128.html.

[320] Women's Caucus for Gender Justice, 'Recommendations and Commentary for the Elements of Crimes and Rules of Procedure and Evidence, Submitted to the Preparatory Commission for the International Criminal Court', see n. 217, 9.

[321] Ibid., citing: A/RES/48/104, 20 December 1993, Art. 4.

states agreed with the Caucus, hence, the proposal was rejected. While this was a victory for the Women's Caucus, it was not celebrated by all. For example, the North American news service Lifesite, which was started by a Canadian 'pro-life' group,[322] reported that the delegates had 'removed explicit protection for families from the ICC statutes [sic]' after the so-called protection was 'attacked and defeated by radical feminists'.[323] Taking a similarly sympathetic view of the rejected proposal, C-Fam reported:

> UN delegates decided this week to remove explicit protection for families in the evolving International Criminal Court (ICC) statutes ... even mainstream observers believe the feminist reaction to the Arab proposal confirms the broad suspicion that the court will be used for social engineering and attacks on the family.[324]

## 3.3 Conclusion

International criminal law has historically paid little attention to conflict-related sexual violence, and to the significance of gender norms. The Rome Statute departs from this pattern by expressly recognising sexual violence crimes as war crimes and crimes against humanity, and by defining gender-based persecution as a crime against humanity. These gains were put at risk during the negotiations for the Elements of Crimes, during which several states made proposals that would have placed further limits on the ICC's ability to prosecute gender-based crimes. However, those proposals were defeated and some positive developments were included, including an explicit confirmation that sexual violence can be an act of genocide for the purposes of the ICC. On its face then, the ICC's legal framework puts the Court in strong position to prosecute gender-based crimes.

However, as feminist institutionalist Fiona MacKay has argued,

> New formal institutions even those that seem to represent a break with the status quo, are neither blank slates nor free floating. Rather, they are indelibly marked by past institutional legacies and by initial and ongoing

[322] Lifesite, 'About Lifesite' (undated): www.lifesitenews.com/about.

[323] Lifesite, 'International Criminal Court Strips Family Protection' (17 December 1999): www.lifesitenews.com/news/international-criminal-court-strips-family-protection.

[324] A. Ruse, 'Protection for Families Dropped from New International Criminal Court' (C-Fam, 17 December 1999): https://c-fam.org/friday_fax/protection-for-families-dropped-from-new-international-criminal-court/.

> interactions with already existing institutions (formal structures and rules, informal practices, norms and ideas) within which they are 'nested' and interconnected.[325]

This does not mean that the inclusion of a wide range of gender-based crimes in the Rome Statute was a meaningless or empty gesture. However, it means that the ICC is not insulated against gender legacies that interfered with the prosecution of sexual and gender violence crimes in the past. Thus, the tendencies that hampered the recognition and prosecution of gender-based crimes in international tribunals in the 1940s, and which re-surfaced in the 1990s and early 2000s, may likewise have that effect in the ICC. In addition, the contests between women's rights activists and conservative governments and NGOs during the negotiations for the Rome Statute and Elements of Crimes are part of the political context in which the ICC is nested, and are likely to play out again in cases before the Court.

As a result, while the adoption of the Rome Statute on 17 July 1998 and the Elements of Crimes in September 2002 were turning points in efforts to make international criminal law more gender-sensitive, it was not the end of the road. In the following chapter, I follow that road through its twists and turns in the practice of the ICC.

[325] F. Mackay, 'Nested Newness, Institutional Innovation, and the Gendered Limits of Change' (2014) 10(4) *Politics & Gender* 549, 567.

# 4

# The Road from Rome

This chapter identifies and describes key developments in all 24 cases from the International Criminal Court (ICC) under analysis, up until the Rome Statute's 20th anniversary on 17 July 2018. The focus is on the Office of the Prosecutor's (OTP's) practice in charging gender-based crimes and on the outcome of those charges at the pre-trial and (where applicable) trial stage. Out of respect for the victims and consideration for the readers, these crimes are not described in graphic detail. However, readers may follow the citations to the evidence if they require a more detailed account.

The chapter is structured as a series of individual case studies, organised by the starting date of the relevant investigation. A table showing which crimes were charged and their outcome is given for each case, and details of the modes of liability can be found at the end of the book (Appendix). For ease of reference, a timeline of relevant events is included in Table 4.1. This chapter is fairly dense and technical, and is intended as a reference for readers interested in the details of individual cases. A different type of analysis can be found in Chapter 5, which draws out patterns and trends in the ICC's case load as a whole.

## 4.1 Democratic Republic of Congo

The territory now called the Democratic Republic of Congo has been the site of conflict and mass crimes since long before the creation of the ICC. In 1884, it became the private colony of Belgian monarch Leopold II, who enslaved virtually the entire country – an offence for which he was not brought to justice, although George Washington Williams, a black American historian and journalist, called in 1890 for an 'international commission' to investigate this crime.[1] In 1908, Leopold was forced to cede

[1] D. Fahey, 'Ituri: Gold, Land, and Ethnicity in North-Eastern Congo' (Rift Valley Institute & Usalama Project, 2013) 18–19; A. Hochschild, *King Leopold's Ghost* (Houghton Mifflin, 1999) 101–114; J. Franklin, *George Washington Williams* (University of Chicago Press, 1985) 243–254.

Table 4.1 Timeline

| | | |
|---|---|---|
| **16-Jun-03** | **Prosecutor Moreno-Ocampo's term begins** | — |
| 23-Jun-04 | Investigation opened: Democratic Republic of Congo | DRC |
| 29-Jul-04 | Investigation opened: Uganda | Uganda |
| 6-May-05 | Arrest warrant request: *Kony et al.* | Uganda |
| 6-Jun-05 | Investigation opened: Darfur, Sudan | Sudan |
| 8-Jul-05 | Arrest warrants issued: *Kony et al.* | Uganda |
| 13-Jan-06 | Arrest warrant request: *Lubanga & Ntaganda* | DRC |
| 10-Feb-06 | Arrest warrant issued: *Lubanga* | DRC |
| 22-Aug-06 | Arrest warrant issued: *Ntaganda* | DRC |
| 28-Aug-06 | Document containing the charges: *Lubanga* | DRC |
| 25-Feb-07 | Arrest warrant/summons request: *Ahmad Harun & Ali Kushayb* | Sudan |
| 27-Jan-07 | Confirmation Decision: *Lubanga* | DRC |
| 27-Apr-07 | Arrest warrant issued: *Ahmad Harun & Ali Kushayb* | Sudan |
| 22-May-07 | Investigation opened: Central African Republic (No. 1) | CAR I |
| 25-Jun-07 | Arrest warrant request: *Katanga & Ngudjolo* | DRC |
| 10-Mar-08 | Joinder of cases: *Katanga & Ngudjolo* | DRC |
| 9-May-08 | Arrest warrant request: *Bemba* | CAR I |
| 23-May-08 | Arrest warrant issued: *Bemba* | CAR |
| 26-Jun-08 | Document containing the charges: *Katanga & Ngudjolo* | DRC |
| 14-Jul-08 | Arrest warrant request: *Bashir* | Sudan |
| 30-Sep-08 | Confirmation decision: *Katanga & Ngudjolo* | DRC |
| 17-Oct-08 | Document containing the charges: *Bemba* | CAR I |
| 20-Nov-08 | Arrest warrant/summons request: *Abu Garda; Banda & Jerbo* | Sudan |
| 26-Jan-09 | Opening statements at trial: *Lubanga* | DRC |
| 3-Mar-09 | Adjournment decision: *Bemba* | CAR I |
| 4-Mar-09 | First arrest warrant issued: *Bashir* | Sudan |
| 30-Mar-09 | Revised document containing the charges (with Art. 28): *Bemba* | CAR I |
| 7-May-09 | Summons issued: *Abu Garda* | Sudan |
| 15-Jun-09 | Confirmation Decision: *Bemba* | CAR I |

| | | |
|---|---|---|
| 27-Aug-09 | Summons issued: *Banda & Jerbo* | Sudan |
| 10-Sep-09 | Document containing the charges: *Abu Garda* | Sudan |
| 24-Nov-09 | Opening statements at trial: *Katanga & Ngudjolo* | DRC |
| 8-Feb-10 | Confirmation decision: *Abu Garda* | Sudan |
| 31-Mar-10 | Investigation opened: Kenya | Kenya |
| 20-Aug-10 | Arrest warrant request: *Mbarushimana* | DRC |
| 28-Sep-10 | Arrest warrant issued: *Mbarushimana* | DRC |
| 19-Oct-10 | Document containing the charges: *Banda & Jerbo* | Sudan |
| 22-Nov-10 | Opening statements at trial: *Bemba* | CAR I |
| 15-Dec-10 | Summons application: *Muthaura et al.; Ruto et al.* | Kenya |
| 3-Mar-11 | Investigation opened: Libya | Libya |
| 7-Mar-11 | Confirmation Decision: *Banda & Jerbo* | Sudan |
| 8-Mar-11 | Summons issued: *Muthaura et al.; Ruto et al.* | Kenya |
| 16-May-11 | Arrest warrant request: *Gaddafi et al.* | Libya |
| 27-Jun-11 | Arrest warrants issued: *Gaddafi et al.* | Libya |
| 3-Aug-11 | Document containing the charges: *Mbarushimana* | DRC |
| 15-Aug-11 | Document containing the charges: *Ruto et al.* | Kenya |
| 19-Aug-11 | Document containing the charges: *Muthaura et al.* | Kenya |
| 3-Oct-11 | Investigation opened: Côte d'Ivoire | Côte d'Ivoire |
| 25-Oct-11 | Arrest warrant request: *(Laurent) Gbagbo* | Côte d'Ivoire |
| 23-Nov-11 | Arrest warrant issued: *(Laurent) Gbagbo* | Côte d'Ivoire |
| 2-Dec-11 | Arrest warrant request: *Hussein* | Sudan |
| 12-Dec-11 | Arrest warrant request: *Blé Goudé* | Côte d'Ivoire |
| 16-Dec-11 | Confirmation Decision: *Mbarushimana* | DRC |
| 21-Dec-11 | Arrest warrant issued: *Blé Goudé* | Côte d'Ivoire |
| 23-Jan-12 | Confirmation decision: *Muthara et al.; Ruto et al.* | Kenya |
| 7-Feb-12 | Arrest warrant request: *(Simone) Gbagbo* | Côte d'Ivoire |
| 29-Feb-12 | Arrest warrant issued: *(Simone) Gbagbo* | Côte d'Ivoire |
| 1-Mar-12 | Arrest warrant issued: *Hussein* | Sudan |
| 14-Mar-12 | Trial judgment: *Lubanga* | DRC |
| 14-May-12 | Second arrest warrant request: *Ntaganda* | DRC |
| 15-May-12 | Arrest warrant application: *Mudacumura* | DRC |

Table 4.1 (*cont.*)

| | | |
|---|---|---|
| **15-Jun-12** | **Prosecutor Bensouda's term begins** | — |
| 4-Jul-12 | Second arrest warrant request: *Mudacumura* | DRC |
| 31-May-12 | Arrest warrant application dismissed: *Mudacumura* | DRC |
| 12-Jul-12 | Second arrest warrant issued: *Bashir* | Sudan |
| 13-Jul-12 | Second arrest warrant issued: *Ntaganda* | DRC |
| 13-Jul-12 | Arrest warrant issued: *Mudacumura* | DRC |
| 21-Nov-12 | Severance of cases: *Katanga & Ngudjolo* | DRC |
| 18-Dec-12 | Trial judgment: *Ngudjolo* | DRC |
| 16-Jan-13 | Investigation opened: Mali | Mali |
| 17-Jan-13 | Document containing the charges: *(Laurent) Gbagbo* | Côte d'Ivoire |
| 18-Mar-13 | Charges withdrawn: *Muthaura* | Kenya |
| 27-Mar-13 | Arrest warrant request: *Al-Tuhamy* | Libya |
| 18-Apr-13 | Arrest warrant issued: *Al-Tuhamy* | Libya |
| 3-Jun-13 | Adjournment decision: *(Laurent) Gbagbo* | Côte d'Ivoire |
| 10-Sep-13 | Opening statements at trial: *Ruto & Sang* | Kenya |
| 10-Jan-14 | Document containing the charges: *Ntaganda* | DRC |
| 13-Jan-14 | Revised document containing the charges: *(Laurent) Gbagbo* | Côte d'Ivoire |
| 12-Jun-14 | Confirmation decision: *(Laurent) Gbagbo* | Côte d'Ivoire |
| 14-Jun-14 | Confirmation decision: *Ntaganda* | DRC |
| 7-Mar-14 | Trial judgment: *Katanga* | DRC |
| 22-Aug-14 | Document containing the charges: *Blé Goudé* | Côte d'Ivoire |
| 24-Sep-17 | Investigation opened: Central African Republic (No. 2) | CAR II |
| 1-Dec-14 | Appeal judgment: *Lubanga* | DRC |
| 11-Dec-14 | Confirmation Decision: *Blé Goudé* | Côte d'Ivoire |
| 6-Feb-15 | Severance of cases: *Ongwen & Kony et al.* | Uganda |
| 27-Feb-15 | Appeal judgment: *Ngudjolo* | DRC |
| 11-Mar-15 | Joinder of cases: *(Laurent) Gbagbo & Blé Goudé* | Côte d'Ivoire |
| 13-Mar-15 | Charges withdrawn: *Kenyatta* | Kenya |
| 2-Sep-15 | Opening statements at trial: *Ntaganda* | DRC |
| 7-Sep-15 | Arrest warrant request: *Al Mahdi* | Mali |
| 18-Sep-15 | Arrest warrant issued: *Al Mahdi* | Mali |
| 21-Dec-15 | Document containing the charges: *Ongwen* | Uganda |

| | | |
|---|---|---|
| 28-Jan-16 | Opening statements at trial: *(Laurent) Gbagbo & Blé Goudé* | Côte d'Ivoire |
| 18-Feb-16 | Confirmation decision: *Al Mahdi* | Mali |
| 21-Mar-16 | Trial judgment: *Bemba* | CAR I |
| 23-Mar-16 | Confirmation decision: *Ongwen* | Uganda |
| 5-Apr-16 | Charges vacated: *Ruto & Sang* | Kenya |
| 22-Aug-16 | Opening statements at trial: *Al Mahdi* | Mali |
| 27-Sep-16 | Trial judgment: *Al Mahdi* | Mali |
| 6-Dec-16 | Opening statements at trial: *Ongwen* | Uganda |
| 15-Jun-17 | Appeals Chamber affirms Counts 6 & 9: *Ntaganda* | DRC |
| 1-Aug-17 | Arrest warrant request: *Al-Werfalli* | Libya |
| 15-Aug-17 | Arrest warrant issued: *Al-Werfalli* | Libya |
| 20-Mar-18 | Arrest warrant request: *Al Hassan* | Mali |
| 22-May-18 | Arrest warrant issued: *Al Hassan* | Mali |
| 8-Jun-18 | Appeal judgment: *Bemba* | CAR I |

'his' colony to the Belgium state, whose rule lasted until 1960. Throughout that period of Belgian rule, the colonial authorities treated the local people differently depending on their ethnicity, often privileging the Hema people (whom Leopold's agent described as having 'almost European features') over the Lendu and Ngiti.[2]

After gaining independence in 1960, the country remained volatile. The presidency was seized by Joseph-Desiré Mobutu in 1965, who ruled until 1997 when, after a two-year conflict, he was toppled by rebel leader Laurent Kabila with support of Uganda and Rwanda (the 'first Congo war'). After 1998, those states turned on Kabila's government, and militias fought with each other and with the government for control of land and resources. These conflicts lasted until 2003 (the 'second Congo war').[3] Since then, hostilities have continued intermittently.[4] The impact of this series of conflicts has been devastating. The second Congo war alone

[2] Fahey, see n. 1, 17, and Chapter 2 generally.

[3] A. Apreotesei, 'The International Criminal Court: First Cases and Situations' (2008) 5(1) *Eyes on the ICC* 1, 3; A. Van Woudenberg, 'Democratic Republic of Congo: On the Brink' (Human Rights Watch, 1 August 2006).

[4] Fahey, see n. 1, 3; Human Rights Watch, 'World Report 2014: Events of 2013' (2014) 103–107.

killed over 3.3 million civilians: the largest civilian death toll of any conflict since World War II.[5] Sexual violence was also endemic in the Congo wars. For example, a 2010 study in Ituri province found that almost 40 per cent of women and 24 per cent of men had experienced sexual violence, most of which was conflict-related.[6]

The ICC's involvement with this state began in July 2003, when Prosecutor Moreno-Ocampo began 'closely analyzing' the situation in Ituri, in the north-east of the Democratic Republic of Congo. Two months later, the Prosecutor announced that he was ready to request authorisation to open an investigation into this situation but that a referral from the Democratic Republic of Congo would 'assist his work'.[7] In March 2004, the government of the Democratic Republic of Congo made the referral, and after conducting a preliminary examination, the Prosecutor opened an investigation on 23 June 2004.[8] Together, Prosecutor Moreno-Ocampo and Prosecutor Bensouda brought six cases from this situation during the period under analysis, which is more than any other situation before the ICC to date.

### *4.1.1 Prosecutor v. Thomas Lubanga Dyilo*

Status at 17 July 2018: Conviction upheld on appeal; sentence and reparations order finalised (Table 4.2).

#### 4.1.1.1 Key Points

As the first case to proceed to trial at the ICC, *Lubanga* has particular significance in the ICC's public image. The case focused on the war crimes of 'conscripting or enlisting children under the age of fifteen years into armed forces or groups or using them to participate actively in hostilities' (henceforth, 'conscripting, enlisting, and using "child soldiers"').[9] Prosecuting these crimes was important: it sent a strong message about the international community's condemnation of this

[5] Human Rights Watch, 'World Report 2004' (2004) 3.

[6] K. Johnson et al., 'Association of Sexual Violence and Human Rights Violations with Physical and Mental Health in Territories of the Eastern Democratic Republic of the Congo' (2010) 204(5) *Journal of the American Medical Association* 553, 558.

[7] ICC OTP, 'The Office of the Prosecutor of the International Criminal Court Opens Its First Investigation' (23 June 2004).

[8] Ibid.

[9] RS, Art. 8(2)(b)(xxvi) and Art. 8(2)(e)(vii).

Table 4.2 *Lubanga* charges

| Crime | Article | Established at ... Arrest Warrant Stage | Confirmation Stage | Trial |
|---|---|---|---|---|
| War crime: Conscripting children into armed group | 8(2)(e)(vii)-1^ | ✓ | ✓ | ✓ |
| War crime: Enlisting children into armed group | 8(2)(e)(vii)-2^ | ✓ | ✓ | ✓ |
| War crime: Using children to participate actively in hostilities | 8(2)(e)(vii)-3^ | ✓ | ✓ | ✓ |

* Denotes any gender-based crimes in the case.
^ The warrant also contained charges for these war crimes in an international armed conflict.

extreme form of child abuse and generated valuable jurisprudence on crimes which, at the time the case began, had received little judicial interpretation by an international court.[10] Yet from a gender perspective, the case was 'disappointing'.[11] In the words of the Prosecutor's Gender Advisor, Patricia Sellers,

> It was disappointing because there was no sexual assault analysis of what was going on in the trial judgment, and there couldn't be, because there were no sexual assault charges. That means that you have no gender analysis in jurisprudence at the trial level, in terms of the Majority, and no gender analysis in jurisprudence at the appellate level, and it also means that at the reparations level, that sexual violence was eventually not included.[12]

The problems arose because, despite leading evidence of sexual violence against female UPC 'child soldiers' at trial, the OTP did not mention this

[10] These war crimes were recognised for the first time in the 1998 Rome Statute, and then in the 2002 Statute for the Special Court for Sierra Leone (SCSL). In January 2006, when the ICC Prosecutor initiated the case against Lubanga, the SCSL had not rendered any trial judgment on these crimes. However, it had ruled that these war crimes existed under customary law by 30 November 1996, when the SCSL's temporal jurisdiction began. See Decision on Preliminary Motion Based on Lack of Jurisdiction (Child Recruitment), *Norman* (SCSL-2004-14-AR72(E)), 31 May 2004.

[11] Interview, February 2018.

[12] Ibid.

violence at the pre-trial stage. As a consequence, there was no accountability for sexual violence in this case and no reparation for the resultant harms.

#### 4.1.1.2 Pre-Trial

On 13 January 2006, the Prosecutor requested an arrest warrant for Thomas Lubanga Dyilo, President of the *Union des Patriotes Congolais* (UPC), a Hema militia involved in the 2002–2003 Ituri conflict.[13] The Prosecutor alleged that, together with Bosco Ntaganda (see §4.1.2) and other members of the UPC, Lubanga was responsible as a co-perpetrator under Art. 25(3)(a) for the war crimes of conscripting, enlisting, or using 'child soldiers' from July 2002 to December 2003.[14] At the time the Prosecutor applied for this arrest warrant, there were reports of UPC troops committing sexual violence crimes throughout Ituri, including raping young female abductees.[15] These reported sexual violence crimes received no mention in the Prosecutor's arrest warrant request.[16] The warrant was issued under seal on 10 February 2006 and made public in March 2006, after the national authorities surrendered Lubanga to the ICC.[17]

The Pre-Trial Chamber set the deadline for the Document Containing the Charges (DCC) as 28 August 2006.[18] One month after that date was set, the Prosecutor decided to 'temporarily suspend' the Ituri investigation because there was not enough time to collect sufficient evidence to expand the charges before the DCC was due.[19] The Prosecutor noted that the investigation 'may' continue after the confirmation proceedings, and

[13] The UPC is sometimes described as a political movement, as distinct from its military arm, '*Forces Patriotiques pour la Libération du Congo*'. However, for brevity, and because several witnesses used the term 'UPC' to describe both the political movement and the military arm, that is the term used in this book.

[14] See ICC-01/04-02/06-20-Anx2, 10 February 2006, [25]–[28], [107].

[15] E.g. Amnesty International, 'Democratic Republic of Congo: Mass Rape - Time for Remedies' (25 October 2004) 13; Human Rights Watch, 'The Prosecution of Sexual Violence in the Congo War' (March 2005) 19–21; UN Organization Mission in the Democratic Republic of the Congo, 'Special Report on the Events in Ituri, January 2002–December 2003, UN DOC. s/2004/573' (16 July 2004), [1]–[2], [24], [37], [80], [153].

[16] The arrest warrant request is not publicly available. However, in the excerpts of that request cited in the Pre-Trial Chamber's arrest warrant decision, there is no reference to acts of sexual violence of any kind, and the OTP has never claimed that such acts were described in the arrest warrant request in this case.

[17] ICC-01/04-01/06-37, 17 March 2006.

[18] ICC-01/04-01/06-126, 24 May 2006, 7.

[19] ICC-01/04-01/06-170, 28 June 2007, [7].

stated that he would seek confirmation of further charges if sufficient evidence could be found.[20] The suspension of the investigation alarmed many local and international human rights groups monitoring the case. In an open letter dated 1 August 2006, eight of the most active NGOs in the Coalition for the ICC urged the Prosecutor to continue to investigate Lubanga's responsibility for rape and other crimes allegedly committed by his troops. They warned:

> The failure to include additional charges in the case against Mr Lubanga could undercut the credibility of the ICC in the DRC. Moreover, the narrow scope of the current charges may result in severely limiting victims' participation [and] negatively impact on the right of victims to reparations. We believe that you, as the prosecutor, must send a clear signal to the victims in Ituri and the people of the DRC that those who perpetrate crimes such as rape, torture and summary executions will be held to account.[21]

One of this letter's signatories, namely Women's Initiatives for Gender Justice, also sent the Prosecutor a confidential submission on 16 August 2006. This submission contained evidence of sexual violence crimes perpetrated by Lubanga's troops against civilians in Ituri and against children recruited by the UPC, including interviews with 31 victims who had allegedly been raped by members of that group.[22] Despite this advocacy, the Prosecutor did not change course: the DCC, filed on 28 August 2006, did not include any additional charges beyond those listed in the arrest warrant. The DCC provided detailed descriptions of certain tasks performed by child recruits in the UPC, including acting as bodyguards, undergoing weapons training, receiving air-dropped weapons, and fighting on the front lines.[23] It made no reference to children being raped themselves but alluded to children being incited to commit sexual violence crimes against third parties, including one incident when a commander 'told the recruits that they were allowed to rape the Lendu women',[24] and another incident when a UPC commander 'ordered [a 'child soldier'] to tie up the

[20] Ibid., [10].

[21] Avocats Sans Frontières et al., 'DR Congo: ICC Charges Raise Concern' (31 July 2006): www.hrw.org/news/2006/07/31/dr-congo-icc-charges-raise-concern.

[22] Women's Initiatives for Gender Justice, 'Public Redacted Version of Confidential Letter to ICC Prosecutor' (16 August 2006): www.iccwomen.org/news/docs/Prosecutor_Letter_August_2006_Redacted.pdf. See also Women's Initiatives for Gender Justice, 'Legal Eye on the ICC' (May 2012).

[23] ICC-01/04-01/06-356-Anx2, 28 August 2006, [23], [35], [39], [40], [48], [57].

[24] Ibid., [55].

testicles of a Lendu prisoner with a wire' (which the child did to avoid being shot, resulting in the death of the Lendu man).[25]

On 7 September 2006, Women's Initiatives for Gender Justice sought leave to file an *amicus curiae* brief in the case. Is application stated that the *amicus curiae* brief, if accepted, would argue that the Pre-Trial Chamber should determine whether the Prosecutor abused his discretion by deciding to charge Lubanga only with the recruitment and use of 'child soldiers' when there had been reports of widespread rape and murder by UPC forced under Lubanga's control.[26] The Defence opposed this request,[27] as did the Prosecutor.[28] The Pre-Trial Chamber declined to accept the proposed *amicus curiae* brief on the basis that Lubanga was not charged with sexual violence crimes, and therefore, the proposed brief would have 'no link' to the case.[29]

The OTP's final opportunity to present the charges was the confirmation hearing, held from 9 to 28 November 2006. At that hearing, the OTP made no reference to sexual abuse of children in the UPC.[30] It also minimised the significance of gender differences in the UPC, stating: 'upon arrival in the camps the children were distributed into groups of new recruits – adult soldiers and children together, boys and girls together, *no distinctions were made*'.[31] One prosecution witness indicated that girls in the UPC were treated differently to their male peers. This witness was Christine Peduto, a child protection advisor with the United Nations (UN) Mission in the Democratic Republic of Congo in 2002 and 2003. She testified about hearing reports of the sexual abuse of young girls in armed groups in Ituri, and of girls in the UPC being forced to do domestic work alongside their military training.[32] These activities were not referenced by the OTP lawyers. The statements by the victims' counsel were marginally more gender-aware: they made fleeting reference to rapes that their 'young clients' were allegedly forced to commit[33] but did not speak of other sexual violence crimes against UPC 'child soldiers'.

25 Ibid., [83].

26 ICC-01/04-01/06-403, 7 September 2006, [20].

27 ICC-01/04-01/06-442, 19 September 2006.

28 ICC-01/04-01/06-478, 25 September 2006.

29 ICC-01/04-01/06-480, 26 September 2006, 3.

30 The Prosecution made no reference to this issue in the publicly available transcripts of the confirmation hearing and has not subsequently claimed to have raised this issue during that hearing. See transcripts ICC-01/04-01/06-T-30-EN to ICC-01/04-01/06-T-47-EN.

31 ICC-01/04-01/06-T-30-EN, 9 November 2006, 49(25)–50(2) (emphasis added).

32 ICC-01/04-01/06-T-37-EN, 15 November 2006, 28(7–9); 49(3–6).

33 ICC-01/04-01/06-T-30-EN, 9 November 2006, 86(3–8).

On January 2007, the Pre-Trial Chamber found that there were substantial grounds to believe that Lubanga was responsible for the crimes charged between September 2002 and August 2003.[34] In interpreting the war crime of using children to participate actively in hostilities, the Chamber held that the concept of 'active participation in hostilities' is not limited to direct participation in hostilities, i.e. combat, but also covers 'combat-related activities'.[35] Activities which it saw as sufficiently 'combat-related' included 'scouting, spying, sabotage and the use of children as decoys, couriers or at military check-points'. Activities which it saw as *insufficiently* 'combat-related' included 'the use of domestic staff in married officers' quarters'.[36] The Chamber's exclusion of such domestic labour discriminated against girls (who generally do the bulk of this work), but aligned with the 1998 Draft ICC Statute.[37] The Chamber made no reference to the evidence of 'child soldiers' being forced to rape or sexually mutilate civilians. Faced with such evidence, a different Bench may have adjourned the proceedings and asked the Prosecutor to consider amending the charges.[38] However, this Bench did not do so, and thus, the case went to trial with no mention of sexual violence in the facts confirmed.

#### 4.1.1.3 Trial

In the lead-up to the trial, the UN Special Representative for Children and Armed Conflict, Radhika Coomaraswamy, took action to surface gender issues in the *Lubanga* case. In March 2008, she filed an *amicus curiae* brief, with leave of the Trial Chamber. The brief explained that 'when the Special Representative spoke to girl combatants in the eastern Democratic Republic of Congo, they spoke of being fighters one minute, a "wife" or "sex slave" the next, and domestic aides and food providers at another time'.[39] These girls included 'Mary', who after being abducted by a militia

[34] ICC-01/04-01/06-803-tEN, 29 January 2007, 156–157. Note: The Prosecutor charged Lubanga with the war crimes of 'conscripting', 'enlisting' and 'using' children in a *non-international* armed conflict, pursuant to RS, Art. 8(2)(e)(vii). The Pre-Trial Chamber confirmed charges under that provision for the period of June–August 2003, but also confirmed charges for the equivalent crimes in an *international* armed conflict from early September 2002 to June 2003 under Art. 8(2)(c)(xxvi).

[35] Ibid., [261].

[36] Ibid., [261]–[262].

[37] Ibid., n. 339, citing 'Report of the Preparatory Committee on the Establishment of an International Criminal Court: Addendum 1, UN Doc. A/CONF.183/2/Add.1 ("1998 Draft ICC Statute")' (14 April 1998), 21.

[38] RS, Art. 61(7)(c)(ii).

[39] ICC-01/04-01/06-1229-AnxA, 18 March 2008, [22].

on her way to school, was used for sex and domestic labour and forced to participate in armed attacks, and 'Eva', who was kept in a state of forced nudity, and used for sex, for domestic chores, and for transporting looted goods.[40] To capture the experiences of these girls and others like them, Coomaraswamy urged the Trial Chamber to interpret the term 'using children to participate actively in hostilities' to include activities performed primarily by female children, including being used for sex.[41]

She also urged the Chamber not to draw a 'bright line' between activities which do and do not constitute 'active participation in hostilities' as the Pre-Trial Chamber had done, because this approach 'threatens to exclude a great number of child soldiers – particularly girl soldiers – from coverage under the crime'.[42] She argued that 'the exclusion of girls from the definition of child soldiers would represent an insupportable break from well-established international consensus', as evinced by the 1997 Cape Town Principles, the 2007 Paris Principles, and the 2003 Protocol to the African Charter on Human and Peoples' Rights (the 'Maputo Protocol').[43] She stated that if a child has been used to 'participate actively in hostilities' for the purposes of the Rome Statute, it does not automatically follow that he or she has 'participated directly in hostilities' (and was therefore a legitimate target for the enemy during such participation in hostilities) for the purposes of international humanitarian law (IHL).[44]

The trial was scheduled to begin on 23 June 2003, but shortly before that date, the Trial Chamber decided to stay the proceedings indefinitely. The stay was a response to the Prosecution's refusal to share certain confidential evidence with the Chamber.[45] The matter was resolved after tense litigation, and the trial commenced on 26 January 2009. Few would have predicted the shift in the Prosecution's case on that day. After having said nothing about the sexual violence against girls in the UPC at the pre-trial stage, the Prosecutor raised this issue within the first minute of his opening address. He stated:

> Lubanga's armed group recruited, trained and used hundreds of young children to kill, pillage, and rape. The children still suffer the consequences ... They cannot forget that they raped and that they were

[40] Ibid., [16], [22].
[41] Ibid., [24]–[26].
[42] Ibid., [20].
[43] Ibid., [24].
[44] Ibid., [18]. The Special Representative made these same arguments in person in January 2010. See ICC-01/04-01/06-T-223-ENG, 7 January 2010, 14(4)–16(10).
[45] The Chamber required the evidence in order to determine if that evidence was exculpatory, and must therefore be disclosed to the defence. ICC-01/04-01/06-1644, 23 January 2009.

> raped. … In the camps child soldiers were exposed to the sexual violence perpetrated by Thomas Lubanga's men in unspeakable ways. … young boys were instructed to rape… girl soldiers were the daily victims of rape by the commanders.[46]

Much of the evidence that the OTP would bring to support these allegations would come from its nine ex-UPC 'child soldier' witnesses, namely eight men, and one woman.[47] They described the UPC as a group dominated by male commanders[48] in which women and girls were marked out as 'the other' by the term 'PMFs' (*personnel militaire féminin).*[49] In line with the Prosecutor's opening remarks, these nine witnesses described a gendered pattern of abuse, with girls being singled out for rape. In particular, the account of P-0010, the only female ex-'child soldier' to testify, echoed Coomaraswamy's observations about the multiple roles played by girls in armed groups. P-0010 stated that after being abducted by UPC as a child, she was forced to take part in military training[50] and was then sent into combat, where she killed several people and was shot herself.[51] She also gave evidence of being sexually abused by UPC commanders, an experience which she said was common to many girls within the group.[52] In her words, 'we couldn't refuse. It was impossible. We didn't have the power to say no'.[53] P-0010's evidence was corroborated by several of the male ex-'child soldiers', who stated that women

[46] ICC-01/04-01/06-T-107-ENG, 26 January 2009, 4(19)–5(3); 11(21–24).

[47] P-0298: ICC-01/04-01/06-T-110-Red3-ENG, ICC-01/04-01/06-T-123-Red3-ENG, ICC-01/04-01/06-T-124-ENG; P-0213: ICC-01/04-01/06-T-132-EN, ICC-01/04-01/06-T-133-Red3-ENG, ICC-01/04-01/06-T-134-Red- ENG; P-0008: ICC-01/04-01/06-T-135-Red3-ENG, ICC-01/04-01/06-T-137-Red-ENG, ICC-01/04-01/06-T-138-ENG; P-0011: ICC-01/04-01/06-T-138-ENG, ICC-01/04-01/06-T-139-Red2-ENG, ICC-01/04-01/06-T-140-ENG, ICC-01/04-01/06-T-142-ENG; P-0010: ICC-01/04-01/06-T-144-Red2-ENG; ICC-01/04-01/06-T-145-Red3-ENG; P-0007: ICC-01/04-01/06-T-148-Red2-ENG, ICC-01/04-01/06-T-149-Red2-ENG, ICC-01/04-01/06-T-150-Red3-ENG; P-0924: ICC-01/04-01/06-T-150-Red3-ENG, ICC-01/04-01/06-T-151-Red2-ENG, ICC-01/04-01/06-T-152-Red3-ENG; P-0157: ICC-01/04-01/06-T-185-Red2-ENG, ICC-01/04-01/06-T-186-Red3-ENG, ICC-01/04-01/06-T-187-Red3-ENG, ICC-01/04-01/06-T-188-Red2-ENG; P-0297: ICC-01/04-01/06-T-285-Red2-ENG, ICC-01/04-01/06-T-286-Red2-ENG, ICC-01/04-01/06-T-287-Red-ENG, ICC-01/04-01/06-T-288-Red2-ENG.

[48] For one exception, see: ICC-01/04-01/06-T-144-Red2-ENG, 5 March 2009, 26(22–25).

[49] Ibid., 28(7–8); ICC-01/04-01/06-T-149-Red2-ENG, 17 March 2009, 14(17)–15(10).

[50] ICC-01/04-01/06-T-144-Red2-ENG, 5 March 2009, 21–35.

[51] Ibid., 49(12)–64(20).

[52] Ibid., 36(16)–37(25); ICC-01/04-01/06-T-145-Red3-ENG, 6 March 2009, 6(17)–8(23).

[53] ICC-01/04-01/06-T-145-Red3-ENG, 6 March 2009, 8(22–23).

and girls were raped and used as 'wives' by members of the UPC,[54] and took part in combat as well.[55]

This evidence of sexual violence was facilitated by the OTP lawyers, who asked questions about the role of girls in the UPC, including direct questions about whether those girls were used for sex.[56] The evidence also emerged due to questions from the judges, in particular Judge Odio Benito, who came to the ICC with experiences as an ICTY trial judge. The responses to these questions indicated that as well as suffering sexual abuse, girls in the UPC were exposed to early pregnancy and associated risks. For example, during his testimony, one of the male ex-'child soldier' witnesses stated: 'if the women got pregnant, they were either driven out of the camp or had an abortion'. Returning to this statement later in the hearing, Judge Odio Benito asked: 'this decision to have an abortion was made by the girls themselves or by somebody else?' The witness confirmed that the decision was made by the commanders. Her Honour then asked if there were abortion facilities in the camp, to which witness responses that no, the girls 'did things themselves', and referred to one girl who had died as a result of a self-administered abortion.[57]

In May 2009, the victims' counsel sought an expansion of the charges. They argued that the evidence of sexual abuse of female 'child soldiers' should be charged as sexual slavery,[58] and other abuses described by the witnesses, including the treatment of girls who became pregnant, should be charged as cruel or inhumane treatment.[59] The victims' counsel asked the Trial Chamber to bring in these charges using Regulation 55, which enables a Trial Chamber to 'change the legal characterisation of facts', so long as this change does not exceed the facts and circumstances confirmed. The Majority of the Chamber, Judge Fulford dissenting, found that it could grant the victims' request.[60] The Defence appealed,[61] as did

[54] E.g. ICC-01/04-01/06-T-135-Red3-ENG, 25 February 2009, 13(8)–14(25); ICC-01/04-01/06-T-138-Red-ENG, 27 February 2009, 65(23)–66(2), 74(2–11); ICC-01/04-01/06- T-148-Red2-ENG, 13 March 2009, 49(11–22); ICC-01/04-01/06-T-133-Red3-ENG, 23 February 2009, 4(17–23).

[55] E.g. ICC-01/04-01/06-T-149-Red2-ENG, 17 March 2009, 14 (15–17).

[56] E.g. ICC-01/04-01/06-T-151-Red2-ENG, 19 March 2009, 5(14–25); ICC-01/04-01/06-T-144-Red2-ENG, 5 March 2009, 36(16–19).

[57] ICC-01/04-01/06-T-150-Red-ENG, 18 March 2009, 35(16)–36(14).

[58] ICC-01/04-01/06-1891-tENG, 22 May 2009, [34]

[59] Ibid., [33].

[60] ICC-01/04-01/06-2049, 14 July 2009.

[61] ICC-01/04-01/06-2073-tENG, 11 August 2009.

the Prosecution, who argued that the proposed change would undermine the Court's appearance of impartiality, compromise Lubanga's fair trial rights, and intrude on the Prosecutor's role.[62] The matter was resolved in December 2009, when the Appeals Chamber unanimously decided that a Trial Chamber cannot use Regulation 55 to introduce charges that exceed the facts described in the confirmation decision, which in this case, meant no new charges for the alleged sexual abuse.[63]

The trial ground to a halt again in July 2010, when the Trial Chamber stayed the proceedings due to the Prosecutor's failure to comply with orders to disclose to the Defence, on a confidential basis, the identity of an intermediary who had assisted with the investigation.[64] However, the Appeals Chamber reversed this stay in October 2010, ruling that although the Prosecutor was obliged to comply with judicial orders, the Trial Chamber should have imposed sanctions on the Prosecutor before resorting to the 'significantly more drastic' step of staying the case.[65] Thus, the trial resumed.

In its closing brief, the OTP urged the Chamber to interpret the crime of 'using children to participate actively in hostilities' in a way that would include 'activities such as the ones described by [Radhika Coomaraswamy] the UN Special Representative'.[66] In particular, it listed evidence of girls being used as bodyguards, 'wives', sexual slaves, cooks and fighters as examples of the 'use of girl child soldiers' in the UPC.[67] Some commentators were sceptical about this apparent evolution in the Prosecution's case. For example, Hayes argued that while the Special Representative's arguments had merit, 'their co-option by the Office of the Prosecutor to retrospectively justify a clearly inept and insufficient range of charges was unbecoming and reeked slightly of panic'.[68]

[62] ICC-01/04-01/06-2074, 12 August 2009.

[63] ICC-01/04-01/06-2205, 8 December 2009.

[64] The Prosecutor's rationale for refusing to comply with the order was as follows: 'The Prosecution is sensitive to its obligation to comply with the Chamber's instructions. However, it also has an independent statutory obligation to protect persons put at risk on account of the Prosecution's actions. It should not comply, or be asked to comply, with an Order that may require it to violate its separate statutory obligation by subjecting the person to a foreseeable risk. The Prosecutor accordingly has made a determination that the Prosecution would rather face adverse consequences in its litigation than expose a person to risk on account of prior interaction with this Office'. ICC-01/04-01/06-2582, 8 October 2010, [12].

[65] Ibid., [60].

[66] ICC-01/04-01/06-2748-Red, 1 June 2011, [143].

[67] Ibid., [227]–[234].

[68] N. Hayes, 'Sisyphus Wept: Prosecuting Sexual Violence at the International Criminal Court' in W. Schabas, Y. McDermott and N. Hayes (eds), *The Ashgate Research Companion to International Criminal Law* (Ashgate, 2013) 7, 24.

On the second-last day of the trial, Judge Odio Benito asked the Prosecution to clarify how the allegations of sexual violence fit into its case. Directing her question to the (then) Deputy Prosecutor Fatou Bensouda, who was the OTP's focal point on gender, Judge Odio Benito asked:

> In the OTP closing brief… and again this afternoon in your presentation, it was stated, and I quote: 'That girls who were recruited were even in a worse situation than boys, as they were used as sex slaves and were subject to systematic sexual abuse. This resulted in pregnancies, abortions and a psychological state that is quite catastrophic'. However, the Prosecution never mentioned sexual violence in the document containing the charges against the accused. Sexual violence was also not included in the charges confirmed against the accused by Pre-Trial Chamber I. Bearing in mind Article 74 [which states that the judgment 'shall not exceed the facts and circumstances described in the charges'], my question is as follows: How is sexual violence relevant to this case, and how does the Prosecution expect the Trial Chamber to refer to the sexual violence allegedly suffered by girls if this is not in the facts and circumstances described in the charges against Mr Lubanga Dyilo?[69]

Rather than allowing Bensouda to respond, the Prosecutor answered himself. He stated:

> We believe the facts are that the girls were abused, used as sexual slaves and raped. We believe this suffering is part of the suffering of the conscription. We did not allege and will not present evidence linking Thomas Lubanga with rapes. We allege that he linked it with the conscription and he knows the harsh conditions. So what we believe in this case is a different way to present the gender crimes. It presents the gender crimes not specific as rapes. Gender crimes were committed as part of the conscription of girls in – in the militias. And it is important to have the charge as confined to the inscription [sic], because if not – and that's the point that Ms. Coomaraswamy did here – if not, the girls are considered wife and ignored as people to be protected and demobilised and cared [sic]. That is why the Prosecutor decided to confine the charges – to present the suffering and the sexual abuse and the gender crime suffered by the girls in the camps just as conscription, showing this gender aspect of the crime … I have to be clear. We agree with the Chamber idea [sic]: their act, they are not used in hostility. However, factually we believe when a commander ordered [sic] to abduct girls to use them as sexual slaves or rape them, this order is using the children in hostility. That is the submission we are doing. So to summarise, we agree with the Chamber there is a line, there's a border between

[69] ICC-01/04-01/06-T-356-ENG, 25 August 2011, 53(12)–54(1).

> hostilities and no hostilities, and cooking could be a good example, maybe, but ordering to abduct girls in order to rape them is an order to – and use children in hostilities.[70]

### 4.1.1.4 Judgment

The judgment was rendered on 14 March 2012. The Trial Chamber unanimously convicted Lubanga as a co-perpetrator for conscripting, enlisting or using 'child soldiers' from September 2002 to August 2003.[71] However, in interpreting those crimes, the Chamber was divided. The Majority held that a child has 'participated actively in hostilities' if 'the support provided by the child to the combatants exposed him or her to real danger as a potential target'.[72] It left open the question of whether this crime could ever be committed through sexual abuse[73] and refused to determine Lubanga's culpability for the alleged acts of sexual violence because these acts exceeded the facts and circumstances confirmed in the case.[74] The Majority recognised evidence that girls in the UPC were used for sex and domestic work as part of their role within the group[75] but did not use this evidence to support the conviction for the 'using' crime.[76]

In a dissenting opinion, Judge Odio Benito argued that by failing to include sexual violence within the concept of using children to participate actively in the hostilities, 'the Majority of the Chamber is making this critical aspect of the crime invisible'.[77] She argued:

> Sexual violence and enslavement are in the main crimes committed against girls and their illegal recruitment is often intended for that purpose (nevertheless they also often participate in direct combat). If the war crimes considered in this case are directed at securing their physical and psychological wellbeing, then we must recognize sexual violence as a failure to afford this protection and sexual violence as acts embedded in the enlisting, conscription and use of children under 15 in hostilities.[78]

[70] Ibid., 54(8)–55(21).

[71] Using Regulation 55, the Trial Chamber re-characterised the charges as war crimes in a non-international armed conflict at all times relevant to the charges. See ICC-01/04-01/06-2842, 14 March 2012, [1359].

[72] Ibid., [628].

[73] Ibid., [630].

[74] Ibid., [629]–[630], [896].

[75] Ibid., [878]–[882], [892]–[895].

[76] Ibid., [915]–[916].

[77] Ibid., (Odio Benito), 14 March 2012, [16].

[78] Ibid., [21].

Applying Article 21(3) of the Rome Statute, Judge Odio Benito concluded that excluding sexual violence from the definition of the crime 'is discriminatory'.[79]

The Defence appealed against the conviction, without success. Among the many findings of the appeals judgment, two deserve particular attention here. First, the Appeals Chamber rejected the Trial Chamber's interpretation of the crime of 'using children to participate actively in hostilities'.[80] It held that in order to determine if a child was used in this manner, one need not ask if the child was exposed to danger as a 'potential target', but must instead 'analyse the link between the activity for which the child is used and the combat in which the armed force or group of the perpetrator is engaged'.[81] Second, the Appeals Chamber held that if a child has been used to 'participate actively in hostilities' for the purposes of the Rome Statute, he or she is not automatically excluded from the category of 'persons taking no active part in hostilities' for the purposes of common Article 3 of the Geneva Conventions. The Chamber reasoned that when used in the Rome Statute, the phrase 'participate actively in hostilities' is intended *to protect children* from being used in armed hostilities. By contrast, in common Article 3 of the Geneva Conventions, the phrase 'active part in hostilities' is intended to set the conditions in which an individual *loses protection* as a civilian. Therefore, because these phrases serve different purposes, they should not be assumed to mean exactly the same thing.[82]

The implications of this decision are discussed further in Chapter 6, which explores the way that sexual violence against 'child soldiers' might be charged as 'using children to participate actively in hostilities' if such sexual violence is linked to the group's engagement in hostilities.

#### 4.1.1.5 Sentence

At sentencing, the OTP argued that the alleged sexual abuse of UPC 'child soldiers' should be regarded as an aggravating factor because it showed that the crimes were committed with particular cruelty and against particularly defenceless victims and involved discrimination

[79] Ibid., [6], [21]. See also L. Chappell, A. Durbach and E. Odio Benito, 'Judge Odio Benito: A View of Gender Justice from the Bench' (2014) 16(4) *International Feminist Journal of Politics* 648, 650.

[80] ICC-01/04-01/06-3121-Red, 1 December 2014, [329]–[340].

[81] Ibid., [335].

[82] Ibid., [324].

on gender grounds (those being aggravating factors under the Rules of Procedure and Evidence).[83] The Majority of the Trial Chamber rejected these arguments. It ruled that sexual violence could not be an aggravating factor in this case because Lubanga's culpability for sexual violence had not been established beyond reasonable doubt.[84] It also excoriated Moreno-Ocampo for raising the issue of sexual violence at the sentencing stage, given that 'not only did the former Prosecutor fail to apply to include sexual violence or sexual slavery at any stage during these proceedings, including in the original charges, but he *actively opposed* taking this step during the trial' by opposing the victims' request to charge the relevant evidence as sexual slavery.[85] It sentenced Lubanga to fourteen years' imprisonment, less the time spent in detention since March 2006.[86] The Prosecution appealed, arguing (among other things) that the Majority erred in refusing to treat the evidence of sexual violence as an aggravating factor.[87] The Defence also appealed, seeking a reduction in the sentence.[88] Both appeals were dismissed.[89]

In a dissenting opinion, Judge Odio Benito accepted that the evidence of sexual violence could be an aggravating sentencing factor in Lubanga's case and recommended a total sentence of 15 years.[90]

#### 4.1.1.6 Reparation

On 7 August 2012, the Trial Chamber announced the reparations principles to be applied in the case. It held that collective reparations could be awarded to direct and indirect victims of the crimes for which the accused was convicted,[91] that reparations must not discriminate on certain grounds including 'gender' and 'sexual orientation'[92] and that priority must be given to victims requiring urgent assistance, including victims of sexual violence.[93] The Defence appealed, arguing (among other things) that the reparation order in this case must not include harms caused

[83] ICC-01/04-01/06-2881, 14 May 2012, [30]–[36]; RPE, rule 145(2)(b)(iii)–(v).
[84] ICC-01/04-01/06-2901, 10 July 2012, [60]–[76].
[85] Ibid., [60] (emphasis added).
[86] Ibid., [107]–[108].
[87] ICC-01/04-01/06-2950, 3 December 2012, [7].
[88] ICC-01/04-01/06-2949-tENG, 3 December 2012.
[89] ICC-01/04-01/06-3122, 1 December 2014.
[90] ICC-01/04-01/06-2901 (Odio Benito), 10 July 2012.
[91] ICC-01/04-01/06-2904, 7 August 2012, [194].
[92] Ibid., [191].
[93] Ibid., [200].

by sexual violence crimes, as Lubanga had not been convicted of those crimes.[94] The Appeals Chamber rendered is reparations decision on 3 March 2016. It left in place the Trial Chamber's finding that, in principle, reparations should not discriminate on the aforementioned grounds.[95] However, it found that there could be no reparation for sexual violence in this case and therefore amended the order to that effect.[96]

### 4.1.2 *Prosecutor v. Bosco Ntaganda*

Status at 17 July 2018: Trial underway (Table 4.3).

#### 4.1.2.1 Key Points

The *Ntaganda* case started off much like the *Lubanga* case: both cases concern crimes allegedly committed by the UPC, and in both cases, the charges were initially confined to conscripting, enlisting and using 'child soldiers'. However, while the charges in *Lubanga* were never modified, the charges in *Ntaganda* were later expanded to include a wide range of gender-based crimes, including sexual violence against women and men. Of particular interest are the counts concerning the alleged sexual abuse of UPC 'child soldiers', which Prosecutor Bensouda has charged using the war crimes of rape and sexual slavery. The Defence challenged those charges on legal grounds, arguing that even if the alleged sexual abuse occurred, it cannot amount to war crimes under the Rome Statute because the putative victims and perpetrators are both members of the same armed group. That argument has now been rejected by the Pre-Trial Chamber,[97] Trial Chamber[98] and Appeals Chamber,[99] all of whom have concluded that these charges are valid at law. In our 2018 interview, the Prosecutor's Special Advisor on Gender, Patricia Sellers, described the Appeals Chamber decision on these charges as a 'high point' in the ICC's evolving jurisprudence, and observed, 'it hasn't really hit the international criminal law consciousness yet'.[100] Closing statements were delivered on 28–30 August 2018, and the trial judgment will deliver its decision in due course.

[94] ICC-01/04-01/06-2972-tENG, 5 February 2013, [124]–[136].
[95] ICC-01/04-01/06-3129-AnxA, 3 March 2015, [16].
[96] ICC-01/04-01/06-3129, 3 March 2015, [198].
[97] ICC-01/04-02/06-309, 9 June 2014, [76]–[82].
[98] ICC-01/04-02/06-1707, 4 January 2017.
[99] ICC-01/04-02/06-1962, 15 June 2017.
[100] Interview, February 2018. See also P.V. Sellers, 'Ntaganda: Re-Alignment of a Paradigm' (International Institute of Humanitarian Law, 2018): www.iihl.org/wp-content/uploads/2018/03/Ntaganda-V.pdf.

Table 4.3 *Ntaganda* charges

| | | Established at ... | | |
|---|---|---|---|---|
| Crime | Article | Arrest Warrant Stage | Confirmation Stage | Trial |
| Crime against humanity: Murder | 7(1)(a) | ✓ | ✓ | Pending |
| Crime against humanity: Attempted murder | 7(1)(a) & 25(3)(f) | n/a | ✓ | Pending |
| Crime against humanity: Forcible transfer | 7(1)(d) | n/a | ✓* | Pending |
| Crime against humanity: Rape | 7(1)(g)-1 | ✓* | ✓* | Pending |
| Crime against humanity: Sexual slavery | 7(1)(g)-2 | ✓* | ✓* | Pending |
| Crime against humanity: Persecution ('ethnic') | 7(1)(h) | ✓* | ✓* | Pending |
| War crime: Murder | 8(2)(c)(i)-1 | ✓ | ✓ | Pending |
| War crime: Attempted murder | 8(2)(c)(i)-1 & 25(3)(f) | n/a | ✓ | Pending |
| War crime: Attacking civilian population | 8(2)(e)(i) | ✓* | ✓* | Pending |
| War crime: Attacking protected objects | 8(2)(e)(iv) | n/a | ✓ | Pending |
| War crime: Pillage | 8(2)(e)(v) | ✓ | ✓ | Pending |
| War crime: Rape | 8(2)(e)(vi)-1 | ✓* | ✓* | Pending |
| War crime: Sexual slavery | 8(2)(e)(vi)-2 | ✓* | ✓* | Pending |
| War crime: Conscripting children into armed group | 8(2)(e)(vii)-1^ | ✓ | ✓ | Pending |
| War crime: Enlisting children into armed group | 8(2)(e)(vii)-2^ | ✓ | ✓ | Pending |
| War crime: Using children to participate actively in hostilities | 8(2)(e)(vii)-3^ | ✓ | ✓* | Pending |
| War crime: Displacement of civilians | 8(2)(e)(viii) | n/a | ✓* | Pending |
| War crime: Destruction of property | 8(2)(e)(xii) | n/a | ✓ | Pending |

* Denotes any gender-based crimes in the case.

^ The warrant also contained charges for these war crimes in an international armed conflict.

#### 4.1.2.2 Pre-Trial

On 13 January 2006, the same day that Prosecutor Moreno-Ocampo request an arrest warrant for Lubanga, he also requested an arrest warrant for Lubanga's associate, Bosco Ntaganda.[101] The Prosecutor alleged that as a high-ranking UPC commander, Ntaganda was responsible as co-perpetrator under Article 25(3)(a) for the war crimes of conscripting, enlisting and using 'child soldiers'.[102] The Pre-Trial Chamber initially refused to issue the arrest warrant on the basis that Ntaganda was not among 'the most senior leaders of the DRC situation', and therefore, the case was not sufficiently grave to be admissible to the ICC.[103] However, the Pre-Trial Chamber later issued the warrant on 22 August 2006 after the Appeals Chamber held that Ntaganda's rank was not a valid reason to refuse the Prosecutor's request.[104] When the warrant was unsealed on 28 April 2008, several NGOs noted the absence of charges for other crimes reportedly committed by the UPC, including rape.[105] However, perhaps because Ntaganda was not in the ICC's custody, and therefore no trial was imminent, the outcry was not as fierce as it had been in Lubanga's case.

Ntaganda's military career continued for several years after the arrest warrant was issued. In 2005, he left the UPC and fought in other armed groups in the Democratic Republic of Congo; in 2009, after announcing a ceasefire, he was named a general in that country's armed forces; in April 2012, he defected and joined another armed group; and in March 2013, following leadership struggles within that group, he arrived at the US Embassy in Rwanda, asking to be transferred to the ICC.[106]

In May 2012, following Ntaganda's defection from the armed forces, Prosecutor Moreno-Ocampo applied for a second warrant for his arrest. This application alleged that Ntaganda was responsible as co-perpetrator under Article 25(3)(a) for a further five war crimes and four crimes against humanity.[107] In public court records, the facts pertaining to each charge were not entirely clear. However, it seems that the charges of rape, sexual

[101] ICC-01/04-02/06-20-Anx2, 10 February 2006, [1].

[102] Ibid., [25]–[28], [107].

[103] Ibid., [89].

[104] ICC-01/04-169, 13 July 2006, [68]–[82]; ICC-01/04-02/06-2-Anx-tENG, 22 August 2006 (in ICC legal tools as ICC-01/04-02/06-2-tENG). The judicial signature on the latter decision is dated 7 August 2006, but 22 August 2006 is used on the first page and in other court records.

[105] Human Rights Watch, 'DR Congo: Suspected War Criminal Wanted' (29 August 2008); Women's Initiatives for Gender Justice, 'Making a Statement' (2008) 10.

[106] ICC-01/04-02/06-203-AnxA, 10 January 2014, [29]–[34].

[107] ICC-01/04-611-Red, 16 May 2012.

slavery, persecution, and attacks on the civilian population were all based on evidence that the UPC soldiers raped civilians and/or forced them to rape one another. The victims of those rapes were mostly identified as women and girls, but the application noted that 'men and boys were also subjected to sexual violence'.[108] The Pre-Trial Chamber issued a warrant containing all charges sought on 13 July 2012, just weeks after Fatou Bensouda's term as Prosecutor commenced.[109] Ntaganda's first appearance before the ICC was on 26 March 2013.[110]

The DCC, filed in January 2014, focused on the UPC's alleged recruitment and use of 'child soldiers' in 2002–2003, as well as crimes allegedly committed by that group during two attacks: one in November–December 2002 on villages in the Banyali-Kilo *collectivité* ('first attack') and one in February 2003 on villages in the Walendu-Djatsi *collectivité* ('second attack'). The Prosecutor alleged that in this context, Ntaganda was responsible for six crimes against humanity and twelve war crimes under Article 25(3)(a) (direct perpetration, or direct or indirect co-perpetration), 25(3)(b) (ordering/inducing), 25(3)(d) (contributing to the commission of crimes by a group acting with a common purpose) or Article 28 (command responsibility).[111] Further details of the charges were provided in the updated DCC and pre-trial brief[112] and the OTP's closing brief.[113]

The charges of rape and sexual slavery were divided into two groups. The first group (Counts 4, 5, 7 and 8) concerned the alleged sexual abuse of 'civilians'. The alleged victims included over 25 female rape victims,[114] three male rape victims[115] and several male and female victims who were forced to perform sexual acts with one another.[116] The second group (Counts 6 and 9) concerned the alleged sexual abuse of UPC 'child soldiers'. The alleged victims were children aged fifteen or under who were allegedly raped and sexually enslaved by UPC soldiers and commanders, some of whom became pregnant as a result of rape, and some of whom were also forced to perform domestic chores.[117] The Prosecutor's decision

[108] Ibid., [113].
[109] ICC-01/04-02/06-36-Red, 13 July 2012.
[110] ICC-01/04-02/06-309, 9 June 2014, [2].
[111] ICC-01/04-02/06-203-AnxA, 10 January 2014.
[112] ICC-01/04-02/06-402-AnxA, 14 November 2014; ICC-01/04-02/06-503-AnxA-Red2, 1 September 2015.
[113] ICC-01/04-02/06-2277-Anx1-Corr-Red, 7 November 2018.
[114] ICC-01/04-02/06-309, 9 June 2014, [49]–[57]; [81]–[82].
[115] Ibid., [52].
[116] Ibid., [50], [52].
[117] ICC-01/04-02/06-2277-Anx1-Corr-Red, 17 November 2018, [779]–[790].

to charge the sexual abuse of these 'child soldiers' as a war crime was groundbreaking, because in the history of international criminal law, violence *within* an armed group has almost never been charged as a war (see §5.3.1).[118]

Sexual violence was relevant to other charges as well: the charges of forcible transfer and displacement of civilians were based on evidence that UPC troops forced the non-Hema population to flee 'through openly criminal conduct such as directly attacking, persecuting, killing, raping and sexually enslaving civilians, destroying property and pillaging';[119] the charge of persecution referred to the rape of civilians by UPC soldiers;[120] and the charge of attacking the civilian population did as well.[121] In addition, the charge of 'using children to participate actively in hostilities' incorporated evidence of sexual violence. To quote the relevant part of the Pre-Trial Brief:

> Many girls were used by commanders to do reconnaissance and gather intelligence prior to battles. So-called 'IS girls' would be given civilian clothes and ordered to go near enemy camps and attract the attention of enemy soldiers, who would let them into the camp to have sex with them, and thereby allow them to gather intelligence such as the number of soldiers and the types of weapons. In addition to being forced to have sex with enemy soldiers, IS girls risked being discovered and killed.[122]

On 9 June 9014, the Pre-Trial Chamber unanimously confirmed all of the charges under several alternative modes of liability. This was the first case in which all charges of sexual and gender-based crimes were confirmed.

#### 4.1.2.3 Trial

The trial began on 2 September 2015. The OTP's opening statements were presented first by Prosecutor Bensouda and then by Nicole Samson, the

[118] For an exception, see ICC-01/04-02/06-309, 9 June 2014, [79], n. 318, citing: Judgment, *Taylor* (SCSL-03-01-T), 30 May 2012, [1179], [1206(vii)], [1207], [1451].

[119] ICC-01/04-02/06-503-AnxA-Red2, 1 September 2015, [324]. See also ICC-01/04-02/06-402-AnxA, 14 November 2014, 63 (Counts 12–13 and paragraphs cited therein).

[120] ICC-01/04-02/06-503-AnxA-Red2, 1 September 2015, [356], [358], [360]; ICC-01/04-02/06-402-AnxA, 14 November 2014, 62 (Count 10 and paragraphs cited therein).

[121] ICC-01/04-02/06-503-AnxA-Red2, 1 September 2015, [132], [265], [268], [273]; ICC-01/04-02/06-402-AnxA, 14 November 2014, 60 (Count 3 and paragraphs cited therein).

[122] ICC-01/04-02/06-503-AnxA-Red2, 1 September 2015, [396].

only woman to lead an ICC trial team to date. The Prosecutor emphasised the scale and gravity of sexual violence within the UPC, stating:

> Rape and sexual enslavement of its own soldiers was so prevalent in the UPC that these girls were referred to as *guduria* – this is a Swahili word for a large communal cooking pot – reduced to objects which soldiers and commanders could pass around and use for sex whenever they pleased.[123]

Samson made it clear that the UPC used sexual violence strategically, explaining: 'sexual violence was used as a tool to persecute non-Hema civilians and as a reward for the UPC troops',[124] and also highlighting the use of 'IS' girls who were typically required to have sex with enemy soldiers in order to gain access to their camps.[125]

Much of the testimony of sexual violence occurred in closed session. However, some occurred in open session. For example, one former-UPC insider stated: 'soldiers who were at the checkpoints occasionally raped girls or women', adding 'this is not hearsay. These are things that occurred that I saw with my own eyes',[126] and a civilian witness testified that while she was detained by the UPC, she saw male soldiers raping male and female civilians.[127] The Chamber also heard accounts of sexual violence from several victim participants, including one woman who stated that her daughter was detained and raped by UPC soldiers,[128] one woman who recalled being raped when she was thirteen by three UPC soldiers,[129] one woman who said she was robbed and then raped by two UPC soldiers in front of her children[130] and one woman who stated that two UPC soldiers raped her and smashed her face with their rifle-butts, causing her to lose several teeth.[131]

During trial, the Defence challenged the legality of the charges of sexual violence against the UPC 'child soldiers'. It argued that these charges fell outside the ICC's jurisdiction, a claim that was rejected by the Trial and Appeal Chamber, as detailed in Chapter 5.[132]

[123] ICC-01/04-02/06-T-23-ENG, 2 September 2015, 14(5–9).
[124] Ibid., 21(11–12).
[125] Ibid., 62(3–7).
[126] ICC-01/04-02/06-T-29-Red-ENG, 21 September 2015, 26(1–12).
[127] ICC-01/04-02/06-T-115-Red-ENG, 6 July 2016, 49(12–19).
[128] ICC-01/04-02/06-T-198-Red-ENG, 1 March 2017, 20(23–25).
[129] Ibid., 58(22)–61(4).
[130] ICC-01/04-02/06-T-199-Red-ENG, 2 March 2017, 7(13–14); 8(10)–(23); 11(8)–(14).
[131] ICC-01/04-02/06-T-202-Red-ENG, 11 April 2017, 18(5–9); 22(4–6); 25(17)–26(19).
[132] See Chapter 5, §5.3.1.

After 248 hearings, in which the Chamber heard from 80 Prosecution witnesses, nineteen Defence witnesses, three witnesses called by the victims' counsel and five victim participants, the parties and participants gathered for closing statements on 28–30 August 2018.[133] The judgment will be issued in due course.

### 4.1.3 *Prosecutor v. Mathieu Ngudjolo Chui*

Status at 17 July 2018: Acquittal upheld on appeal (Table 4.4).

#### 4.1.3.1 Key Points

For most of the proceedings, this case was joined to the *Katanga* case. Both cases concerned an attack on Bogoro, a village in Ituri, in February 2003. The alleged leaders of that attack, Germain Katanga and Mathieu Ngudjolo Chui, were the first people to be charged with sexual violence crimes at the ICC. The Trial Chamber found that those crimes occurred, but that the responsibility of the accused had not been proven. In *Ngudjolo*, the Chamber reached that conclusion for *all* of the crimes, whereas in *Katanga*, it applied specifically to the sexual violence crimes.

#### 4.1.3.2 Pre-Trial

On 25 June 2007, Prosecutor Moreno-Ocampo requested arrest warrants for Katanga and Ngudjolo.[134] The Prosecutor charged both suspects for three crimes against humanity and six war crimes in relation to the Bogoro attack, including two gender-based crimes, namely sexual slavery as a war crime and a crime against humanity.[135] The Pre-Trial Chamber issued the warrants against Katanga and Ngudjolo on 2 and 6 July 2007, respectively, finding that there were reasonable grounds to believe that both men were responsible under Article 25(3)(a) (perpetration) or Article 25(3)(b) (ordering).[136] Katanga was surrendered to the ICC on 17 October 2007 and Ngudjolo on 6 February 2008. Soon after, the Chamber joined the two cases for efficiency.[137]

The DCC, filed on 26 June 2008, provided details of the attack. It stated that the village was attacked by two groups: the *Force de Résistance*

[133] ICC, 'ICC Trial Chamber VI to Deliberate on the Case against Bosco Ntaganda' (30 August 2018).

[134] See ICC-01/04-01/07-1-US-tENG, 2 July 2007, 2; ICC-01/04-02/07-1-tENG, 6 July 2007, 2.

[135] ICC-01/04-01/07-1-US-tENG, 2 July 2007, 6; ICC-01/04-02/07-1-tENG, 6 July 2007, 6.

[136] ICC-01/04-01/07-1-US-tENG, 2 July 2007, 6; ICC-01/04-02/07-1-tENG, 6 July 2007, 6. The Chamber did not specify which form of perpetration under Article 25(3)(a) applied.

[137] ICC-01/04-01/07-307, 10 March 2008.

Table 4.4 *Ngudjolo* charges

| | | Established at … | | |
|---|---|---|---|---|
| Crime | Article | Arrest Warrant Stage | Confirmation Stage | Trial |
| War crime: Murder | 8(2)(a)(i)^ | ✓ | ✓ | ✗ |
| War crime: Inhuman or cruel treatment | 8(2)(a)(ii)-1^ | ✓ | ✗ | n/a |
| War crime: Attacking civilian population | 8(2)(b)(i)^ | ✓ | ✓ | ✗ |
| War crime: Destruction of property | 8(2)(b)(xiii)^ | n/a | ✓ | ✗ |
| War crime: Pillage | 8(2)(b)(xvi)^ | ✓ | ✓ | ✗ |
| War crime: Outrages on personal dignity | 8(2)(b)(xxi)^ | n/a | ✗* | n/a |
| War crime: Rape | 8(2)(b)(xxii)-1^ | n/a | ✓* | ✗* |
| War crime: Sexual slavery | 8(2)(b)(xxii)-2^ | ✓* | ✓* | ✗* |
| War crime: Using children to participate actively in hostilities | 8(2)(b)(xxvi)-3^ | ✓ | ✓ | ✗ |
| Crime against humanity: Murder | 7(1)(a) | ✓ | ✓ | ✗ |
| Crime against humanity: Rape | 7(1)(g)-1 | n/a | ✓* | ✗* |
| Crime against humanity: Sexual slavery | 7(1)(g)-2 | ✓* | ✓* | ✗* |
| Crime against humanity: Other inhumane acts | 7(1)(k) | ✓ | ✗ | n/a |

* Denotes any gender-based crimes in the case.
^ The warrant also contained charges for these war crimes in a non-international armed conflict.

*Patriotique en Ituri* (FPRI), composed of Ngiti people, and the *Front des Nationalistes et Intégrationnistes* (FNI), composed of Lendu people.[138] They allegedly targeted Bogoro because it was inhabited mainly by Hema

[138] ICC-01/04-01/07-649-Anx1A, 26 June 2008, [3]–[14]. The OTP later conceded that Ngudjolo's militia may have had a different name: ICC-01/04-01/07-T-336-ENG, 15 May 2012, 10(21)–13(13).

people, was beside the base of a Hema militia (the UPC) and was strategically located (the Lendu and Ngiti fighters needed to cross Bogoro to access the main road to Bunia from the south and to coordinate with one another).[139] The Prosecutor alleged that as the respective leaders of the FPRI and FNI, Katanga and Nugdjolo were responsible for nine war crimes and four crimes against humanity as co-perpetrators under Article 25(3)(a) because they made essential contributions to the implementation of a common plan to 'wipe out' the village[140] or under Article 25(2)(b) because they ordered the attack.[141] Five of the charges were based on evidence of sexual violence against civilian women and girls: sexual slavery as a war crime and a crime against humanity, rape as a war crime and a crime against humanity and the war crimes of outrages on personal dignity. The latter charge was based on evidence that the attackers made Witness P-287 strip to her blouse and briefs in public, and that a combatant later cut off her briefs with his knife.[142]

The Pre-Trial Chamber issued the confirmation of charges decision on 30 September 2008. In relation to the sexual violence crimes, the Chamber was divided: all three judges agreed that these crimes were committed,[143] however, they disagreed as to the suspects' responsibility for these crimes. The Majority found that there were substantial grounds to believe that the suspects were responsible for these crimes as indirect co-perpetrators under Article 25(3)(a) because they implemented the plan to wipe out the village, knowing that women would be raped and sexually enslaved in the 'ordinary course of the events'.[144] It based this conclusion on evidence that rape and sexual slavery were a 'common practice' in the Ituri conflict, that this practice was 'widely acknowledged' by the combatants, that the groups that attacked Bogoro had 'repeatedly' committed sexual violence crimes in previous and subsequent attacks, that they trained in camps where women were 'constantly raped' and that Katanga and Ngudjolo had visited these camps and received frequent reports of activities therein.[145]

[139] ICC-01/04-01/07-649-Anx1A, 26 June 2008, [64].
[140] Ibid., [91]–[93].
[141] Ibid., [94].
[142] Ibid, 33–34 (Counts 6–10), [89]; ICC-01/04-01/07-717, 30 September 2008, [373]–[377]; ICC-01/04-01/07-T-129-Red-ENG, 19 April 3010, 41(1–9).
[143] ICC-01/04-01/07-717, 30 September 2008, [436], [444]; ICC-01/04-01/07-717 (Ušacka), 30 September 2008, [13]–[14].
[144] ICC-01/04-01/07-717, 30 September 2008, [576], [580].
[145] Ibid., [568].

However, for Judge Ušacka, this evidence was not enough to prove that Katanga and Ngudjolo would have known that as a result of the attack, women would be subjected to sexual violence in the 'ordinary course of events.'[146] As Women's Initiatives has observed, Judge Ušacka's dissent on this point was 'an early and important indication' that the Prosecution's arguments about the suspect's responsibility for rape and sexual slavery 'would need to be refined and reinforced at trial'.[147]

The Chamber was also divided over the charge of 'other inhumane acts', which was based on evidence that the attackers wounded villagers with firearms and machetes. The Majority declined to confirm this charge because in its view, the attackers intended to cause death, not just serious harm.[148] However, Judge Ušacka would have confirmed this charge.[149] As to the remaining charges, the Chamber was unanimous. It declined to confirm the charges of inhuman treatment and outrages on personal dignity, because although there was sufficient evidence that these crimes occurred,[150] there was 'no evidence' that the suspects had the requisite knowledge and intent.[151] However, it found that there were substantial grounds to believe that the suspects were responsible for the war crime of using 'children soldiers' as *direct* co-perpetrators under Article 25(3)(a)[152] and also for one crime against humanity (murder) and four war crimes (murder, pillage, destruction of property and attacking the civilian population) as *indirect* co-perpetrators under Article 25(3)(a).[153] Of those charges, pillage was the outlier: the Chamber found that the suspects did not mean for this crime to happen, but they knew it would occur in the 'ordinary course of events' (which under Article 30 of the Rome Statute is enough to satisfy the ICC's 'intent and knowledge' requirement).[154]

[146] ICC-01/04-01/07-717 (Ušacka), 30 September 2008, [13]–[29].

[147] Women's Initiatives for Gender Justice, 'Appeals Withdrawn by Prosecution and Defence: The Prosecutor vs. Germain Katanga' (26 June 2014) 2.

[148] ICC-01/04-01/07-717, 30 September 2008, [456]–[465].

[149] ICC-01/04-01/07-717 (Ušacka), 30 September 2008, [35].

[150] ICC-01/04-01/07-717, 30 September 2008, [361]–[364] (inhuman treatment by detaining civilians in a room filled with corpses and later using them to lure out other civilians); [365]–[377] (outrages on personal dignity through forced nudity).

[151] Ibid., [570]–[571].

[152] Ibid., [574].

[153] Ibid., [575].

[154] Ibid., [575], [579].

#### 4.1.3.3 Trial

The *Katanga & Ngudjolo* trial began on 24 November 2009. In his opening statements, the Prosecutor stated that the attack on Bogoro started at 5:30 am when 'hundreds of women, men and children, under the command of Mr Katanga and Mr Ngudjolo, armed with automatic weapons, machetes and spears, descended on the village centre'.[155] He told the Court that the attackers killed UPC soldiers and civilians indiscriminately, and that they 'raped and then killed women'.[156] He further alleged that in the afternoon, when the village was strewn with bodies, the attackers put down chairs and 'got drunk'.[157] The next day, they allegedly forced captured civilians to call out to other villagers hiding in the bush, and when those people emerged, they too were 'brutally executed'.[158] The Prosecutor continued:

> The joint attack achieved its goal, but the horror was not over yet for the women of Bogoro. Once captured, some women hid their Hema identity to save their lives. Those later revealed as Hema were killed. The others were raped and forced into marriage as combatant wife [sic], or detained to serve as sexual slaves by Mr Katanga or Mr Ngudjolo's soldiers. All these women were victimised *on the basis of their gender*. They were attacked in particular *because they were women*.[159]

This attention to gender was progressive. However, it raised a question as to why, if this was the OTP's interpretation of the facts, the crime of gender-based persecution had not been charged. Similar questions about absent charges were raised throughout trial. For example, several witnesses testified that they became pregnant while detained,[160] a claim that the Trial Chamber found credible for at least one witness,[161] which raised a question as to whether 'forced pregnancy' could also have been charged. Moreover, one Prosecution witness recalled that the attackers cut off men's and women's genitals, noting that one soldier wore a woman's genitals as a bracelet.[162] Although this evidence was captured

[155] ICC-01/04-01/07-T-80-ENG, 24 November 2009, 23(25)–24(2).
[156] Ibid., 24(25).
[157] Ibid., 25(14–15).
[158] Ibid., 25(17–19).
[159] Ibid., 25(19–25) (emphasis added).
[160] ICC-01/04-01/07-T-336-ENG, 15 May 2012, 7(7–8).
[161] ICC-01/04-01/07-3436-tENG, 7 March 2014, [1006].
[162] ICC-01/04-01/07-T-206-Red, 17(14–19).

by the charges of attacking the civilian population and murder, it seemed capable of satisfying the more specific war crime of 'sexual violence'.[163]

Notwithstanding those possible gaps in the charges, the Prosecution brought strong evidence of the gender-based crimes which *were* charged. It questioned several witnesses about women being captured for use as 'wives' after the attack on Bogoro,[164] and it called three witnesses to testify about their own experiences of being raped and sexually enslaved during and after this attack,[165] all of whom identified the perpetrators of these crimes as men.[166] Some of these witnesses became upset when testifying about sexual violence, leading to departures from the standard 'question and answer' script.[167] For example, when Judge Cotte asked P-132 whether the men who raped her were drunk, she responded: 'My body was affected. My God, I was very ashamed. Now I have become useless'.[168] Judge Diarra and Judge Cotte consoled the witness and commended her for giving evidence to the Court.[169] Judge Van den Wyngaert, the third judge, did not add her own remark.

Throughout the trial, witnesses for both parties referred to *fétiches*, meaning spiritual protections that supposedly shielded fighters from bullets or increased their strength. Several witnesses stated that these *fétiches* only worked if certain conditions were upheld, for example, if the fighter refrained from pillage and rape.[170] However, according to Prosecution witness P-280, no such conditions applied during attacks on villages inhabited only by the Hema. In those attacks, the fighters 'were told to do whatever we wanted. We had permission to do anything'.[171]

[163] See RS, Art. 8(2)(b)(xxii)-6.

[164] ICC-01/04-01/07-T-206-Red-ENG, 19 October 2010, 40(14)–48(25).

[165] P-249: ICC-01/04-01/07-T-135-Red-ENG, 4 May 2010, 41(4–17); 50(1–9); 54(6)–56(5); ICC-01/04-01/07-T-136-Red-ENG, 5 May 2010, 48(5–15); 75(21–24). P-132: ICC-01/04-01/07-T-139-Red-ENG, 11 May 2010, 14(1–9); 19(2)–20(24); 46(2)–(54)(13); ICC-01/04-01/07-T-141-Red-ENG, 14 May 2010, 36(15)–42(18). P-353: ICC-01/04-01/07-T-213-Red-ENG, 4 November 2010, 58(1–12); 60(11)–61(19).

[166] Ibid.

[167] See Women's Initiatives for Gender Justice, 'Gender Report Card 2010' (2010) 165–176.

[168] ICC-01/04-01/07-T-141-Red-ENG, 14 May 2010, 39(1–9).

[169] Ibid., 39(13)–40(16).

[170] E.g. ICC-01/04-01/07-T-149-Red-ENG, 28 May 2010, 8(11)–14(14); ICC-01/04-01/07-T-157-Red-ENG, 16 June 2010, 7(3)–8(22); ICC-01/04-01/07-T-159-Red-ENG, 22 June 2010, 74(18)–77(22); ICC-01/04-01/07-T-279-Red-ENG, 10 June 2011, 28(21)–29(16).

[171] ICC-01/04-01/07-T-157-Red-ENG, 16 June 2010, 17(5)–19(6). Note: The Trial Chamber ultimately found that Witness P-280's testimony could not be relied upon. See ICC-01/04-02/12-3-tENG, 18 December 2012, [219].

Towards the end of the trial, both accused chose to testify. On the topic of sexual violence, Katanga claimed that he had never heard of rape before the case and that this crime was 'impossible' in Ngiti culture. In his words, 'when you do that, you die … Rape is prohibited in our area. It is a taboo'.[172] Ngudjolo did not initially answer questions on this topic directly. When asked whether he was aware of rape in the Ituri conflict, he referred to his culture's practice of dowry-giving, stating 'we are aware of the value of a woman'.[173] However, when pressed by the Prosecution, he conceded: 'I'm not contesting the fact that there were rapes, I'm not saying that there were no rapes, but I'm saying that personally I never saw any. I never saw a rape'.[174]

In closing arguments, the Defence argued that the evidence of sexual violence was unreliable due to inconsistencies in the witness's accounts. The Prosecution refuted this claim, arguing that the Defence had exaggerated and in some cases invented these inconsistencies, and that in any case, 'none of these alleged inconsistencies go to the heart of the witnesses′ accounts of their rape'.[175] The Prosecution also noted that victims of rape may struggle to recall specific facts due to trauma, but this does not mean their evidence is inherently unreliable,[176] a point stressed by the victims' counsel also.[177]

The Defence also sought to distance their clients from the alleged sexual violence crimes, with Ngudjolo's counsel arguing that the OTP had not established who committed the rapes, or how those people were connected to Ngudjolo,[178] and Katanga's counsel claiming that Katanga neither intended any rapes nor knew that rape would occur in the 'ordinary course of events', citing Judge Ušacka's dissenting opinion.[179] The Prosecution disputed these arguments. It maintained that the accused

[172] ICC-01/04-01/07-T-316-ENG, 4 October 2011, 45(13)–46(12).

[173] ICC-01/04-01/07-T-332-Red-ENG, 10 November 2011, 21(20–23). Note: In some parts of the eastern DRC, a marriage cannot proceed unless the woman's family has received a satisfactory dowry payment from the prospective husband. See I. Bjørkhaug and M. Bøås, 'Men, Women and Gender-Based Violence in North Kivu, DRC' (Fafo, 2014) 16, 19; M. Hallward-Driemeier and T. Hasan, *Empowering Women: Legal Rights and Economic Opportunities in Africa* (Agence Française de Développement and World Bank, 2013) 72.

[174] ICC-01/04-01/07-T-332-Red-ENG, 10 November 2011, 22(3–5).

[175] See ICC-01/04-01/07-T-336-ENG, 15 May 2012, 47(14)–49(23).

[176] Ibid.

[177] ICC-01/04-01/07-T-337-Red-ENG, 16 May 2012, 73(2)–74(14).

[178] ICC-01/04-01/07-3265-Corr2-Red, 8 November 2012, [516].

[179] ICC-01/04-01/07-3266-Corr2-Red, 29 June 2012, [1002]–[1010].

were both present at the Bogoro attack, and that they were the leaders of the attacking groups.[180] It conceded that rape and sexual slavery did not form part of the common plan to attack the village, but it maintained that Katanga and Ngudjolo were responsible for those crimes because they were aware that as a result of that attack, rape and sexual slavery would occur in the 'ordinary course of events'.[181] This argument about Katanga and Ngudjolo's mental state was based on several pieces of circumstantial evidence, including evidence that the Lendu and Ngiti fighters were encouraged to target all civilians (including women) in Bogoro because it was a primarily Hema village; that before the attack, the Ngiti fighters sung songs in front of Katanga and other commanders, the lyrics of which dehumanised Hema people and made degrading references to their sexual organs; that according to one witness, the usual *fétiche* conditions were not enforced during attacks on Hema villages; that the attackers were given a 'carte blanche' to do as they pleased after battle; that several witnesses testified about having experienced sexual slavery or having heard of women being used in this way by the commanders of Katanga and Ngudjolo's groups; that Katanga was aware of women being forcibly 'married' to fighters in his group; and that rape and sexual slavery were reportedly committed by all militias involved in the Ituri armed conflict, including the Ngiti and Lendu forces.[182]

On 21 November 2012, after both parties had presented closing statements, the Majority of the Trial Chamber (Judge Van den Wyngaert dissenting) gave notice that it might consider Katanga's responsibility under a different mode of liability to that charged by the Prosecutor. This potential change would affect all charges except the war crime of using 'child soldiers'.[183] As this change would not affect Ngudjolo, the Chamber severed the two cases at that point. Katanga appealed the Majority's decision, but his appeal was dismissed.[184] Hence, the cases remained severed.

On 18 December 2012, the Trial Chamber handed down a unanimous judgment in the *Ngudjolo* case. It found that there was a 'wealth of evidence' to show that all of the crimes charged, including rape and sexual slavery,

[180] ICC-01/04-01/07-T-336-ENG, 15 May 2012, 10(17)–30(8).

[181] ICC-01/04-01/07-3251-Corr-Red, 3 July 2012, [668]; ICC-01/04-01/07-T-336-ENG, 15 May 2012, 50(2–10).

[182] ICC-01/04-01/07-3251-Corr-Red, 3 July 2012, [669]–[688].

[183] ICC-01/04-01/07-3319-tENG/FRA, 21 November 2012, [7].

[184] ICC-01/04-01/07-3363, 27 March 2013.

had been committed during the Bogoro attack.[185] However, it found that the Prosecution had not established that Ngudjolo was the leader of the Lendu group at the time of the Bogoro attack, and therefore, he was acquitted on all charges.[186] The Prosecution appealed the judgment, arguing that the Trial Chamber applied an 'impossible' standard of proof that exceeded the 'beyond reasonable doubt' standard required by the Rome Statute.[187] The Appeals Chamber rejected this appeal and confirmed the acquittal in full.[188]

### 4.1.4 *Prosecutor v. Germain Katanga*

Status at 17 July 2018: Partial conviction rendered; judgment not appealed (Table 4.5).

#### 4.1.4.1 Key Points

The *Katanga* case clearly demonstrates the difficulties in establishing criminal responsibility for sexual violence crimes. After a late change to the mode of liability, the Majority of the Trial Chamber convicted Katanga on all applicable charges *except* rape and sexual slavery. Despite weaknesses in the Chamber's decision, the Prosecutor did not appeal. Thus, the Chamber's decision stood unchallenged.

#### 4.1.4.2 Pre-Trial

At the pre-trial stage, the *Katanga* case was joined to the *Ngudjolo* case (see § 4.1.3.2).

#### 4.1.4.3 Trial

At the end of Katanga & Ngudjolo's trial, the Majority gave notice that it might judge Katanga according to a different mode of liability to that with which he had been charged: rather than judging him as a direct or indirect co-perpetrator under Article 25(3)(a), it would judge his responsibility under Article 25(3)(d). According to this provision, a person is responsible for a crime if he or she 'contributes to the commission or attempted commission of such a crime by a group of persons acting with a common purpose'.

[185] ICC-01/04-02/12-3-tENG, 18 December 2012, [338]. Notably, the Chamber did not refer to the three women who had testified about being sexually abused during and after the attack in support of its finding that there was a 'wealth of evidence' to show that the crimes had been committed.

[186] Ibid., [503].

[187] ICC-01/04-02/12-39-Red2, 3 April 2013, [2].

[188] ICC-01/04-02/12-271, 27 February 2015.

Table 4.5 *Katanga* charges

| | | Established at … | | |
|---|---|---|---|---|
| Crime | Article | Arrest Warrant Stage | Confirmation Stage | Trial |
| War crime: Murder | 8(2)(a)(i)^ | ✓ | ✓ | ✓ |
| War crime: Inhuman or cruel treatment | 8(2)(a)(ii)-1^ | ✓ | ✗ | n/a |
| War crime: Attacking civilian population | 8(2)(b)(i)^ | ✓ | ✓ | ✓ |
| War crime: Destruction of property | 8(2)(b)(xiii)^ | n/a | ✓ | ✓ |
| War crime: Pillage | 8(2)(b)(xvi)^ | ✓ | ✓ | ✓ |
| War crime: Outrages on personal dignity | 8(2)(b)(xxi)^ | n/a | ✗* | n/a |
| War crime: Rape | 8(2)(b)(xxii)-1^ | n/a | ✓* | ✗* |
| War crime: Sexual slavery | 8(2)(b)(xxii)-2^ | ✓* | ✓* | ✗* |
| War crime: Using children to participate actively in hostilities | 8(2)(b)(xxvi)-3^ | ✓ | ✓ | ✗ |
| Crime against humanity: Murder | 7(1)(a) | ✓ | ✓ | ✓ |
| Crime against humanity: Rape | 7(1)(g)-1 | n/a | ✓* | ✗* |
| Crime against humanity: Sexual slavery | 7(1)(g)-2 | ✓* | ✓* | ✗* |
| Crime against humanity: Other inhumane acts | 7(1)(k) | ✓ | ✗ | n/a |

* Denotes any gender-based crimes in the case.

^ The warrant also contained charges for these war crimes in a non-international armed conflict. In the DCC, all war crimes were charged for an international *or* non-international armed conflict. The Pre-Trial Chamber confirmed these charges for an international armed conflict. However, the Trial Chamber analysed them as war crimes in a non-international armed conflict.[189]

[189] ICC-01/04-01/07-3436-tENG, 7 March 2014, [1229]–[1230].

The OTP argued that the evidence presented at trial 'clearly' satisfied that provision.[190] Citing relevant parts of the trial record, it argued that Katanga assisted a 'group of persons acting with a common purpose', namely, the Ngiti combatants from Walendu-Bindi,[191] by helping them to obtain weapons and ammunition for the attack, and by organising and participating in planning meetings.[192] As to the 'common purpose', it argued that 'the Ngiti and Lendu combatants devised a plan to attack Bogoro and eliminate the presence of its predominantly Hema population and UPC soldiers',[193] and that on the day of the attack, the attackers descended on Bogoro 'with the plan to wipe out the village by targeting the predominantly Hema civilian population, killing indiscriminately women, children and elderly, raping and sexually enslaving women, destroying and looting the property of civilians'.[194] The OTP argued that the concept of a 'common purpose' was 'functionally identical' to the concept of a 'common plan' that had hitherto been part of the Prosecutor's case.[195] It directed the Chamber to its closing brief, in which the evidence relating to the 'common plan' was analysed at length.[196] This reference to the closing brief raised a concern, because that brief stated: 'les crimes de viol et esclavage sexuel *ne faisaient pas* partie du plan commun' (the crimes of rape and sexual slavery *did not form* part of the common plan).[197] The OTP did not appear to reconcile this potential inconsistency in its case.

The Trial Chamber rendered its judgment on 7 March 2014. All three judges agreed that the alleged sexual violence crimes occurred.[198] They also agreed that Katanga was not responsible for the crimes under Article 25(3)(a) as initially charged.[199] The Majority then considered whether he was responsible for any crimes under Article 25(3)(d),

190 ICC-01/04-01/07-3367, 8 April 2013, [4].

191 Ibid., [30]–[42].

192 Ibid., [50].

193 Ibid., [49].

194 Ibid., [45].

195 Ibid., [43].

196 Ibid., [44].

197 ICC-01/04-01/07-3251-Corr-Red, 3 July 2012, [668] (emphasis added).

198 In relation to rape, the Chamber found that Witnesses 132, 249 and 353 were vaginally penetrated in coercive circumstances, namely, by soldiers who were armed, who threatened the women with death, and who outnumbered the women (in one incident, six to one). In relation to sexual slavery, it found that after the attack, these three women were detained in camps where they were raped by multiple men (including men who took them as 'wives') and that Witnesses 132 and 249 were also forced to perform household chores. ICC-01/04-01/07-3436-tENG, 7 March 2014, [988]–[1019].

199 Ibid., [1417]–[1421].

and found that he was guilty under that provision of one crime against humanity (murder) and four war crimes (murder, directing attacks against the civilian population, destruction of property and pillage). However, it found that he was *not* responsible under Article 25(3)(d) for rape and sexual slavery on the basis that there was insufficient evidence to show that those crimes 'necessarily' fell within the 'common purpose' of the group.[200] Based on the partial conviction, the Majority sentenced Katanga to twelve years' imprisonment, including the time spent in detention at the ICC since 18 September 2007.[201] In a dissenting opinion, Judge Van den Wyngaert found that the introduction of charges under Article 25(3)(d) at the end of the trial violated Katanga's fair trial rights, and that in any case, there was insufficient evidence to convict him under that mode of liability for any of the crimes charged.[202]

On 9 April 2014, both parties gave notice of their intent to appeal the judgment, with the Defence seeking a full acquittal, and the Prosecution seeking convictions for rape and sexual slavery.[203] However, on 25 June 2014, the Defence withdrew its appeal, confirmed that it would accept the sentence, and published a short statement in which Katanga expressed his '*sincères regret*'.[204] That same day, the OTP withdrew its appeal.[205] Thus, the acquittals for sexual violence stood unchallenged.

#### 4.1.4.4 Reparation

On 24 March 2017, the Trial Chamber held that Katanga was liable for $US 1 million in reparations to victims of the crimes for which he was convicted.[206] The order comprised $250 to each of the 297 victims found eligible to receive individual reparations. The Chamber described this sum as 'symbolic award', stating that a payment of $250 'is not intended as compensation for the harm in its entirety. Yet, the Chamber believes that that award may provide some measure of relief for the harm suffered by the victims'.[207] The Chamber also ordered collective reparations to support victims in the four areas that they had identified, namely: housing,

[200] Ibid., [1663]–[1664].
[201] ICC-01/04-01/07-3484-tENG-Corr, 23 May 2014.
[202] ICC-01/04-01/07-3436-AnxI (Van den Wyngaert), 7 March 2014.
[203] ICC-01/04-01/07-3459, 9 April 2014; ICC-01/04-01/07-3462, 9 April 2014.
[204] ICC-01/04-01/07-3497, 25 June 2014 (with Annex A).
[205] ICC-01/04-01/07-3498, 25 June 2014.
[206] ICC-01/04-01/07-3728-tENG, 24 March 2017, [264].
[207] Ibid., [300].

income-generating activity, education and psychological rehabilitation.[208] However, it declined a request to order reparations for five children who claimed to be suffering transgenerational psychological harm as a result of the attack (which occurred before they were born). The Chamber explained that while these children were 'in all likelihood' suffering from transgenerational harm, there was insufficient evidence to show that this suffering was the result of the Bogoro attack.[209] After reviewing that decision as directed by the Appeals Chamber, the Trial Chamber made a final decision not to order reparations for transgenerational harm on 19 July 2018.[210]

### *4.1.5 Prosecutor v. Callixte Mbarushimana*

Status at 17 July 2018: Charges not confirmed (Table 4.6).

#### 4.1.5.1 Key Points

The *Mbarushimana* case concerned crimes allegedly committed in the Kivu provinces in 2009–2010 by the *Forces Démocratiques pour la Liberation du Rwanda* (FLDR), a group formed by Hutu forces who fled Rwanda after the 1994 genocide. The case included a record number of gender-based crimes,[211] including the ICC's first charge of persecution on 'gender' grounds, which the Prosecutor later changed to persecution on 'political' grounds. Due to weaknesses in the Prosecution's evidence, none of the charges were confirmed. As this case illustrates, a wide range of gender-based crimes does not necessarily lead to greater accountability: much depends on the quality of the supporting evidence.

#### 4.1.5.2 Pre-Trial

On 20 August 2010, Prosecutor Moreno-Ocampo requested an arrest warrant for Callixte Mbarushimana, Executive Secretary of the FLDR, who at that time lived in France. The application alleged that in December 2009, the Democratic Republic of Congo and Rwandan armies launched a joint operation aimed at stopping the FDLR's criminal activities in North and South Kivu. In response, Mbarushimana and two other FDLR leaders, Ignace Murwanashyaka (who, in 2015, was convicted on related charges

[208] Ibid., [302]–[304].
[209] Ibid., [132]–[135].
[210] ICC-01/04-01/07-3804-Red, 19 July 2018.
[211] Hayes, see n. 68, 37.

Table 4.6 *Mbarushimana* charges

| Crime | Article | Established at … Arrest Warrant Stage | Confirmation Stage | Trial |
|---|---|---|---|---|
| War crime: Attacking civilian population | 8(2)(e)(i)^ | ✓ | ✗* | n/a |
| Crime against humanity: Murder | 7(1)(a) | ✓ | ✗ | " " |
| War crime: Murder | 8(2)(c)(i)-1^ | ✓ | ✗ | " " |
| War crime: Mutilation | 8(2)(c)(i)-2 or 8(2)(e)(xi)-1 | n/a | ✗* | " " |
| Crime against humanity: Other inhumane acts | 7(1)(k) | ✓* | ✗ | " " |
| War crime: Inhuman treatment | 8(2)(a)(ii)-2 | ✓* | n/a | " " |
| War crime: Cruel treatment | 8(2)(c)(i)-3 | n/a | ✗ | " " |
| Crime against humanity: Rape | 7(1)(g)-1 | ✓* | ✗* | " " |
| War crime: Rape | 8(2)(e)(vi)-1^ | ✓* | ✗* | " " |
| Crime against humanity: Torture | 7(1)(f) | ✓* | ✗* | " " |
| War crime: Torture | 8(2)(c)(i)-4^ | ✓* | ✗* | " " |
| War crime: Destruction of property | 8(2)(e)(xii)^ | ✓ | ✗ | " " |
| War crime: Pillage | 8(2)(e)(v) | n/a | ✗ | " " |
| Crime against humanity: Persecution ('gender') | 7(1)(h) | ✓* | n/a | " " |
| Crime against humanity: Persecution ('political') | 7(1)(h) | n/a | ✗* | " " |

* Denotes any gender-based crimes in the case.

^ The warrant also contained charges for these war crimes in an international armed conflict.

by a German court)[212] and Sylvestre Mudacumura (who is the subject of another ICC case) created a 'humanitarian catastrophe' in the Kivus in an effort to force Rwanda to negotiate with them.[213] This catastrophe allegedly resulted in five crimes against humanity and six war crimes for which Mbarushimana was responsible as a co-perpetrator under Article 25(3)(a) and as a contributor under Article 25(3)(d).[214]

The charges of rape and torture were based on evidence of sexual violence.[215] So too were the charges of inhuman treatment and other inhumane acts, which among other things, were based on evidence that civilian women had spears inserted into their vaginas and fetuses ripped from their bellies, and that civilian men were forced to rape civilian women.[216] The charge of persecution was based on those acts of sexual violence, among other things.[217] As to the grounds of persecution, the Prosecution alleged that Mbarushimana and the other co-perpetrators 'intentionally and in a discriminatory manner targeting women and men seen to be affiliated with the FARDC on the basis of their gender'.[218] Elaborating on this point, the Prosecution alleged:

> When carried out at the rates reported by international organisations in the Kivu Provinces, [sexual violence] amounts to sexual violence against the individual that is also persecution *on the basis of gender* against the collective. The rape of women and girls is carried out because they, as females, are easily targeted and can be put forth as objects of FDLR domination vis-à-vis the men in their families. Men and boys, who for example are forced to rape, suffer from persecution on the basis of gender, targeted to show FDLR dominance through violating their manhood in this manner.[219]

The arrest warrant was issued on 28 September 2010. It included all of the crimes charged, albeit under Article 25(3)(d) only. The Chamber made no comment on the definition of 'gender' in relation to the persecution

[212] In November 2009, FDLR president Ignace Murwanashyaka and vice president Straton Musoni were arrested in Germany. On 28 September 2015, Murwanashyaka was convicted by the Stuttgart Higher Regional Court in relation to war crimes committed by members of the FDLR in the DRC between January 2008 and November 2009. The conviction has been appealed. See: 'Make Way for Justice #4' (Trial International, 2018) 59–60.

[213] ICC-01/04-01/10-11-Red2, 20 August 2010, 4–5.

[214] Ibid., [20]–[21].

[215] Ibid., 15–16 (Counts 5–8).

[216] Ibid., 16 (Counts 9 and 10), read together with [106].

[217] Ibid., 17 (Count 11).

[218] Ibid.

[219] Ibid., 97 (emphasis added).

charge.[220] Mbarushimana was arrested in France in October 2010, and on 25 January 2011, he arrived in The Hague.[221]

In the DCC, the Prosecutor charged Mbarushimana with five crimes against humanity and eight war crimes.[222] As the Pre-Trial Chamber would later observe, the DCC did not clearly specify the facts relevant to each charge.[223] However, it is clear that at least seven charges in the DCC were based on evidence of sexual violence: rape as a war crime and crime against humanity, based on evidence that numerous women were raped or gang-raped;[224] torture as a war crime and crime against, based on those rapes, as well as evidence that victims had fetuses cut from their bodies or spears inserted into their vaginas and that family members were forced to watch these acts;[225] the war crime of mutilation, based on the evidence that three women were found with sticks in their vaginas and crushed skulls, and two men's genitals were cut off;[226] the war crime of attacking the civilian population, based on evidence of those mutilations as well as evidence that women were raped, held captive and beaten;[227] and the crime against humanity of persecution through rape, among other things.[228] This time, the persecution charge referred to 'political' grounds, but the OTP still argued that the crimes were gendered in their *effects*. As an OTP lawyer explained at the confirmation hearing:

> By committing rapes, sexual torture, and genital mutilations, the FDLR attacked and damaged the very identity of these victims and the role that they are assigned in their communities as men and women. Women whose foetuses were extracted from their womb were attacked in a way that can affect only women. They were deprived of being able to give birth and to be mothers. Women who were victims of rapes were humiliated and broken down as both women and spouses. Men who went through - who were castrated before the people, their families, were deprived of their masculinity, as it is defined socially, or else as they identify with it. The effect of this is to vilify them before their families.[229]

220 ICC-01/04-01/10-2-tENG, 28 September 2010. See also ICC-01/04-01/10-1, 28 September 2010.
221 ICC-01/04-01/10-465-Red, 16 December 2011, [15].
222 ICC-01/04-01/10-330-AnxA-Red, 3 August 2011.
223 ICC-01/04-01/10-465-Red, 16 December 2011, [110].
224 ICC-01/04-01/10-330-AnxA-Red, 3 August 2011, [74]–[83].
225 Ibid.
226 Ibid., [66]–[70], [80].
227 Ibid., [52], [56], [58], [59].
228 Ibid., [96], [101], [104].
229 ICC-01/04-01/10-T-7-Red-ENG, 19 September 2011, 17(10–23). See also: ICC-01/04-01/10-T-6-Red2-ENG, 16 September 2011(33), 8–12.

The Prosecution alleged that Mbarushimana was responsible for all of these crimes under Article 25(3)(d) because he contributed to the commission of crimes by a group acting with a 'common purpose'. That 'common purpose' was allegedly to direct attacks against the civilian population in order to create a 'humanitarian catastrophe' while also conducting an international media campaign aimed at concealing the FDLR's responsibility for the attacks and persuading the international community that the FDLR could not be defeated by military force.[230] As to Mbarushimana's contribution, the Prosecution alleged that he led this media campaign and thereby helped to communicate the FDLR's demands and to provide encouragement to its troops.[231]

The Defence challenged the contention that Mbarushimana's media activities contributed to the commission of any crimes. It argued that his press releases were not extortive, and there was 'no evidence' that FDLR soldiers read them, or that they would have been more likely to commit crimes if they did.[232] The Defence also challenged the Prosecution's reliance on hearsay evidence, arguing that such evidence is 'extremely weak'.[233] In response, the Prosecution noted that the ICC's legal framework does not prohibit the admission of hearsay evidence, and asserted that in previous cases, the Pre-Trial Chamber had given such evidence 'credence and weight' at the confirmation of charges stage.[234] The Prosecution did not mention that in each of the cases in support of that assertion, the Chamber had cautioned that although even anonymous hearsay evidence is admissible, it has low probative value and will generally not, on its own, satisfy the standard of proof at the confirmation stage.[235]

The Pre-Trial Chamber issued its confirmation decision on 16 December 2011. It began by noting that the DCC was 'articulated in such vague terms that the Chamber had serious difficulties in determining, or

[230] ICC-01/04-01/10-330-AnxA-Red, 3 August 2011, [110].

[231] Ibid., [115]–[122]. See also ICC-01/04-01/10-448-Red, 6 October 2011, [65]–[68].

[232] ICC-01/04-01/10-450, 21 October 2011, [29]–[32].

[233] ICC-01/04-01/10-T-7-Red-ENG, 19 September 2011, 82(4). See also ICC-01/04-01/10-T-8-Red-ENG, 20 September 2011, 39(19)–41(13), 44(2–8); ICC-01/04-01/10-T-9-ENG, 21 September 2011, 26(20)–27(2).

[234] ICC-01/04-01/10-448-Red, 6 October 2011, [107], citing ICC-01/04-01/06-803-tEN, 7 February 2007, [101]; ICC-01/05-01/08-424,15 June 2009, [47], [51]; ICC-01/04-01/07-717, 30 September 2008, [118], [137].

[235] ICC-01/04-01/06-803-tEN, 7 February 2007, [106]; ICC-01/05-01/08-424, 15 June 2009, [47] paired with [51]; ICC-01/04-01/07-717, 30 September 2008, [118]–[120], [137]–[141].

could not determine at all, the factual ambit of a number of the charges'.[236] The Majority then declined to confirm any of the charges, for three main reasons. First, several of the allegations were based solely on hearsay evidence. For instance, regarding the rapes in Manje, the only evidence was a statement that Human Rights Watch claimed to have taken from a victim,[237] and regarding the rapes in Mianga, the only evidence was a statement by a witness who claimed to have heard soldiers bragging about acts of sexual violence during a previous attack.[238] Second, the Majority was not persuaded that the FDLR pursued a 'policy' of attacking the civilian population, as required by the ICC's definition of crimes against humanity. Instead, it appeared that the FDLR's attacks were directed at military targets or at civilians who were perceived as supporting those targets, and that 'accordingly, such attacks cannot be considered to be part of any larger organised campaign specifically designed to be directed against the civilian population'.[239] Third, the OTP had not shown that Mbarushimana was responsible for any of the alleged crimes under Article 25(3)(d). Specifically, it had not shown that the FDLR constituted 'a group of persons acting with a common purpose', or that Mbarushimana had provided a 'significant contribution' to the commission of the crimes by members of the group.[240] In the Chamber's view, 'there is very little of an extortionate nature to be found in the press releases' and in any case, it was contradictory for the Prosecution to argue that the FDLR's media campaign was aimed at concealing the FDLR's involvement in the crimes *and* persuading Rwanda that the crimes would continue unless it agreed to the FDLR's demands.[241]

In a dissenting opinion, Judge Monageng agreed with the Majority's point about the lack of evidence for particular criminal acts.[242] However, based on the remaining criminal acts, her Honour found that there was sufficient evidence to charge Mbarushimana under Article 25(3)(d) on all counts except torture as a war crime, torture as a crime against humanity and persecution.[243]

[236] ICC-01/04-01/10-465-Red, 16 December 2011, [110].
[237] Ibid., [194], citing Human Rights Watch, '"You Will Be Punished": Attacks on Civilians in Eastern Congo' (December 2009).
[238] Ibid., [220]–[221].
[239] Ibid., [263]–[267].
[240] Ibid., [291]–[340].
[241] Ibid., [311].
[242] ICC-01/04-01/10-465-Red (Monageng), 16 December 2011, [27].
[243] For her Honour's findings on torture and persecution, see [29]–[37].

The Prosecution appealed the Majority's decision, but its appeal was unanimously dismissed.[244] The dismissal of all charges in this case significantly dragged down the OTP's early track record in establishing charges for gender-based crimes. If there is something positive to be said for the decision, it is that it clarified that a DCC can include charges based on facts that were not alleged in the arrest warrant request.[245] This enables the OTP to conduct investigations after obtaining an arrest warrant, which is particularly useful for sexual violence crimes, as victims often need more time before they are comfortable speaking to investigators about these crimes.

### 4.1.6 *Prosecutor v. Sylvestre Mudacumura*

Status at 17 July 2018: Arrest warrant issued; suspect not in ICC custody (Table 4.7).

#### 4.1.6.1 Key Points

Like the *Mbarushimana* case, this case focuses on crimes allegedly committed by the FDLR in North and South Kivu from January 2009–September 2010. Should the suspect appear before the ICC, that would provide an opportunity to prosecute many of the same crimes, including numerous gender-based crimes, that did not proceed to trial in the *Mbarushimana* case.

#### 4.1.6.2 Pre-Trial

On 15 May 2012, Prosecutor Moreno-Ocampo requested an arrest warrant in respect of Sylvestre Mudacumura, Supreme Commander of the FDLR.[246] The Pre-Trial Chamber rejected this application for lack of specificity.[247] The OTP then applied a second time, with Prosecutor Bensouda signing the application.[248] This second application alleged that Mudacumura and other FDLR leaders developed a plan to 'conduct a widespread and systematic attack against the civilian population of the Kivus and a simultaneous

[244] ICC-01/04-01/10-514, 30 May 2012. Judge Fernandez de Gurmendi also penned a separate opinion finding that the Pre-Trial Chamber erred in finding that to satisfy Article 25(3)(d), the persons' contribution to the crimes must have been 'significant'.

[245] ICC-01/04-01/10-465-Red, 16 December 2011, [86]–[92].

[246] ICC-01/04-612-Red-Corr, 15 May 2012.

[247] ICC-01/04-613, 31 May 2012.

[248] ICC-01/04-616-Red2, 4 July 2012; ICC-01/04-01/12-1-Red, 13 July 2012, 1.

Table 4.7 *Mudacumura* charges

| | | Established at ... | | |
|---|---|---|---|---|
| Crime | Article | Arrest Warrant Stage | Confirmation Stage | Trial |
| Crime against humanity: Murder | 7(1)(a) | ✗ | Pending | Pending |
| Crime against humanity: Rape | 7(1)(g)-1 | ✗* | Pending | Pending |
| Crime against humanity: Torture | 7(1)(f) | ✗* | Pending | Pending |
| Crime against humanity: Persecution (political grounds) | 7(1)(h) | ✗* | Pending | Pending |
| Crime against humanity: Other inhumane acts | 7(1)(k) | ✗ | Pending | Pending |
| War crime: Attacking civilian population | 8(2)(e)(i) | ✓ | Pending | Pending |
| War crime: Murder | 8(2)(c)(i)-1 | ✓ | Pending | Pending |
| War crime: Mutilation | 8(2)(c)(i)-2 | ✓* | Pending | Pending |
| War crime: Cruel treatment | 8(2)(c)(i)-3 | ✓ | Pending | Pending |
| War crime: Rape | 8(2)(e)(vi)-1 | ✓* | Pending | Pending |
| War crime: Torture | 8(2)(c)(i)-4 | ✓* | Pending | Pending |
| War crime: Destruction of property | 8(2)(e)(xii) | ✓ | Pending | Pending |
| War crime: Pillage | 8(2)(e)(v) | ✓ | Pending | Pending |
| War crime: Outrages on personal dignity | 8(2)(c)(ii) | ✓ | Pending | Pending |

*Denotes any gender-based crimes in the case.

international media campaign together designed to extort political concessions for the FDLR in Rwanda.'[249] It alleged that in connection to this plan, Mudacumura was responsible for five crimes against humanity and nine war crimes under Article 25(3)(a) (indirect co-perpetration),

[249] Ibid., [2].

25(3)(b) (ordering) and 28(a) (command responsibility).[250] The charges of rape, torture, persecution and mutilation were all based on evidence of sexual violence.[251]

The Pre-Trial Chamber issued the arrest warrant on 13 July 2012, finding that there were reasonable grounds to believe that Mudacumura was responsible under Article 25(3)(b) for the nine war crimes alleged by the Prosecutor, although there was insufficient evidence for particular indicants of murder and rape.[252] As in the *Mbarushimana* case, the Chamber found that the evidence did not satisfy the 'policy' requirement for crimes against humanity. Thus, no charges for crimes against humanity were included.[253]

## 4.2 Uganda

Uganda has been a State Party to the Rome Statute since 14 June 2002. In December 2003, it became the first State Party to make a 'self-referral' to the ICC. The referral asked the ICC Prosecutor to investigate the 'situation concerning the Lord's Resistance Army',[254] referring to the rebel group led by alleged spirit medium Joseph Kony, that had been trying to overthrow the Ugandan government since 1987 and was reportedly responsible for widespread crimes against civilian in Uganda, including murder, rape, torture and abducting hundreds of thousands of people for use as soldiers, domestic servants, 'wives' and sexual slaves.[255] On 29 January 2004, after conducting a preliminary examination, Prosecutor Moreno-Ocampo announced that he had decided to open an investigation into the situation in 'Northern Uganda'.[256] While this investigation was not limited to the Lord's Resistance Army (LRA), the Prosecutor

[250] Ibid., [31]. C.f. [24].

[251] Ibid., 20–21 (Counts 7–10), 22 (Count 13), see also ICC-01/04-01/12-1-Red, 13 July 2012, [42]–[43]. Due to redactions in the public version of the arrest warrant application and arrest warrant decision, it is not possible to determine if other charges also involved sexual and/or gender-based violence.

[252] ICC-01/04-01/12-1-Red, 13 July 2012, [41], [48].

[253] Ibid., [23]–[29].

[254] ICC, 'President of Uganda Refers Situation Concerning the Lord's Resistance Army (LRA) to the ICC' (29 January 2004).

[255] ICC-02/04-01/05-53, 27 September 2005, [5]; 'Report of the Secretary-General Pursuant to Resolutions 1653 (2006) and 1663 (2006), UN Doc. S/2006/478' (29 June 2006), [10]; Human Rights Watch, 'Stolen Children: Abduction and Recruitment in Northern Uganda' (March 2003), 5–18.

[256] ICC OTP, 'Prosecutor of the International Criminal Court Opens an Investigation into Northern [Sic] Uganda' (29 July 2004).

explained that he chose to 'start' with that group as its crimes appeared to be graver than those of the Ugandan army or other fighting groups.[257] As at 17 July 2018, all announced cases from the Uganda situation concern leaders of the LRA.[258]

### 4.2.1 *Prosecutor v. Joseph Kony & Vincent Otti*

Status at 17 July 2018: Arrest warrant issued; suspects not in ICC custody (Table 4.8).

#### 4.2.1.1 Key Points

This case was the first case to be brought before the ICC. It focuses on crimes allegedly committed by LRA fighters in Uganda since 1 July 2002. It initially included five suspects: Kony, who remains at large; Raska Lukwiya and Okot Odhiambo, whose deaths have been acknowledged by the ICC;[259] Vincent Otti, who is reportedly also dead;[260] and Dominic Ongwen, whose case was severed from Kony's in February 2015.[261] Of these five suspects, Kony and Otti were charged with rape and sexual slavery; the other arrest warrant requests did not include gender-based crimes.

#### 4.2.1.2 Pre-Trial

On 6 May 2005, Prosecutor Moreno-Ocampo requested arrest warrants for the five suspects, alleging:

> Since at least 1987 … the LRA has engaged in a cycle of violence and established a pattern of 'brutalization of civilians' by acts including murder, abduction, sexual enslavement, mutilation, as well as mass burnings of houses and looting of camp settlements; that abducted civilians, including children, are said to have been forcibly 'recruited' as fighters, porters and sex slaves to serve the LRA and to contribute to attacks against the Ugandan army and civilian communities.[262]

The Pre-Trial Chamber issued the warrants on 8 July 2005, finding that there were reasonable grounds to believe that Kony was responsible for

[257] S. Nouwen and W. Werner, 'Doing Justice to the Political: The International Criminal Court in Uganda and Sudan' (2010) 21(4) *European Journal of International Law* 941, 251.

[258] For a thoughtful analysis of the political implications of the Prosecutor's selection of cases in Uganda, see: Nouwen and Werner, 2010.

[259] ICC-02/04-01/05-248, 11 July 2007; ICC-02/04-01/05-431, 7 September 2015.

[260] ICC-02/04-01/15-T-26-ENG, 6 December 2016, 26(25)–27(1).

[261] ICC-02/04-01/05-424, 6 February 2015.

[262] ICC-02/04-01/05-53, 28 September 2005, [5].

Table 4.8 *Kony & Otti* charges

| | | Established at ... | | |
|---|---|---|---|---|
| Crime | Article | Arrest Warrant Stage | Confirmation Stage | Trial |
| Crime against humanity: Murder | 7(1)(a) | ✓ | Pending | Pending |
| Crime against humanity: Enslavement | 7(1)(c) | ✓ | Pending | Pending |
| Crime against humanity: Rape | 7(1)(g)-1 | ✓* | Pending | Pending |
| Crime against humanity: Sexual slavery | 7(1)(g)-2 | ✓* | Pending | Pending |
| Crime against humanity: Other inhumane acts | 7(1)(k) | ✓ | Pending | Pending |
| War crime: Murder | 8(2)(c)(i)-1 | ✓ | Pending | Pending |
| War crime: Cruel treatment | 8(2)(c)(i)-3 | ✓ | Pending | Pending |
| War crime: Attacking civilian population | 8(2)(e)(i) | ✓ | Pending | Pending |
| War crime: Pillage | 8(2)(e)(v) | ✓ | Pending | Pending |
| War crime: Rape | 8(2)(e)(vi)-1 | ✓* | Pending | Pending |
| War crime: Enlisting children into armed group | 8(2)(e)(vii)-1 | ✓ | Pending | Pending |

* Denotes any gender-based crimes in the case.

five crimes against humanity and six war crimes under Article 25(3)(b) (ordering),[263] and that his co-accused were responsible under the same provision for some of the same crimes.[264] Kony was also charged with rape under a different mode of liability, seemingly 'direct perpetratorship'

[263] Ibid., [42].

[264] ICC-02/04-01/05-54, 8 July 2005; ICC-02/04-01/05-55, 8 July 2005; ICC-02/04-01/05-56, 8 July 2005; ICC-02/04-01/05-57, 5 July 2005.

under Article 25(3)(a).[265] The case will not proceed to the confirmation stage unless Kony appears at the ICC[266] or the Pre-Trial Chamber schedules a confirmation hearing in his absence.[267]

### 4.2.2 *Prosecutor v. Dominic Ongwen*

Status at 17 July 2018: Trial underway (Table 4.9).

#### 4.2.2.1 Key Points

After an unpromising start, this case has become one of the most innovative case on gender-based crimes in the ICC to date. It focuses on attacks allegedly carried by the LRA on four internally displaced persons (IDP) camps in Uganda between July 2002 and December 2005 during an armed conflict between the Ugandan army and the LRA. The case includes numerous charges of sexual violence as well as *non-sexual* gender-based crimes, such as forcing abducted women and girls to cook and clean for the LRA. At the time of writing, the case is in trial. Regardless of the verdict, this case has already advanced the ICC's jurisprudence on forced pregnancy and 'forced marriage', and has demonstrated the utility of prior-recorded testimony and DNA evidence to the prosecution of gender-based crimes.

Throughout the case, both parties have acknowledged that LRA abductees were forced to commit heinous crimes, thereby fulfilling the roles as 'victim' and 'perpetrator' at once.[268] Such acknowledgment is rare in international trials: the format favours neat dichotomies, e.g. guilty or not guilty, victim or perpetrator.[269] The narratives presented in this case challenge such dichotomies, thereby shedding light on what Erin Baines

[265] ICC-02/04-01/05-53, 28 September 2005, [16], read together with Count 2 and the 'Case Information Sheet', which refers to Kony's responsibility under 'articles 25(3)(a) and 25(3)(b) of the Statute'. See ICC, 'The Prosecutor v. Joseph Kony and Vincent Otti (ICC-PIDS-CIS-UGA-001-006/18_Eng)' (April 2018): www.icc-cpi.int/CaseInformationSheets/KonyEtAlEng.pdf.

[266] RS, Art. 61(1).

[267] RS, Art. 61(2).

[268] E.g. ICC-02/04-01/15-533, 6 September 2016, [54] (see evidence of P-0200, P-0314, P-0340 and P-0351).

[269] M. Drumbl, 'Victims Who Victimise' (2016) 4(2) *London Review of International Law* 217, 218. For a similar critique, see M. Elander, 'The Victim's Address: Expressivism and the Victim at the Extraordinary Chambers in the Courts of Cambodia' (2013) 7 *International Journal of Transitional Justice* 95.

Table 4.9 *Ongwen* charges

| | | Established at ... | | |
|---|---|---|---|---|
| Crime | Article | Arrest Warrant Stage | Confirmation Stage | Trial |
| Crime against humanity: Murder | 7(1)(a) | ✓ | ✓ | Pending |
| Crime against humanity: Attempted murder | 7(1)(a) & 25(3)(f) | n/a | ✓ | Pending |
| Crime against humanity: Enslavement | 7(1)(c) | ✓ | ✓* | Pending |
| Crime against humanity: Torture | 7(1)(f) | n/a | ✓* | Pending |
| Crime against humanity: Rape | 7(1)(g)-1 | n/a | ✓* | Pending |
| Crime against humanity: Sexual slavery | 7(1)(g)-2 | n/a | ✓* | Pending |
| Crime against humanity: Forced pregnancy | 7(1)(g)-4 | n/a | ✓* | Pending |
| Crime against humanity: Persecution ('political') | 7(1)(h) | n/a | ✓* | Pending |
| Crime against humanity: Other inhumane acts | 7(1)(k) | ✓ | ✓* | Pending |
| War crime: Murder | 8(2)(c)(i)-1 | ✓ | ✓ | Pending |
| War crime: Attempted murder | 8(2)(c)(i)-1 & 25(3)(f) | n/a | ✓ | Pending |
| War crime: Cruel treatment | 8(2)(c)(i)-3 | ✓ | ✓* | Pending |
| War crime: Torture | 8(2)(c)(i)-4 | n/a | ✓* | Pending |
| War crime: Outrages on personal dignity | 8(2)(c)(ii) | n/a | ✓* | Pending |
| War crime: Attacking civilian population | 8(2)(e)(i) | ✓ | ✓* | Pending |
| War crime: Pillage | 8(2)(e)(v) | ✓ | ✓ | Pending |

| | | | | |
|---|---|---|---|---|
| War crime: Rape | 8(2)(e)(vi)-1 | n/a | ✓* | Pending |
| War crime: Sexual slavery | 8(2)(e)(vi)-2 | n/a | ✓* | Pending |
| War crime: Forced pregnancy | 8(2)(e)(vi)-4 | n/a | ✓* | Pending |
| War crime: Conscripting children into armed group | 8(2)(e)(vii)-1 | n/a | ✓ | Pending |
| War crime: Using children to participate actively in hostilities | 8(2)(e)(vii)-3 | n/a | ✓ | Pending |
| War crime: Destruction of property | 8(2)(e)(xii) | n/a | ✓ | Pending |

*Denotes any gender-based crimes in the case.

describes as 'a "space-in-between" victim and perpetrator'.[270] Ongwen's story is one example. He was allegedly abducted by the LRA when he was nine years old, and from that point on, was raised to believe in Kony's supernatural power and forced to perform 'unspeakable acts'.[271] He remained in the LRA for roughly 28 years until his surrender to US forces in the Central African Republic (CAR) in January 2015.

#### 4.2.2.2 Pre-Trial

Ongwen's arrest warrant, issued in July 2005, did not include any charges of gender-based crimes.[272] That changed soon after Ongwen appeared before the ICC in January 2015. His case was severed from the *Kony et al.* case in February 2015,[273] and the DCC was filed on 21 December 2015.[274] In the period between Ongwen's initial appearance and the filing of the

[270] E. Baines, *Buried in the Heart Women, Complex Victimhood and the War in Northern Uganda* (Cambridge University Press, 2017) 7.

[271] ICC-02/04-01/15-404-Red3, 25 May 2016, [45].

[272] ICC-02/04-01/05-57, 8 July 2005; ICC-02/04-01/15-5, 8 July 2005.

[273] ICC-02/04-01/05-424, 6 February 2015.

[274] ICC-02/04-01/15-375-AnxA-Red, 22 December 2015 (confidential version filed on 21 December 2015).

DCC, the OTP conducted further investigations in Uganda.[275] The result was a DCC that alleged 22 crimes split into 70 counts, for which Ongwen was charged under Articles 25(3)(a) (indirect co-perpetration and direct perpetration), 25(3)(b) (ordering), 25(3)(c) (aiding or abetting), 25(3)(d) (contributing to the commission of crimes by a group acting with a common purpose) and/or 28(a) (command responsibility). Sexual or gender-based violence was relevant to fourteen of the 22 crimes with which Ongwen was charged. For ease of analysis, these sexualised or gendered crimes can be arranged into three groups.

First, although there were no rape charges associated with the camp attacks, the attack on Odek camp allegedly included an incident in which a female LRA fighter sexually assaulted a civilian woman. That incident formed part of the *actus reus* for the charge of attacking the civilian population, amongst other crimes.[276] As the goal was seemingly to attack the camp's population irrespective of gender, some may consider this a 'sexual but not gender-based' crime. The second group covered the abuse of women and girls who were abducted by the LRA and used by various members of the group as sexual slaves, 'ting tings' (household servants) or 'wives' (the term used for women who were assigned to a specific soldier and made to work in his house, submit to his sexual demands, and refrain from having sex with anyone else).[277] The Prosecution charged the sexual abuse, forced labour and beatings allegedly suffered by these victims as torture, rape, sexual slavery and enslavement, and charged the imposition of the 'forced marriages' using the crime against humanity of 'other inhumane acts'.[278] The third group covered crimes allegedly committed against eight women who were assigned as 'wives' to Ongwen. The crimes in this group included everything in group two, as well as forced pregnancy.[279]

The OTP argued that all of the above gender-based crimes were committed for strategic purposes, rather than as purely opportunistic crimes. As explained by Senior Trial Lawyer Ben Gumpert at the confirmation hearing, the LRA sought to ensure its continued existence through two long-term plans:

> One plan was aimed at sustaining the fighting strength of the LRA. Young civilians were kidnapped and recruited to become child soldiers … There was a second plan also involving abduction but this time of girls and

[275] These further investigations are referenced in numerous documents, e.g. ICC-02/04-01/15-256-Red, 27 May 2016, [14] (confidential version filed on 26 June 2015).

[276] ICC-02/04-01/15-375-AnxC-Red, 15 February 2016 (confidential version filed on 21 December 2015), Counts 11, 16, 17, 18, 19 and 23 paired with [251].

[277] Ibid., [433]–[437].

[278] Ibid., Counts 61–68, [540]–[575].

[279] See ICC-02/04-01/15-533, 6 September 2016, Counts 50–60, [515]–[590].

> young women with the express aim of forcing them to act as wives of LRA commanders and fighters ... Many of them became pregnant without any choice in the matter, and some gave birth to numerous children who were themselves then ingested into the ranks of the LRA.[280]

There was some indication that the first plan, involving the recruitment of 'child soldiers', also involved gender-based crimes. For example, the DCC alleged that 'male abductees to be conscripted and used as soldiers and female abductees to serve primarily as domestic servants, sex slaves and forced exclusive conjugal partners'.[281] However, for the most part, the crimes of conscripting, enlisting or using 'child soldiers' were described in gender-neutral terms,[282] and at the confirmation hearing, Gumpert specifically noted that: '[i]t wasn't just young boys who were conscripted and used as child soldiers. One of the four individuals on whom the Prosecution rely [sic] to provide firsthand accounts of their experience as child soldiers was a girl aged about 10 when she was abducted on her way to school in June 2003'.[283] The charges of conscripting, enlisting or using 'child soldiers' are therefore not classified as gender-based crimes in this case, but the ambiguity is noted.

As noted previously, this case was the first in the ICC to use prior-recorded video testimony. The testimony was given by Ongwen's eight alleged 'wives' in closed session, with questions by both parties. Their testimony was recorded in accordance with Article 56, which allows the Pre-Trial Chamber to preserve evidence that may be unavailable at trial. The OTP requested this measure because there was a risk that, due to social pressures (including pressure from Ongwen himself, who had already called some of the women while he was in ICC detention), these witnesses would change their account or withdraw their testimony later on. The OTP also argued that taking these women's testimony at the pre-trial stage, with a view to playing the video at trial, would be better for their mental health than calling them back to the stand.[284]

[280] ICC-02/04-01/15-T-20-Red-ENG, 21 January 2016, 13(9)–14(16).

[281] For example, the DCC alleged that the LRA abducted civilians, with 'male abductees to be conscripted and used as soldiers and female abductees to serve primarily as domestic servants, sex slaves and forced exclusive conjugal partners'. ICC-02/04-01/15-375-AnxA-Red, 22 December 2015, [3] (confidential version filed on 21 December 2015). See also ICC-02/04-01/15-375-AnxC-Red, 15 February 2016 (confidential version filed on 21 December 2015), [617]; ICC-02/04-01/15-T-27-ENG, 7 December 2016, 36(9–13).

[282] ICC-02/04-01/15-375-AnxA-Red, 22 December 2015, [135]–[141].

[283] ICC-02/04-01/15-T-20-Red-ENG, 21 January 2016, 13(17–20).

[284] ICC-02/04-01/15-256-Red, 27 May 2016; ICC-02/04-01/15-310-Red, 27 May 2016.

On 23 March 2016, the Pre-Trial Chamber confirmed all 70 counts against Ongwen.[285] The Chamber found that all but one of the 'wives' gave credible evidence of being abducted by the LRA, being made Ongwen's 'wife' and sometimes also his 'ting ting', being deprived of their liberty, being forced into sexual intercourse with Ongwen, and becoming pregnant as a result.[286] The testimony of the remaining seven 'wives', together with other witness testimony and radio intercepts, played a central part in the Chamber's determination. The Pre-Trial Chamber rejected the Defence's legal challenges to the charges of forced pregnancy and 'forced marriage', as detailed in Chapter 5. It also rejected the Defence's claim that the case should be dismissed due to Ongwen's status as a former 'child soldier'[287] or because he had suffered 'duress' within the meaning of Article 31(1)(d) of the Rome Statute.[288] The Chamber rejected the first claim because it lacked any legal basis[289] and also dismissed the 'duress' claim because the defence had not shown that the threats Ongwen allegedly faced as an adult LRA soldier were sufficiently imminent or serious,[290] or that his conduct was proportionate to such threats,[291] and because in the Chamber's view, these threats could not be seen as beyond Ongwen's control, given that other LRA abductees had escaped.[292]

#### 4.2.2.3 Trial

In the lead-up to the trial, the Trial Chamber recognised as formally submitted the prior-recorded testimony from the seven 'wives' whose evidence had been deemed reliable by the Pre-Trial Chamber.[293] Also before trial, the Prosecutor filed a brief that summarised the charges and the evidence it would seek to rely on, including the testimony of those 'wives' and other witnesses, documentary evidence, and radio intercepts, along with DNA evidence which went towards showing that Ongwen fathered the children of several of his alleged 'wives'.[294]

[285] ICC-02/04-01/15-422-Red, 23 March 2016.
[286] Ibid., [104].
[287] ICC-02/04-01/15-404-Red3, 26 May 2016, [36]–[49].
[288] Ibid., [50]–[57].
[289] ICC-02/04-01/15-422-Red, 23 March 2016, [150].
[290] Ibid., [153].
[291] Ibid., [155].
[292] Ibid., [154].
[293] ICC-02/04-01/15-520, 10 August 2016.
[294] ICC-02/04-01/15-533, 6 September 2016, [604]–[605]. This evidence showed it is 99.99% more likely that there is a match between the DNA samples because Ongwen is the father than that the match is a random one.

The trial began on 6 December 2016. In the Prosecution's opening statements, gender-based crimes – and not only the sexual ones – were highlighted.[295] For instance, Gumpert stated that several of Ongwen's 'forced wives' were 'beaten, sometimes to a state of unconsciousness, by Ongwen personally or by his escorts on his orders. The reasons varied: failing to make his bed, giving food to other women while preparing a meal for him or even appearing to look dirty'.[296] Gumpert also drew attention to the evidence provided by Ongwen's 'wives', showing that in addition to being physically and sexually abused, these women were denied choice in relation to becoming mothers, doing household chores and remaining in the 'marriage' with Ongwen.[297] Both sets of victims' counsel also emphasised the prevalence of gender-based crimes in the LRA and explained the lasting physical, psychological, social and economic impact of these crimes.[298]

The prosecution called numerous witnesses of sexual violence, most of whom testified in private session.[299] An interesting witness was P-0045, a high-ranking female LRA fighter who participated in one of the attacks relevant to the case.[300] Her presence disrupted assumptions about soldiers as necessarily male, and her testimony offered a glimpse into the way that in the LRA, as in many cultures around the world, rape within marriage was seen as a contradiction in terms because once a woman is married, it is presumed that her husband can expect sex on demand.[301] For example, when asked about sexual relations between LRA fighters and their 'wives', she replied: 'We don't label that the same as rape because you have already been given to this man and then it's between you and that man that you have to make things work'.[302]

[295] ICC-02/04-01/15-T-26-ENG, 6 December 2016, 33(3)–35(21); ICC-02/04-01/15-T-27-ENG, 7 December 2016, 10(15)–35(23).

[296] ICC-02/04-01/15-T-26-ENG, 6 December 2016, 60(16–20).

[297] ICC-02/04-01/15-T-27-ENG, 7 December 2016, 15(21)–27(1).

[298] Ibid., 59(21)–60(22), 74(3–10).

[299] E.g. After Witness P-0448 gave evidence in private session, she was asked by the victims' counsel and the Presiding Judge about physical and mental harms of the rapes that she had apparently described. See ICC-02/04-01/15-T-156-Red-ENG, 21 February 2018, 36(9)–38(20); 41(6)–42(5).

[300] See ICC-02/04-01/15-375-AnxC-Red, 15 February 2016, [32].

[301] S. Mandal, 'The Impossibility of Marital Rape: Contestations Around Marriage, Sex, Violence and the Law in Contemporary India' (2014) 29(1) *Australian Feminist Studies* 255; T. Fus, 'Criminalizing Marital Rape' (2006) 39 *Vanderbilt Journal of Transnational Law* 481.

[302] ICC-02/04-01/15-T-105-Red2-ENG, 14 September 2017, 13(19–20).

In February 2018, the victims' counsel applied to present evidence prior to the start of the Defence's case.[303] Among other things, they asked to present testimony of three men who had allegedly sexually assaulted by the LRA and/or forced to desecrate dead bodies during one of the attacks relevant to the case.[304] The Defence objected to this request. It declared the evidence (which it had yet not heard) to be 'highly incredulous' because 'homosexual acts were not ordered, condoned or tolerated in the LRA'.[305] The Chamber rejected that argument[306] but nonetheless denied leave for the three men to testify on the basis that their evidence would go 'beyond the scope of the charges' in the case.[307] The victims' counsel urged the Chamber to reconsider its decision because 'the conscious *exclusion* of material about sexual violence against men has the consequence of entrenching the misconception that such violence did not happen'.[308] They explained that challenging this misconception was particularly important in Uganda, where the social stigmatisation of male victims of sexual violence, coupled with the country's anti-sodomy laws, mean that male victims very rarely speak out about their experiences of sexual violence.[309] The Trial Chamber was not persuaded. It affirmed its decision to exclude the evidence, with the result that the testimony of male sexual violence was not heard.[310]

The Prosecution closed its presentation of evidence on 13 April 2018, after presenting 69 witnesses over 142 days.[311] The victims' counsel then gave their evidence, including expert evidence from a professor of psychiatry who specialises in treating victims of sexual violence crimes,[312] and on 18 September 2018, the Defence began its case.

[303] The Rome Statute does not give victims a right to lead evidence, but several Trial Chambers have allowed victims to do so via Article 69(3), which provides that: 'the Court shall have the authority to request the submission of all evidence that it considers necessary for the determination of the truth'. See ICC-01/04-01/06-1432, 11 July 2008, [86]–[105].

[304] ICC-02/04-01/15-1166, 2 February 2018, [16]–[26].

[305] ICC-02/04-01/15-1182-Red, 22 February 2018, [38]–[39].

[306] ICC-02/04-01/15-1199-Red, 6 March 2018, [58].

[307] Ibid., [57].

[308] ICC-02/04-01/15-1203, 12 March 2018, [33] (emphasis original).

[309] Ibid., [29]–[31].

[310] ICC-02/04-01/15-1210, 26 March 2018. For a critique of this decision, see J. O'Donohue, R. Grey and L. Krasny, 'Evidence of Sexual Violence against Men and Boys Rejected in the Ongwen Case' on *Human Rights in International Justice* (10 April 2018).

[311] ICC-02/04-01/15-1225, 13 April 2018; T. Maliti, 'The Ongwen Trial: The Prosecution's Case in Numbers' on *International Justice Monitor* (6 June 2018).

[312] ICC-02/04-01/15-T-175-Red-ENG, 14 May 2018, from 13(12).

## 4.3 Sudan

Since at least August 2002, there has been a non-international armed conflict in Darfur, Sudan, between the government and affiliated groups against various rebel groups.[313] On 25 January 2005, a UN Commission of Inquiry reported that the Sudanese government and janjaweed militia were responsible for 'indiscriminate attacks' in Darfur, targeting people from the Fur, Zaghawa and Masalit groups, and subjecting them to 'killing of civilians, torture, enforced disappearances, destruction of villages, rape and other forms of sexual violence, pillaging and forced displacement'.[314] The Commission also reported that rebel forces may have committed war crimes in Darfur, although it did not find a 'widespread or systematic pattern' to these rebel-authored crimes.[315] On 31 March 2005, the UN Security Council referred the situation in Darfur since 1 July 2002 to the ICC Prosecutor.[316] The Prosecutor opened an investigation on 6 June 2005[317] and subsequently initiated cases against individuals on both sides of the conflict, including, in 2009, President Omar Al-Bashir.

In this situation, obtaining custody of the suspect has been extremely difficult. As noted by the Prosecutor in her June 2018 report to the Security Council, 'all the suspects in the Darfur situation remain at large'.[318] This is due largely to inaction by states with a legal duty to cooperate with the ICC, including Sudan, which has not transferred the suspects to the Court[319] and several ICC States Parties, which have declined to arrest the suspects when on their territory,[320] and by two

[313] ICC-02/05-02/09-91-Red, 24 September 2009, 6, [7]; ICC-02/05-02/09-243-Red, 8 February 2010, [17]. Elsewhere, the conflict is said to have started in March 2003. E.g. ICC-02/05-157-AnxA, 14 July 2008, [9].

[314] 'Report of the International Commission of Inquiry on Darfur to the United Nations Secretary-General Pursuant to Security Council Resolution 1564 (2004) of 18 September 2004, UN Doc S/2005/60' (1 February 2005) 3.

[315] Ibid., 4.

[316] S/RES/1593 (2005), 31 March 2005.

[317] ICC OTP, 'The Prosecutor of the ICC Opens Investigation in Darfur' (6 June 2005).

[318] ICC OTP, 'Twenty-Seventh Report of the Prosecutor of the International Criminal Court to the United Nations Security Council Pursuant to UNSCR 1593 (2005)' (20 June 2018), [3].

[319] In its resolution referring the situation in Darfur to the ICC, the Security Council decided that the government of Sudan 'shall cooperate fully with and provide any necessary assistance to the Court and the Prosecutor'. Sudan is obliged to comply with that decision pursuant to UN Charter, Art. 25.

[320] These states include Malawi, Chad, Democratic Republic of Congo, Djibouti, Uganda, South Africa and Jordan. See: ICC-02/05-01/09-139-Corr, 13 December 2011; ICC-02/05-01/09-151, 26 March 2013; ICC-02/05-01/09-195, 9 April 2014; ICC-02/05-01/09-266, 11 July 2016; ICC-02/05-01/09-267, 11 July 2016; ICC-02/05-01/09-302, 6 July 2017; ICC-02/05-01/09-309, 11 December 2017 (appeal pending).

permanent members of the Security Council, namely Russia and China, which have hosted Al-Bashir since the ICC issued the warrants for his arrest.[321] The remaining ICC States Parties and members of the Security Council also bear some responsibility, for having not taken stronger measures against states who have been found to have breached their obligation to cooperation with the ICC.

### *4.3.1 Prosecutor v. Ahmad Muhammad Harun ('Ahmad Harun') & Ali Muhammad Ali Abd-Al-Rahman ('Ali Kushayb')*

Status at 17 July 2018: Arrest warrants issued; suspects not in ICC custody (Table 4.10).

#### 4.3.1.1 Key Points

This case focuses on crimes allegedly committed by the Sudanese armed forces and janjaweed militia against the civilian population in Darfur. The alleged crimes include sexual violence crimes against women and girls from the Fur ethnic group, as well as massacres of men from that group. On their face, these facts present an opportunity to recognise the intersection between persecution on ethnic and gender grounds. However, the OTP's filings do not make this intersection explicit; the focus is on the ethnic dimensions of the crimes.

#### 4.3.1.2 Pre-Trial

On 27 February 2007, Prosecutor Moreno-Ocampo requested an arrest warrant or summons for Ahmad Harun, Minister of State for the Interior at the time of the alleged crimes, and Ali Kushayb, a tribal leader and member of the Sudanese army.[322] The Prosecutor alleged that from August 2003–March 2004, the army and janjaweed carried out indiscriminate attacks in Darfur, targeting civilians as well as rebels from the Fur, Masalit and Zaghawa groups. The charges covered thirteen crimes, split into 51 counts. The suspects were charged with contributing to these crimes under Article 25(3)(d).[323] Specifically, the OTP alleged that Ahmad Harun recruited, armed and funded the janjaweed and incited them to

[321] ICC OTP, 'Twenty-Sixth Report of the Prosecutor of the International Criminal Court to the UN Security Council Pursuant to UNSCR 1593 (2005)' (17 December 2017), [28]; BBC News, 'China Defends Visit by Sudan President Omar Al-Bashir' (21 June 2011).

[322] ICC-02/05-56, 25 February 2007, [29]–[37].

[323] Ibid., Part II.

Table 4.10 *Ahmad Harun & Ali Kushayb* charges

| | | Established at … | | |
|---|---|---|---|---|
| Crime | Article | Arrest Warrant Stage | Confirmation Stage | Trial |
| Crime against humanity: Murder | 7(1)(a) | ✓* | Pending | Pending |
| Crime against humanity: Forcible transfer | 7(1)(d) | ✓ | Pending | Pending |
| Crime against humanity: Deprivation of Liberty | 7(1)(e) | ✓* | Pending | Pending |
| Crime against humanity: Torture | 7(1)(f) | ✓* | Pending | Pending |
| Crime against humanity: Rape | 7(1)(g)-1 | ✓* | Pending | Pending |
| Crime against humanity: Persecution ('ethnic') | 7(1)(h) | ✓* | Pending | Pending |
| Crime against humanity: Other inhumane acts | 7(1)(k) | ✓ | Pending | Pending |
| War crime: Murder | 8(2)(c)(i)-1 | ✓* | Pending | Pending |
| War crime: Outrages on personal dignity | 8(2)(c)(ii) | ✓* | Pending | Pending |
| War crime: Pillage | 8(2)(c)(v) | ✓ | Pending | Pending |
| War crime: Attacking civilian population | 8(2)(e)(i) | ✓* | Pending | Pending |
| War crime: Rape | 8(2)(e)(vi)-1 | ✓* | Pending | Pending |
| War crime: Destruction of property | 8(2)(e)(xii) | ✓ | Pending | Pending |

*Denotes any gender-based crimes in the case.

carry out indiscriminate attacks,[324] while Ali Kushayb directed and participated in several of the relevant attacks and also mobilised, recruited, armed and provided supplies to the militia that he led.[325] Ahmad Harun was also charged under Article 25(3)(b) for inducing the war crime of pillage;[326] and Ali Kushayb was charged under Article 25(3)(a) for directly co-perpetrating the crimes of murder, attacks against the civilian population and outrages on personal dignity.[327]

Five of the crimes charged were based on evidence of sexual violence: rape as a crime against humanity,[328] rape as a war crime,[329] outrages on personal dignity,[330] attacking the civilian population[331] and persecution.[332] The latter charge referred to the persecution 'of the primarily Fur population',[333] which the OTP would later describe as an 'ethnic' group (see *Al Bashir* case). The OTP did not refer to intersecting gender and ethnic persecution, although the alleged facts seem to support that claim. For example, the victims of rape were all identified as women and girls from primarily Fur towns,[334] and several counts related to the alleged massacre, detention and assault of Fur men, which are charged as murder, attacks against the civilian population, torture, deprivation of liberty and persecution.[335]

The Pre-Trial Chamber issued the arrest warrants on 27 April 2007, finding there were reasonable grounds to believe the suspects committed the crimes charged.[336] In May 2010, the Pre-Trial Chamber informed the Security Council of Sudan's failure to comply with its legal duty to arrest them and surrender them to the ICC.[337] The suspects remain at large.

### 4.3.2 *Prosecutor v. Omar Hassan Ahmad Al-Bashir*

Status at 17 July 2018: Arrest warrant issued; suspect not in ICC custody (Table 4.11).

[324] Ibid., [119]–[142], [177].
[325] Ibid., [161]–[164], [177].
[326] Ibid., [181] and Count 37.
[327] Ibid., [180] and Counts 7, 16, 25, 27, 29, 31, 33, 45, and 47.
[328] Ibid., Counts 13, 42.
[329] Ibid., Counts 14, 43.
[330] Ibid., Counts 46, 47.
[331] Ibid., Counts 15, 16, 32, 33, 44, 45 and [210]–[212], [219], [242], [244]–[247].
[332] Ibid., Counts 10, 39.
[333] Ibid., Counts 1, 10, 21 and 39.
[334] Ibid., Counts 13, 14, 42, 43, 46, 47 and [210]–[212], [219], [242], [244]–[247].
[335] E.g. Ibid., Counts 21–35 paired with [223]–[230].
[336] ICC-02/05-01/07-2, 27 April 2007; ICC-02/05-01/07-3, 27 April 2007.
[337] ICC-02/05-01/07-57, 25 May 2010.

Table 4.11 *Al-Bashir* charges

| Crime | Article | Established at ... Arrest Warrant Stage | Confirmation Stage | Trial |
|---|---|---|---|---|
| Genocide: Killing | 6(a) | ✓ | Pending | Pending |
| Genocide: Causing serious bodily or mental harm | 6(b) | ✓* | Pending | Pending |
| Genocide: Inflicting destructive conditions | 6(c) | ✓ | Pending | Pending |
| Crime against humanity: Murder | 7(1)(a) | ✓* | Pending | Pending |
| Crime against humanity: Extermination | 7(1)(b) | ✓* | Pending | Pending |
| Crime against humanity: Forcible transfer | 7(1)(d) | ✓ | Pending | Pending |
| Crime against humanity: Torture | 7(1)(f) | ✓* | Pending | Pending |
| Crime against humanity: Rape | 7(1)(g)-1 | ✓* | Pending | Pending |
| War crime: Attacking civilian population | 8(2)(e)(i) | ✓* | Pending | Pending |
| War crime: Pillage | 8(2)(e)(v) | ✓ | Pending | Pending |

* Denotes any gender-based crimes in the case.

#### 4.3.2.1 Key Points

The *Al-Bashir* case exemplifies the difficulties that the ICC Prosecutor may face when seeking to prosecute leaders who are still in power. As President of Sudan, Al-Bashir has the means to commit serious crimes, including gender-based crimes, on a massive scale. Yet his position as president also makes it extremely difficult to ensure his arrest and surrender to the ICC. As a result, Al-Bashir continues to enjoy impunity for his alleged crimes in Darfur.

#### 4.3.2.2 Pre-Trial

On 14 July 2008, Prosecutor Moreno-Ocampo requested an arrest warrant for Al-Bashir, alleging that he was responsible as indirect perpetrator or indirect co-perpetrator under Article 25(3)(a) for war crimes, crimes against humanity and genocide. The Prosecutor alleged that from March 2003–July 2008, Al-Bashir had committed the crimes through the army and through janjaweed militia under his control.[338] There were numerous allegations of sexual violence, which the OTP cited as evidence for four charges: genocide through causing serious bodily or mental harm,[339] the crime against humanity of extermination,[340] the crime against humanity of rape[341] and the war crime of attacking the civilian population.[342] The victims of these sexual violence crimes were almost exclusively women and girls, 'thousands' of whom were allegedly subjected to gang-rape, rape at gunpoint, rape with forced nudity, rape while physically restrained and/or rape in front of family members.[343] The charge of genocide through causing serious bodily or mental harm also referred to an incident in which seven men from a primarily Fur camp were stripped naked and flogged.[344] There were also several examples of *non-sexual* gender-based crimes. For example, the charge of murder referred, *inter alia*, to a killing in which all 73 victims were men,[345] and the charge of torture referred, *inter alia*, to two incidents in which the victims were all men.[346]

The Pre-Trial Chamber issued the arrest warrant on 4 March 2009, finding there were reasonable grounds to believe that Al-Bashir was responsible for the alleged war crimes and crimes against humanity as indirect perpetrator or indirect co-perpetrator under Article 25(3)(a). In relation to the charge of genocide, all three judges accepted the Prosecution's argument that the Fur, Masalit and Zaghawa groups constituted 'ethnic' groups for the purposes of the 1948 Genocide Convention.[347] However, the Majority did not accept that the 'only reasonable conclusion' to be drawn from the evidence was that Al-Bashir intended to *destroy* these

[338] ICC-02/05-157-AnxA, 14 July 2008.
[339] Ibid., 22 (Count 2); [121]–[145].
[340] Ibid., 21–22 (Count 5); [235].
[341] Ibid., 22 (Count 8); [218]–[219], [232(b)].
[342] Ibid., 22–23 (Count 9), [16], [243].
[343] Ibid., [16]. See also [24], [121]–[145], [213], [218]–[219], [232(b)].
[344] Ibid., [150].
[345] Ibid., [216].
[346] Ibid., [220], [232(c)]. Note: in one of these incidents, a victim was allegedly restrained with 'a stove left burning between his legs'. This could arguably constitute sexual violence.
[347] The majority regarded the Fur, Masalit and Zaghawa people as three ethnic groups, each with its own language, customs and links to the land. However, Judge Ušacka characterised these groups as one ethnic group, which she described as 'African tribes'. ICC-02/05-01/09-3, 4 March 2009, [137]. C.f. ICC-02/05-01/09-3 (Ušacka), 4 March 2009, [26]. For the Prosecution's view, see ICC-02/05-157-AnxA, 14 July 2008, [77]–[88].

groups, and therefore, did not include the genocide charge on the warrant.[348] The Prosecutor appealed, arguing that the Majority had applied the wrong standard of proof in assessing the genocidal intent.[349] The Appeals Chamber agreed, and directed the Pre-Trial Chamber to determine whether there were 'reasonable grounds to believe' that the suspect was responsible for genocide.[350] After applying that standard, the Pre-Trial Chamber issued a second arrest warrant which included the genocide charge on 12 July 2010.[351]

### 4.3.3 *Prosecutor v. Bahar Idriss Abu Garda*

Status at 17 July 2018: Charges not confirmed (Table 4.12).

#### 4.3.3.1 Key Points

This case concerns a 2007 attack on an African Union peacekeeping base in Darfur by roughly 1,000 soldiers who had splintered off from certain armed groups at war with the Sudanese government.[352] These soldiers allegedly killed twelve peacekeepers, injured eight and stole vehicles and supplies.[353] There is no indication that this attack involved gender-based crimes: the African Union's report on the incident says nothing to that effect,[354] nor did the victims' counsel in this case.[355]

#### 4.3.3.2 Pre-Trial

On 20 November 2008, Prosecutor Moreno-Ocampo requested an arrest warrant or summons for Abu Garda, one of the alleged commanders of the attacking force.[356] The Prosecutor alleged that Abu Garda was responsible as direct or indirect co-perpetrator under Article 25(3)(a) for war crimes committed during the attack on the base.[357] The Pre-Trial Chamber issued

[348] ICC-02/05-01/09-3, 4 March 2009, [205]. C.f. ICC-02/05-01/09-3 (Ušacka), 4 March 2009, [86].
[349] ICC-02/05-01/09-25, 6 July 2009.
[350] ICC-02/05-01/09-73, 3 February 2010.
[351] ICC-02/05-01/09-95, 12 July 2010.
[352] ICC-02/05-02/09-1, 7 May 2009, [12]; ICC-02/05-03/09-1-RSC, 27 August 2009, [7].
[353] ICC-02/05-02/09-1, 7 May 2009, [5].
[354] African Union, 'Investigation Report on the Attack on MGS Haskanita on 29/30 Sep 07 by Armed Faction to the Darfur Conflict' (9 October 2007).
[355] ICC-02/05-02/09-236, 23 November 2009.
[356] The request was later modified to seek a summons only. ICC-02/05-02/09-1, 7 May 2009, 3.
[357] Ibid., [2], [23]–[24].

Table 4.12 *Abu Garda* charges

| | | Established at … | | |
|---|---|---|---|---|
| Crime | Article | Arrest Warrant Stage | Confirmation Stage | Trial |
| War crime: Murder and attempted murder | 8(2)(c)(i)-1 | ✓ | ✗ | n/a |
| War crime: Attacking peacekeepers | 8(2)(e)(iii) | ✓ | ✗ | n/a |
| War crime: Pillage | 8(2)(e)(v) | ✓ | ✗ | n/a |

*Denotes any gender-based crimes in the case.

the summons on 7 May 2009, and the suspect appeared voluntarily before the Court on 18 May 2009. In the DCC, the Prosecutor alleged that Abu Garda was responsible as a direct or indirect co-perpetrator under 25(3)(a) for the crimes listed on his summons.[358] The Chamber declined to confirm the charges because there was insufficient evidence that Abu Garda was responsible under Article 25(3)(a).[359] Having made that finding, it did not determine whether the alleged crimes were actually committed.[360]

### 4.3.4 *Prosecutor v. Abdallah Banda Abakaer Nourain & Saleh Mohammed Jerbo Jamus*

Status at 17 July 2018: Charges confirmed (Table 4.13).

#### 4.3.4.1 Key Points

This case is based on the same incident as the *Abu Garda* case. As with that case, there are no charges of gender-based crimes and no indication that such charges could or should have been included.

#### 4.3.4.2 Pre-Trial

On 20 November 2008, Prosecutor Moreno-Ocampo requested an arrest warrant or summons for both suspects, who together with Abu Garda, had allegedly directed the attack on the peacekeeping base.[361] The charges

[358] ICC-02/05-02/09-91-Red, 24 September 2009, [117].
[359] ICC-02/05-02/09-243-Red, 8 February 2010, [233].
[360] Ibid., [234]–[235].
[361] The request was later modified to seek a summons only. See ICC-02/05-03/09-1-RSC, 27 August 2009, 3.

Table 4.13 *Banda & Jerbo* charges

| Crime | Article | Established at ... Arrest Warrant Stage | Confirmation Stage | Trial |
|---|---|---|---|---|
| War crime: Murder and attempted murder | 8(2)(c)(i)-1 | ✓ | ✓ | Pending |
| War crime: Attacking peacekeepers | 8(2)(e)(iii) | ✓ | ✓ | Pending |
| War crime: Pillage | 8(2)(e)(v) | ✓ | ✓ | Pending |

* Denotes any gender-based crimes in the case.

and modes of liability were the same as the *Abu Garda* case.[362] The Pre-Trial Chamber issued a summons for both suspects on 27 August 2009, and they both appeared voluntarily before the ICC on 17 June 2010. The same charges were alleged in the DCC, filed on 19 October 2010.[363] The Chamber confirmed the charges, finding there were substantial grounds to believe that Banda and Jerbo were responsible as direct co-perpetrators under Article 25(3)(a).[364] Jerbo's case ceased on 4 October 2013 due to his death.[365] In September 2014, due to Sudan's failure to transfer Banda to The Hague, the Trial Chamber vacated the scheduled trial date and issued a warrant for his arrest.[366] Sudan has not executed that warrant despite its legal duty to do so. The Trial Chamber has notified the Security Council of that fact.[367]

### 4.3.5 *Prosecutor v. Abdel Raheem Muhammad Hussein*

Status at 17 July 2018: Arrest warrant issued; suspect not in ICC custody (Table 4.14).

#### 4.3.5.1 Key Points

This case concerns Sudan's Minister for National Defence since 2005, who is alleged to have committed numerous crimes, including gender-based crimes, in Darfur. Like the President of Sudan, who is also wanted

[362] Ibid., [16], [27].

[363] ICC-02/05-03/09-79-Red, 11 November 2010. (confidential version filed on 19 October 2010)

[364] ICC-02/05-03/09-121-Corr-Red, 7 March 2011.

[365] ICC-02/05-03/09-512-Red, 4 October 2013.

[366] ICC-02/05-03/09-606, 11 September 2014; ICC-02/05-03/09-632-Red, 3 March 2015.

[367] ICC-02/05-03/09-641, 19 November 2015.

Table 4.14 *Hussein* charges

| Crime | Article | Established at … Arrest Warrant Stage | Confirmation Stage | Trial |
|---|---|---|---|---|
| Crime against humanity: Murder | 7(1)(a) | ✓* | Pending | Pending |
| Crime against humanity: Forcible transfer | 7(1)(d) | ✓ | Pending | Pending |
| Crime against humanity: Deprivation of liberty | 7(1)(e) | ✓* | Pending | Pending |
| Crime against humanity: Torture | 7(1)(f) | ✓* | Pending | Pending |
| Crime against humanity: Rape | 7(1)(g)-1 | ✓* | Pending | Pending |
| Crime against humanity: Persecution ('ethnic') | 7(1)(h) | ✓* | Pending | Pending |
| Crime against humanity: Other inhumane acts | 7(1)(k) | ✓ | Pending | Pending |
| War crime: Murder | 8(2)(c)(i)-1 | ✓* | Pending | Pending |
| War crime: Outrages on personal dignity | 8(2)(c)(ii) | ✓* | Pending | Pending |
| War crime: Pillage | 8(2)(c)(v) | ✓ | Pending | Pending |
| War crime: Attacking civilian population | 8(2)(e)(i) | ✓* | Pending | Pending |
| War crime: Rape | 8(2)(e)(vi)-1 | ✓* | Pending | Pending |
| War crime: Destruction of property | 8(2)(e)(xii) | ✓ | Pending | Pending |

*Denotes any gender-based crimes in the case.

by the ICC, Hussein has thus far evaded arrest even when traveling to states which are legally obligated to cooperate with the ICC.

#### 4.3.5.2 Pre-Trial

On 2 December 2011, Prosecutor Moreno-Ocampo requested a warrant for the arrest of Hussein. The application alleged that as Minister of the Interior and the President's Special Representative in Darfur at the time of the alleged crimes, Hussein was responsible as direct or indirect co-perpetrator under Article 25(3)(a) for the same crimes charged in the *Ahmad Harun & Ali Kushayb* case.[368] The Pre-Trial Chamber issued the warrant on 1 March 2012, finding that there were reasonable grounds to believe that Hussein was responsible for all crimes as indirect co-perpetrator under Article 25(3)(a).[369] On 26 June 2015, the Chamber informed the Security Council of Sudan's failure to arrest Hussein and surrender him to the ICC.[370]

## 4.4 Central African Republic

There have been two ICC investigations in the Central African Republic: one concerning conflict in 2002–2003[371] and another concerning crimes allegedly committed after 1 August 2012.[372] As of the Rome Statute's twentieth anniversary (17 July 2018) no cases from that second investigation had been announced. However, the first investigation led to one case, *Bemba*.

The case focuses primarily on events in and around Bangui, the national capital, towards the end of Ange-Félix Patassé's presidency. After surviving two attempted coups in 2001, Patassé faced a third on 25 October 2002, this time by his former chief of staff François Bozizé.[373] This upset led to a non-international armed conflict, with the armed forces and aligned groups on one side and the rebels on the other.[374] Reports from that conflict pointed to a surge in sexual violence, with many of the alleged perpetrators belonging to the *Mouvement de Libération du Congo* (MLC), an armed group from the Democratic Republic of Congo that President Patassé had invited in to help suppress the rebels. Key reports included a February 2003 report by International Federation for Human Rights (in French, FIDH) in which 79 women and girls described being gang-raped and subjected to invasive body searches (including vaginal searches) by

[368] ICC-02/05-237-Red, 24 January 2012, [4], [11].
[369] ICC-02/05-01/12-2, 1 March 2012.
[370] ICC-02/05-01/12-33, 26 June 2015.
[371] ICC OTP, 'Prosecutor Opens Investigation in the Central African Republic' (22 May 2007).
[372] ICC OTP, 'Statement of the Prosecutor of the International Criminal Court, Fatou Bensouda, on Opening a Second Investigation in the Central African Republic' (24 September 2014).
[373] FIDH, 'Crimes de Guerre En République Centrafricaine: "Quand Les Éléphants Se Battent, c'est l'herbe Qui Souffre"' translated by Women's Initiatives for Gender Justice (FIDH, 2006) 6.
[374] See ICC-01/05-01/08-3343, 21 March 2016, [650]–[663].

MLC soldiers,[375] and a 2004 report by Amnesty International, which described alleged rapes by MLC soldiers and the rebels.[376]

By 15 March 2003, the MLC had withdrawn from the CAR and the rebels had taken hold of Bangui.[377] On 22 December 2004, President Bozizé (as he was then) referred the situation to the ICC. After conducting a preliminary examination, Prosecutor Moreno-Ocampo opened an investigation on 22 May 2007.[378] The following year, the Prosecutor sought an arrest warrant against the MLC's alleged President and Commander-in-Chief, Jean-Pierre Bemba Gombo ('Bemba'). In the years since, the OTP has not announced any other case in relation to the 2002–2003 CAR conflict. In addition to limiting the ICC's capacity to do justice for the victims in the CAR, this has raised questions about the OTP's approach to case selection.[379]

### 4.4.1 *Prosecutor v. Jean-Pierre Bemba Gombo*

Status as at 17 July 2018: Conviction overturned on appeal (Table 4.15).

#### 4.4.1.1 Key Points

This was the ICC's first case to include charges for the rape of male and female victims, and the first to consider the principle of 'command responsibility', as defined in Article 28 of the Rome Statute. In March 2016, Bemba was convicted under that mode of liability for acts of rape, murder and pillage committed by his troops in the CAR.[380] Together with some of his (then) Defence team, he was subsequently convicted for corruptly influencing witnesses in connection to the main case.[381] The conviction for 'witness tampering' was partly upheld,[382] but in June 2018, the conviction for rape, murder and pillage was overturned.[383] Thus concluded a saga of impunity for the crimes allegedly committed by Bemba's troops in the CAR: impunity in the MLC's disciplinary system, and ultimately, impunity in the ICC.

[375] FIDH, see n. 373, 26–29.

[376] Amnesty International, 'Central African Republic: Five Months of War Against Women' (10 November 2004).

[377] ICC-01/05-01/08-3343, 21 March 2016, [560]–[562].

[378] ICC OTP, 'Prosecutor Opens Investigation in the Central African Republic', see n. 371.

[379] E.g. Human Rights Watch, 'Unfinished Business: Closing Gaps in the Selection of ICC Cases' (September 2011) 31–33.

[380] ICC-01/05-01/08-3343, 21 March 2016.

[381] ICC-01/05-01/13-1989-Red, 19 October 2016.

[382] ICC-01/05-01/13-2275-Red, 8 March 2018.

[383] ICC-01/05-01/08-3636-Red, 8 June 2018. C.f. ICC-01/05-01/08-3636-Anx1-Red (Monageng and Hofmański), 8 June 2018.

Table 4.15 *Bemba* charges

| | | Established at … | | |
|---|---|---|---|---|
| Crime | Article | Arrest Warrant Stage | Confirmation Stage | Trial |
| Crime against humanity: Murder | 7(1)(a) | ✓ | ✓ | ✗ |
| Crime against humanity: Torture | 7(1)(f) | ✓* | ✗* | n/a |
| Crime against humanity: Rape | 7(1)(g)-1 | ✓* | ✓* | ✗* |
| Crime against humanity: Other sexual violence | 7(1)(g)-6 | ✗* | n/a | n/a |
| War crime: Murder | 8(2)(c)(i)-1 | ✓ | ✓ | ✗ |
| War crime: Torture | 8(2)(c)(i)-4 | ✓* | ✗* | n/a |
| War crime: Outrages on personal dignity | 8(2)(c)(ii) | ✓* | ✗* | n/a |
| War crime: Pillage | 8(2)(e)(v) | ✓ | ✓ | ✗ |
| War crime: Rape | 8(2)(e)(vi)-1 | ✓* | ✓* | ✗* |
| War crime: Other sexual violence | 8(2)(e)(vi)-6 | ✗* | n/a | n/a |

* Denotes any gender-based crimes in the case.

As the arguments on Article 28 proved to be the main issue on appeal, it is useful to briefly explain that provision here. Under Article 28, a commander is responsible for crimes committed by forces under his or her effective control if he or she had sufficient knowledge of the crimes[384] and yet 'failed to take all necessary and reasonable measures within his or her power to prevent or repress their commission or to submit the matter to the competent authorities for investigation and prosecution'. The phrase 'within his or her power' means that a commander is not required to do

[384] The Prosecutor must show that the commander 'either knew or, owing to the circumstances at the time, should have known that the forces were committing or about to commit such crimes'.

the impossible.[385] Indeed, a commander need not even do everything that *is* possible; it is enough to take 'all necessary *and reasonable* measures within his or her power', meaning that they must only clear a certain bar. It falls to the Chamber to decide how high that bar sits, provided it does not penalise the accused for failing to do something that was outside his or her power at the time. For the three judges on the Trial Chamber in this case, Bemba's actions fell short of the bar. While two of the appeal judges found the Trial Chamber's reasoning adequate, the other three did not. Hence, Bemba's conviction was overturned.

#### 4.4.1.2 Pre-Trial

In the arrest warrant application, filed on 9 May 2008, Prosecutor Moreno-Ocampo charged Bemba as direct co-perpetrator under Article 25(3)(a) for four crimes against humanity and six war crimes allegedly committed by MLC forces during the 2002–2003 mission in the CAR.[386] The Prosecutor alleged that Bemba was responsible for those crimes because he sent the troops into the CAR at the request of Patassé, with both men accepting that these crimes would occur as a 'normal outcome' of their plan.[387] Of the ten charges listed in the application, seven were gender-based crimes: rape as a crime against humanity and a war crime, 'other forms of sexual violence' as a crime against humanity and a war crime, torture as a crime against humanity and a war crime and the war crime of outrages on personal dignity, all committed 'through acts of rape or other forms of sexual violence'.[388] Regarding the gendered nature of these crimes, the application stated:

> These crimes occurred partly as a deliberate tactic to punish and humiliate civilians that were perceived to be sympathetic to Bozize's rebel troops. Women were raped on the pretence that they were rebel sympathisers. Men were also raped as a deliberate tactic to humiliate civilian men and demonstrate their powerlessness to protect their families.[389]

The Pre-Trial Chamber issued the arrest warrant on 23 May 2008.[390] The warrant included all charges except murder and 'sexual violence', because

[385] ICC-01/05-01/08-3636-Red, 8 June 2018, [167]–[169]; ICC-01/05-01/08-3636-Anx1-Red (Monageng and Hofmański), 8 June 2018, [50].

[386] ICC-01/05-01/08-26-Red, 9 May 2008.

[387] Ibid., [74].

[388] Ibid., Counts 1–7.

[389] Ibid., [50].

[390] ICC-01/05-01/08-1-tENG-Corr, 23 May 2008. See also ICC-01/05-01/08-14-tENG, 10 June 2008, [6]–[7].

the Chamber was awaiting further information on those crimes.[391] On 24 May 2003, Bemba was arrested in Belgium.[392]

Three days later, the OTP filed further information on the charges of murder and 'sexual violence'. The 'sexual violence' charges were based on three incidents: one in which several male MLC soldiers forced a civilian woman to undress; one in which a civilian man was forced to undress by several female MLC soldiers; and one in which another civilian man was forced to undress by a female MLC soldier, who also forced him to have sex with her (the Prosecution did not explain why that forced sex was charged as 'other forms of sexual violence' instead of rape).[393] After receiving that information, the Chamber issued a revised warrant, which it sent to Belgium along with a request to surrender Bemba to the ICC.[394] This revised warrant included charges of murder but did not include charges of 'sexual violence' because, in the Chamber's view, the incidents of forced nudity were captured by the charge of outrages on personal dignity[395] and were not sufficiently grave to justify a separate charge of 'other sexual violence' as a crime against humanity under Article 7(1)(g).[396] The Chamber said nothing in respect to the allegations of rape. The Prosecution did not seek leave to appeal.

In the DCC, filed in October 2008, the Prosecutor alleged that Bemba was responsible for three crimes against humanity and five war crimes as an indirect co-perpetrator under Article 25(3)(a).[397] Of the eight crimes listed in the DCC, five were gender-based crimes: rape as a crime against humanity and a war crime, torture 'through acts of rape or other forms of sexual violence' as a crime against humanity and a war crime and the war crime of outrages on personal dignity.[398] As detailed at the confirmation hearing and afterwards, in the Prosecution's In-Depth Analytical Chart, the charges of torture and outrages on personal dignity were based on evidence that rape victims were humiliated and degraded because they were raped by multiple perpetrators (sometimes sequentially, sometimes simultaneously), often at gunpoint, in public, and/or in a state of undress,

391 ICC-01/05-01/08-14-tENG, 10 June 2008, [5].

392 Ibid., [8].

393 ICC-01/05-01/08-29-Red, 27 May 2008, [6(c)(v)]. See also Amnesty International, 'Central African Republic: Five Months of War Against Women', see n. 376, 5–6, 9.

394 ICC-01/05-01/08-14-tENG, 10 June 2008, [10].

395 Ibid., [63].

396 Ibid., [39]–[40].

397 ICC-01/05-01/08-169-Anx3A, 17 October 2008, [57].

398 Ibid., Counts 1–5.

and that other victims, mainly family members, were forced to witness this sexual abuse.[399] The Prosecution argued that this sexual violence was committed for a prohibited purpose as required for the war crime of torture, namely, to punish the victims for supposedly supporting Bozizé's rebels.[400]

After reviewing the DCC, the Chamber asked the Prosecutor to consider amending the charge to include the mode of liability found in Article 28.[401] Four weeks later, the Prosecution filed a revised DCC which alleged that Bemba was responsible for the crimes 'primarily' as an indirect co-perpetrator under Article 25(3)(a) or Article 28(a) or (b).[402]

The Pre-Trial Chamber issued a unanimous decision on the charges on 15 June 2009.[403] It confirmed charges of two crimes against humanity (rape and murder) and three war crimes (rape, murder and pillage) on the grounds that Bemba *knew* that his troops were committing or were about to commit the crimes[404] and yet failed to take all necessary and reasonable measures within his power in accordance with Article 28.[405] However, the Chamber dismissed the charges of torture and outrages on personal dignity on the basis that the allegations of forced penetration were already charged as rape, and that the other allegations were not identified with sufficient precision in the amended DCC.[406] It also dismissed the charge of torture as a war crime on the basis that the Prosecution had not specified facts showing that the pain was inflicted for a prohibited purpose.[407]

The OTP sought leave to appeal the dismissal of the charges of torture and outrages on personal dignity, citing relevant parts of the DCC, amended DCC and In-Depth Analysis Chart that the Chamber had not acknowledged.[408] The OTP's arguments were supported by the victims' counsel[409] and by Women's Initiatives for Gender Justice, acting as

[399] ICC-01/05-01/08-T-11-ENG, 14 January 2009, 10(4)–14(13). See also excerpts from the In-Depth Analysis Chart cited in ICC-01/05-01/08-427, 22 June 2009, [34].

[400] ICC-01/05-01/08-427, 22 June 2009, [34]. For the war crime of torture, the Prosecutor must show that the perpetrator inflicted pain 'for such purposes as: obtaining information or a confession, punishment, intimidation or coercion or for any reason based on discrimination of any kind'. EoC, Art. 8(2)(a)(ii) and 8(2)(c)(i).

[401] ICC-01/05-01/08-388, 3 March 2009.

[402] ICC-01/05-01/08-395-Anx3, 30 March 2009, [57].

[403] ICC-01/05-01/08-424, 15 June 2009.

[404] Ibid., [478]–[489].

[405] Ibid., [490]–[501].

[406] Ibid., [199]–[209], [307]–[312].

[407] Ibid., [291]–[300].

[408] ICC-01/05-01/08-427, 22 June 2009, [29]–[45].

[409] ICC-01/05-01/08-428, 26 June 2009.

*amicus curiae*.[410] All of these submissions made the point that the rape charges captured only one aspect of the alleged conduct, and the OTP's in particular showed that the Chamber had not engaged with the evidence in depth. However, the Pre-Trial denied leave to appeal, with the result that the charges of torture and outrages of personal dignity were lost.[411] Thus, in a case that initially had seven charges of gender-based crimes, only two of those crimes (rape as a war crime and crime against humanity) went to trial.

#### 4.4.1.3 Trial

After a delay caused by errors in the second amended DCC,[412] the trial began on 22 November 2010. In its opening address, the OTP argued that Bemba was responsible under Article 28 for acts of rape, murder and pillage committed by his troops in the CAR because he 'had knowledge of the crimes', as well as 'the capacity to prevent, repress or punish', and yet 'he failed to do anything … not because of incapacity, but because he did not want to take serious actions'.[413] In particular, the OTP argued that Bemba's response to rape was demonstrably weak. In its words:

> After evidence was presented by nongovernmental organisations and the media, Bemba purported to convene an investigative commission in December 2002, which resulted in a court martial proceeding. But the commission's actions were irrelevant in relation to the crimes committed and their scale. Only a handful of persons were charged. No civilian victims in the Central African Republic were called as witnesses, and the offenders, convicted of petty theft, were not seriously punished. The trials were concluded in December 2002. *None of the soldiers was tried for rapes*.[414]

[410] ICC-01/05-01/08-466, 31 July 2009.
[411] ICC-01/05-01/08-532, 18 September 2009.
[412] The Trial Chamber requested a second amended DCC which would reflect the charges as confirmed by the Pre-Trial Chamber. The Prosecution complied, but its amendments were not entirely accurate: whereas the Pre-Trial Chamber had found that Bemba satisfied the Article 28 knowledge standard because he 'knew' that MLC soldiers were committing or were about to commit the relevant crimes, the second amended DCC alleged that he either 'knew or, owing to the circumstances at the time, should have known' of that fact. The Prosecution later rectified that discrepancy, following a motion by the Defence and an order from the Trial Chamber. See ICC-01/05-01/08-593-Anx-Red, 4 November 2009. C.f. ICC-01/05-01/08-950-Red-AnxA, 13 October 2010.
[413] ICC-01/05-01/08-T-32-ENG, 22 November 2010, 19(23)–20(16).
[414] Ibid., 21(23)–22(5) (emphasis added).

During his opening address, the Prosecutor argued that 'the massive rapes were not just sexually motivated; as *gender crimes*, they were crimes of domination and humiliation directed against women, but also directed against men with authority'.[415] This claim found support in the testimony of expert witness Dr André Tabo, head of psychiatry at the National Hospital in Bangui. Based on his studies and his clinic work, Dr Tabo stated that sexual violence in the CAR conflict was linked to the fact that women and girls were seen as 'war booty'.[416] He explained: 'women are thought of as the spoils of war and so women had become what you would call in psychology the object of sexual pleasure. And so a soldier bearing arms thinks that he can make use of this object as he wishes when he wishes'.[417] Dr Tabo also stated that civilians were raped as punishment if they were suspected to have supported the rebels, and to 'destabilise the enemy troops' by assaulting the people close to them.[418] In response to the Prosecution's questions about male rape victims in the CAR, Dr Tabo returned to gender norms, stating: 'raping a man in the time of a conflict is humiliating him … Humiliating a man also means that you have humiliated his family and the people close to him, so there's also that concept of punishment associated with the rape of men'.[419]

As the trial progressed, the Prosecution led extensive evidence of rape. Ten witnesses (eight women and two men) testified about being raped by MLC soldiers,[420] and several of those witnesses also gave evidence of the rape of family members.[421] A further three witnesses testified about seeing MLC soldiers raping civilian women,[422] and several gave hearsay evidence to that effect. The rapes that they described followed a similar

[415] Ibid., 10(14–16) (emphasis added).

[416] ICC-01/05-01/08-T-100-ENG, 13 April 2011, 4(19).

[417] Ibid., 8(16–19).

[418] Ibid., 4(23)–5(6).

[419] Ibid., 11(21)–12(1).

[420] These ten witnesses were P68 (female), P87 (female), P23 (male), P80 (female), P81 (female), P82 (female), P69 (male), P22 (female), P79 (female) and P29 (female). See transcripts cited in ICC-01/05-01/08-3343, 21 March 2016, [464], [472]–[473], [488]–[494], [498]–[501], [508], [510]–[513], [545].

[421] E.g. P68 testified about the rape of her sister-in-law; P23, P80, P81 and P82 (all related) testified about the rape of each other, and of some other family members; P69 testified about the rape of his wife; and P79 also testified about the rape of her daughter. Ibid., [464]–[466], [488]–[494], [498], [511].

[422] P1119 testified about the rape of two unknown girls, P47 testified about the rape of eight unknown women, and P75 testified about the rape of another woman. Ibid., [467], [481], [522].

pattern: most were gang-rapes, committed at gunpoint, in front family members and involving multiple forms of penetration (i.e. vaginal, oral and anal).[423] In addition to these OTP witnesses, a victim participant gave evidence of being raped by MLC soldiers: fourteen soldiers in all.[424] This pattern corresponded to the testimony of expert witness Dr Adeyinka Akinsulure-Smith, a psychologist with expertise in treating victims of sexual violence in the CAR.[425]

In closing statements, the Prosecution team reiterated the description of rape as a 'gender crime'.[426] The expressive potential of the case was highlighted by Senior Trial Lawyer Jean-Jacques Badibanga, who stated:

> This is a unique opportunity for you, your Honours, to send a message to tell the entire world that women, particularly women, cannot be considered to be spoils that soldiers are entitled to during an armed conflict. You can tell the world that these barbaric acts violating the intimacy of a person cannot be tolerated by humanity and must come to an end.[427]

On 21 March 2016, Bemba was unanimously convicted on all charges pursuant to Article 28(a). The conviction was based on three murders,[428] approximately 22 cases of pillage[429] and the rape of 28 people: 25 female prosecution witnesses, two male prosecution witness, and one female victim participant,[430] all of whom were raped by male MLC soldiers.[431]

In applying Article 28(a), the Chamber found that Bemba took *some* actions to prevent, repress or punish the crimes: he established a commission of inquiry ('the Mondonga Inquiry') which went to Bangui to investigate the allegations, leading to the prosecution of seven MLC soldiers for pillage in an MLC military court;[432] he created another commission of inquiry to investigate whether goods pillaged from the CAR were being sold in Zongo (the city in the Democratic Republic of Congo closest Bangui);[433] he visited the CAR to give his troops a speech about respecting

[423] E.g. P38: ICC-01/05-01/08-T-33-Red2-ENG, 23 November 2010, 55(16–25); ICC-01/05-01/08-T-34-Red2-ENG, 24 November 2010, 11(25)–12(5).
[424] VI: ICC-01/05-01/08-T-220-ENG, 1 May 2012, 30(1–7); 36(4–23).
[425] ICC-01/05-01/08-T-38-ENG, 29 November 2010, 23(12–17).
[426] ICC-01/05-01/08-T-364-Red-ENG, 12 November 2014, 21(22).
[427] Ibid., 8(16–22).
[428] ICC-01/05-01/08-3343, 21 March 2016, [624].
[429] Ibid., [640].
[430] Ibid., [633] and paragraphs cited therein.
[431] Ibid.
[432] Ibid., [582]–[589], [597].
[433] Ibid., [601]–[603].

the civilian population;[434] he met in person with President Patassé and the UN Special Representative in the CAR to discuss the alleged crimes;[435] he sent a letter to the Special Representative, which among other things, sought assistance in conducting an investigation into the allegations;[436] he also sent a letter to the head of FIDH, which offered to work with that NGO to establish 'the whole truth' of what happened in Bangui;[437] and finally, he sent MLC soldiers, officials and accompanying journalists to meet with local people and community leaders in Sibut, CAR, to hear their views on the MLC.[438] However, in the Chamber's view, these actions constituted 'a grossly inadequate response to the consistent information of widespread crimes'.[439] It also found that Bemba had failed to submit the matter to competent authorities, because he had not empowered MLC officials to fully investigate and prosecute the crimes and he made 'no effort' to refer the matter to the CAR authorities or cooperate with international efforts to investigate the crimes.[440]

The Chamber held that given his 'extensive material ability to prevent and repress the crimes', other measures that Bemba could have taken included: ensuring that his troops were properly trained in IHL, ensuring that they were properly supervised in the CAR, initiating 'genuine and full investigations' into the commission of crimes, properly prosecuting and punishing any soldiers suspected of committing crimes, giving his commanders in the CAR further orders to prevent the commission of crimes, altering troop deployment to minimise contact with civilians, removing soldiers who had been found to commit or condone crimes in the CAR, sharing information with the CAR authorities, supporting external efforts to investigate the crimes and withdrawing the MLC from the CAR sooner than March 2003.[441] In finding that those measures were within Bemba's power, the Chamber dismissed the Defence's arguments about the difficulties of conducting comprehensive investigations in the CAR during the conflict, difficulties that (so argued the Defence) also plagued the CAR and ICC investigators after the conflict and were heightened for

[434] Ibid., [594]–[596].
[435] Ibid., [590]–[593].
[436] Ibid., [604]–[606].
[437] Ibid., [607]–[611].
[438] Ibid., [612]–[620].
[439] Ibid., [727].
[440] Ibid., [733].
[441] Ibid., [729]–[730].

Bemba because he could not send investigators into the CAR without permission from that state.[442] In the Chamber's view, the evidence of Bemba's dependence on the CAR authorities was unreliable,[443] and the difficulties faced by investigators from the CAR and ICC were 'irrelevant' to the evaluation of Bemba's own response.[444]

The Chamber sentenced Bemba to eighteen years' imprisonment, deducting time spent in detention since his arrest on 24 May 2008.[445] When determining the sentence for rape, the Chamber acknowledged the serious physical damage to the victims, including infertility and HIV, as well as the psychological damage, and the rejection of several victims by their community as a result of being raped.[446] It also considered loss of 'virginity' as a relevant harm, stating 'some of the victims lost their virginity as a result of their rape, a harm that cannot be underestimated, particularly in the cultural context in which the crimes were committed'.[447] It also considered the nature of the rapes (e.g. that they were gang-rapes, committed in front of others, and involving multiple forms of penetration) as aggravating factors.[448]

In September 2016, the Defence filed its appeal against the conviction.[449] Meanwhile, the Trial Chamber moved ahead with the reparations proceedings, a decision that the Defence challenged several times, before requesting that all three trial judges be recused from the reparations proceedings on the grounds of apprehended bias.[450] The Defence would later withdraw that request after the conviction was overturned, rendering the reparations proceedings moot.[451]

#### 4.4.1.4 Appeal

On 8 June 2018, the Appeals Chamber issued its decision. It was a split decision, with three judges reversing the conviction and two upholding it. The decision sparked a wave of online commentaries, with much contention

[442] ICC-01/05-01/08-3121-Red, 22 April 2016, [919]–[935].
[443] ICC-01/05-01/08-3343, 21 March 2016, [448].
[444] Ibid., [732].
[445] ICC-01/05-01/08-3399, 21 June 2016, [96]–[97].
[446] Ibid., [38]–[40].
[447] Ibid., [38].
[448] Ibid., [44]–[47].
[449] ICC-01/05-01/08-3434-Red, 28 September 2018.
[450] ICC-01/05-01/08-3611-Red, 9 March 2018.
[451] ICC-01/05-01/08-3638, 11 June 2018.

over the standard of review applied.[452] Important though that concern is, the main point for this book is how the Chamber approached the issue of Bemba's liability under Article 28.[453] The Majority of the Appeals Chamber (Judges Van den Wyngaert, Eboe-Osuji and Morrison) found the Trial Chamber's findings on Article 28 errant in several respects. Errors included paying insufficient attention to the difficulties that Bemba, as a 'remote commander', faced in investigating the conduct of his troops in a foreign state,[454] and finding that Bemba had made 'no effort' to refer the matter to the CAR authorities, without acknowledging contrary evidence about a letter he supposedly sent to the CAR president.[455]

The Majority did not suggest that Bemba's measures were *actually* effective in preventing, repressing or ensuring accountability for the crimes. However, it found that 'measures taken by a commander cannot be faulted merely because of shortfalls in their execution'. In other words, if the measures initiated by Bemba did not accomplish much, it was not

[452] E.g. L. Sadat, 'Fiddling While Rome Burns? The Appeals Chamber's Curious Decision in Prosecutor v. Jean-Pierre Bemba Gombo' on *EJIL Talk!* (12 June 2018); D Amann, 'In Bemba and Beyond, Crimes Adjudged to Commit Themselves' on *EJIL Talk!* (13 June 2018); A Whiting, 'Appeals Judges Turn the ICC on Its Head with Bemba Decision' on *Just Security* (14 June 2018); S. SáCouto, 'The Impact of the Appeals Chamber Decision in Bemba: Impunity for Sexual and Gender-Based Crimes?' on *International Justice Monitor* (22 June 2018); Amnesty International, 'The Bemba Appeals Judgment Warrants Better Investigations and Fair Trials – Not Efforts to Discredit the Decision' on *Human Rights in International Justice* (19 June 2018); A. Heinze, 'Some Reflections on the Bemba Appeals Chamber Judgment' on *Opinio Juris* (18 June 2018); J. Trahan, 'Bemba Acquittal Rests on Erroneous Application of Appellate Review Standard' on *Opinio Juris* (25 June 2018); J. Powderly and N. Hayes, 'The Bemba Appeal: A Fragmented Appeals Chamber Destabilises the Law and Practice of the ICC' on *PhD Studies in Human Rights* (26 June 2018); ICC OTP, 'Statement of ICC Prosecutor, Fatou Bensouda, on the Recent Judgment of the ICC Appeals Chamber Acquitting Mr Jean-Pierre Bemba Gombo' (13 June 2018); ICC, 'Statement of the President of the Court in Relation to the Case of Mr Jean-Pierre Bemba Gombo' (14 June 2018).

[453] With thanks to Valerie Oosterveld, for observing that the standard of review applied by the Majority is linked to its subsequent findings on Article 28. The Majority showed less deference to the Trial Chamber's assessment of the evidence than is the general practice in international criminal law, including the evidence regarding Bemba's capacity to control the troops in the CAR and the measures that he took in response to the reported crimes.

[454] ICC-01/05-01/08-3636-Red, 8 June 2018, [171].

[455] Ibid., [174]–[175]. It is noted that no such letter was adduced into evidence. The evidence of its existence came from Defence witness D48, whose testimony the Trial Chamber deemed largely unreliable. See ICC-01/05-01/08-3343, 21 March 2016, [448]; ICC-01/05-01/08-3636-Anx1-Red (Monageng and Hofmański), 8 June 2018, [67]; ICC-01/05-01/08-T-267-Red2-ENG, 6 November 2012, 51(3–11); 55(1–10).

necessarily his fault; that would depend on whether he knew about the problems in execution, how serious those problems were and whether he had the capacity to remedy them – factors which the Trial Chamber did not consider in this case.[456]

The Majority also faulted the Trial Chamber for assuming that it would have been reasonable for Bemba to redeploy the MLC so as to avoid contact with the civilian population, a measure which, according to the Defence, Bemba 'heard about for the first time in his judgment'.[457] The Majority agreed that Bemba was not given a sufficient opportunity to challenge the claim that this measure would have been 'reasonable'. In its view, he lacked that opportunity even though the DCC alleged that he had the powers to redeploy his troops during the CAR mission, because that detail was not specified in the part of the DCC regarding the 'all necessary and reasonable measures' test.[458] From one angle, this reading of the DCC was overly 'compartmentalised'.[459] On the other hand, describing relevant measures in another part of the DCC may not be adequate notice because 'charges are not a loose collection of names, places and events that can be ordered and reordered at will'.[460]

Having determined that the Trial Chamber's findings on the 'failure to take all necessary and reasonable measures' test were 'tainted by serious errors',[461] the Majority had a choice: to acquit Bemba or to order a re-trial. Judge Eboe-Osuj initially favoured a re-trial.[462] However, for his two colleagues in the Majority, a re-trial was 'not an option' because:

> Mr Bemba, who now benefits from the presumption of innocence again, has already been in the Court's detention for over ten years. Ordering a retrial at this stage would inevitably prolong these proceedings by several more months, if not years. In light of the scope and nature of the charges, this would be excessive in our view. We are also concerned that ordering a retrial after such a long time would create a perverse incentive for the Trial Chamber to arrive at a conviction in order to 'justify' the extended detention. In addition, we would not find it fair to give the Prosecutor a 'second chance' to prosecute this case, given the serious problems we have detected in the Prosecution case.[463]

[456] ICC-01/05-01/08-3636-Red, 8 June 2018, [180]–[181].
[457] ICC-01/05-01/08-T-373-ENG, 10 January 2018, 59(9–10).
[458] ICC-01/05-01/08-3636-Red, 8 June 2018, [185]–[188]. See also ICC-01/05-01/08-950-Red-AnxA, 13 October 2010, [27], [68], [70].
[459] ICC-01/05-01/08-3636-Anx1-Red (Monageng and Hofmański), 8 June 2018, [96].
[460] ICC-01/05-01/08-T-373-ENG, 10 January 2018, 60(7–8).
[461] ICC-01/05-01/08-3636-Red, 8 June 2018, [166].
[462] ICC-01/05-01/08-3636-Anx2 (Van den Wyngaert and Morrison), 8 June 2018, [73]; ICC-01/05-01/08-3636-Anx3 (Eboe-Osuji), 14 June 2018, [22].
[463] ICC-01/05-01/08-3636-Anx2 (Van den Wyngaert and Morrison), 8 June 2018, [73].

In their dissenting opinion, Judges Monageng and Hofmański detected no error or unreasonableness in the trial judgment.[464] They rejected the Majority's 'uncritical acceptance' of the Defence's submission about the difficulties of conducting investigations in the CAR, noting that Bemba had not cited any investigation that he had *tried* to initiate, but was *unable* to initiate, in that country.[465] They also found that he had sufficient opportunity to challenge the conclusions about measures that he *could* have taken (including the measure of redeploying MLC troops), because these powers were listed in the final DCC, albeit in the section regarding effective control.[466] Unlike the Majority, the dissenting judges accepted the Trial Chamber's finding that Bemba bore some responsibility for the fact that his measures produced unsatisfactory results. They reasoned:

> If the results of measures taken are unsatisfactory and a commander *does not follow up* with other measures that are available in the circumstances, it cannot be said that he or she has discharged his or her duty to prevent, repress or punish crimes committed by his or her subordinates.[467]

The dissenting opinion validated the trial judgment and, by extension, the case of the OTP. However, it did not alter the outcomes of the case. These outcomes were, first, an acquittal for Bemba, who in August 2018 returned to the Democratic Republic of Congo. Second, a wrenching disappointment for the victims, who through their lawyers, expressed their 'deep disappointment and loss of confidence in justice'.[468] In particular, victims of sexual violence 'expressed their feeling of having suffered a triple punishment: from the crimes suffered in their own flesh; from the consequent sufferings and stigmatisation by their communities; and, finally, from the acquittal and the end of these proceedings, which were perceived as an insult to their sufferings'.[469] Third, a troubling precedent on Article 28. I say 'troubling' because this case sets such low expectations about what a so-called 'remote commander', armed with the knowledge that his or her troops are committing very serious crimes during a mission abroad, must do to avoid being held responsible under Article 28.

[464] ICC-01/05-01/08-3636-Anx1-Red (Monageng and Hofmański), 8 June 2018, [43].
[465] Ibid., [45]. See also [54]–[64].
[466] Ibid., [96]–[100]. See also ICC-01/05-01/08-3472-Corr-Red, 19 January 2017, [202].
[467] ICC-01/05-01/08-3636-Anx1-Red (Monageng and Hofmański), 8 June 2018, [80] (emphasis added).
[468] ICC-01/05-01/08-3649, 12 July 2018, [21].
[469] Ibid., [32].

As observed by Diane Marie Amann, the Prosecutor's Special Advisor on Children in and Affected by Armed Conflict:

> Command responsibility doctrine recognizes war's awful consequences, and so imposes extra duties of care upon officers who accept to lead others in the use of lethal, armed force … Evincing scant regard for the ethical roots of the doctrine that imposes extra duties of care upon military leaders, the [*Bemba*] appellate majority thus transformed command responsibility into an admonition with little effect, a legal burden too easily shirked.[470]

The rape charges in *Bemba* exemplify this concern of 'a legal burden too easily shirked'. Rape was a major focus, arguably *the* major focus, of the case. Bemba was convicted for the rape of 28 people, along with three murders and approximately 22 cases of pillage.[471] After the Appeals Chamber excluded from that list all acts not specified in the DCC and auxiliary filings at the pre-trial stage, the conviction still covered the rape of twenty people, along with one murder and five cases of pillaging.[472] Yet Bemba did almost nothing to address the crime of rape.[473] To explain, there is some evidence that rape was prohibited by the MLC's military code.[474] There is also some evidence that the troops were informed of this code and of relevant IHL standards, although the degree to which they were informed is a matter of dispute.[475]

However, the remaining measures were ill-equipped, if not totally incapable, of preventing, redressing or ensuring accountability for rape. The Zongo Commission was only mandated to investigate pillage and was (to quote the Defence) 'stuck in Congolese territory'.[476] There is a dispute as to whether the Mondonga Inquiry's mandate was also limited to pillage,[477] but in any case, the Trial Chamber found that this body did

[470] Amann, see n. 452.
[471] ICC-01/05-01/08-3343, 21 March 2016, [624], [633], [640].
[472] ICC-01/05-01/08-3636-Red, 8 June 2018, [119].
[473] Following the appeal judgment, a similar concern was raised in several commentaries, e.g. SáCouto, see n. 452; Powderly and Hayes, see n. 452.
[474] ICC-01/05-01/08-3343, 21 March 2016, [392].
[475] Ibid., [393], [736]. See also ICC-01/05-01/08-3121-Red, 22 April 2016, [944]–[955]; ICC-01/05-01/08-3434-Red, 28 September 2016, [396]–[398]; ICC-01/05-01/08-3472-Corr-Red, 19 January 2017, [265]–[269].
[476] ICC-01/05-01/08-3343, 21 March 2016, [722]; ICC-01/05-01/08-3636-Anx1-Red (Monageng and Hofmański), 8 June 2018, [103]; ICC-01/05-01/08-3121-Red, 22 April 2016, [713].
[477] ICC-01/05-01/08-3343, 21 March 2016, [726]. C.f. ICC-01/05-01/08-3434-Red, 28 September 2016, [374]–[375].

not follow up on reports of rape (a finding deemed reasonable by the dissenting appeal judges, given that 'there is no evidence that any action was taken [by the Mondonga Inquiry] in respect of allegations of rape').[478] The Sibut mission was conducted in public and in the presence of armed MLC soldiers,[479] which would not have encouraged disclosures of any rapes that MLC soldiers may have committed there.[480] Even in his speech in the CAR, in which he warned the assembled troops to respect the civilian population, it appears that Bemba did not expressly prohibit or refer to rape.[481]

It is a sobering thought that although Bemba was found to have known that his troops were committing rape,[482] and although his response to that crime was minimal, the result was an acquittal. It is possible that the acquittal was justified on the facts: without access to all of the evidence, it is not possible to form an independent view of reasonableness of Bemba's responses in light of the constraints he faced, and one must decide whether to place more trust in the findings of the Trial Chamber

[478] ICC-01/05-01/08-3343, 21 March 2016, [589], [720]; ICC-01/05-01/08-3636-Anx1-Red (Monageng and Hofmański), 8 June 2018, [102]; C.f. ICC-01/05-01/08-3121-Red, 22 April 2016, [1008].

[479] ICC-01/05-01/08-3343, 21 March 2016, [616].

[480] For allegations of rape by MLC soldiers in Sibut, see ICC-01/05-01/08-3343, 21 March 2016, [531]. Regarding good practice in investigating sexual violence crimes, see M. Jarvis and N. Nabti, 'Policies and Institutional Strategies for Successful Sexual Violence Prosecutions' in S. Brammertz and M. Jarvis (eds), *Prosecuting Conflict-related Sexual Violence at the ICTY* (Oxford University Press, 2016) 73; D. Luping, 'Investigation and Prosecution of Sexual and Gender-Based Crimes Before the International Criminal Court' (2009) 17(2) *American University Journal of Gender, Social Policy and the Law* 433; X. Agirre Aranburu, 'Sexual Violence beyond Reasonable Doubt: Using Pattern Evidence and Analysis for International Cases' (2000) 23(3) *Leiden Journal of International Law* 609; M. Marcus, 'Investigation of Crimes of Sexual and Gender-Based Violence under International Criminal Law' in A. de Brouwer et al. (eds), *Sexual Violence as an International Crime: Interdisciplinary Approaches* (Intersentia, 2013) 211; B. Nowrojee, *Shattered Lives: Sexual Violence During the Rwandan Genocide and Its Aftermath* (Human Rights Watch/FIDH, 1996) 25–26, 91–93.

[481] In the transcripts that are publicly available, none of the witnesses who reportedly attended Bemba's speech mentioned him telling the troops not to rape. Nor is such an instruction mentioned in the relevant parts of the judgment. See ICC-01/05-01/08-3343, 21 March 2016, [594]–[595], [721]; P-36: ICC-01/05-01/08-T-215-Red2-ENG, 15 March 2012, 20(17)–21(20), 66(17–21); P-42: ICC-01/05-01/08-T-65-Red2-ENG, 14 February 2011, 14(2)–15(8); D-51: ICC-01/05-01/08-T-261-ENG, 24 October 2012, 56(11–18); D-19: ICC-01/05-01/08-T-285-Red2-ENG, 26 February 2013, 5(20–25); ICC-01/05-01/08-T-293-Red2-ENG, 13 March 2013, 12(21–24).

[482] ICC-01/05-01/08-3343, 21 March 2016, [706]–[718]. This finding was not reversed on appeal.

or Appeals Chamber in this respect. What we do know is that, as a result of the final decision, 'remote commanders' with little interest or motivation in repressing rape may breathe a sigh of relief. When it comes to assessing 'all necessary and reasonable measures', the bar for preventing and responding to reports that one's troops have committed this crime – especially if those troops are part of a multilateral force operating abroad – has been set low.

A more granular analysis of command responsibility, in which the judges differentiated between the adequacy of measures taken in response to reports of pillage versus reports of rape (for example), may have produced a different result. It is also troubling that in this first case on Article 28, the Appeals Chamber did not decide what causal link is required between the commander's failure to take appropriate measures and the commission of the crimes.[483] It left this question unanswered at a time that two other trials (*Ntaganda and Ongwen*) include charges under Article 28, leaving a shadow of uncertainty over those cases.

## 4.5 Kenya

On 27 December 2007, Kenyans went to the polls to elect a new president. The election was contested by two major parties: the Party of National Unity (PNU) and the Orange Democratic Movement (ODM). Support for each party tended to correlate with ethnicity, with the PNU drawing votes mainly from the Kikuyu, Embu and Meru communities and backing a Kikuyu candidate, (then) sitting President Mwai Kibaki, and the ODM drawing votes mainly from the Luo, Luhya and Kalenjin communities and backing a Luo candidate, Raila Odinga.[484] According to Human Rights Watch, '[t]he election campaign itself was virulently divisive, with

[483] There is a debate as to whether the crimes must be 'the result of' the commander's failure to properly exercise control, and if so, what standard of causation applies. In *Bemba*, the majority of the Appeals Chamber left the standard of causation unresolved. See ICC-01/05-01/08-3636-Red, 8 June 2018, [30]–[32]. For a range of views, see: ICC-01/05-01/08-406, 20 April 2009, [30]–[47] (Amnesty International as *amicus curiae*); ICC-01/05-01/08-412, 27 April 2009; ICC- 01/05-01/08-424, 15 June 2009, [423]–[426]; ICC-01/05-01/08-3121-Red, 22 April 2016, [1049]–[1051]; ICC-01/05-01/08-3343-AnxI (Steiner), 21 March 2016, [4]–[9]; ICC-01/05- 01/08-3343-AnxII (Ozaki), 21 March 2016, [8]–[11]; ICC-01/05-01/08-3472-Corr-Red, 19 January 2017, [220]; ICC-01/05-01/08-3636-Anx1-Red (Monageng and Hofmański), 8 June 2018, [319]–[339]; ICC-01/05-01/08-3636-Anx3 (Eboe-Osuji), 14 June 2018, Part VII–IX.

[484] International Crisis Group, 'Kenya in Crisis: Africa Report No. 137' (21 February 2008) 1; Z. Nyambura, 'In Kenya, Politics Split on Ethnic Divide' (DW, 26 October 2017).

politicians on both sides characterizing their opponents in derogatory terms linked to their ethnicity'.[485] For example:

> The opposition [ODM] built a political coalition based on the widespread perception that the Kibaki government had entrenched tribalism and governed in the interests of the Kikuyu community. The PNU, on the other hand, made Luo cultural traditions a target, claiming that an uncircumcised man could not rule Kenya.[486]

The Kenyan Electoral Commission named Kibaki as the victor, but Odinga contested that result and made allegations of electoral fraud. In a context of long-running political violence, deep-seated grievances over land and power, and high youth unemployment, this dispute quickly erupted into violence, with ODM supporters attacking perceived PNU supporters and PNU supporters retaliating with force throughout February 2008.[487] These attacks reportedly left 1,133 people dead, 350,000 forcibly displaced, 3,561 injured and 117,700 properties destroyed.[488] Reports also point to an unspecified number of sexual violence crimes, including rape, gang-rape and mutilation of both men's and women's genitals.[489]

On 5 February 2008, while this crisis was unfolding, Prosecutor Moreno-Ocampo initiated a preliminary examination in Kenya using his powers under Article 15 of the Rome Statute. Meanwhile, an international mediation team led by former UN Secretary-General Kofi Annan endeavoured to broker a power-sharing agreement between Kibaki and Odinga, which by 28 February 2008, led to a pact that Kibaki would continue as president and Odinga would serve as prime minister. The pact also mandated the creation of several commissions to examine Kenya's

[485] Human Rights Watch, 'Ballots to Bullets: Organized Political Violence and Kenya's Crisis of Governance' (March 2008) 20.

[486] Ibid., 4.

[487] Ibid., 1–6; International Crisis Group, see n. 484, 6–8. For an examination of pre-existing grievances, see Commission of Inquiry into Post-Election Violence, 'Final Report' (16 October 2008): Chapter 2 http://reliefweb.int/sites/reliefweb.int/files/resources/15A00F569813F4D549257607001F459D-Full_Report.pdf.

[488] Commission of Inquiry into Post-Election Violence, see n. 487, 345–352.

[489] Ibid., 348 ('the sexual violence experienced took the form of gang and individual rapes, many of which were ethnically driven, as well as horrendous female and male genital mutilation. Women and children's labia and vaginas were cut using sharp objects and bottles were stuffed into them. Men and boys, in turn, had their penises cut off and were traumatically circumcised, in some cases using cut glass. Furthermore, entire families, including children often were forced to watch their parents, brothers and sisters being sexually violated'.)

electoral system, including a Commission of Inquiry on Post-Election Violence.[490] In its final report, the Commission recommended the creation of a special tribunal in Kenya to prosecute those most responsible for the post-election violence, or failing that, for the list of suspects to be sent to the ICC Prosecutor.[491] Kibaki and Odinga agreed to set up the special tribunal, but the Kenyan legislature declined to pass the required constitutional amendment.[492] Moreno-Ocampo then met with Kenya's government on 3 July 2009 to discuss the options for accountability. The government agreed that by the end of September 2009, it would either provide the Prosecutor with a report on the national accountability process or refer the situation to the ICC.[493]

On 26 November 2009, having concluded that the criteria for opening an investigation were satisfied and having not received a referral from Kenya, the Prosecutor requested judicial authorisation to open an investigation on his own motion. The Prosecutor's request alleged that during the post-election violence, supporters of both parties committed crimes against humanity within the jurisdiction of the ICC.[494] As to the organised nature of these crimes, it argued:

> While the violence initially appeared to be spontaneous, triggered by the perceived rigging of the elections, the organised aspect of the violence became apparent as it emerged that political leaders, businessmen and others had enlisted criminal elements and ordinary people to carry out attacks against specifically targeted groups.[495]

The Majority of the Pre-Trial Chamber authorised the investigation, although Judge Kaul dissented on the grounds that there was insufficient evidence of a 'State or organizational policy' behind the alleged attacks.[496] On 15 December 2010, the Prosecutor initiated two cases from the Kenya situation: one case against the leaders of the PNU and another case against the leaders of the ODM.[497] There were six suspects in all: the 'Ocampo six', to use a term popularised by the press.[498] With the support of the African Union, in March 2011, Kenya asked the UN Security Council to defer

[490] ICC-01/09-3, 26 November 2009, [6].
[491] Commission of Inquiry into Post-Election Violence, see n. 487, 472–473.
[492] ICC-01/09-3, 26 November 2009, [10]–[12].
[493] Ibid., [14].
[494] Ibid., [48], [74]–[75].
[495] Ibid., [63].
[496] ICC-01/09-19-Corr, 31 March 2010.
[497] ICC-01/09-31-Red, 15 December 2010; ICC-01/09-30-Red, 15 December 2010.
[498] E.g. Al Jazeera, 'ICC Judges Summon Ocampo Six' (9 March 2011); E. Kwamboka, 'Sigh of Relief for Ocampo Six' (The Standard, 11 May 2011).

the cases.[499] That same month, it argued before the ICC that the cases were inadmissible because recent constitutional and legislative reforms had 'opened the way for Kenya to conduct its own prosecutions in Kenya for the post-election violence in respect of persons at the highest levels of authority and for the most serious crimes'.[500] Neither of these efforts to stall or avoid further action by the ICC succeeded,[501] and in January 2012, charges against four of the 'Ocampo six' were confirmed.[502]

In March 2013, two of the suspects, Uhuru Kenyatta and William Ruto, were elected President and Vice President of Kenya. This did not render either man immune from prosecution in the ICC,[503] but it enabled both suspects to ask to be excused from continuous presence at trial in order to fulfill their official duties.[504] The Trial Chamber partially granted that request on certain conditions,[505] however, that decision was reversed on appeal.[506] With support from the African Union, Kenya again lobbied the Security Council to defer the proceedings, but once against its request was rejected.[507] Kenya then lobbied the Assembly of States Parties to amend the Rome Statute so that heads of state and their deputies would be exempt from prosecution while in office. The Assembly declined to adopt the statutory amendment proposed by Kenya, but agreed to amend the Rules of Procedure and Evidence to specify that persons who had been summoned to appear, and who were held 'extraordinary public duties at the highest national level', could be excused from attending certain parts of their trial.[508] In the face of Kenya's posture towards the ICC, and

[499] African Union (Assembly), 'Decision on the Implementation of the Decisions of the International Criminal Court, EX.CL/639(XVIII)' (30 January 2011), [6]; 'Letter Dated 23 March 2011 from the Permanent Representative of Kenya to the United Nations Addressed to the President of the Security Council Request of Kenya for Deferral under Article 16 of the Rome Statute of the International Criminal Court, UN Doc. S/2011/201' (29 March 2011).

[500] ICC-01/09-02/11-26, 31 March 2011, [5].

[501] ICC-01/09-02/11-274, 30 August 2011; ICC-01/09-01/11-307, 30 August 2011.

[502] ICC-01/09-02/11-382-Red, 23 January 2012; ICC-01/09-01/11-373, 23 January 2012.

[503] RS, Art. 27.

[504] ICC-01/09-01/11-685, 17 April 2013; ICC-01/09-02/11-809, 23 September 2013.

[505] ICC-01/09-01/11-777, 18 June 2013; ICC-01/09-02/11-830, 18 October 2013.

[506] ICC-01/09-01/11-1066, 25 October 2013; ICC-01/09-02/11-863, 26 November 2013.

[507] African Union (Assembly), 'Decision on Africa's Relationship with the International Criminal Court, Ext/Assembly/AU/Dec.1(Oct.2013)' (13 October 2013); UN Security Council, 'Press Release: Security Council Resolution Seeking Deferral of Kenyan Leaders' Trial Fails to Win Adoption' (15 November 2013).

[508] ICC RPE, Rule 134 *quarter*; Women's Initiatives for Gender Justice, 'Gender Report Card 2013' (March 2014) 31–34.

Table 4.16 *Muthaura et al.* charges

| | | Established at ... | | |
|---|---|---|---|---|
| Crime | Article | Arrest Warrant Stage | Confirmation Stage | Trial |
| Crime against humanity: Murder | 7(1)(a) | ✓ | ✓ | n/a |
| Crime against humanity: Rape | 7(1)(g)-1 | ✓* | ✓* | n/a |
| Crime against humanity: Other sexual violence | 7(1)(g)-6 | ✗* | ✗* | n/a |
| Crime against humanity: Forcible transfer | 7(1)(d) | ✓ | ✓ | n/a |
| Crime against humanity: Persecution ('political') | 7(1)(h) | ✓* | ✓* | n/a |
| Crime against humanity: Other inhumane acts | 7(1)(k) | ✓ | ✓ | n/a |

* Denotes any gender-based crimes in the case.

alleged offences against the administration of justice in relation to both Kenya cases,[509] the OTP could not obtain sufficient evidence to bring the cases to trial. Prosecutor Bensouda withdrew all remaining charges for that reason, as explained subsequently.

### 4.5.1 *Prosecutor v. Francis Kirimi Muthaura, Uhuru Muigai Kenyatta and Mohammed Hussein Ali*

Status at 17 July 2018: Charges against Ali not confirmed; charges against Muthaura & Kenyatta withdrawn (Table 4.16).

#### 4.5.1.1 Key Points

In this case, the Prosecution faced both legal and political challenges to prosecuting sexual and gender-based crimes. The legal challenges related to the Prosecution's attempt to charge acts of forced circumcision and genital mutilation as 'other forms of sexual violence', which sparked a

[509] ICC-01/09-01/13-1-Red2, 2 August 2013; ICC-01/09-01/15-1-Red, 10 March 2015.

debate between the Prosecution and Pre-Trial Chamber about what constitutes a 'sexual' act. This debate remains unresolved because the charges were withdrawn before a final judicial decision was made.

#### 4.5.1.2 Pre-Trial

On 15 December 2010, Prosecutor Moreno-Ocampo requested a summons in respect of Francis Muthaura and Uhuru Kenyatta, both prominent PNU politicians, and Mohammed Ali, the former police commissioner. The Prosecutor alleged that following the 2007 election result, the suspects, working together with a gang called the Mungiki, developed a plan to stage counter-attacks on perceived ODM supporters and to keep the PNU in power.[510] The plan allegedly resulted in the commission of six crimes against humanity for which the suspects were responsible under Articles 25(3)(a) (indirect co-perpetration) or 25(3)(d) (contributing to the commission of crimes by a group acting with a common purpose).[511] The persecution charge referred to acts of rape, among other things.[512] While the alleged mode of 'sexual violence' was redacted in the summons request, it was later revealed that the charge was based on evidence that PNU supporters of Kikuyu ethnicity had subjected perceived ODM supporters of Luo ethnicity to forced nudity and genital mutilation. For example, one witness alleged that her brother had died after his penis was 'cut and placed in his mouth',[513] and another witness alleged:

> The Kikuyu militias were forcibly circumcising Luo men … They grabbed one man, about 30 years old, and told him to remove his pants … they forcibly removed his pants. One person was holding his penis, and another one was cutting his foreskin with a piece of a broken Fanta bottle.[514]

The Pre-Trial Chamber issued a summons for all three suspects on 8 March 2011. The Majority of the Chamber, Judge Kaul dissenting, found that were reasonable grounds to believe that Muthaura and Kenyatta were responsible under Article 25(3)(a) for the crimes against humanity of murder, rape, forcible deportation or transfer, 'political' persecution and

[510] ICC-01/09-31-Red, 15 December 2010, [5]–[8].
[511] Ibid., [31]. C.f. Part F, which describes the suspects as 'co-perpetrators'.
[512] Ibid., Count 5.
[513] ICC-01/09-02/11-T-5-Red-ENG, 22 September 2011, 63(9–10).
[514] Ibid., 88(22)–89(5).

inhumane acts, and that Ali was responsible under Article 25(3)(d) for the same crimes.[515] The rape charge was narrower than requested because the OTP had brought allegations of rape in two locations, but had only provided evidence for one.[516] The Chamber excluded the charge of 'sexual violence' on the ground that 'the acts of forcible circumcision cannot be considered acts of a "sexual nature" … but are to be more properly qualified as "other inhumane acts"'.[517] The OTP sought leave to appeal that finding, but the Chamber refused leave, given that the Prosecutor could still bring the 'sexual violence' charge at the confirmation stage.[518]

In the DCC, the Prosecutor alleged that the suspects were responsible for the same six crimes against humanity listed previously because, together with other PNU supporters and the Mungiki, they 'agreed to pursue an organizational policy to keep the PNU in power through every means, including by orchestrating a police failure to prevent the commission of crimes'.[519] The OTP alleged that Muthaura and Kenyatta were responsible for these crimes as indirect co-perpetrators under Article 25(3)(a),[520] while Ali was responsible for contributing under Article 25(3)(d) because, as police commissioner, he ensured that the police did not prevent the attacks against perceived supporters of the ODM.[521] At the confirmation hearing, the Prosecution made further arguments as to why acts of genital mutilation constituted 'sexual violence', as detailed in Chapter 5.[522]

The Pre-Trial Chamber issued the confirmation decision on 23 January 2012. The Majority found that there were substantial grounds to believe that Muthaura and Kenyatta were responsible as indirect co-perpetrators under Article 25(3)(a) for the crimes against humanity of murder, rape, forced transfer, 'political' persecution and other inhumane acts. It therefore confirmed those charges against Muthaura and Kenyatta, but none for Ali.[523] This time, the rape charge included the allegations related to the town of Naivasha, which had previously failed at the summons stage.[524]

[515] ICC-01/09-02/11-1, 8 March 2011, [56].
[516] Ibid., [26].
[517] Ibid., [27].
[518] ICC-01/09-02/11-27, 1 April 2011.
[519] ICC-01/09-02/11-280, 2 September 2011, [35] (original filed on 19 August 2011).
[520] Ibid., [76]–[93]. C.f. Part VII, which describes Muthaura and Kenyatta as 'co-perpetrators'.
[521] Ibid., [94]–[102].
[522] Chapter 5, §5.3.5.
[523] ICC-01/09-02/11-382-Red, 23 January 2012, [428]–[430].
[524] Ibid., [415], [428(d)].

The Majority declined to confirm the charge of 'sexual violence' because, in its view, the relevant conduct was captured by the charge of 'other inhumane acts' and was not 'sexual' in nature.[525] In a dissenting opinion, Judge Kaul dismissed all of the charges on the grounds that there was insufficient evidence of a 'State or organizational policy'.[526]

#### 4.5.1.3 Trial

The debate as to whether the alleged acts of genital mutilation constituted 'sexual violence' continued at trial, by which time Fatou Bensouda had commenced as Prosecutor. On 3 July 2012, before opening statements, the OTP asked the Trial Chamber to give notice that the acts of genital mutilation might be re-characterised as 'other forms of sexual violence' pursuant to Regulation 55.[527] The victims' counsel supported that request.[528] In August 2012, while waiting for a decision on that request, the OTP filed an updated summary of charges. The summary did not include any new charges, but it contained references to 'sexual violence' that could be interpreted as a descriptor of the acts against the Luo men.[529] In response to objections from the Defence, the Trial Chamber directed the OTP to remove those references to 'sexual violence', noting that this direction did not affect its pending decision on the request to re-characterise the acts as 'sexual violence' using Regulation 55.[530]

The description of these acts did not continue to be litigated. In March 2013, Prosecutor Bensouda withdrew the charges against Muthaura because there was 'no reasonable prospect of conviction'.[531] The Prosecutor made this decision because several witnesses had died, become unwilling to testify, or admitted to taking bribes, and because the Kenyan government had 'failed to assist it in uncovering evidence that would have been crucial, or at the very least, may have been useful'.[532] This left Kenyatta, the sitting president, as the sole accused in the case.

On 3 December 2014, the Trial Chamber found that Kenya had breached its duty to cooperate with the ICC by providing the Prosecutor

[525] Ibid., [260]–[271].
[526] ICC-01/09-02/11-382-Red (Kaul), 23 January 2012.
[527] ICC-01/09-02/11-445, 3 July 2012, [13]–[14].
[528] ICC-01/09-02/11-458, 24 July 2012.
[529] ICC-01/09-02/11-468-AnxC, 24 August 2012, [31], [60], [71].
[530] ICC-01/09-02/11-584, 28 December 2012, [63]–[67].
[531] ICC-01/09-02/11-687, 11 March 2013, [1].
[532] Ibid., [11]. See also ICC-01/09-02/11-696, 18 March 2013.

with evidence related to the case, but declined to refer the matter to the Assembly of States Parties.[533] That same day, the Chamber rejected the Prosecutor's request for an adjournment and gave her one week to either withdraw the charges or confirm her intention to proceed to trial.[534] Two days later, the Prosecutor withdrew the charges, stating 'today is a dark day for international criminal justice'.[535] Kenyatta, by contrast, felt 'vindicated'.[536] Referring to the charges against Vice President William Ruto and broadcaster Joshua Sang, he tweeted: 'one case down, two more to go'.[537]

### 4.5.2 *William Samoei Ruto, Henry Kiprono Kosgey and Joshua Arap Sang*

Status at 17 July 2018: Charges against Kosgey not confirmed; charges against Ruto and Sang vacated (Table 4.17).

#### 4.5.2.1 Key Points

The *Ruto et al.* case focuses on crimes allegedly committed by ODM supporters during Kenya's 2007–2008 post-election crisis. Although there were reports of ODM supporters committing sexual violence crimes in this period, there were no charges of such crimes in this case. The reason for this gap in the charges is unclear: there was a suggestion from the victims' counsel that the OTP did not investigate these crimes;[538] there is also information that the relative powerlessness of women in Kenyan society, coupled with cultural sensitivities, would have made the investigation of sexual violence crimes very difficult;[539] or there may simply have been insufficient evidence linking the sexual violence crimes reportedly

[533] ICC-01/09-02/11-982, 3 December 2014. Note: The OTP successfully appealed this decision. The Trial Chamber subsequently rendered a decision which found that Kenya failed to cooperate and that the matter should be referred to the ASP. See ICC-01/09-02/11-1037, 19 September 2016.

[534] ICC-01/09-02/11-981, 3 December 2014.

[535] ICC OTP, 'Statement of the Prosecutor of the International Criminal Court, Fatou Bensouda, on the Withdrawal of Charges against Mr Uhuru Muigai Kenyatta' (5 December 2014).

[536] BBC News, 'Uhuru Kenyatta Denounces ICC as Kenya Charges Dropped' (5 December 2014).

[537] Ibid.

[538] ICC-01/09-01/11-367, 9 November 2011, [11(b)(ii)].

[539] Commission of Inquiry into Post-Election Violence, see n. 487, 272–273.

Table 4.17 *Ruto et al.* charges

| Crime | Article | Established at … Arrest Warrant Stage | Established at … Confirmation Stage | Established at … Trial |
|---|---|---|---|---|
| Crime against humanity: Murder | 7(1)(a) | ✓ | ✓ | n/a |
| Crime against humanity: Forcible transfer | 7(1)(d) | ✓ | ✓ | n/a |
| Crime against humanity: Torture | 7(1)(f) | ✗ | n/a | n/a |
| Crime against humanity: Persecution ('political') | 7(1)(h) | ✓ | ✓ | n/a |

* Denotes any gender-based crimes in the case.

committed by ODM supporters to the suspects in this case. It is also possible that the OTP made no effort to investigate sexual violence crimes committed by the ODM. However, that seems unlikely, given that there were charges of sexual violence in the other Kenya case.

#### 4.5.2.2 Pre-Trial

On 15 December 2010, Prosecutor Moreno-Ocampo requested a summons in respect of William Ruto and Henry Kosgey, both senior ODM politicians, and Joshua Sang, a pro-ODM radio broadcaster. The Prosecutor alleged that in the lead-up to the 2007 election, the suspects made a plan to attack supporters of the PNU and began establishing a network to carry out such attacks, with a view to strengthening the ODM's power in the Rift Valley and expelling PNU supporters from that area.[540] The network allegedly commenced the attacks immediately after the election result was announced, resulting in four crimes against humanity (murder, deportation or forced transfer, 'political' persecution, and torture) for which the suspects were responsible under Articles 25(3)(a) (direct or indirect co-perpetratorship) or 25(3)(d) (contributing).[541] The Pre-Trial Chamber issued the summons on 8 March 2011. The majority of the Chamber, Judge Kaul dissenting, found that there were reasonable grounds to believe that Ruto and Kosgey were responsible for the crimes against humanity of murder, forced transfer and persecution as indirect

[540] ICC-01/09-30-Red, 15 December 2010, [1], [17]–[25].
[541] Ibid., [23], [26]–[27].

co-perpetrators under Article 25(3)(a) and Sang was responsible for the same crimes under Article 25(3)(d).[542] It found that there was insufficient evidence of torture.[543]

In the DCC, filed on 15 August 2011, the Prosecutor charged Ruto and Kosgey as indirect co-perpetrators under Article 25(3)(a)[544] and Sang as a contributor under Article 25(3)(d) for the crimes against humanity of murder, forcible transfer and persecution.[545]

The Pre-Trial Chamber issued the confirmation of charges decision on 23 January 2012. The Majority confirmed the charges against Ruto and Sang, finding that there were substantial grounds to believe the suspects were responsible as an indirect co-perpetrator under Article 25(3)(a) and a contributor under 25(3)(d), respectively.[546] It found that there was insufficient evidence to confirm the charges against Kosgey.[547] As in *Muthaura et al.*, Judge Kaul declined to confirm the charges on the grounds that there was insufficient evidence of a 'State or organizational policy' behind the alleged attacks.[548]

#### 4.5.2.3 Trial

The trial commenced on 10 September 2013. In her opening statements, Prosecutor Bensouda alluded to the African Union's concerns about the ICC's involvement in Kenya, stating that the trial was 'not about meddling in African affairs' but about 'obtaining justice for the many thousands of victims of the post-election violence and ensuring that there is no impunity for those responsible, regardless of power or position'.[549] The Prosecutor also highlighted the difficulties that her Office faced in investigating the case, stating:

> This trial is the culmination of a long and difficult investigation. It has been fraught with cooperation challenges and obstacles relating to the security of witnesses. Many victims and witnesses have been too

[542] ICC-01/09-01/11-1, 8 March 2011, [57].

[543] Ibid., [33].

[544] ICC-01/09-01/11-261-AnxA, 15 August 2011, [198]–[123]. Note: Although para. 98 of the DCC describes Ruto and Kosgey as 'co-perpetrators', the DCC sets out the elements for 'indirect co-perpetration'. Hence, the Pre-Trial Chamber deemed 'indirect co-perpetration' to be the mode of liability charged. See ICC-01/09-01/11-373, 23 January 2012, [285].

[545] ICC-01/09-01/11-261-AnxA, 15 August 2011, [124]–[133].

[546] ICC-01/09-01/11-373, 23 January 2012, [349], [367].

[547] Ibid., [293].

[548] ICC-01/09-01/11-373 (Kaul), 23 January 2012.

[549] ICC-01/09-01/11-T-27-ENG, 10 September 2013, 19(24)–20(3).

> frightened to come forward. Others have given statements, but subsequently sought to withdraw from the process, citing intimidation or fear of harm.[550]

After the Prosecution closed its evidence on 10 September 2015, Ruto and Sang argued that there was no case to answer.[551] The majority of the Trial Chamber, Judge Herrera Carbuccia dissenting, declared a mistrial and vacated the charges on 5 April 2016.[552] Prosecutor Bensouda did not appeal.

## 4.6 Libya

In February 2011, following the popular uprisings in Tunisia and Egypt, thousands of Libyans took to the streets to protest against their unelected leader, Colonel Muammar Gaddafi, and his military regime.[553] The Libyan authorities responded with force, sealing off the most active neighborhoods and opening fire on the protesters.[554] On 26 February 2011, in response to reports of this state-authored violence, the UN Security Council referred the situation in Libya since 15 February 2011 to the ICC.[555] After conducting a rapid preliminary examination, the Prosecutor opened an investigation on 3 March 2011.[556] Meanwhile, the violence in Libya escalated into an armed conflict between pro-Gaddafi forces and forces aligned with Libya's interim government, the National Transitional Council.[557] On 17 March 2011, the Security Council authorised member states to take 'all necessary measures' bar establishing an occupying force to protect civilians in Libya.[558] Based on that resolution, NATO forces were deployed to repress the use of force against

[550] Ibid., 18(22)–19(1).

[551] ICC-01/09-01/11-1991-Red, 6 November 2015; ICC-01/09-01/11-1990-Corr-Red, 26 October 2016.

[552] ICC-01/09-01/11-2027-Red-Corr, 5 April 2016.

[553] 'Report of the High Commissioner under Human Rights Council Resolution S-15/1, UN Doc. A/HRC/17/45' (7 June 2011), [5]. See also Human Rights Watch, 'World Report 2012: Events of 2011' (2012) 595.

[554] Ibid., [22].

[555] S/RES/1970 (2011), 26 February 2011.

[556] ICC OTP, 'ICC Prosecutor to Open an Investigation in Libya' (2 March 2011).

[557] 'Report of the High Commissioner under Human Rights Council Resolution S-15/1, UN Doc. A/HRC/17/45', see n. 553, [22].

[558] S/RES/1973 (2011), 17 March 2017, [4].

civilians in Libya.[559] In August 2011, the National Transitional Council took control of Tripoli, and on 20 October 2011, Colonel Gaddafi was killed in Sirte.[560]

On 15 March 2011, while this conflict was unfolding, the UN Human Rights Council established a commission of enquiry to examine the situation in Libya.[561] This commission found that during the conflict, Gaddafi's forces reportedly 'executed and tortured to death large numbers of prisoners in detention centres'.[562] Methods of torture documented by the international commission of enquiry included: 'severe beatings including on the soles of the feet (falaqa), electric shocks on genitalia, burning, threatening with dogs, suspension over doors, hanging from bars, and locking in small spaces or in solitary confinement for extended periods'.[563] In addition to that pattern of sexual violence in detention, which reportedly affected male and female detainees, the commission received reports of a second pattern of sexual violence in which women were raped by armed men in their homes.[564]

Prosecutor Moreno-Ocampo initiated one case from this situation, against Colonel Gaddafi, his son Saif al-Islam Gaddafi, and his chief of military intelligence Abdullah Al Senussi.[565] Prosecutor Bensouda subsequently initiated two further cases: one against the head of Libya's Internal Security Agency, Al-Tuhamy Mohamed Khaled,[566] and the other against Mahmoud Mustafa Busayf Al-Werfalli, a commander from one of the groups that fought against the Gaddafi regime in 2011 (although Al-Werfalli joined it after the regime fell).[567] The proceedings against Colonel Gaddafi were terminated on 22 November 2011 due to his death,[568] and the proceedings against Saif Gaddafi and Al-Senussi were split on 4 May 2012 when the Pre-Trial Chamber decided to examine Libya's admissibility challenge

[559] 'Report of the High Commissioner under Human Rights Council Resolution S-15/1, UN Doc. A/HRC/17/45', see n. 553, [23]; Human Rights Watch, 'World Report 2012: Events of 2011', see n. 553, 596.

[560] 'Report of the International Commission of Inquiry on Libya, UN Doc. A/HRC/19/68' (2 March 2012), [32].

[561] Ibid., [2].

[562] Ibid., [35]. See also Human Rights Watch, 'World Report 2012: Events of 2011', see n. 553, 596–597.

[563] Ibid., [45].

[564] Ibid., [66]–[67].

[565] ICC-01/11-4-Red, 16 May 2011.

[566] ICC-01/11-01-13-1, 18 April 2013, [2].

[567] ICC-01/11-01/17-2, 15 August 2017, [7]–[9].

[568] ICC-01/11-01/11-28, 22 November 2011.

Table 4.18 *Gaddafi* charges

| | | Established at ... | | |
|---|---|---|---|---|
| Crime | Article | Arrest Warrant Stage | Confirmation Stage | Trial |
| Crime against humanity: Murder | 7(1)(a) | ✓ | Pending | Pending |
| Crime against humanity: Persecution ('political') | 7(1)(h) | ✓* | Pending | Pending |

* Denotes any gender-based crimes in the case.

to each case separately.[569] As a result, one can speak of four cases from the situation in Libya: the *(Saif Al-Islam) Gaddafi* case, the *Al Senussi* case, the *Al-Tuhamy* case, and the *Al-Werfalli* case. Libya is yet to comply with its legal duty to surrender the suspects to the ICC.[570]

### 4.6.1 *Prosecutor v. Saif Al-Islam Gaddafi*

Status at 17 July 2018: Arrest warrant issued; suspect not in ICC custody (Table 4.18).

#### 4.6.1.1 Key Points

There are some charges of sexual violence in the *Gaddafi* case, based on evidence that political prisoners were subjected to sexualised torture in detention. However, there are no charges of rape in either case, despite reports that prisoners were also subjected to this crime.[571]

#### 4.6.1.2 Pre-Trial

On 16 May 2011, Prosecutor Moreno-Ocampo requested warrants for the arrest of Colonel Gaddafi, Saif Al-Islam Gaddafi and Abdullah Al-Senussi. The Prosecutor alleged that all three suspects were responsible for crimes

[569] ICC-01/11-01/11-134, 4 May 2012, [8].

[570] In its resolution referring the situation in Libya to the ICC, the Security Council decided that 'the Libyan authorities shall cooperate fully with and provide any necessary assistance to the Court and the Prosecutor'. Libya is obliged to comply with that decision pursuant to UN Charter, Art. 25.

[571] E.g. 'Report of the International Commission of Inquiry on Libya, UN Doc. A/HRC/19/68', see n. 560, [67].

against humanity committed in Libya from 15 February 2011 because they developed and implemented a plan to 'suppress any challenge to [Colonel Gaddafi's] absolute authority through killings and other acts of persecution executed by Libyan Security Forces'.[572] Colonel Gaddafi was charged as an indirect perpetrator under Article 25(3)(a); the other suspects were charged as indirect *co*-perpetrators under that article.[573] The persecution charge was based on evidence of violence, including sexual violence, against suspected dissidents who were arrested by Libyan security forces. According to the Prosecutor, numerous victims were 'kept naked in small cells and tortured', including by 'tying electric wires around victims' genitals and shocking them with electricity'.[574]

The Pre-Trial Chamber issued the arrest warrants on 27 June 2011. It found there were reasonable grounds to believe that both Gaddafis were responsible as indirect co-perpetrators for the crimes against humanity of murder and persecution throughout Libya from 15 to 28 February 2011, and that Al-Senussi was responsible as an indirect perpetrator of those the same crimes in Benghazi from 15 to 20 February 2011.[575] The day after the arrest warrants were issued, the Prosecutor stated that his Office 'will continue investigating new crimes regarding the situation in Libya since 15 February 2011, in particular allegations of rapes and efforts to cover up the crimes; we will eventually add new charges to the same case'.[576] As of 17 July 2018, no further charges have been added to this case, but Prosecutor Bensouda has initiated a separate case which includes allegations of rape (see *Al-Tuhamy* case, §4.6.3).

On 1 May 2012, Libya challenged the admissibility of the case against Saif Gaddafi on the grounds that he was being investigated in Libya for similar crimes to those listed in the ICC arrest warrant.[577] On 31 May 2013, the Pre-Trial Chamber dismissed that admissibility challenge because Libya had not established that the domestic case covered the same criminal conduct as alleged in the ICC, or that it was able to conduct

[572] ICC-01/11-4-Red, 16 May 2011, [1]–[2].

[573] Ibid., [3].

[574] Ibid., [25], [27].

[575] ICC-01/11-01/11-1, 27 June 2011, [71].

[576] ICC OTP, 'Statement of the International Criminal Court Prosecutor, Luis Moreno-Ocampo, on Decision by Pre-Trial Chamber I to Issue Three Warrants of Arrest for Muammar Gaddafi, Saif Al-Islam Gaddafi and Abdulla [Sic] Al-Senussi' (28 June 2011).

[577] Libya's principal submission was that its admissibility challenge related to the *Gaddafi* case only. In the alternative, it argued that the challenges related to Al-Senussi also. See ICC-01/11-01/11-130-Red, 1 May 2012, [73]–[74].

those proceedings genuinely.[578] That decision was upheld on appeal.[579] Relevantly, during the admissibility proceedings, Libya claimed that the domestic case against Gaddafi included charges of rape under domestic law.[580] The truth of this claim is unclear because Libya did not provide sufficient evidence to establish the 'actual contours' of its case.[581] If it *was* accurate at the time, it suggests that the continuance of the ICC case came at the cost of prosecuting rape.

On 10 December 2014, the Pre-Trial Chamber informed the UN Security Council of Libya's failure to surrender Gaddafi to the ICC.[582] On 5 June 2018, the Defence brought its own challenge, arguing that the case was inadmissible to the ICC because Gaddafi had been convicted by an independent and impartial Libyan court in June 2015 for substantially the same conduct as alleged in the ICC, sentenced to death, and then released from prison pursuant to a law promulgated in September 2015.[583] According to the excerpt of that conviction provided by the Defence, Gaddafi was also held accountable for certain acts not charged in the ICC, including rape.[584] The decision on that admissibility challenge awaits.

### 4.6.2 *Prosecutor v. Abdullah Al-Senussi*

Status at 17 July 2018: Arrest warrant issued; case deemed inadmissible (Table 4.19).

#### 4.6.2.1 Key Points

The *Al-Senussi* case concerns the same charges as the *Gaddafi* case, albeit in Benghazi specifically. However, in this case, Libya's admissibility challenge was successful.[585] The persecution charge in this case was based on 'political' grounds. However, as explained below, the analysis of that charge in the admissibility decision has relevance for persecution on 'gender' grounds also.

[578] ICC-01/11-01/11-344-Red, 31 May 2013.
[579] ICC-01/11-01/11-547-Red, 21 May 2014.
[580] ICC-01/11-01/11-130-Red, 1 May 2012, [25]; ICC-01/11-01/11-370-Red3, 24 June 2013, [87].
[581] ICC-01/11-01/11-344-Red, 31 May 2013, [135].
[582] ICC-01/11-01/11-577, 10 December 2014.
[583] ICC-01/11-01/11-640, 5 June 2018.
[584] Ibid., [62(vi),(xv) and (xvi)].
[585] ICC-01/11-01/11-466-Red, 11 October 2013. Upheld on appeal: ICC-01/11-01/11-565, 24 July 2014.

Table 4.19 *Al-Senussi* charges

| Crime | Article | Established at … Arrest Warrant Stage | Confirmation Stage | Trial |
|---|---|---|---|---|
| Crime against humanity: Murder | 7(1)(a) | ✓ | n/a | n/a |
| Crime against humanity: Persecution ('political') | 7(1)(h) | ✓* | n/a | n/a |

* Denotes any gender-based crimes in the case.

#### 4.6.2.2 Pre-Trial

On 2 April 2013, Libya filed an admissibility challenge on the grounds that the same case was under investigation in Libya.[586] That challenge was accepted by the Pre-Trial Chamber on 11 October 2013.[587] The Chamber recognised that the Libyan investigation did not cover 'political persecution' as such, and that the requirement that the victims were targeted because of their political affiliation was not an element of any of the crimes with which Al-Senussi could be charged under domestic law. However, it noted that under the Libyan criminal code, the fact that victims were targeted by reason of their membership of a group could constitute an aggravating sentencing factor. Therefore,

> The national provisions with which Libya contemplates charging Mr Al-Senussi, together with the provisions under articles 27 and 28 of the Libyan Criminal Code, sufficiently capture Mr Al-Senussi's commission, between 15 and at least 20 February 2011 in Benghazi, of murders and inhuman acts severely depriving civilians of fundamental rights contrary to international law, *by reason of their political identity*, as alleged in the proceedings before the Court.[588]

The Defence appealed that decision. Among other things, it argued that the Pre-Trial Chamber erred in taking sentencing factors into account as evidence that the *charges* were sufficiently similar, and observed

[586] ICC-01/11-01/11-307-Red2, 2 April 2013.
[587] ICC-01/11-01/11-466-Red, 11 October 2013.
[588] Ibid., [166] (emphasis added).

that articles 27 and 28 of the Libyan Criminal Code make no mention of aggravating factors, much less persecution or discrimination of any kind.[589] The Defence's appeal was rejected. On the 'persecution' point, the Appeals Chamber noted that 'the overall context of the case as a whole (both before this Court and the relevant part of the case in Libya) is the use of the Security Forces to suppress demonstrators against a political regime, necessarily arising out of the opposition of civilians to the regime', and that the Pre-Trial Chamber did not base its decision *solely* on possible sentencing factors; it also considered the crimes for which Al-Senussi was likely to be charged under Libyan law.[590] Therefore, in the view of the Appeals Chamber, the Pre-Trial Chamber made 'no error' in finding that the Libyan case covered 'substantially the same conduct' as the case in the ICC.[591]

This application of the 'same case' test indicates that in an admissibility challenge, the discriminatory motive of the crimes is not irrelevant. Rather, it was necessary for Libya to show that its case sufficiently captured the charge of 'political persecution', even if that exact crime did not exist under Libyan law. By analogy, if the ICC Prosecutor brings a charge of 'gender persecution', and a state or accused challenges the admissibility of the case, the ICC should examine whether the domestic case sufficiently captures the allegation of targeting on gender grounds. That approach would be consistent with the *Al-Senussi* case and would ensure that the gendered nature of the violence is recognised in whichever jurisdiction the case is tried.

### *4.6.3 Prosecutor v. Al-Tuhamy Mohamed Khaled*

Status at 17 July 2018: Arrest warrant issued; suspect not in ICC custody (Table 4.20).

#### 4.6.3.1 Key Points

The *Al-Tuhamy* case was initiated in 2013 but was only made public in April 2017 when the reasons for its confidential status ceased.[592] Most of the records detailing the charges remain confidential. Hence, the most that can be offered is a preliminary analysis of the case.

[589] ICC-01/11-01/11-565, 24 July 2014, [113]–[115].
[590] Ibid., [118]–[121].
[591] Ibid., [122].
[592] ICC-01/11-01/13-18, 24 April 2017.

Table 4.20 *Al-Tuhamy* charges

| | | Established at ... | | |
|---|---|---|---|---|
| Crime | Article | Arrest Warrant Stage | Confirmation Stage | Trial |
| Crime against humanity: Imprisonment | 7(1)(e) | ✓ | Pending | Pending |
| Crime against humanity: Torture | 7(1)(f) | ✓* | Pending | Pending |
| Crime against humanity: Persecution 'political' | 7(1)(h) | ✓* | Pending | Pending |
| Crime against humanity: Other inhumane acts | 7(1)(k) | ✓* | Pending | Pending |
| War crime: Torture | 8(2)(c)(i)-4 | ✓* | Pending | Pending |
| War crime: Cruel treatment | 8(2)(c)(i)-3 | ✓* | Pending | Pending |
| War crime: Outrages on personal dignity | 8(2)(c)(ii) | ✓* | Pending | Pending |

* Denotes any gender-based crimes in the case.

### 4.6.3.2 Pre-Trial

On 27 March 2013, Prosecutor Bensouda requested a warrant for the arrest of Al-Tuhamy, alleged head of Libya's Internal Security Agency from 15 February to 24 August 2011.[593] The Prosecutor alleged that in that role, Al-Tuhamy had powers to carry out Gaddafi's orders to arrest, detain, conduct raids, conduct surveillance, investigate, monitor and torture political prisoners.[594] She charged Al-Tuhamy with four crimes against humanity and three war crimes under Articles 25(3)(a) or (d), or 28(b).[595] The Pre-Trial Chamber issued the arrest warrant on 18 April 2013. It found that there were reasonable grounds to believe that in the

593 ICC-01/11-01-13-1, 18 April 2013, [2], [11].

594 Ibid., [11].

595 Ibid., [2].

period relevant to the charges, members of the Internal Security Agency and other state security forces:

> Arrested and detained persons perceived to be opponents of the Gaddafi regime, who were subjected to various forms of mistreatment, including severe beatings, electrocution, acts of sexual violence and rape, solitary confinement, deprivation of food and water, inhumane conditions of detention, mock executions, threats of killing and rape in various locations throughout Libya including Zawiya, Tripoli, Tajoura, Misratah, Sirte, Benghazi and Tawergha.[596]

In that context, the Chamber found that there were reasonable grounds to believe that Al-Tuhamy was responsible for the crimes charged under Articles 25(3)(a) or (d), or 28(b).[597] The Chamber did not specify the ground(s) on which the alleged persecution occurred, so for consistency with the other Libya cases, it is anticipated that 'political' grounds will be charged. Although the warrant was issued in April 2013, Al-Tuhamy is yet to appear before the Court.

### 4.6.4 *Prosecutor v. Mahmoud Mustafa Busayf Al-Werfalli*

Status at 17 July 2018: Arrest warrant issued; suspect not in ICC custody (Table 4.21).

#### 4.6.4.1 Key Points

In December 2015, Al-Werfalli allegedly became a commander of the Al-Saiqa Brigade, a group which had once been an 'elite unit' in Gaddafi's army but joined the revolutionary forces early in 2011.[598] This group was part of 'Operation Dignity', a joint operation launched in May 2014 with the stated goal of combating terrorism in Benghazi.[599] The case focuses on his role in seven mass killings that occurred in 2016–2017, which were filmed and posted online. As has been noted elsewhere, this was 'the first ICC arrest warrant to be based largely on evidence collected from social media'.[600]

[596] Ibid., [7].

[597] Ibid., [10], [12]. The public records provide further details on liability under Article 25(3)(a).

[598] ICC-01/11-01/17-2, 15 August 2017, [7], [9].

[599] Ibid., [6].

[600] E. Irving, 'And So It Begins … Social Media Evidence in an ICC Arrest Warrant' on *Opinio Juris* (17 August 2017).

Table 4.21 *Al-Werfalli* charges

| | | Established at ... | | |
|---|---|---|---|---|
| Crime | Article | Arrest Warrant Stage | Confirmation Stage | Trial |
| War crime: Murder | 8(2)(c)(i)-1 | ✓ | Pending | Pending |

* Denotes any gender-based crimes in the case.

The case is notable for that reason, but does not appear to contain allegations of gender-based crimes.[601]

#### 4.6.4.2 Pre-Trial

On 1 August 2017, Prosecutor Bensouda requested an arrest warrant for Al-Werfalli, charging him with the war crime of murder in and around Benghazi between June 2016 and July 2017.[602] The Prosecutor alleged that Al-Werfalli was responsible for this crime under 25(3)(a), 25(3)(b) or 25(3)(d).[603] The Pre-Trial Chamber issued the warrant on 15 August 2017. It found that there was a reasonable basis to believe that Al-Werfalli either killed or ordered the killing of 33 people, none of whom appeared to be legitimate military targets,[604] and that these killings occurred in the context of a non-international armed conflict in Libya since at least March 2011.[605] On 4 July 2018, the Pre-Trial Chamber issued a second arrest warrant against Al-Werfalli in response to an eighth mass killing which allegedly occurred Benghazi in January 2018.[606] Al-Werfalli is yet to appear before the ICC.

## 4.7 Côte d'Ivoire

On 1 October 2003, the OTP opened a preliminary examination into the situation in Côte d'Ivoire. Côte d'Ivoire was not a State Party at that time, but it had made a declaration accepting the ICC's jurisdiction over acts

[601] The first arrest warrant refers to the killing of 33 victims, some of whom are described as 'men', and some described as 'persons'. The second arrest warrant describes the killing of ten 'persons'.
[602] ICC-01/11-01/17-2, 15 August 2017, [2].
[603] Ibid. The public records provide further details on liability under Article 25(3)(a).
[604] Ibid., [10].
[605] Ibid., [25]–[27].
[606] ICC-01/11-01/17-13, 4 July 2018.

committed on its territory since 19 September 2002.[607] While there was violence in Côte d'Ivoire at the time of that declaration, the level of violence reached new heights after the November 2010 presidential election, in which (then) President Laurent Gbagbo and his opponent Allasane Ouattara both claimed victory.[608] Although the African Union and the UN Security Council recognised Ouattara as the new president,[609] Gbagbo did not relinquish power. On 11 April 2011, he was arrested by Ouattara's forces, with assistance of UN and French troops.[610]

In December 2010, Ouattara confirmed Côte d'Ivoire's acceptance of the ICC's jurisdiction, and in June 2011, Prosecutor Moreno-Ocampo requested authorisation to open an investigation into crimes allegedly committed in that state since 28 November 2010.[611] In that request, the Prosecutor alleged that pro-Gbagbo forces had committed crimes against humanity against perceived Ouattara supporters following the 2010 election, and that supporters of both candidates had committed war crimes during a non-international armed conflict that commenced on 25 February 2011.[612] The Pre-Trial Chamber authorised the investigation on 3 October 2011.[613] To date, cases have been announced against three individuals from this situation, namely, Laurent Gbagbo, his political ally and wife Simone Gbagbo and another political ally, Charles Blé Goudé. The cases against Laurent Gbagbo and Blé Goudé were joined after confirmation of charges, consolidating these three cases to two.[614] No case has been announced against Ouattara's supporters, although the Pre-Trial Chamber found that there was a reasonable basis to believe that they committed war crimes and crimes against humanity, including rape, in the post-election period.[615]

### *4.7.1 Prosecutor v. Laurent Gbagbo & Charles Blé Goudé*

Status at 17 July 2018: Outcome of 'no case to answer' motion pending (Table 4.22).

[607] ICC-02/11-3, 23 June 2011, [15].
[608] Ibid., [12]–[13].
[609] Ibid., [12]. See also S/RES/1975 (2011), 20 March 2011, [1].
[610] Ibid., [14].
[611] Ibid., [1], [17].
[612] Ibid., [3]–[4].
[613] ICC-02/11-14, 3 October 2011; ICC-02/11-14-Corr, 15 November 2011.
[614] ICC-02/11-01/15-1, 11 March 2015.
[615] ICC-02/11-14-Corr, 15 November 2011, [111], [161].

Table 4.22 *Gbagbo & Blé Goudé* charges

| | | Established at … | | |
|---|---|---|---|---|
| Crime | Article | Arrest Warrant Stage | Confirmation Stage | Trial |
| Crime against humanity: Murder | 7(1)(a) | ✓ | ✓ | Pending |
| Crime against humanity: Rape | 7(1)(g)-1 | ✓* | ✓* | Pending |
| Crime against humanity: Other sexual violence | 7(1)(g)-6 | ✓* | n/a | n/a |
| Crime against humanity: Persecution ('political, national, ethnic or religious') | 7(1)(h) | ✓* | ✓* | Pending |
| Crime against humanity: Other inhumane acts or attempted murder | 7(1)(k) | ✓ | ✓ | Pending |

*Denotes any gender-based crimes in the case.

#### 4.7.1.1 Key Points

Gbagbo was the first former head of state to be prosecuted in the ICC. He was charged, among other things, for sexual violence crimes committed during Côte d'Ivoire's post-election violence. The case got off to a rocky start, with the Pre-Trial Chamber finding that there was insufficient evidence to confirm the charges against Gbagbo and criticising the OTP for relying too heavily on hearsay evidence. However, after the Prosecutor brought stronger evidence and charged different modes of liability, the charges were confirmed in June 2014. After the Prosecution called its last witness in January 2018, the Defence filed a 'no case to answer' motion (a motion seeking an acquittal without the need for the Defence to present its case). In January 2019, after this study's cut-off date, the Trial Chamber granted the Defence's request.[616] The Prosecutor has a right to appeal.

[616] ICC-02/11-01/15-T-232-ENG, 15 January 2019.

#### 4.7.1.2 Pre-Trial

On 25 October 2011, Prosecutor Moreno-Ocampo requested a warrant for the arrest of Laurent Gbagbo in relation to five crimes against humanity allegedly committed during Côte d'Ivoire's post-election violence.[617] The Prosecutor alleged that Gbagbo was responsible for these crimes as an indirect co-perpetrator under Article 25(3)(a) because, together with his 'inner circle', he developed and implemented a policy to attack Ouattara's supporters in order 'to retain power by all means, including by lethal force'. These attacks were allegedly carried out by the Côte d'Ivoire Defence and Security Forces, together with pro-Gbagbo youth and mercenaries.[618] The facts charged as rape and 'other forms of sexual violence' were redacted[619] and the persecution charge referred back to these redacted facts as well.[620] The Pre-Trial Chamber issued the arrest warrant on 23 November 2011, albeit noting that the alleged mode of liability 'may well need to be revisited in due course'.[621] Gbagbo was surrendered to the ICC on 30 November 2011.[622]

The DCC was filed in January 2013, by which time Fatou Bensouda had commenced as Prosecutor.[623] The DCC alleged that Gbagbo was responsible for four crimes against humanity under Article 25(3)(a) (indirect co-perpetration)[624] or Article 25(3)(d) (contributing to the commission of the crimes by a group acting with a common purpose).[625] Unlike in the arrest warrant, there was no charge of 'other forms of sexual violence'. In a decision rendered on 3 June 2013, the Pre-Trial Chamber expressed its 'serious concern' with the OTP's reliance on anonymous hearsay evidence to substantiate elements of its case.[626] It observed that 'such pieces of evidence cannot in any way be presented as the fruits of a full and proper investigation by the Prosecutor'.[627] However, the Majority of the Chamber, Judge Fernández de Gurmendi dissenting, did not decline to confirm the

[617] ICC-02/11-01/11-9-Red, 30 November 2011, [4], [6]. The grounds of persecution are enumerated at [62].
[618] Ibid., [5]–[6].
[619] Ibid., [59].
[620] Ibid., [63].
[621] ICC-02/11-01/11-1, 23 November 2011; ICC-02/11-01/11-9-Red, 30 November 2011, [77].
[622] ICC-02/11-01/11-432, 3 June 2013, [2].
[623] Ibid., [9].
[624] ICC-02/11-01/11-357-Anx1-Red, 25 January 2013.
[625] Ibid., 56–57 (Counts 5–8).
[626] ICC-02/11-01/11-432, 3 June 2013, [35].
[627] Ibid.

charges at that point. Instead, it invited the OTP to file a revised DCC which described the charges 'in detail and with precision'.[628]

On 13 January 2014, Prosecutor Bensouda filed a revised DCC which charged Gbagbo with the same four crimes listed previously under Article 25(3)(a) (indirect co-perpetration), 25(3)(b) (ordering), 25(3)(d) (contributing) or 28 (command responsibility).[629] The murder charge referred to the killing of 167 people, including seven women who were allegedly killed when pro-Gbagbo forces opened fire on protesters during a pro-Ouattara rally on 3 March 2011.[630] The rally was organised by women, and the 3,000 protesters were apparently female.[631] However, there is no indication that they were targeted because of their gender; it appears that like the other 160 alleged murder victims, they were targeted due to their pro-Ouattara stance. By contrast, all 38 of the alleged rape victims were female (as well as pro-Ouattara), which suggests that gender played a part in those crimes.[632] The persecution charge was based on those alleged rapes, among other crimes.[633] However, gender was not one of the grounds of persecution alleged in this case. Rather, the Prosecutor brought charges of persecution on 'political, national, ethnic or religious' grounds.[634]

On 24 June 2014, the Majority of the Pre-Trial Chamber confirmed the charges against Gbagbo under Article 25(3)(a) (indirect co-perpetrator), 25(3)(b) or 25(3)(d).[635] It declined to confirm any charges under Article 28, notwithstanding evidence that Gbagbo had control over the perpetrators, was aware of the crimes and yet failed to take adequate measures to prevent or repress them: in the Chamber's view, this failure was part of his '*deliberate* effort to achieve the purpose of retaining power at any cost', making Article 28 inapplicable.[636] In a dissenting opinion, Judge van den Wyngaert held that there was insufficient evidence to confirm the charges under Article 25(3)(a), (b) or (d), but there *was* sufficient evidence to confirm the charges Article 28 in respect of crimes allegedly committed by

[628] Ibid., [45].

[629] ICC-02/11-01/11-592-Anx1, 13 January 2014, [6].

[630] Ibid., [63], [120], [217(ii)], [232].

[631] Ibid., [120].

[632] Ibid., [218], [233].

[633] Ibid., [235] citing, *inter alia*, [218].

[634] Ibid., [220]. Translated in ICC-02/11-01/11-656-Red, 12 June 2014, [274].

[635] ICC-02/11-01/11-656-Red, 12 June 2014, [230]–[259].

[636] Ibid., [264] (emphasis added). For a critique, see M. Gillet, 'Has the Pre-Trial Chamber Jeopardized the Gbagbo Trial at the International Criminal Court' on *Beyond The Hague* (29 December 2014).

state-controlled forces, but not the crimes allegedly committed by other pro-Gbagbo groups.[637]

The *Blé Goudé* pre-trial proceedings overlapped with those developments in Gbagbo's case. On 12 December 2011, Prosecutor Moreno-Ocampo requested a warrant for the arrest of Charles Blé Goudé, a member of Gbagbo's 'inner circle'.[638] The Prosecutor alleged that Blé Goudé was responsible as indirect co-perpetrator under Article 25(3)(a) for the same crimes listed in Gbagbo's arrest warrant.[639] The Pre-Trial Chamber issued the warrant on 21 December 2011, but Blé Goudé was not surrendered until 22 March 2014.[640] In the DCC, filed on 22 August 2014, Prosecutor Bensouda broadened the modes of liability to also include 25(3)(b) (ordering), (25)(3)(c) (aiding or abetting) or 25(3)(d) (contributing).[641] The Majority of the Pre-Trial Chamber confirmed the charges under all modes of liability alleged.[642] In a partly dissenting opinion, Judge van den Wyngaert confirmed the charges under Article 25(3)(b) and (c), but only for some of the incidents charged.[643]

#### 4.7.1.3 Trial

The *Gbagbo & Blé Goudé* trial began on 28 January 2016. As at the pre-trial stage, the OTP argued that the victims were targeted because of their political affiliation, nationality, ethnicity or religion, without citing gender as an intersecting ground.[644] The Prosecutor indicated that over the months ahead, the OTP would call 138 witnesses to support its case.[645] It called the last of those witnesses on 19 January 2018.[646] On 23 April 2018, having heard the Prosecution's evidence, both accused sought leave to file a 'no case to answer' motion.[647] The Trial Chamber gave leave for those motions to be filed[648] and scheduled a hearing for the Defence, Prosecution and victims' counsel to give their views on the matter on 1 October 2018.[649]

637 ICC-02/11-01/11-656-Anx (Van den Wyngaert), 12 June 2014.
638 ICC-02/11-02/11-1, 21 December 2011, [2], [12].
639 Ibid., [7]–[9].
640 ICC-02/11-02/11-186, 11 December 2014, [4].
641 Ibid., [10].
642 Ibid., [194].
643 ICC-02/11-02/11-186-Anx (Van den Wyngaert), 11 December 2014.
644 ICC-02/11-01/15-T-9-ENG, 28 January 2016, 39(25)–80(4), esp. 51(19); ICC-02/11-01/15-T-10-ENG, 29 January 2016, 1(20)–40(16).
645 ICC-02/11-01/15-T-9-ENG, 28 January 2016, 46(6).
646 ICC-02/11-01/15-1174, 4 June 2018, [1].
647 Ibid., [4].
648 Ibid., [10].
649 ICC-02/11-01/15-1189, 22 June 2010.

Table 4.23 *Gbagbo* charges

| Crime | Article | Established at … Arrest Warrant Stage | Confirmation Stage | Trial |
|---|---|---|---|---|
| Crime against humanity: Murder | 7(1)(a) | ✓ | Pending | Pending |
| Crime against humanity: Rape | 7(1)(g)-1 | ✓* | Pending | Pending |
| Crime against humanity: Other sexual violence | 7(1)(g)-6 | ✓* | Pending | Pending |
| Crime against humanity: Persecution ('political, national, ethnic or religious') | 7(1)(h) | ✓* | Pending | Pending |
| Crime against humanity: Other inhumane acts or attempted murder | 7(1)(k) | ✓ | Pending | Pending |

* Denotes any gender-based crimes in the case.

### 4.7.2 *Prosecutor v. Simone Gbagbo*

Status at 17 July 2018: Arrest warrant issued; suspect not in ICC custody (Table 4.23).

#### 4.7.2.1 Key Points

From a gender perspective, the most notable feature of this case is that the suspect's gender identity marks her as 'the Other'. Simone Gbagbo, Côte d'Ivoire's former first lady and a former university professor in Abidjan,[650] is one of a handful of women to be charged by an international or internationalised tribunal. She joins Biljana Plavšić at the ICTY, Pauline Nyiramasuhuko at the ICTR, Rasema Handanović at the War Crimes Chamber of the Court of Bosnia and Herzegovina, and Ieng Thirith and Im Chaem at the ECCC. There has been some thoughtful commentary on how these defendants challenge stereotypes about women, and how gendered narratives are deployed in their cases by the Prosecution,

[650] ICC-02/11-01/12-39, 8 April 2014, [40].

judges and Defence.[651] As suggested elsewhere, the disruptive presence of a female suspect provokes questions about the 'typical' suspect in an international criminal tribunal. It prompts us to ask why these suspects are almost always male, what this indicates about gender balance in high-level military and political positions and whether the type of violence seen in international trials would decrease, increase or change if armies and rebellions were led mostly by women rather than by men.[652]

#### 4.7.2.2 Pre-Trial

Prosecutor Moreno-Ocampo requested an arrest warrant for Simone Gbagbo on 7 February 2012. The Prosecutor alleged she was responsible as indirect co-perpetrator under Article 25(3)(a) for the same five crimes listed on Laurent Gbagbo's arrest warrant because as part of his 'inner circle', she helped to plan the attacks on supporters of Ouattara.[653] The Pre-Trial Chamber issued the warrant on 29 February 2012, finding Simone Gbagbo 'was ideologically and professionally very close to her husband' and that '[a]lthough not elected, Ms Gbagbo acted as an *alter ego* for her husband, exercising the power to make state decisions'.[654]

On 30 September 2013, Côte d'Ivoire challenged the admissibility of the case on the grounds that Simone Gbagbo was being investigated or prosecuted at the national level.[655] The OTP opposed this admissibility challenge on the basis that Côte d'Ivoire had not demonstrated that its proceedings covered substantially the same conduct as the ICC case.[656] The Defence neither opposed nor joined the admissibility challenge but stated that because of her 'unwavering espousal' of Côte d'Ivoire's sovereignty, Simone Gbagbo preferred to be tried there rather than in the ICC.[657] The Pre-Trial Chamber rejected the admissibility challenge on 11 December 2014, finding that the domestic authorities were not taking 'tangible, concrete and progressive steps' to determine whether the

[651] E.g. N. Hodgson, 'Gender Justice or Gendered Justice? Female Defendants in International Criminal' (2017) 25(3) *Feminist Legal Studies* 337; 'A Wife Accused of War Crimes: The Unprecedented Case of Simone Gbagbo' (*The Atlantic*, 3 December 2012).

[652] See R. Grey and L. Chappell, 'Simone Gbagbo & the International Criminal Court: The Unsettling Spectre of the Female War Criminal' on *Int Law Grrls* (26 November 2012).

[653] ICC-02/11-01/12-1, 29 February 2012, [2], [10].

[654] Ibid., [10] (emphasis original).

[655] ICC-02/11-01/12-11-Red, 30 September 2013.

[656] ICC-02/11-01/12-41-Red, 24 June 2014.

[657] ICC-02/11-01/12-39, 8 April 2014, [42].

suspect was responsible for the conduct alleged before the ICC.[658] That decision was upheld on appeal.[659]

In Côte d'Ivoire, Simone Gbagbo was convicted of related crimes in 2015 and sentenced to twenty years' imprisonment,[660] but acquitted in 2017 in a separate domestic prosecution for war crimes and crimes against humanity.[661] In August 2018, Gbagbo was released from jail when her former opponent, President Ouattara, pardoned her and 800 others involved in the 2010–2011 post-election violence.[662] It remains to be seen how the ICC will respond to her release.

## 4.8 Mali

In January 2012, political tensions in Mali rose to the level of a non-international armed conflict between the armed forces and various rebel factions, including several Islamist groups.[663] While the conflict took place across northern Mali, the ICC cases have focused on events in one northern city, Timbuktu. To briefly set out those events,[664] in April 2012, Timbuktu was invaded by the separatist group *Mouvement National de Libération de L'Azawad* (MNLA), which was toppled within days by its once-allies Al-Qaeda in the Islamic Maghreb (AQIM) and Ansar Dine ('أنصار الدين', meaning 'defenders of the faith').[665] Those groups

[658] ICC-02/11-01/12-47-Red, 11 December 2014, [36].

[659] ICC-02/11-01/12-75-Red, 27 May 2015.

[660] 'Ivory Coast Court Sentences Wife of Ex-President to 20 Years in Prison' (*The Guardian*, 10 March 2015).

[661] 'Ivory Coast's Former First Lady Simone Gbagbo Acquitted of War Crimes' (*The Guardian*, 29 March 2017).

[662] R. Maclean, 'Ivory Coast President Pardons 800 People Including Ex-First Lady' (*The Guardian*, 7 August 2018); A. Aboa, 'Ivory Coast's Simone Gbagbo Leaves Detention after Amnesty' (*Reuters*, 8 August 2018).

[663] ICC OTP, 'Situation in Mali Article 53(1) Report' (16 January 2013), [3].

[664] This summary is drawn primarily from ICC documents, as cited throughout. Other sources included: 'Report of the Secretary-General on the Situation in Mali, UN Doc. S/2012/894' (28 November 2012); A. Thurston and A. Lebovich, 'A Handbook on Mali's 2012–2013 Crisis' (Institute for the Study of Islamic Thought in Africa, 2 September 2013); Human Rights Watch, 'World Report 2013: Events of 2012' (2013) 134–139. G. Lydon, 'Inventions and Reinventions of Sharia in African History and the Recent Experiences of Nigeria, Somalia and Mali' (2018) 40(1) *Ufahamu: A Journal of African Studies* 67; K. Gänsler, 'Life in Timbuktu after the Islamists' (DW) 8 May 2013; Al Jazeera, 'Explainer: Tuareg-Led Rebellion in North Mali' (4 April 2012).

[665] ICC-01/12-01/15-171, 27 September 2016, [31]; ICC-01/12-01/18-1-Red, 31 March 2018, [56].

remained in control until January 2013, when they were driven out by French and Malian forces.[666]

During their ten-month rule, AQIM and Ansar Dine forcefully imposed their ideology, which was ostensibly based on Shariah law, onto the primarily Muslim population of Timbuktu.[667] They allegedly outlawed music, cigarettes and alcohol,[668] banned prayers at the shrines of Muslim saints and destroyed ten of those buildings[669] and imposed numerous rules that discriminated on the basis of sex and/or governed relations between men and women, such as forcing women to wear a veil, banning women from socialising with men other than their husband or relatives and making 'adultery' (i.e. extra-marital sex) a punishable offence.[670] To enforce these rules, AQIM and Ansar Dine created the 'Islamic Police', which, together with a so-called 'morality brigade' ('Hesbah') and security battalions, patrolled streets, markets and homes, day and night.[671] They also established an 'Islamic Court', which imposed sentences for supposed violations and operated with scant regard for basic fair trial rights. These bodies fell under the management of a presidency of three men, who were ultimately under the control of Ansar Dine's leader, Iyad Ag Galy.[672]

On July 2012, while this Islamist take-over was unfolding, the Malian government referred the situation in its territory since January 2012 to the ICC.[673] After conducting a preliminary examination, Prosecutor Bensouda opened an investigation on 16 January 2013.[674] To date, this investigation has led to cases against two members of Ansar Dine: the *Al Mahdi* case, which focuses on the destruction of protected buildings in Timbuktu; and the *Al Hassan* case, which concerns a wider range of crimes allegedly committed in that city in 2012–2013. To date, no case has been announced against Ag Ghaly[675] or against members of AQIM.

[666] ICC-01/12-01/18-1-Red, 31 March 2018, [26]–[27].
[667] Ibid., [3]–[4]. See also: ICC-01/12-01/15-T-4-Red-ENG, 22 August 2016, 105 (9–11).
[668] ICC-01/12-01/18-1-Red, 31 March 2018, [41], [71], [77], [80], [113], [141].
[669] Ibid., [141], [152]; ICC-01/12-01/15-171, 27 September 2016, [34]–[41].
[670] ICC-01/12-01/18-1-Red, 31 March 2018, [77], [114], [149].
[671] Ibid., [43]; ICC-01/12-01/15-171, 27 September 2016, [31].
[672] ICC-01/12-01/18-1-Red, 31 March 2018, [61]–[62].
[673] ICC OTP, 'Situation in Mali Article 53(1) Report', see n. 663, [5].
[674] ICC OTP, 'ICC Prosecutor Opens Investigation into War Crimes in Mali: "The Legal Requirements Have Been Met. We Will Investigate"' (16 January 2013).
[675] ICC-01/12-01/15-70-AnxA-Corr, 17 December 2015, [8].

Table 4.24 *Al Mahdi* charges

| Crime | Article | Established at … | | |
|---|---|---|---|---|
| | | Arrest Warrant Stage | Confirmation Stage | Trial |
| War crime: Attacking protected objects | 8(2)(e)(iv) | ✓ | ✓ | ✓ |

* Denotes any gender-based crimes in the case.

### 4.8.1 *Prosecutor v. Ahmad Al Faqi Al Mahdi*

Status at 17 July 2018: Conviction, sentence and reparations order rendered (Table 4.24).

#### 4.8.1.1 Key Points

The *Al Mahdi* case concerns the destruction of property in Timbuktu, also known as 'the city of 333 saints' because it is the final resting place of many Muslim scholars and imams dating back to the thirteenth century.[676] In 2012, several of these tombs were reduced to rubble on the pretext that their architectural style was offensive to Islamic teachings.[677] Al Mahdi, who pleaded guilty to the war crime of attacking protected objects[678] was the first person to be tried for the destruction of cultural heritage property in the ICC.[679] When the charge against *Al Mahdi* was made public, there was a broad call from civil society for the ICC to also prosecute gender-based crimes in Mali, based on investigations indicating that Ansar Dine also 'persecuted women, imprisoning them, and subjecting them to forced

[676] ICC-01/12-01/15-84-Red, 24 March 2016, 22; ICC-01/12-01/15-T-6-ENG, 24 August 2016, 23(2); UNESCO, 'Director-General Praises the People of Timbuktu for the Reconstruction of the City's Mausoleums' (19 July 2015).

[677] ICC-01/12-01/15-171, 27 September 2016, [34]; ICC-01/12-01/15-T-4-Red-ENG, 22 August 2016, 13(14)–14(8).

[678] ICC-01/12-01/15-78-Anx1-Red2, 19 August 2016.

[679] The war crime of attacking protected objects pursuant to Article 8(2)(e)(iv) had been charged previously in the *Ntaganda* case. The *Al Mahdi* case was the first ICC case in which this crime was charged in relation to attacks on cultural heritage property. For a critical view on this case's messaging about the value of cultural heritage, see L. Lixinski and S. Williams, 'The ICC's Al-Mahdi Ruling Protects Cultural Heritage, but Didn't Go Far Enough' on *The Conversation* (18 October 2016).

marriages', and that Al Mahdi 'also sanctioned rape and sexual slavery'.[680] The Prosecutor later did so in the *Al Hassan* case, which includes charges of gender-based crimes.

In researching the *Al Mahdi* case, I was struck by the gap between the emerging feminist literature on cultural heritage and the narrative heard in the ICC. In the feminist literature, and in publications that approach the topic of cultural heritage from a gender perspective, questions are constantly asked about who speaks on behalf of a people about their shared values, who decides which tangible or intangible property embodies those values and therefore warrants protection, who has access to that property and how that property either normalises or challenges received wisdom about the respective roles of men and women.[681] Often, these questions reveal a male bias in recognition and enjoyment of cultural heritage and suggest that the history told by the property is not representative of the whole society, but of certain power-holders within it. They also show that 'gender is largely ignored in heritage discourse'[682] and warn that 'female knowledge holders, when discussing women's affairs, may not share this information with a male recorder, and likewise for men's affairs'.[683] These issues received some attention in the *Al Mahdi* reparations phase but were largely overlooked until then. I return to this issue in Chapter 6.

#### 4.8.1.2 Pre-Trial

On 7 September 2015, Prosecutor Bensouda requested an arrest warrant for Al Mahdi, former head of Hesbah, the unit created by Ansar Dine to prevent 'vice' and promote 'virtue' in Timbuktu.[684] He was charged with one offence: the war crime of 'intentionally directing attacks against buildings dedicated to religion, education, art, science or charitable purposes, historic monuments, hospitals and places where the sick and

[680] See FIDH, 'Mali: The Hearing of Al Mahdi before the ICC Is a Victory, but Charges Must Be Expanded' (30 September 2015).

[681] E.g. L. Smith, 'Heritage, Gender and Identity' in B. Graham and P. Howard (eds), *The Ashgate Research Companion to Heritage and Identity* (Ashgate, 2008) 159; UNESCO, 'Gender Equality: Heritage and Creativity' (2014).

[682] J. Blake, 'Intangible Cultural Heritage' in UNESCO, *Gender Equality: Heritage and Creativity* (UNESCO, 2014) 48, 49.

[683] UNESCO, 'Overview' in UNESCO, *Gender Equality: Heritage and Creativity* (UNESCO, 2014) 32, 42.

[684] ICC-01/12-01/15-4-Red2, 1 November 2015. Regarding Hesbah's role, see: ICC-01/12-01/15-T-5-Red-ENG, 23 August 2016, 5(16); ICC-01/12-01/15-70-AnxA-Corr, 17 December 2015, [6].

wounded are collected, provided they are not military objectives'.[685] The charge was based on the destruction of ten tombs and mosques, nine of which were on UNESCO's World Heritage list.[686] These ten buildings were of great significance to Islamic history and were cherished by worshippers from Timbuktu and afar. As one worshipper explained to Karima Bennoune, UN Special Rapporteur in the field of cultural rights, 'the mausoleums are like confidantes. You can say everything you have in your heart'.[687]

For his role in the crime, Al Mahdi was charged under Article 25(3)(a) (direct perpetrator or co-perpetrator), 25(3)(c) (aiding, abetting or assisting) or 25(3)(d) (contributing to the commission of the crime by a group acting with a common purpose).[688] A warrant listing all of these modes of liability was issued on 18 September 2015, and the suspect was surrendered by the authorities of Niger (where he was detained on separate charges relating to the supply of weapons) on 26 September 2015.[689]

In the DCC, filed on 17 December 2015, the Prosecution charged Al Mahdi under all modes of liability listed on the arrest warrant plus 'soliciting or inducing' under Article 25(3)(b).[690] The DCC alleged that Al Mahdi agreed to Ag Ghaly's plan to destroy the buildings, drummed up support for that plan in a sermon given on the eve of the attack, supplied the necessary equipment to carry out the plan, supervised the destruction of all ten sites and physically participated in the destruction of five.[691] In February 2016, Al Mahdi agreed to plead guilty on all modes of liability, and on 24 March 2016, the Pre-Trial Chamber confirmed the charge.[692] In accordance with Article 65, the case was then sent to trial. The plea deal negotiated by the parties was contingent on the suspect's 'voluntary decision to accept responsibility for this actions' as well as other conditions that were not made public.[693]

[685] RS, 8(2)(e)(iv).
[686] ICC-01/12-01/15-4-Red2, 1 November 2015, [14]; ICC-01/12-01/15-171, 27 September 2017, [45]–[46].
[687] ICC-01/12-01/15-214-AnxI-Red3, 27 April 2017, 21.
[688] ICC-01/12-01/15-4-Red2, 1 November 2015, [130]–[146].
[689] ICC-01/12-01/15-1-Red, 18 September 2015, [14].
[690] ICC-01/12-01/15-70-AnxA-Corr, 17 December 2015.
[691] Ibid., [18]–[20].
[692] ICC-01/12-01/15-84-Red, 24 March 2016.
[693] ICC-01/12-01/15-78-Anx1-Red2, 19 August 2016, [15]–[18].

#### 4.8.1.3 Trial

The trial lasted three days, commencing 22 August 2016. In her opening statements, the Prosecutor emphasised the importance of destroyed sites to the people of Timbuktu, to Africa and to Muslim people worldwide.[694] She also drew attention to the value protected by this crime, stating:

> What is so serious about this crime is that it is a deep attack upon the identity of a population, their memory and their very future. This is a crime, a crime for which there is a victim. And I speak of the true wealth of communities, entire communities. This is a crime that leaves us all diminished, a crime that strikes a blow and does great harm to the universal values that we must protect.[695]

The idea of gender was not referenced in the Prosecution's opening statements, except for the statement that 'the heritage of mankind was ransacked'[696] – an uncharacteristically sexist phrase that echoed the wording of international treaties on cultural heritage,[697] and recalled feminist critiques of the perceived interchangeability of the terms 'humanity' and 'men'.[698]

As the trial progressed, the OTP called three witnesses: Witness 182, an OTP investigator;[699] Witness 151, a UNESCO representative;[700] and Witness 431, an expert in Malian history and heritage.[701] All three witnesses were men, and none spoke about gender at length. The OTP investigator mentioned the 'dress code for women' and 'the issue of women being out in the street on their own' when explaining the context in which buildings were attacked;[702] the UNESCO representative observed that local men and women both participated in the maintenance of the

[694] ICC-01/12-01/15-T-4-Red-ENG, 22 August 2016, 14(23)–23(11).

[695] Ibid., 16(7–12.)

[696] Ibid., 16(3–4). In French: 'le patrimoine des hommes est l'objet de saccages répétés': ICC-01/12-01/15-T-4-Red-FRA, 22 August 2016, 16(17–18).

[697] Convention for the Protection of Cultural Property in the Event of Armed Conflict, 14 May 1954, 249 UNTS 240 (entered into force 7 August 1956), preamble; Convention concerning the Protection of World Cultural and Natural Heritage, 23 November 1972, 1037 UNTS 151 (entered into force 15 December 1975), preamble and Art. 1.

[698] E.g. H. Charlesworth and C. Chinkin, *The Boundaries of International Law: A Feminist Analysis* (Manchester University Press, 2000) 232; S. de Beauvoir, *The Second Sex (1949)* (Vintage, 2011) 6–7.

[699] ICC-01/12-01/15-T-4-Red-ENG, 22 August 2016, 41(17–21); 89(21) to ICC-01/12-01/15-T-5-Red-ENG, 23 August 2016, 20(13).

[700] ICC-01/12-01/15-T-5-Red-ENG, 23 August 2016, 21(6)–61(16).

[701] Ibid., 62(7)–96(23).

[702] ICC-01/12-01/15-T-4-Red-ENG, 22 August 2016, 105(9–25).

shrines, albeit in different roles;[703] and the expert on Malian history explained that these buildings signified 'the virtues of man'.[704] Other than that, gender issues were not discussed by the Prosecution or in the submissions of the victims' counsel.[705]

On 27 September 2016, the Chamber unanimously accepted the guilty plea and convicted Al Mahdi as a direct co-perpetrator under Article 25(3)(a).[706] It sentenced him to nine years' imprisonment, deducting time spent in detention since his arrest on 18 September 2015.[707]

#### 4.8.1.4 Reparation

Gender issues were not a focus of the three *amici curiae* briefs filed at the reparations stage[708] or the submissions of Trust Fund.[709] The victims' counsel's filings were similarly gender-blind, although he noted in passing that women were not allowed to enter the mausoleums, although they used to pray outside.[710] By contrast, in the reports of experts appointed by the Chamber, a deeper gender perspective began to emerge. Interestingly, it arose in relation to the reparations *process*, more than quantum of harm.

To explain: at the beginning of the reparations process, the victims' counsel had suggested that 'local and traditional leaders' should play a role in implementing the reparations order.[711] This view was later challenged by Dr Marina Lostal, a lecturer in international law at The Hague University. Dr Lostal warned that although the idea of engaging with traditional leaders had some merit, the Court should be aware that women's interests are often sidelined in the justice processes that such leaders promote.[712]

703 ICC-01/12-01/15-T-5-Red-ENG, 23 August 2016, 39(8)–40(5). See also ICC-01/12-01/15-214-AnxIII-Red2, 4 August 2017, 26.

704 ICC-01/12-01/15-T-5-Red-ENG, 23 August 2016, 44(18–20.) In French: 'Pour les musulmans, ce sont les vertus de l'homme: la sagesse, la connaissance, l'engagement religieux, un exemple de vie idéale'. ICC-01/12-01/15-T-5-Red-FRA, 23 August 2016, 43(18–19).

705 ICC-01/12-01/15-T-6-ENG, 24 August 2016, 18(14)–33(25).

706 ICC-01/12-01/15-171, 27 September 2016, [53]–[56].

707 Ibid., [109]–[111].

708 There were three *amicus curiae* briefs: one from UNESCO, one from FIDH and its Malian branch and one from University Belfast Human Rights Centre and Redress. None of these briefs discussed gender issues in depth, although FIDH noted that in terms of community consultation, the Malian people would likely be more comfortable speaking to someone of their own sex. See ICC-01/12-01/15-194, 2 December 2016 (UNESCO brief); ICC-01/12-01/15-189-tENG, 2 December 2016 (FIDH and AMDH brief); ICC-01/12-01/15-188, 2 December 2016 (Queen's University Belfast Human Rights Centre and Redress Trust brief).

709 ICC-01/12-01/15-187, 2 December 2016; ICC-01/12-01/15-225, 16 June 2017.

710 ICC-01/12-01/15-224-Corr-Red-tENG, 14 July 2017, [31].

711 ICC-01/12-01/15-190-Red-tENG, 3 January 2017, [22], [131].

712 ICC-01/12-01/15-214-AnxII-Red2, 28 April 2017 (amended 3 May 2017), [115].

She explained: 'women occupy a submissive position in society, so their ability to negotiate or stand up for themselves in this type of process is curtailed *ab initio*'.[713] She advised the Court to bear this point in mind when deciding what role (if any) traditional leaders would play in distributing reparations ordered by the ICC.[714]

The same concern about traditional justice process was raised by Karima Bennoune.[715] In addition, Bennoune referred to the restriction on women's access to the destroyed buildings, indicating that this rule was linked to women's capacity for menstruation.[716] As a more general point, Bennoune emphasised that respect for the preservation of cultural heritage does not require a static definition of culture or a blind acceptance of practices that discriminate against women and girls. In her words:

> Culture is constituted by social practices that change over time. Sometimes, cultural change is mandated by human rights law when practices violate human rights, as required, for example, under article 5(a) of the Convention on the Elimination of All Forms of Discrimination against Women [CEDAW]. While cultural diversity is to be celebrated, cultural rights, being firmly embedded in the universal human rights framework, *cannot be invoked to excuse human rights violations, discrimination, or violence*.[717]

After hearing these views, the Chamber issued the reparations order on 17 August 2017. It found Al Mahdi liable for reparations of €2.7 million: €97,000 to restore the buildings, €2.12 million for economic loss and €483,000 for moral harm.[718] The award was to be paid collectively to the community of Timbuktu, except for a portion of the sum for economic loss, which would go to individuals whose livelihood depended 'exclusively' on the destroyed sites.[719] In addition, the Malian government and UNESCO would receive a 'symbolic' payment of €1 each.[720] To avoid the risk of discrimination against women, the Chamber decided against including traditional justice processes in the implementation of the award.[721] It did not directly cite Bennoune's argument that discriminatory cultural practices need not be protected in the name of 'cultural heritage'.

[713] Ibid., [114].
[714] Ibid., [114].
[715] ICC-01/12-01/15-214-AnxI-Red3, 27 April 2017, 48–49.
[716] Ibid., 22.
[717] Ibid., 7 (emphasis added).
[718] ICC-01/12-01/15-236, 17 August 2017, [116]–[134].
[719] Ibid., [81].
[720] Ibid., [106]–[107].
[721] Ibid., [147].

However, it observed that 'reparations should reflect local cultural and customary practices *unless these are discriminatory or exclusionary or they deny victims equal access to their rights*'.[722]

In its commentary on this decision, Amnesty International argued that limiting individual reparations to those whose livelihood depended 'exclusively' on the destroyed sites could discriminate against women, who could not work on site, and were less likely to be business owners than men.[723] The decision was also challenged by the victims' counsel, but on different grounds (namely, that the Chamber's restriction on individual reparations was too narrow, and that the Chamber improperly delegated the task of determining which victims were eligible to receive reparations to the Trust Fund).[724] The Appeals Chamber rejected the first ground but was persuaded by the second. It, therefore, amended the order to require that any decision on eligibility made by the Trust Fund would be subject to judicial approval.[725]

It is positive to see that the Trust Fund's draft implementation plan, which is yet to be approved, has been written with the principle of gender equality in mind. The plan states that in reparation aimed at economic rehabilitation, such as training in basic accounting and access to micro-credits, priority will be given to people who are women and/or elderly, as these groups are in 'dire financial circumstances as a result of the loss of livelihoods and tools of the trade'.[726] The plan also refers to trauma-healing activities organised according to gender and age (i.e. different activities for older women, younger women, older men and younger men), in order promote free expression and respect cultural practices in Timbuktu.[727] By approving these measures, the Chamber can hopefully increase access to justice for women in the affected community and set a precedent for gender-sensitive reparations in cases concerning the destruction of cultural heritage sites.

### 4.8.2 *Prosecutor v. Al Hassan Ag Abdoul Aziz Ag Mohamed Ag Mahmoud*

Status at 17 July 2018: Confirmation of charges hearing scheduled to begin on 6 May 2019 (Table 4.25).

[722] Ibid., [34] (emphasis added).

[723] A. Ringin, 'Women and Girls Must Not Be Excluded from Reparation in the Al Mahdi Case' on *Human Rights in International Justice* (2 October 2017).

[724] ICC-01/12-01/15-244-tENG, 17 October 2017.

[725] ICC-01/12-01/15-259-Red2, 8 March 2018.

[726] ICC-01/12-01/15-265-Corr-Red, 18 May 2018, [245].

[727] Ibid., [259].

Table 4.25 *Al Hassan* charges

| | | Established at … | | |
|---|---|---|---|---|
| Crime | Article | Arrest Warrant Stage | Confirmation Stage | Trial |
| Crime against humanity: Persecution ('religious') | 7(1)(h) | ✓* | Pending | Pending |
| Crime against humanity: Persecution ('gender') | 7(1)(h) | ✓* | Pending | Pending |
| Crime against humanity: Rape | 7(1)(g)-1 | ✓* | Pending | Pending |
| Crime against humanity: Sexual slavery | 7(1)(g)-2 | ✓* | Pending | Pending |
| Crime against humanity: Torture | 7(1)(f) | ✓* | Pending | Pending |
| Crime against humanity: Other inhumane acts | 7(1)(k) | ✓* | Pending | Pending |
| War crime: Cruel treatment | 8(2)(c)(i)-3 | ✓* | Pending | Pending |
| War crime: Torture | 8(2)(c)(i)-4 | ✓* | Pending | Pending |
| War crime: Outrages on personal dignity | 8(2)(c)(ii) | ✓* | Pending | Pending |
| War crime: Rape | 8(2)(e)(vi)-1 | ✓* | Pending | Pending |
| War crime: Sexual slavery | 8(2)(e)(vi)-2 | ✓* | Pending | Pending |
| War crime: Attacking protected objects | 8(2)(iv) | ✓ | Pending | Pending |
| War crime: Imposition of sentences by improper court | 8(2)(c)(iv) | ✓* | Pending | Pending |

* Denotes any gender-based crimes in the case.

#### 4.8.2.1 Key Points

*Al Hassan* will potentially be a landmark case in the ICC's jurisprudence on gender-based crimes. The arrest warrant, issued in May 2018, contains twelve gender-based crimes. These crimes include persecution on the grounds of 'gender', a crime that has never before been charged at the confirmation stage. The case is a timely recognition of the threat that religious fundamentalists, especially militant Islamist groups, pose to women's human rights. As Naureen Chowdhury Fink and Alison Davidian have observed, 'despite the glorification of female roles in their narratives, control over women, their lives, and their bodies lies at the heart of the agenda of many violent extremist and terrorist groups'.[728]

By way of example, Fink and Davidian refer to Ansar Dine, the Taliban, Boko Haram and the so-called Islamic State (IS).[729] Notably, all of these groups are on the OTP's radar: Ansar Dine is at the centre of the *Al Mahdi* and *Al Hassan* cases, the Prosecutor has applied for authorisation to open an investigation into crimes committed by the Taliban (and others) in Afghanistan,[730] the OTP is examining alleged crimes by Boko Haram in the preliminary examination in Nigeria[731] and it has received a request to investigate gender-based crimes allegedly committed by IS.[732] Thus, in addition to being an important case in its own right, the *Al Hassan* case could potentially be the first in a series of thematic prosecutions on gender-based violence which is committed by religious extremists/Islamists who seek to enforce their interpretation of religion through violent rule.

#### 4.8.2.2 Pre-Trial

On 20 March 2018, Prosecutor Bensouda requested an arrest warrant against Al Hassan, a member of Ansar Dine and de facto leader of the Islamic Police in 2012–2013.[733] The request alleged that during

[728] N. Chowdhury Fink and A. Davidian, 'Complementarity and Convergence? Women, Peace and Security and Counterterrorism' in F. Ní Aoláin et al. (eds), *The Oxford Handbook of Gender and Conflict* (Oxford University Press, 2018) 158, 160.

[729] Ibid.

[730] ICC-02/17-7-Conf-Exp ICC-02/17-7-Red, 20 November 2017.

[731] ICC OTP, 'Report on Preliminary Examination Activities 2017' (4 December 2017), [204]–[229].

[732] CUNY Law School, MADRE, and Organization of Women's Freedom in Iraq, 'Communication to the ICC Prosecutor Pursuant to Article 15 of the Rome Statute Requesting a Preliminary Examination into the Situation of: Gender-Based Persecution and Torture as Crimes Against Humanity and War Crimes Committed by the Islamic State of Iraq and the Levant (ISIL) in Iraq' (8 November 2017).

[733] ICC-01/12-01/18-1-Red, 31 March 2018, [6], [22].

this period, the people of Timbuktu were subjected to oppressive and discriminatory rules, in line with Ansar Dine and AQIM's religious ideology.[734] These rules extended into gender relations in the private sphere. For example, the Prosecution cited video evidence of a couple being flogged in public by members of the Islamic Police, among others, to give effect to a sentence for 'adultery' imposed by the Islamic Court.[735]

The request paid particular attention to the plight of women during Ansar Dine and AQIM's rule. It alleged that women were not allowed to speak to each other in the street, or socialise with men to whom they were not related, or refrain from wearing a veil.[736] Women who breached these rules were allegedly beaten and flogged by the Islamic Police, sometimes with authorisation from the Islamic Court.[737] In addition, female rule-breakers were allegedly detained in a hot, $2m^2$ cell with no toilets at the former bank that served as the base for Islamic Police and Hesbah,[738] where women were allegedly raped.[739] The Islamists also allegedly forced women into marriages, both to gain a foothold in the local population, and to legitimise the resultant sexual abuse in the perpetrators' eyes.[740] As one witness explained, men were encouraged to satisfy their so-called 'sexual needs', so long as they did so within marriage.[741] These forced marriages were allegedly encouraged by AQIM and Ansar Dine, and in some cases, made official by the Islamic Court.[742]

In this case, sexual and gender-based violence formed the basis of charges of six war crimes (rape, sexual slavery, torture, cruel treatment, outrages on personal dignity and imposition of sentences by an improper court) and five crimes against humanity (rape, sexual slavery, torture, persecution and other inhumane acts including 'forced marriage'), for

[734] Ibid., [4].
[735] Ibid., [149].
[736] Ibid., [114].
[737] Ibid., [164].
[738] Ibid., [166].
[739] Ibid., [123].
[740] Ibid., [48], [114], [124], [168]–[170]. See also 'Report of the Secretary-General on the Situation in Mali, UN Doc. S/2012/894', see n. 664, [25].
[741] ICC-01/12-01/18-1-Red, 31 March 2018, [168].
[742] Ibid., [169].

which Al Hassan was allegedly responsible under 25(3)(a) (including as direct perpetrator, and direct and indirect co-perpetrator), 25(3)(b), 25(3)(c) and 25(3)(d). In addition, he was charged with the war crime of attacking protected objects, the same charge brought in the *Al Mahdi* case, under 25(3)(a), 25(3)(c) and 25(3)(d).[743]

The persecution charge was interesting. The Prosecutor alleged that the perpetrators targeted local people who were perceived not to conform to their vision of religion,[744] that such targeting was based on 'religious' grounds,[745] that it occurred in connection with other Rome Statute crimes (namely torture, attacks on dignity of the person, cruel treatment, other inhumane acts and attacks on protected objects)[746] and that it involved the deprivation of fundamental rights including the right to equality between men and women,[747] the right to freedom of assembly (due to the ban on women talking to each other in the street)[748] and the right to privacy (due, among other things, to the punishment of 'adultery').[749] In addition, the Prosecutor alleged that women and girls were targeted on 'gender' grounds through the restriction of women's freedom, the enforcement of sexist dress codes, and the pattern of forced marriage.[750] The Prosecution alleged that this persecution involved the deprivation of fundamental rights including the right against sex discrimination and the right against arbitrary imprisonment,[751] and occurred in connection with the crimes of torture, cruel treatment, other inhumane acts, rape and sexual slavery.[752]

On 22 May 2018, the Pre-Trial Chamber issued the warrant, including all charges listed in the Prosecutor's request.[753] The Chamber found that there were reasonable grounds to believe that Al Hassan was responsible for these crimes under 25(3)(a) (direct perpetratorship and direct

743 Ibid., [50], [232]–[287].
744 Ibid., [155]–[161].
745 Ibid.
746 Ibid., [50(a)]; [153]–[154].
747 Ibid., [142].
748 Ibid., [143].
749 Ibid., [149].
750 Ibid., [138], [162]–[172].
751 Ibid., [162], fn 414.
752 Ibid., [50(b)], [173].
753 ICC-01/12-01/18-35-Red2, 22 May 2018; ICC-01/12-01/18-2-tENG, 27 March 2018.

co-perpetratorship, depending on the charge) and 25(3)(b) (ordering).[754] Malian authorities transferred the suspect to the ICC on 31 March 2018 and he made his first appearance before the Court on 4 April 2018.[755] The confirmation of charges hearing is scheduled to commence on 6 May 2019.[756]

754 ICC-01/12-01/18-35-Red2, 22 May 2018, [161]–[191].

755 ICC, 'Press Release: Al Hassan Ag Abdoul Aziz Ag Mohamed Ag Mahmoud Makes First Appearance before the ICC' (4 April 2018).

756 ICC-01/12-01/18-94-Red, 20 July 2018.

# 5

# Finding the Positives

Based on the 24 case studies in the previous chapter, this chapter assesses the International Criminal Court's (ICC's) practice in prosecuting gender-based crimes as a whole. In particular, it comments on where the Office of the Prosecutor (OTP) has succeeded in prosecuting these crimes, where it has foundered, and what obstacles it has faced in this regard. Where relevant, the chapter also considers the practice of other courtroom actors, including the judges, the victims' counsel, and the Defence. Bearing in mind the discussion in Chapter 1 about what would constitute a 'successful' practice in prosecuting gender-based crimes at the ICC, this chapter does not simply count the number of convictions for these crimes. Rather, it presents a qualitative and quantitative analysis of charging strategies, charging outcomes, legal precedents and trial narratives. The analysis is informed by feminist critiques of previous international criminal tribunals, as detailed in Chapter 3.

This chapter concludes that, although the OTP has so far struggled to ensure accountability for gender-based crimes, it is making progress in that regard. The OTP has also spearheaded some significant advances in the international jurisprudence on gender-based crimes, brought charges for a wide range of gender-based crimes against male and female victims, and on some occasions, has taken steps to draw attention to gender hierarchies and roles in trial narratives. From time to time, the tendencies that have undermined accountability for gender-based crimes in the past have recurred in the ICC. These include a tendency to overlook gender as a basis of victimisation and the tendency to require more evidence to establish criminal liability for sexual violence crimes than other common wartime offences. A feminist institutionalist approach suggests that these regressions are not unusual: actors in newly designed institutions often fall back on previous practices, because habits of thought and action are not erased by the creation of new formal rules (see Chapter 1, §1.3.3).

I write this chapter at a time when many people in and outside the ICC are still processing the June 2018 *Bemba* judgment, in which the Appeals Chamber overturned the Court's first (and, thus far, only) conviction for rape. That decision was rendered just two weeks before the Rome Statute's twentieth anniversary, with the result that the ICC passed that milestone without having held any individual accountable for rape or indeed any other gender-based crimes. An assessment of the ICC's practice in prosecuting these crimes is especially timely in this context.

## 5.1 Charging Strategies

The first area to be assessed is charging strategies, namely, decisions made within the OTP about whether to bring charges of gender-based crimes, which provisions to use and which victims' experiences to focus on. Bringing charges of gender-based crimes does not *guarantee* that these crimes will go to trial, or that the victims of these crimes will receive reparations for the harms caused. However, it is a prerequisite for those outcomes to be achieved: if the relevant facts are not charged by the Prosecutor and confirmed by the Pre-Trial Chamber, they cannot form part of a subsequent conviction or reparations order in the case.

### *5.1.1 Sexual Violence Crimes*

It is sensible to start by reviewing charges of sexual violence crimes, as these comprise the majority of gender-based crimes charged in the ICC. Within the first four years of his term, which began in June 2003, Prosecutor Moreno-Ocampo initiated four cases: the *Kony et al.* case, concerning the Lord's Resistance Army (LRA) in Uganda; the *Lubanga* and *Ntaganda* cases, concerning the *Union des Patriotes Congolais* (UPC) in the Democratic Republic of Congo; and the *Ahmad Harun & Ali Kushayb* case, concerning the Sudanese army and affiliated *janjaweed* fighters in Darfur. It was reasonable to expect that each of these cases would include charges of sexual violence crimes, because each of the relevant groups had reportedly committed these crimes on a large scale.[1] However, sexual violence was not charged in all of these cases: the *Kony et al.* and *Ahmad*

[1] Regarding the LRA, see Human Rights Watch, 'Stolen Children: Abduction and Recruitment in Northern Uganda' (March 2003) 2; Human Rights Watch, 'Abducted and Abused: Renewed Conflict in Northern Uganda' (July 2003) 28–31. Regarding the UPC, see Amnesty International, 'Democratic Republic of Congo: Mass Rape-Time for Remedies' (25 October 2004) 14; Human Rights Watch, 'Seeking Justice: The Prosecution

*Harun & Ali Kushayb* did include charges of such crimes but the *Lubanga* and *Ntaganda* cases did not. Rather, in the latter two cases, the charges were limited to the recruitment and use of 'child soldiers'. The Prosecutor later added charges of sexual violence in *Ntaganda*, as discussed subsequently. However, in *Lubanga*, he did not seek to amend the charges, nor make allegations of sexual violence in relation to the existing charges, before the charges were confirmed, or between that date and the start of the trial.[2]

The decision had lasting consequences for the *Lubanga* case, which as the first case to proceed to trial at the ICC, had a major influence on public perceptions of the Court. International and local NGOs were highly critical of the Prosecutor's decision not to charge Lubanga with a broader range of crimes, including sexual violence crimes. As detailed in Chapter 4, these groups urged the Prosecutor to add charges of sexual violence before the confirmation of charges stage, but he did not do so.[3] After the charges were confirmed, the OTP sought to make amends at trial. At that stage, it introduced evidence of sexual violence crimes committed against UPC 'child soldiers' by their commanders, arguing that this sexual abuse was covered by the existing charges of conscripting, enlisting or using 'child soldiers'. The argument did not succeed: in 2009, the Appeals Chamber held that the charges could not exceed the facts and circumstances confirmed by the Pre-Trial Chamber;[4] in 2012, the Trial Chamber therefore declined to determine Lubanga's accountability for any sexual violence crimes;[5] and in 2015, the Appeals Chamber held that he was therefore not liable to pay any reparations for such crimes.[6]

of Sexual Violence in the Congo War' (March 2005) 19–21; UN Organization Mission in the Democratic Republic of the Congo, 'Special Report on the Events in Ituri, January 2002–December 2003, UN DOC. s/2004/573' (16 July 2004), [2], [24] [37], [80], [153]. Regarding the Sudanese army and Janjaweed, see 'Report of the International Commission of Inquiry on Darfur to the United Nations Secretary-General Pursuant to Security Council Resolution 1564 (2004) of 18 September 2004, UN Doc S/2005/60' (1 February 2005) 3.

2 RS, Art. 61(9).

3 E.g. Avocats Sans Frontières et al., 'DR Congo: ICC Charges Raise Concern' (31 July 2006) www.hrw.org/news/2006/07/31/dr-congo-icc-charges-raise-concern. See also P. Kambale, 'A Story of Missed Opportunities' in C. De Vos, S. Kendall and C. Stahn (eds), *The Politics and Practice of International Criminal Court Interventions* (Cambridge University Press, 2015) 171, 180–181.

4 *Lubanga* (ICC-01/04-01/06-2205), 17 December 2009, [77].

5 *Lubanga* (ICC-01/04-01/06-2842), 14 March 2012, [629]–[629].

6 *Lubanga* (ICC-01/04-01/06-3129), 3 March 2015, [196]–[199].

Unsurprisingly, women's rights activists and feminist scholars were dismayed at the Prosecutor's approach to charging sexual violence in this case. For instance, Patricia Sellers, current Special Advisor on Gender to the ICC Prosecutor, has described the case as 'disappointing' from a gender perspective.[7] Other terms used included 'shocking',[8] 'shambolic'[9] and a 'colossal failure'.[10]

It appears that numerous factors contributed to the failure to charge sexual violence crimes in this first trial. First, the ICC's status as a new institution seems to have created a sense of urgency and anxiety around starting cases without delay. Reflecting on this pressure in a 2008 interview with the Institute for War and Peace Reporting (IWPR), one former senior official in the OTP explained 'the idea was if we want to get the Court started, there was no way we could investigate for years and years and not have cases. Once we have sufficient evidence, we have to move.'[11]

Second, the investigation in Ituri, a region devastated by decades of war, was very difficult. According to the investigation leader Bernard Lavigne, whose deposition the ICC heard in 2011, these difficulties arose from the 'insufficient' number of ICC investigators, coupled with the unstable security situation in Ituri, which was 'still in the hands of militia groups' at the time.[12] Another difficulty was the Prosecutor's inconsistent objectives for the investigation, to which Lavigne alluded in his deposition[13] and again in 2016, when he told *The New York Times*:

> We accumulated a lot of information about one militia [in the DRC]. Then suddenly, because of a political decision by Luis or his political committee, we were obliged to change our planning and our investigative work and concentrate on a new target. It was completely crazy.[14]

[7] Interview, February 2018.

[8] Women's Initiatives for Gender Justice, 'Reflection: Gender Issues and Child Soldiers – the Case of Prosecutor v. Thomas Lubanga Dyilo' (25 August 2011) 2.

[9] N. Hayes, 'Sisyphus Wept: Prosecuting Sexual Violence at the International Criminal Court' in W. Schabas, Y. McDermott and N. Hayes (eds), *The Ashgate Research Companion to International Criminal Law* (Ashgate, 2013) 7, 16.

[10] K. O'Smith, 'Prosecutor v. Lubanga: How the International Criminal Court Failed the Women and Girls of the Congo' (2013) 54(2) *Howard Law Journal* 467, 474.

[11] K. Glassborrow, 'ICC Investigative Strategy Under Fire' (Institute for War and Peace Reporting, 27 October 2008).

[12] See ICC-01/04-01/06-Rule68Deposition-Red2-ENG, 16 November 2011, 16(16); 22(11–12).

[13] Ibid., 24(8–24); 29(9–12). See also the next two hearings, bearing the same number, on 17 and 18 November 2011.

[14] J. Verini, 'The Prosecutor and the President' (*New York Times*, 22 June 2016).

Third, there were additional time pressures in the *Lubanga* case. In January 2006, roughly eighteen months into the investigation, Prosecutor Moreno-Ocampo received information that Lubanga was due to be released from detention in the Democratic Republic of Congo imminently, possibly 'within the next three to four weeks.'[15] The Prosecutor therefore wanted to obtain an arrest warrant quickly, so that Lubanga could be transferred to The Hague before he had a chance to flee. At that time, the only crimes that the OTP had sufficient evidence to charge were the war crimes of conscripting, enlisting and using 'child soldiers'. As explained by the Prosecutor in 2009:

> I knew to arrest Lubanga I had to move my case fast. So, I had strong evidence about child soldiers, I was not ready to prove the connection between Lubanga and some of the killings and the rapes. And then I decided to move just with the case I had proofs [sic].[16]

This point about the state of the evidence is important: had the Prosecutor included sexual violence charges without sufficient evidence, those charges would surely not have been confirmed – a scenario later illustrated by the *Mbarasuhimana* case. Yet behind this point lie some larger questions: why was there so little evidence to prove crimes of sexual violence at the time that Lubanga's release became imminent? Was this the unavoidable outcome of a rigorous and gender-sensitive investigation in which a sincere effort to collect evidence of sexual violence crimes was made? The aforementioned IWPR report presents conflicting views in this regard. According to Christine Chung, a former OTP Senior Trial Attorney, 'pressure to start cases was there, but that factor did not cause planning for the investigation of sexual violence crimes to be impaired.'[17] Former OTP investigators presented a different view. One told IWPR: 'we knew that during killings, rapes happened [but] the idea was that the first ICC trial could not fail. To organise a good trial, the prosecutor selected child soldiers as the only charge against Lubanga and to drop the others … against the will of many investigators.' Another stated:

> For a year and a half, we didn't just investigate the use of child soldiers – sexual violence was part of the overall investigation – but the decision to focus meant that all the things we had done for the last year and

[15] ICC-01/04-02/06-20-Anx2, 10 February 2006, [33].

[16] P. Yates, *The Reckoning: The Battle for the International Criminal Court* (Skylight Pictures, 2009) 00:38:24. See also ICC OTP, 'Report on the Activities Performed during the First Three Years (June 2003–June 2006)' (12 September 2006) 8, 12–13; R. Irwin, 'Interview with Fatou Bensouda, ICC Deputy Prosecutor' on *International Justice Monitor* (31 July 2009).

[17] Glassborrow, see n. 11.

> a half was gone. I cannot remember how and when the explanation was given, but it was important for the office to present a case before the court.

In that same report, an ex-investigator stated that sexual violence crimes 'were not specifically investigated' in Uganda either; rather, these crimes were only included in the *Kony et al.* case after female witnesses raised the issue when investigators were pursuing other leads.[18] These statements suggest that in the early years, the investigation of sexual violence was not a high priority for the OTP leadership. The Prosecutor himself gave that same impression at a hearing in February 2006, three weeks after he applied for Lubanga's arrest warrant. At that hearing, the Prosecutor listed several crimes that his staff were continuing to investigate in relation to Lubanga, none of which were sexual violence crimes.[19]

These findings suggest that in the early years, the OTP's approach to charging sexual violence crimes was inconsistent and seemingly reactive, rather than planned from the outset. That the former Prosecutor seemed to have de-prioritised accountability for of sexual violence crimes may have been surprising, given the prevalence of these crimes in the situations under investigation and their prominence in the Rome Statute. However, it is not so surprising if one considers the historical tendency to overlook or trivialise sexual violence crimes in international criminal law, or to assume that these crimes are too difficult to investigate, as detailed in Chapter 3. A feminist institutionalist approach suggests that these tendencies will not cease immediately following a change in the formal rules, but will seep into a new institution in ways unanticipated by its designers. As Louise Chappell has persuasively argued, this understanding of how new institutions generally operate helps to contextualise the de-prioritisation of accountability for sexual violence crimes in the ICC's early years.[20]

In my discussions and interviews with OTP staff, there appears to be a further reason that the OTP did not charge Lubanga for the rapes allegedly committed against 'child soldiers' (as distinct from the other sexual violence crimes reportedly committed by the UPC throughout Ituri). That is, the OTP assumed that because the putative victims and perpetrators of

[18] Ibid.

[19] ICC-01/04-01/06-170, 28 June 2007, [3].

[20] See L. Chappell, 'Conflicting Institutions and the Search for Gender Justice at the International Criminal Court' (2014) 67(1) *Political Research Quarterly* 183; L. Chappell, *The Politics of Gender Justice at the International Criminal Court: Legacies and Legitimacy* (Oxford University Press, 2016) 110–117.

these sexual violence crimes were all part of the same armed group, this sexual violence could not be charged as a war crime. As one OTP interviewee stated, 'the feeling at the time' of the *Lubanga* case was that sexual violence *within* an armed group was not a war crime because 'if you look at it from a classical point of view, war crimes are crimes that you commit against the Other', that is, against persons and property associated with the opposing side.[21] Later, in the *Ntaganda* case, the OTP successfully refuted that 'classical view' of war crimes (see §5.3.1). However, when Lubanga was charged in 2006, the Office had not yet invested the time nor sought out the expertise that would enable it to make that legal argument.

It is positive to see that over time, the proportional representation of sexual violence crimes in ICC cases has increased. As of 17 July 2018, gender-based crimes – most of which are sexual violence crimes – account for almost half of all crimes charged at the ICC. Specifically, they account for 85 out of 173 charges (49.13 per cent) in requests for arrest warrants/summons to appear and 50 of 110 charges (45.45 per cent) in charging documents (see Figures 5.1 and 5.2). These percentages take into account developments in the *Ongwen* and *Ntaganda* cases, in which charges for sexual violence crimes were added *after* an initial arrest warrant was issued, as well as the fifteen cases that have included charges for these crimes from the start.[22] It would take some time

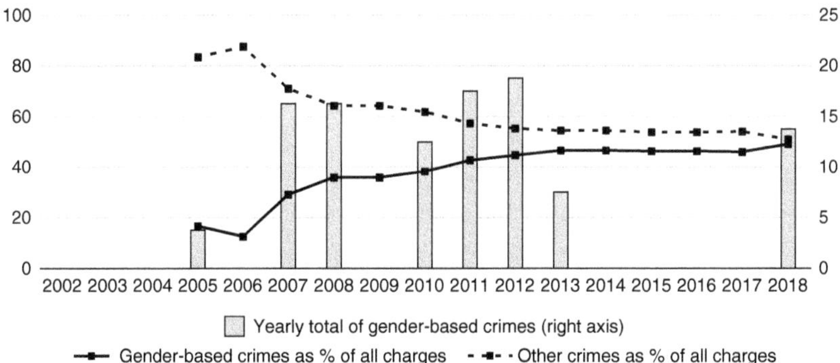


**Figure 5.1** Gender-based crimes as a percentage of all charges in OTP's request for arrest warrant/summons (1 July 2002 to 17 July 2018).

[21] Interview A, ICC OTP, 2017.

[22] These cases are: *Ahmad Harun & Ali Kushayb; Al Hassan; Al-Senussi; Al-Tuhamy; Bashir; Bemba; Gaddafi; Gbagbo & Blé Goudé; Gbagbo; Hussein; Katanga; Mbarushimana; Mudacumura; Muthaura et al.*; and *Ngudjolo*.

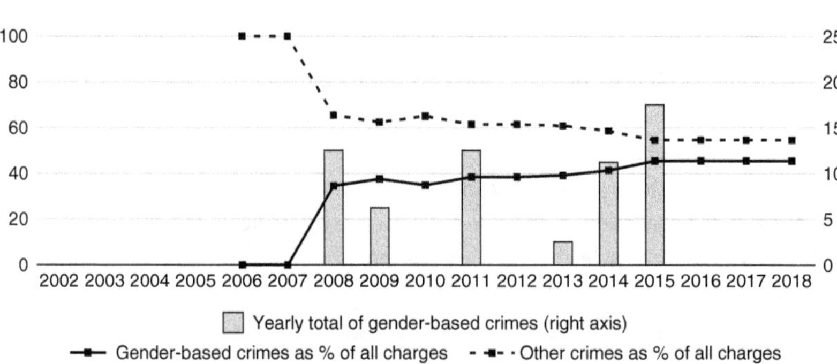


**Figure 5.2** Gender-based crimes as a percentage of all charges in OTP's request for confirmation of charges (1 July 2002 to 17 July 2018).

before the OTP's willingness to include charges of sexual violence crimes was matched with the ability to present sufficiently strong evidence for these charges to be confirmed. However, since 2014, the Office has consistently succeeded on that metric also (see §5.2.3).

### 5.1.2 *Whose Experiences of Sexual Violence?*

For the most part, the victims of sexual violence crimes have been identified as females, ranging from young children to grandmothers. More specifically, they have been female 'civilians', in the sense of people who were not part of armed group. An exception can be seen in the *Ntaganda* case, which includes charges of sexual violence against female 'child soldiers' as well as sexual violence against 'civilians' in Ituri. The OTP's attention to sexual violence against women and girls, including civilians and combatants, is to be commended. It signals that the welfare of women and girls is an issue worthy of international attention, and it helps to educate a global audience about the scale and gravity of conflict-related sexual violence against women and girls. In a 'best-case' scenario, it may also be valuable to the victims – more so if the crimes are proven (in which case, they may receive reparation) – but potentially, even if that outcome is not achieved. This point was emphasised by Paolina Massidda, Principal Counsel of the OPCV, in our 2017 interview. Massidda referred to the *Lubanga* case, in which the OTP did not charge the sexual abuse of female 'child soldiers', but nonetheless put evidence of this sexual violence on record at trial. That evidence was acknowledged in the trial judgment[23] and in

[23] ICC-01/04-01/06-2842, 14 March 2012, [890]–[896].

Judge Odio Benito's dissent.[24] This acknowledgment did not amount to a finding that the sexual violence crimes occurred, nor did it enable the victims to receive reparations for sexual violence crimes. Yet according to Massidda, it meant something to the victims. She explained:

> While there was no formal re-classification of the facts [relating to sexual violence], in the judgment there is recognition that victims were also subjected to gender crimes ... the Chamber acknowledged that witnesses have testified about these events. We went back to the victims, they were happy. Because for them, it was the way in which the story had to be told.[25]

In several cases, male experiences of sexual violence have also been charged. Examples include the *Bemba* case, which included charges for the rape of both male and female civilians in the Central African Republic (CAR); the *Ntaganda* case, which included charges for the alleged rape of male and female civilians by UPC troops, as well as allegations of civilians being forced to rape one another; the *Muthaura et al.* case, which included charges for the alleged genital mutilation of men during Kenya's post-election violence; the *Mbarushimana* and *Mudacumura* cases, which included charges for mutilating men's genitals, raping male civilians and forcing them to rape other female victims during the conflict in North and South Kivu, Democratic Republic of Congo; and potentially the *Gaddafi*, *Al-Senussi* and *Al-Tuhamy* cases, which contain charges for the alleged rape and sexualised torture of political dissidents in Libya (in the public court records, the victims' sex is not disclosed, but the UN commission of inquiry found that both male and female detainees reported this kind of abuse).[26] The recognition of these male experiences of sexual violence is important, especially when contrasted with the inattention to this issue in the past.[27] This recognition is not only important for the victims; it is also important for a global audience of policy-makers, healthcare providers, humanitarian actors and accountability mechanisms because 'without envisioning the violated male body we can neither hope to prevent its violation nor seek redress for violence committed against it.'[28]

That said, there are signs that the OTP may have missed some opportunities to recognise and prosecute sexual violence against men and boys.

[24] Ibid. (Odio Benito), [271].

[25] Interview, 15 June 2017.

[26] 'Report of the International Commission of Inquiry on Libya, UN Doc. A/HRC/19/68' (2 March 2012), [48].

[27] See Chapter 3, §3.1.4.

[28] R. Grey and L. Shepherd, '"Stop Rape Now?" Masculinity, Responsibility, and Conflict-Related Sexual Violence' (2013) 16(1) *Men and Masculinities* 115, 122.

For example, in *Lubanga*, there were signs that male 'child soldiers' in the UPC were incited to commit and participate in sexual violence crimes against women and girls – which can be considered a form of sexual violence towards the male children, as well as towards the women and girls concerned. The Prosecutor flagged this issue on the first day of trial, stating that the victims 'cannot forget that *they raped* and that they were raped',[29] that 'young boys were instructed to rape'[30] and that one such boy told the investigators that the commanders 'really encouraged us to rape women'.[31] Yet as the trial progressed, the OTP's evidence for these allegations was not extensive. Public records suggest that just one witness gave first-hand evidence in this regard. That witness was P-0008, who stated that as a 'child soldier' in the UPC, he was sent by the commanders to 'carry out activities that were not good', which meant 'taking girls by force, that is raping them and taking them to the place where we lived'.[32] When asked by the Prosecution lawyer whether he had personally followed those instructions, P-0008 replied: 'yes, I raped once', and identified the victim as a girl his own age.[33] At that juncture, Judge Fulford intervened to ask whether further questions on this topic were 'strictly necessary'.[34] The Prosecutor lawyer replied:

> It is the prosecution's case that these types of activities were *part and parcel of the use of children in combat,* and it also, in our submission, may provide insight into – to the impact and, therefore, for sentencing. But I understand your Honour's concern, and I'm happy to move on.[35]

In response to questions from Judge Odio Benito, P-008 stated that boys in the UPC were not themselves raped, only girls were raped.[36] The issue was also touched on by P-0031, an intermediary who had worked with the OTP, who referred to a twelve-year-old child in the UPC who 'had to rape a woman of 60'.[37] It appears that the OTP could have raised this issue proactively with other witnesses, without asking impermissible leading

[29] ICC-01/04-01/06-T-107-ENG, 26 January 2009, 5(2–3) (emphasis added).
[30] Ibid., 11(23).
[31] Ibid., 10(8–9).
[32] ICC-01/04-01/06-T-135-Red2-ENG, 25 February 2009, 37(24)–38(6).
[33] Ibid., 38(14).
[34] Ibid., 38(19–25).
[35] Ibid., 39(1–5) (emphasis added).
[36] ICC-01/04-01/06-T-138-Red-ENG, 27 February 2009, 21(24)–22(1).
[37] ICC-01/04-01/06-T-201-Red2-ENG, 30 June 2009, 69(22)–70(5). In the public transcript, the sex of this child is not disclosed. Thus, the sex of this child is inferred here.

questions.[38] By the end of the trial, the issue of sexual violence against male 'child soldiers' was not central to Prosecution's case. It was mentioned only twice in the closing brief: first, as an example of how the children were 'used to participate actively in hostilities', the brief noted that 'during battles, they were incited to pillage and to steal money from the population and sometimes to rape';[39] and second, in reference to P-008's rape admission, as 'a factor in assessing his credibility'.[40]

In the OTP's closing statements, which were delivered by seven advocates over a full day's hearing, the issue of male children being forced to commit rape was mentioned only once – namely, by the (then) Deputy Prosecutor, who stated that UPC 'child soldiers' 'were used to kill, rape, and pillage throughout the 12-month period of these charges.'[41] One advocate also cited evidence of boys being told to abduct girls for their *commanders* to sexually abuse. However, when asked to clarify this argument by Judge Fulford, she confirmed that the OTP did not mean that selecting young women *by itself* constitutes participating in hostilities, rather 'you have to look at the position in the round.'[42] Perhaps because of its obscurity in the Prosecution's case, the sexualised use of male 'child soldiers' was not mentioned in the trial judgment or in Judge Odio Bentio's dissent.

More recently, in the *Ongwen* case, the victims' counsel requested leave to present the testimony of three men who claimed to have been sexually abused by LRA forces during one of the attacks charged in the case. This request, which the Trial Chamber rejected and the OTP did not respond to publically, raises a question as to whether sexual violence against males was adequately investigated in this case. In our 2018 interview,

[38] In *Lubanga*, the Trial Chamber permitted the Prosecution to ask several questions that the Defence viewed as 'leading'. For example, it allowed the Prosecution ask a witness whether girls played a combat role in a particular battle, although the Defence thought this question was too directive. In allowing in such questions, the Chamber was mindful of the need to steer the witnesses towards topics that are relevant to the case. To quote Judge Fulford: 'Questions have got to take the witness to the right area, otherwise the witness will not know what he's expected to deal with.' See ICC-01/04-01/06-T-149-Red2-ENG, 17 March 2009, 14(15)–15(5); ICC-01/04-01/06-T-135-Red3-ENG, 25 February 2009, 33(9–10).

[39] ICC-01/04-01/06-2748-Red, 1 June 2011, [211].

[40] Ibid., [427].

[41] ICC-01/04-01/06-T-356-ENG, 25 August 2011, 4(4–6).

[42] Ibid., 22(6)–23(17). For relevant testimony, see: ICC-01/04-01/06-T-149-Red2-ENG, 17 March 2009, 26(18)–27(18); ICC-01/04-01/06-T-151-Red2-ENG, 19 March 2009, 9(25)–12(1).

this incident was noted by Melinda Reed, Executive Director of Women's Initiatives for Gender Justice. In her words, 'sexual violence against men and boys has been overlooked historically everywhere, and I think in the *Ongwen* case there was a missed opportunity to include evidence of these crimes.'[43] For the three men whose testimony the Chamber declined to hear, and for other male victims of sexual violence who might feel similarly silenced, the Chamber's decision was a great shame.[44] As the victims' counsel explained:

> Where so many other aspects of victims' experiences are highlighted publicly, the conscious *exclusion* of material about sexual violence against men has the consequence of entrenching the misconception that such violence did not happen… Secondly, for those individuals who have bravely spoken up about their experiences of sexual violence despite the barriers to reporting mentioned above, the Chamber's decision risks reinforcing the harmful social messages they have internalised and which form disincentives to disclosure. Their experience is treated as something which is not 'about' the crimes which were committed against them. It is therefore something about them (their gender identity: masculinity or lack of it).[45]

### *5.1.3 Non-Sexual Gender-based Crimes*

As noted previously, most gender-based crimes brought before the ICC have been sexual violence crimes. However, a smaller proportion are non-sexual gender-based crimes. Examples include the alleged massacres of men from the Fur ethnic group in Darfur (*Ahmad Harun & Ali Kushayb* and *Hussein*); the forced domestic labour allegedly performed by female UPC 'child soldiers' (*Ntaganda*); the deprivation of women's civil and political rights, such as the right to freely assemble, by Islamist militants in Mali (*Al Hassan*); the forced domestic labour performed by younger girls known as 'ting tings' in the LRA (*Ongwen*); and the imposition of 'forced marriages', namely, relationships in which the 'wives' were allegedly subjected to forced domestic labour as well as sexual abuse (*Ongwen* and *Al Hassan*).

For the most part, these crimes have not been described in the OTP's filings or opening and closing statements as 'gender-based crimes'. This

[43] Interview, 9 July 2018.

[44] For a critique of this decision, see J. O'Donohue, R. Grey and L. Krasny, 'Evidence of Sexual Violence against Men and Boys Rejected in the Ongwen Case' on *Human Rights in International Justice* (10 April 2018).

[45] *Ongwen* (ICC-02/04-01/15-1203), 12 March 2018, [33]–[34].

is perhaps myopic, but not surprising. As explained by gender expert Niamh Hayes, who at the time of our interview was based in the OTP on secondment from UN Women:

> [First], you have to get people to understand that of course there's a gender component to sexual violence, and that extends to men as well as women. … *Then* you have to get them to understand that there are gender-based crimes with no sexual component.[46]

The interviews conducted for this book suggest that, at least for high-level staff of the OTP, this lesson has been internalised. As detailed in Chapter 2, all but one OTP interviewee defined the term 'gender-based crime' as broader than sexual violence crimes. More concretely, this definition is starting to be applied in cases before the Court. For example, in the *Ongwen* case, the forced domestic labour performed by women and girls in the LRA has been described as a 'gender-based crime'. Moreover, as detailed subsequently, there are indications that the OTP will seek to prosecute various non-sexual acts directed against women and girls as 'gender-based persecution' in the Afghanistan situation, the Nigeria situation, and the *Al Hassan* case from the situation in Mali (see §5.3.2). The fact that these charges of 'gender-based persecution' are not based solely on evidence of sexual violence is progressive. As observed by Hayes, 'it's still really rare to see something that's completely non-sexual be *presented* as a gender-based crime.'[47]

### *5.1.4 Legal Characterisation*

Gender-based crimes, most of which are crimes of sexual violence, have been charged in a wide variety of ways at the ICC. The crimes most often used for this purpose have been rape and persecution, both as crimes against humanity. In addition, other frequently used crimes include torture and sexual slavery as crimes against humanity, and rape, sexual slavery, torture, and outrages on personal dignity as war crimes (see Figure 5.3).

This integrated charging approach accords with the views of women's rights activists at the 1998 Rome Conference, who argued that in the ICC, acts of sexual violence should be charged as such (i.e. as rape, as sexual

[46] Interview, July 2017 (emphasis added).
[47] Ibid.

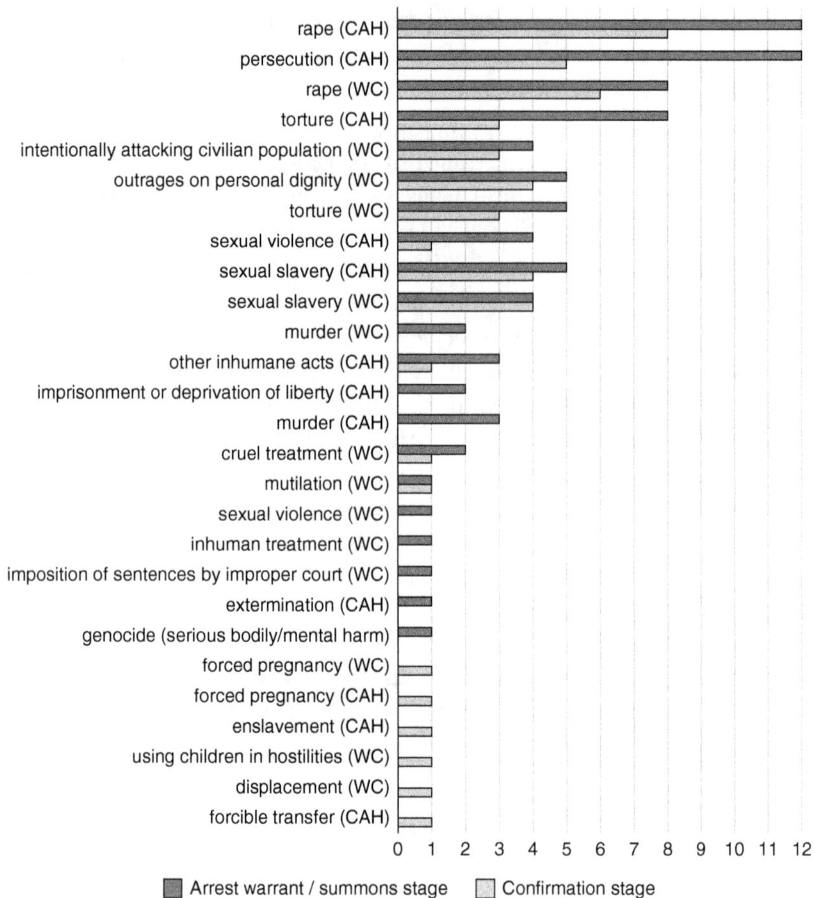


**Figure 5.3** Number of times provision used by Prosecutor to charge gender-based crimes (1 July 2002 to 17 July 2018).

slavery, etc.), and should also be read into other crimes such as torture and genocide, as was the practice at the ICTY and ICTR.[48] This same call continues twenty years later. For example, in a 2018 *amicus curiae* brief in the proceedings regarding a possible ICC investigation into the alleged deportation of Rohingya people from Myanmar and Bangladesh, Women's Initiatives for Gender Justice and their co-authors argued that 'sexual and

[48] Chapter 3, §3.1.2.

gender-based crimes may constitute a coercive act underlying the crime of deportation or forcible transfer',[49] a position with which the OTP agrees[50] and has used in the past, namely, in the *Ntaganda* case.[51]

Since 2014, the OTP's strategy for charging gender-based crimes has become increasingly progressive, including relying on legal arguments that have not previously been made in other international criminal courts. Standout examples include the charges relating to the sexual abuse of 'child soldiers' in the *Ntaganda* case; the charges of forced pregnancy in the *Ongwen* case; and the charge of gender-based persecution in the *Al Hassan* case. These groundbreaking charges are discussed in §5.3.

### 5.1.5 *Internal Reforms*

The previous discussion shows that over time, the OTP has charged an increasing proportion of gender-based crimes, particularly sexual violence crimes, and has begun to develop some novel legal strategies in this regard. What explains these developments in charging practices? In the course of researching this book, several reasons were identified.

The first is that a commitment to investigating and prosecuting gender-based crimes has been institutionalised in the OTP. Fatou Bensouda, who during Luis Moreno-Ocampo's term was the OTP's gender focal point and the Deputy Prosecutor, has consistently articulated a commitment to prosecuting these crimes since she was sworn in as Prosecutor in June 2012.[52] This commitment has been reinforced in OTP planning documents, including the 2014 *Policy Paper on Sexual and Gender-Based Crimes*[53] and the OTP's two most recent Strategic Plans, published in 2013 and 2015.[54] Hence, as Hayes told me in our 2017 interview, the message that the OTP is committed to investigation and prosecuting these crimes is 'absolutely everywhere'.[55]

Second, external criticism over the lack of sexual violence charges in the *Lubanga* case did not cease after the initial outcry, but was sustained

[49] ICC-RoC46(3)-01/18-22, 18 June 2018, [13].

[50] ICC-RoC46(3)-01/18-33, 11 July 2018, [7].

[51] ICC-01/04-02/06-503-AnxA-Red2, 1 September 2015, [324].

[52] F. Bensouda, 'Statement' (at the Ceremony for the solemn undertaking of the Prosecutor of the International Criminal Court, The Hague, 15 June 2012).

[53] OTP, Policy Paper on Sexual and Gender-Based Crimes (June 2014), [51], [71].

[54] ICC OTP, 'Strategic Plan June 2012–2015' (11 October 2013) Goal 3; ICC OTP, 'Strategic Plan 2016–2018' (16 November 2015) Goal 2.

[55] Interview, July 2017.

throughout the case.[56] Prosecutor Bensouda has acknowledged that this advocacy had some effect, stating:

> In the ICC's first trial, against Thomas Lubanga Dyilo, the Prosecution explained the gender dimension of the crime of enlisting and conscripting children under the age of 15. It took note, however, of the reaction of civil society's preference [sic] for these aspects to be explicitly charged. Sexual and gender crimes were included directly in the charges in [the] *Katanga, Ngudjolo, Mbarushimana* and *Mudacumura* cases, as well as in the additional charges presented against Bosco Ntaganda.'[57]

Even more significant than this shift to 'explicitly' charging gender-based crimes is the OTP's current practice of *timely* charging of these crimes. That is, it has not repeated the error of introducing new factual allegations of sexual violence at trial, having made no such allegations at the pre-trial stage.

Third, following critiques of its early investigative strategy[58] and several negative in-court experiences (e.g. the loss of all charges in the *Mbarushimana* case), the OTP has reformed its investigation practices. One reform has been a shift from 'focused investigations' to 'in-depth, open-ended investigations', which means following more leads *before* deciding on the boundaries of the case.[59] Another reform is that team leaders must either specify concrete steps for investigating gender-based crimes in their investigation plan, or justify to OTP colleagues why these steps are not there. As one of my OTP interviewees explained, 'it's making sure that there had to be reasons given why [sexual and gender-based] crimes are *not* incorporated in the charges.'[60] Describing this same change, another interview stated:

> One of the lessons that we have learned to ensure that [the investigation of sexual and gender-based crime] is not put on the backburner, and that's part of our working practice now – if a team leader does not include the investigation of SGBC in the investigations plan, that person has to justify it in writing.[61]

[56] E.g. Women's Initiatives for Gender Justice, 'Reflection: Gender Issues and Child Soldiers – the Case of Prosecutor v. Thomas Lubanga Dyilo', see n. 8; Chappell, 'Conflicting Institutions', see n. 20; Hayes, see n. 9; O'Smith, see n. 10.

[57] F. Bensouda, 'Gender Justice and the ICC' (2014) 16(4) *International Feminist Journal of Politics* 538, 540.

[58] E.g. Hayes, see n. 9; Glassborrow, see n. 11; C. De Vos, 'Investigating from Afar: The ICC's Evidence Problem' (2013) 26(4) *Leiden Journal of International Law* 1009.

[59] OTP, *Strategic Plan June 2012–2015* (11 October 2013), 4(a), [23], [90]; OTP, *Strategic Plan 2016–2018* (16 November 2015), [35], [36].

[60] Interview K, ICC OTP, 2017.

[61] Interview H, ICC OTP, 2017.

These changes have apparently influenced the way that ICC investigators approach their work. As one OTP interviewee who works closely with the investigations unit explained:

> Looking at sexual and gender-based crimes has become part of the general workflow, starting from the initiation of an investigation, right through to trial. So it's become part and parcel of the work of investigation teams – it is something they don't have to leave until half way through the investigation, but it's something that has to be looked at right at the beginning and followed through. For me, that's one indicator of 'success', maybe not as a result, but an outcome of the Office elevating it to a strategic goal. So that for me is one indicator – how much the staff, especially the investigators embrace it, and how much effort they put into proactively investigating it.[62]

Fourth, the process of reviewing the evidence to determine which charges can be sustained has become more formalised. This formalised 'evidence review' process, which was introduced after 2012,[63] was identified as an important change by several OTP interviewees. One stated:

> There were always evidence reviews by independent people outside the team, senior people, to look at 'what's going on there?', 'is that right?', 'have you thought of this, have you thought of that?', 'oh that's a gap, you guys are going to need to address that.' But everything's been made a bit more formal, which I think is a good thing. In all the divisions, there's a checklist for gender analysis.[64]

Another observed:

> In terms of lessons learned, it's also very important for trial teams to have evidence reviews, prior to charging individuals … That's super important: to have a number of eyes in the Office look at a case. Because a trial team can go down a certain path and see things in a certain way. But the beauty of having an evidence review, which involves people from different areas of the Office, who each bring different expertise and have different gender perspectives as well, can really help to see things properly … we really thrash things out in those evidence reviews. I think that process led to appropriate charges being brought in the *Ongwen* case, namely, sexual slavery, forced marriage, and forced pregnancy. I think there was never any doubt regarding the sexual slavery charges. But with forced marriage and forced pregnancy, there were arguments on both sides and it was good to bring out all the relevant issues.[65]

[62] Ibid.
[63] Interview B, ICC OTP, 2017.
[64] Interview K, ICC OTP, 2017.
[65] Interview B, ICC OTP, 2017.

Fifth, the OTP now has increased legal expertise. Its lawyers have had the opportunity to develop their knowledge of the ICC's law and procedure over the sixteen years that the Rome Statute has been in force. Moreover, as the ICTY started to come to a close, a number of highly experienced prosecutors have relocated to the ICC, bringing expertise in the prosecution of gender-based crimes with them. In addition, both ICC Prosecutors have made use of Article 42(9) of the Rome Statute, which requires the Prosecutor to appoint advisors with legal expertise on issues including 'sexual and gender violence'. For the purposes of this book, the most relevant appointments have been Professor Catharine MacKinnon, a widely publicised feminist legal scholar, as Gender Advisor from November 2008 (i.e. after the *Lubanga* confirmation of charges process) to August 2012; Brigid Inder, former Executive Director of Women's Initiatives for Gender Justice, as Gender Advisor from August 2012 to August 2016; and Professor Patricia Sellers, former Gender Advisor to the ICTY Prosecutor, as the ICC Prosecutor's Advisor on International Criminal Law Prosecution Strategies from December 2012, and then as Gender Advisor since December 2017.

Complementing those appointments, increased expertise on other topics has enabled the OTP to develop new strategies for prosecuting gender-based crimes. For example, from March 2010 onward, Professor Tim McCormack has served as the Prosecutor's Advisor on International Humanitarian Law (IHL), also known as the laws of war. During this period, the OTP has revisited its views about the options for prosecuting the sexual abuse of 'child soldiers' by their own commanders, and has determined that this conduct *can* be prosecuted in the ICC using the war crimes of rape and sexual slavery. The OTP made this argument for the first time in the *Ntaganda* case, as detailed subsequently. Reflecting on this shift in approach in our 2017 interview, Fabricio Guariglia, head of the OTP's Prosecution Division, explained:

> It's the Office of the Prosecutor being more curious and self-critical. In *Lubanga*, we took this position, we thought this [sexual abuse of 'child soldiers'] is not a war crime because it's a crime committed against your own [troops]… But there is something there that doesn't feel right, so let's have a second look and task some experts to also have a look with us. And we had a full discussion, and we said actually, this is a war crime.[66]

[66] Interview, ICC OTP, 2017 (ellipses omitted).

Collectively, these reforms have enabled and encouraged the increased investigation and prosecution of gender-based crimes. While it is still early days, these shifts in practice are starting to bear fruit. For example, the case in which the highest number of gender-based crimes has been charged and confirmed to date, namely *Ongwen*, included investigations and an 'evidence review' process that post-dated the aforementioned changes behind the scenes.

## 5.2 Charging Outcomes

Turning now to outcomes, this section assess how well gender-based crimes have fared once they have been brought before the Court. It examines how effective the OTP has been in establishing charges of gender-based crimes – which means proving that the crimes occurred *and* that the accused was responsible for those crimes.

### *5.2.1 Grounds for Concern*

In the ICC, as in most domestic courts, the Prosecution must clear several hurdles before a conviction can theoretically be rendered. At each of hurdle, the evidentiary standard is raised. Specifically, the Prosecution must satisfy a 'reasonable grounds' standard to obtain an arrest warrant or summons to appear, a 'substantial grounds' standard for confirmation of the charges, and 'beyond reasonable doubt' for a conviction.[67] The analysis undertaken for this book shows that at each of these stages of proceedings, a decreasing proportion of gender-based crimes has been confirmed: just under 93 per cent at the arrest warrant/summons to appear stage; 74 per cent at the confirmation stage; and zero per cent at the end of the trial (see Figure 5.4). The mere fact of this decrease does not raise a concern. Across any category of crimes, a decrease is expected: this is a function of the fact that the Prosecution must meet a higher evidentiary standard at each stage of proceedings. However, it is significant that at the ICC, the decrease for gender-based crimes has been *so* sharp, culminating in a conviction rate of zero out of ten charges of gender-based crimes.[68]

[67] RS, Art. 58(1)(a), 61(7), and 66(3).

[68] These ten charges of gender-based crimes include: four from the *Ngudjolo* case (rape as a war crime, rape as a crime against humanity, sexual slavery as a war crime, and sexual slavery as a crime against humanity); four from the *Katanga* case (rape as a war crime, rape as a crime against humanity, sexual slavery as a war crime, and sexual slavery as a

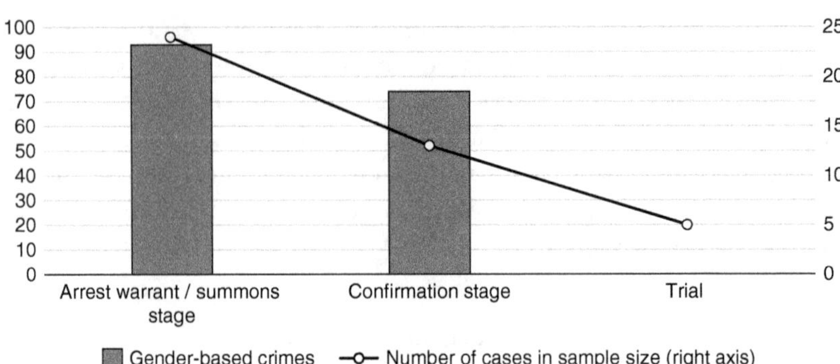


**Figure 5.4** Percentage of charges established at each stage of proceedings: Gender-based crimes (1 July 2002 to 17 July 2018).

The record begins to look more concerning when a comparison with other crimes is introduced (see Figure 5.5). One can see that every stage of proceedings, the OTP has been less successful in establishing charges of gender-based crimes than other crimes. The gap widens at each stage of proceedings, ending in a conviction rate of zero per cent (zero out of ten) for gender-based crimes and 47 per cent (nine out of nineteen) for other crimes. In our 2017 interview, Guariglia acknowledged that this

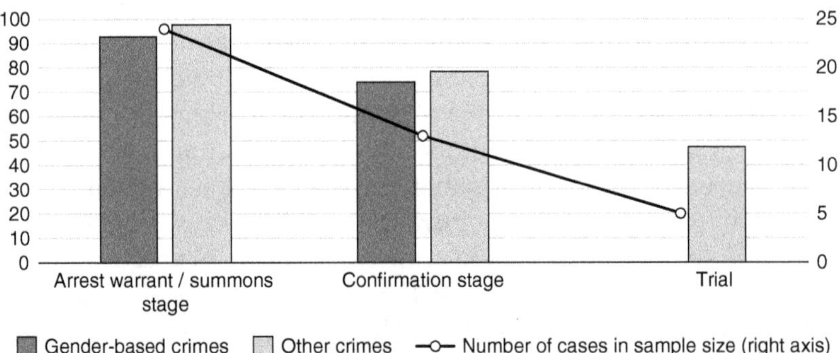


**Figure 5.5** Percentage of charges established at each stage of proceedings: Gender-based crimes v. other crimes (1 July 2002 to 17 July 2018).

crime against humanity); and two from the *Bemba* case (rape as a war crime, and rape as a crime against humanity). As detailed in Chapter 4, there were no charges of gender-based crimes in the *Lubanga* case, although the Prosecution introduced evidence of such crimes at trial. There were also no charges of gender-based crimes in the fifth case where judgment has been rendered (*Al Mahdi*).

pattern raises a concern. He explained that when it comes to convictions and confirmation of gender-based crimes:

> This is an area where basically we were not doing well. Either we were failing to bring [the charges], to properly explore and to bring charges of gender violence when gender crimes had occurred, or we were bringing shaky charges that were not being accepted by the judges.[69]

### 5.2.2 *Contributing Factors*

There is no single reason for this pattern. Rather, there are multiple contributing factors, as summarised in the following sub-sections.

#### 5.2.2.1 Proving the Commission of the Crimes

In certain cases, the evidence regarding the commission of gender-based crimes was not robust. In particular, the OTP relied too heavily on 'hearsay evidence', meaning statements about facts that the witness did not personally observe, which is tendered with a view to proving that the stated facts occurred (such as when the date of a crime is evinced by a witness stating that she *heard* it occurred on a given date).[70] In the ICTY and ICTR, hearsay evidence was admissible, but its probative value was generally considered low.[71] Consistent with that approach, in several early ICC cases, the Pre-Trial Chamber warned that although it would allow the OTP to lead hearsay evidence, it would generally not confirm charges based on that evidence alone.[72] Despite that, the OTP still sought to rely solely on hearsay evidence to substantiate certain incidents of rape in the *Mbarushimana* case. The Pre-Trial Chamber held that this evidence was insufficient to establish that the alleged rapes occurred. Another example

[69] Interview, ICC OTP, 2017 (ellipses omitted).

[70] In the words of the ICTY Appeals Chamber, hearsay evidence is 'the statement of a person made otherwise than in the proceedings in which it is being tendered, but nevertheless being tendered in those proceedings in order to establish the truth of what that person says.' Decision on Prosecutor's Appeal on Admissibility of Evidence, *Aleksovski* (IT-95-14/1), 16 February 1999, [14].

[71] R. Cryer et al., *An Introduction to International Criminal Law and Procedure* (3rd edn) (Cambridge University Press, 2014), 469, citing: Decision on Prosecutor's Appeal on Admissibility of Evidence, *Aleksovski* (IT-95-14/1), 16 February 1999, [15]; Appeal Judgment, *Ndindabahizi* (ICTR-01-71-A), [115].

[72] See ICC-01/04-01/06-803-tEN, 7 February 2007, [106]; ICC-01/05-01/08-424, 15 June 2009, [47] and [51]; ICC-01/04-01/07-717, 11 October 2008, [118]–[120], [137]–[141].

can be seen in the *Mudacumura* case, in which there was insufficient evidence to prove an allegation of rape at the lower evidentiary standard applicable at the arrest warrant stage.[73]

Having said that, proving the commission of gender-based crimes has not been a major problem at the ICC. As Sellers noted in our February 2018 interview, 'the Office has on two different occasions put forward sufficient evidence that the judges have bent over backwards to say that we believe this sexual violence evidence, but it's the [mode of liability] evidence that's missing.'[74] Those two occasions were the *Katanga* and *Ngudjolo* cases, where the Trial Chamber was satisfied that the alleged sexual violence crimes associated with the Bogoro attacked had occurred. We can now say 'three occasions', including the *Bemba* case, in which the Appeals Chamber left in place the Trial Chamber's finding that 28 civilians had been raped by MLC troops in the Central African Republic.

Credit is due here first to the witnesses, whose testimony has been essential to proving the commission of the crimes, and secondly to the OTP, which has identified relevant witnesses and led them through examination-in-chief, and also corroborated their testimonies with pattern evidence (such as hospital data), radio intercepts and logbooks, and DNA evidence, which in the *Ongwen* case, has been advanced to prove the paternity of children that were allegedly conceived through rape. In addition, the OTP has recently started to seek and obtain permission to use prior-recorded testimony to substantiate allegations of sexual violence at trial. The first case to use this procedure was *Ongwen*, in which several women who were allegedly forced to serve as Ongwen's 'wives' gave testimony at the pre-trial stage, with that testimony recorded with a view to using it at trial. Not only is this use of technology useful to the Prosecution (because it ensures that the evidence is available even if the victims are later unable or unwilling to testify); it is also a way of 'reducing the trauma that a victim might have to go through in giving his or her evidence again in court.'[75]

Other courtroom actors deserve credit as well. This includes victims' counsel, who in some cases, have presented evidence that relates to the commission of gender-based crimes. An example can be seen in the

[73] ICC-01/04-01/12-1-Red, 13 July 2012, [48].
[74] Interview, February 2018.
[75] Interview B, ICC OTP, 2017.

*Bemba* case, in which the rape conviction rendered by the Trial Chamber was based, among other things, on testimony of a victim participant known as 'V1'.[76] It also includes the Defence, who on several occasions, have refrained from challenging certain statements where a witness has appeared distressed. For instance, in *Bemba*, the Defence often agreed not to challenge a witness's statement that sexual penetration had occurred.[77] This concession was not fatal to the Defence's case, because the Prosecution still had to prove that the sexual act occurred by threat, force, or coercion, and that Bemba, who was not physically at the scene, was criminally responsible for the crime. However, it potentially eased the process of giving evidence for the witnesses concerned.

Moreover, in assessing the evidence, judges have often shown awareness of the social and psychological factors that can preclude witnesses from giving a detailed and consistent account of their own experiences of sexual violence. For example, in the *Katanga* case, the Trial Chamber found that women had been raped and sexually enslaved in connection to the Bororo attack, as alleged by the OTP. That finding was based primarily on the testimonies of Witness 132, 249 and 353, whom the Chamber deemed credible notwithstanding some discrepancies and gaps in their evidence, which it attributed to the difficulties in testifying about an experience as traumatic as rape.[78]

A more recent example can be seen in the *Ongwen* case, in relation to the testimony of P-227, one of Ongwen's alleged 'wives'. When interviewed by an NGO in Uganda in 2010 shortly after leaving the LRA, P-227 said that she had *not* experienced any sexual violence crimes. However, when interviewed by ICC investigators in 2015, she said the opposite. In response to some strategic questioning by the Prosecution, P-227 explained that she found it easier to talk with the ICC investigators because she was no longer exhausted at the time, and unlike the NGO staff who interviewed her, they were female.[79] The Pre-Trial Chamber accepted this explanation, and deemed P-227's evidence of

[76] ICC-01/05-01/08-3343, 21 March 2016, [548], [551], [553], [633(l)]. The Majority of the Appeals Chamber determined that the rapes of V1 did not validly fall within the conviction because the relevant facts exceeded the scope of the charges as confirmed by the Pre-Trial Chamber. See ICC-01/05-01/08-3636-Red, 8 June 2018, [116(xvi)].

[77] E.g. P80: ICC-01/05-01/08-T-61-Red2-ENG, 6(11)–7(25), P79: ICC-01/05-01/08-T-77-Red3-ENG, 1 March 2011, 12(13)–13(12).

[78] ICC-01/04-01/07-3436-tENG, 7 March 2014, [204], [986] [988]–[992], [994].

[79] ICC-02/04-01/15-T-11-Red-ENG, 19 September 2015, 22(23)–24(5); 43(7)–45(10).

sexual violence to be credible.[80] Had it not been for the Prosecution's questioning, and P-227's ability to rationalise her choices, her testimony would most likely have been deemed unreliable.

#### 5.2.2.2 Proving the Responsibility of the Accused

In terms of proving gender-based crimes, the major issue continues to be showing that the accused person is responsible for the crimes according to one of more modes of liability found in Article 25 or Article 28 of the Rome Statute.[81] In several cases, the Defence has successfully refuted this aspect of the Prosecution's case. To be clear, this issue has not *only* arisen in relation to gender-based crimes. For example, in the *Abu Garda* case, which included no charges of gender-based crimes, the case did not proceed to trial as there was insufficient evidence to show that Abu Garda was responsible as charged. There have also been several cases where the Prosecution's arguments on criminal responsibility failed across all charges, only *some* of which were gender-based crimes. This includes the aforementioned *Mbarushimana* case, in which the Pre-Trial Chamber found that there was insufficient evidence to confirm any charges under Article 25(3)(d) (contributing), the *Ngudjolo* case, in which the accused was acquitted on all charges because there was insufficient evidence of his responsibility as an indirect co-perpetrator under Article 25(3)(a); and the *Bemba* cases, in which the Majority of the Appeals Chamber overturned the conviction under Article 28 (command responsibility). By contrast, in *Katanga*, the issue arose in relation to gender-based crimes specifically.

As detailed in Chapter 4, the Prosecutor charged Katanga with a range of crimes, including rape and sexual slavery, as an indirect co-perpetrator under Article 25(3)(a). The Trial Chamber found that Katanga was not responsible under that mode of liability for any of the crimes charged. The Majority of the Chamber then re-characterised the facts in order to consider Katanga's responsibility under Article 25(3)(d) (contributing to the commission of the crimes by a group of persons acting with a 'common purpose'). It found that he *was* responsible under that provision for murder, directing attacks against a civilian population, destruction of property and pillage, but *not* for rape and sexual slavery. In the Majority's view, those sexual violence crimes were not part of the 'common purpose'

[80] ICC-02/04-01/15-422-Red, 23 March 2016, [118].

[81] N. Hayes, 'La Lutte Continue: Investigating and Prosecuting Sexual Violence at the ICC' in C. Stahn (ed.), *The Law and Practice of the International Criminal Court* (Oxford University Press, 2015) 801, 813.

of the group, being to 'wipe out' the Hema militia based at Bogoro and the Hema civilian population of the village.[82]

The Prosecutor gave notice that she would appeal the acquittal for rape and sexual slavery 'including legal, procedural and factual findings that led to those acquittals.'[83] However, she later withdrew her appeal, stating:

> I have taken note of Germain Katanga's decision and of his acceptance of the Judges' conclusions in their Judgment as to his role and conduct during the attack on Bogoro. In particular, I have noted the 'sincere regret' expressed by Germain Katanga to 'all those who have suffered as a result of [his] conduct, including the victims of Bogoro.' For this reason and mindful of the interest of the victims to see justice finally done in this case, I have decided to discontinue the Office's own appeal against the Judgment, and as a consequence, not to appeal the sentence.[84]

Several people criticised the Prosecutor's decision to let the judgment stand, given that Katanga's actions could not have remedied any errors of law, process or fact that she had previously identified. For example, the victims' counsel stated that he had not been consulted prior to the Prosecutor's decision and would never have agreed with it.[85] He also conveyed his clients' '*étonnement, désarroi, [et] déception*' (astonishment, confusion, [and] disappointment) at the Prosecutor's decision to let the acquittals for sexual violence stand.[86] Further criticism came from Women's Initiative for Gender Justice, whose Executive Director, Brigid Inder, was the Prosecutor's Special Advisor on Gender at the time. As this NGO observed:

> Yesterday's statement by Katanga accepting the judgment, along with his expression of regret to victims, does not seem like an obvious or compelling basis for withdrawing the appeal on Katanga's acquittal of charges for rape and sexual slavery. These concessions, in our view, do not readily explain or justify a decision not to pursue accountability for acts of sexual violence in this case, and not to invest in sound jurisprudence in relation to these crimes.[87]

[82] ICC-01/04-01/07-3436-tENG, 7 March 2014, [1654].
[83] ICC-01/04-01/07-3462) 9 April 2014, [3].
[84] ICC OTP, 'Statement of the Prosecutor of the International Criminal Court, Fatou Bensouda, on Germain Katanga's Notice of Discontinuance of His Appeal against His Judgment of Conviction' (25 June 2014).
[85] ICC-01/04-01/07-3499, 26 June 2014, [3].
[86] Ibid., [5].
[87] Women's Initiatives for Gender Justice, 'Appeals Withdrawn by Prosecution and Defence: The Prosecutor vs. Germain Katanga' (26 June 2014) 1.

The *Katanga* judgment itself (as opposed to the Prosecutor's decision not to challenge it) was also widely criticised. Several critics sided with the dissenting judge, who had refused to change the mode of liability so late in the trial.[88] Others, including Inder, focused on the issue of impunity for sexual violence. They argued that the judges seemed less willing to accept evidence showing that these sexual violence crimes were part of the 'common plan' than was true for other crimes, and observed that this double standard had long been a problem in international criminal law.[89] These criticisms were well-founded: it appears that the Majority gave little weight to the Prosecution's circumstantial evidence about the foreseeability of sexual violence in the Bororo attack. Arguably, the Majority's approach was also incorrect at law. In the relevant part of the judgment the Majority stated that it was not persuaded that rape or sexual slavery formed part of the 'common purpose' of the group who attacked Bogoro because, and I quote, the Prosecution had not shown at this attack 'perforce' or 'necessarily' entailed these crimes.[90] That is a higher standard of certainty than is required by law,[91] and was also higher than the standard applied to other charges in the case.[92]

#### 5.2.2.3 Legal Challenges

In some instances, charges of gender-based crimes were dismissed on legal grounds. That is, the problem was not the evidence – the problem was the Court found that the charges were not in accordance with law.

[88] E.g. S. Rigney, '"The Words Don't Fit You": Recharacterisation of the Charges, Trial Fairness, and Katanga' (2014) 15(2) *Melbourne Journal of International Law* 515; K. Heller, 'Stick to Hit the Accused With': The Legal Recharacterization of Facts under Regulation 55' in C. Stahn (ed.), *The Law and Practice of the International Criminal Court* (Oxford University Press, 2015) 981, 1000–1002.

[89] B. Inder, 'A Critique of the Katanga Judgment' (at the Global Summit to End Sexual Violence in Conflict, London, 11 June 2014) www.iccwomen.org/documents/Global-Summit-Speech.pdf; K. Askin, 'Katanga Judgment Underlines Need for Stronger ICC Focus on Sexual Violence' on *Open Society Foundations* (11 March 2014); Chappell, *The Politics of Gender Justice*, see n. 20, 119–121.

[90] ICC-01/04-01/07-3436-tENG, 7 March 2014, [1663]–[1664].

[91] To convict a person of a crime under Article 25(3)(d), it will suffice to show that the group members implemented the common plan, knowing that the crime would occur in the 'ordinary course of events'. That does not mean that the group members knew with 'absolute certainty that the crime will occur'; rather, 'near' certainty is enough. Ibid., [776], [1630].

[92] For the other crimes, the majority hewed closely to the language of Article 30(2). Specifically, it found that the Ngiti combatants 'meant' to commit the crimes of murder and attacking the civilian population, and were aware that pillage and the destruction of property 'would occur on 24 February 2003 in the ordinary course of events'. Ibid., [1658], [1662].

Examples include the rejection of the 'sexual violence' charges in relation to forced nudity in the *Bemba* case, and genital mutilation in the *Muthaura et al.* case, which are discussed further in §5.3.5. A third example is the Pre-Trial Chamber's refusal to confirm charges of sexual violence based on overlapping facts in the *Bemba* case. As noted in Chapter 4, the Pre-Trial Chamber's reasoning was unsound, but the OTP was denied leave to appeal. Hence, in this particular instance, the prosecution of gender-based crimes seems to have been disabled by the Chamber, rather than the OTP.[93]

### 5.2.3 *Signs of Progress*

Despite the aforementioned challenges, outcomes for gender-based crimes have been improving over time. As shown in Figures 5.6 and 5.7, the proportion of gender-based crimes that have been established at the arrest warrant/summons stage and confirmation stage is still lower than the proportion of other based crimes, but only marginally. The largest improvement can be seen at the confirmation stage, which has been completed in thirteen cases,[94] and will soon be completed in a fourteenth (*Al Hassan*). After a largely unsuccessful period in 2011–2013, the proportion of gender-based crimes that have been confirmed has steadily increased. In 2014,

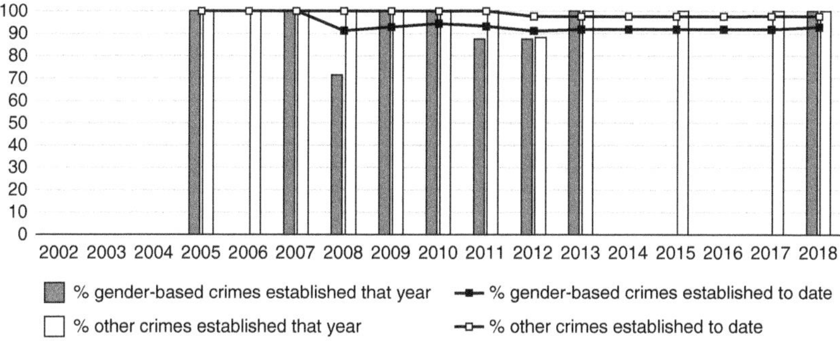


**Figure 5.6** Percentage of crimes established at arrest warrant/summons stage by year (1 July 2002 to 17 July 2018).

[93] See §4.4.1.2. See also Hayes, see n. 9, 40; Chappell, *The Politics of Gender Justice*, see n. 20, 118–119.

[94] Namely: Ongwen; Lubanga; Ntaganda; Ngudjolo; Katanga; Mbarushimana; Bemba, Abu Garda; Banda & Jerbo; Muthaura et al.; Ruto et al.; Gbagbo & Blé Goudé; and Al Mahdi.

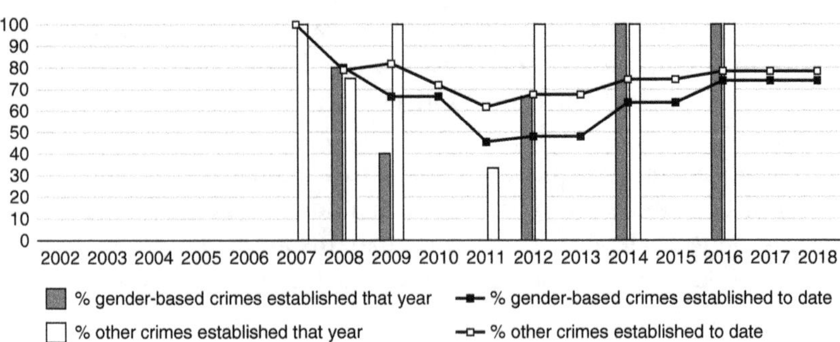


**Figure 5.7** Percentage of crimes established at confirmation stage by year (1 July 2002 to 17 July 2018).

all eleven charges of gender-based crimes were confirmed, and in 2016, all fourteen charges of gender-based crimes were confirmed. Those years brought the total number of gender-based crimes confirmed as at 17 July 2018 up to 37 out of 50 (74 per cent), as compared to 47 out of 60 (just over 78 per cent) for other crimes.

The reasons include a decreased reliance on hearsay evidence, stronger legal arguments, and a shift to charging multiple alternative modes of liability as permitted by the 2015 Pre-Trial Practice Manual.[95] After a disappointing early track record in prosecuting gender-based crimes, these signs of progress at the confirmation stage offer reason for hope.

## 5.3 Establishing Precedents

In several cases, the OTP has presented novel interpretations of the law when prosecuting gender-based crimes. Such interpretations, even if accepted by the judges, do not necessarily lead to convictions: the Prosecution must still prove that the crimes occurred and that the person on trial was responsible. However, they function as *persuasive precedents* for future case in the ICC or other forums that seek guidance from the Court.

### *5.3.1 Rape and Sexual Slavery of 'Child Soldiers'*

Of the sexual violence crimes that are expressly enumerated in the Rome Statute, rape and sexual slavery have been the most frequently charged. A review of all jurisprudence on these crimes would be too lengthy.

[95] ICC, 'Pre-Trial Practice Manual' (September 2015), 18.

Instead, I will focus on a question of utmost importance: can the rape and sexual slavery of 'child soldiers' constitute war crimes under the Rome Statute if the alleged victim and perpetrator are part of the same military force as each other?

Until June 2017, when the ICC Appeals Chamber unanimously answered this question in the affirmative, this was a contested issue. There was no dispute as to the gravity of the alleged sexual abuse; rather, the debate turned on whether sexual violence *within* an armed group involves a violation of IHL, which is a precondition to any war crime. The issue was resolved in the *Ntaganda* case, in which the Prosecution pioneered a new strategy for charging the sexual abuse of 'child soldiers' by members of the same military group. To understand the decisions on these charges, it is useful to briefly review the four categories of war crimes enshrined in Article 8(2) of the Rome Statute. Those categories are:

(a) Grave breaches of the Geneva Conventions of 12 August 1949...
(b) Other serious violations of the laws and customs applicable in international armed conflict, within the established framework of international law...
(c) In the case of an armed conflict not of an international character, serious violations of article 3 common to the four Geneva Conventions of 12 August 1949...
(d) [omitted]
(e) Other serious violations of the laws and customs applicable in armed conflicts not of an international character within the established framework of international law.[96]

In *Ntaganda,* the relevant charges were rape and sexual slavery as war crimes under Article 8(2)(e)(vi). As shown here, Article 8(2)(e) refers to '*other* serious violations' of IHL in a non-international armed conflict, meaning *other than those listed in* Article 3 of the Geneva Conventions (henceforth 'Common Article 3') (which prohibits inhumane or degrading treatment against 'persons taking no active part in the hostilities, including members of armed forces who have laid down their arms and those placed *hors de combat* [out of combat] by sickness, wounds, detention, or any other cause.')

The Defence challenged these charges at the pre-trial and trial stage.[97] Its central claim was that 'crimes committed by members of armed forces on members of the same armed force do not come within the jurisdiction of international humanitarian law nor within international

[96] RS, Art. 8(2).

[97] ICC-01/04-02/06-292-Red2, 14 April 2014, [250]–[263]; ICC-01/04-02/06-804, 1 September 2015; ICC-01/04-02/06-1256, 7 April 2016; ICC-01/04-02/06-1754, 26 January 2017.

criminal law'.[98] More specifically, it argued that: (a) the victim of a war crime in a non-international conflict must be a 'protected person' under Common Article 3; (b) the definition of 'protected persons' excludes crimes committed by commanders and soldiers against fellow 'members' of the same armed group; and (c) the charges relating to the sexual abuse of 'child soldiers' were therefore invalid because the Prosecution had described the victims as 'part of the UPC/FPLC' and the perpetrators as 'their own commanders and other UPC/FPLC soldiers'.[99] The Defence conceded that these charges may have been legally valid if Prosecution described victims as 'civilians', but because the Prosecution had *not* described them in such terms, the charges fell outside the ICC's jurisdiction and needed to be dismissed.[100]

The Prosecution refuted these arguments in numerous filings.[101] Its key arguments at trial were as follows. First, for war crimes under Article 8(2)(e) of the Rome Statute, there is no need to show that the victim was a 'protected person' under Common Article 3, or that he or she was not part of the perpetrator's armed group: such requirements are not imposed by Article 8(2)(e), nor incorporated into that provision by reference to the established framework of international law.[102] Second, even if Article 8(2)(e) only applies to victims who were 'protected persons' under Common Article 3, that would not be fatal in this case: the Trial Chamber might find that the victims were still protected against sexual violence under Common Article 3 *notwithstanding their role in the UPC*. It could do so by finding that the victims' position under IHL was unaltered but for the fact that they could be targeted *by an adverse party* for the specific time that they took part in hostilities, or by finding that the victims were *hors de combat* as a result of mistreatment at the time of the sexual abuse.[103] Third, even if Article 8(2)(e) is inapplicable where the victim and perpetrator share an 'allegiance' in the sense of being part of the same armed group, there was no legally relevant 'allegiance' here: the victims were children, and children cannot lawfully consent to joining

[98] ICC-01/04-02/06-T-10-Red-ENG, 13 February 2014, 27(15–17).

[99] ICC-01/04-02/06-1256, 7 April 2016, [1]–[2].

[100] Ibid., [40].

[101] ICC-01/04-02/06-276-Red, 24 March 2014, [182]–[193]; ICC-01/04-02/06-503-AnxA-Red2, 1 September 2015, [461]–[465]; ICC-01/04-02/06-1278, 14 April 2016; ICC-01/04-02/06-1794-Corr, 21 February 2017; ICC-01/04-02/06-2277-Anx1-Corr-Red, 7 November 2018, [763]–[764].

[102] ICC-01/04-02/06-1278, 14 April 2016, [27]–[57]; ICC-01/04-02/06-1794-Corr 21 February 2017, [12]–[94].

[103] ICC-01/04-02/06-1278, 14 April 2016, [58]–[94]; ICC-01/04-02/06-1794-Corr, 21 February 2017, [95]–[117].

armed groups.[104] Finally, the OTP argued that if the Defence's logic was accepted, it would mean that:

> A soldier intending to rape a child in the context of an armed conflict (a war crime) would be encouraged first to unlawfully conscript the child (another war crime), in order to escape international liability for the rape.[105]

All three Chambers sided with the OTP, albeit for slightly different reasons. For the Pre-Trial Chamber, the lawfulness of these charges turned on whether the victims were taking 'active' or 'direct' part in hostilities when the alleged acts of sexual violence occurred.[106] In the Chamber's view, it was logically impossible for a person to take an 'active' or 'direct' part in hostilities at the exact same time as being forced to engage in a sexual act.[107] Accordingly, at the specific time that the alleged acts of sexual violence occurred, the victims could not take been taking an 'active' or 'direct' part in hostilities.[108]

For the Trial Chamber, the question of whether the victims were taking an 'active' or 'direct' part in hostilities was moot because, in its view, Article 8(2)(e) imposed no 'status requirements' on the victims (i.e. Article 8(2)(e) does not require that the victims are 'protected persons' under the 1949 Geneva Conventions, or under Common Article 3),[109] nor are any 'status requirements' brought into Article 8(2)(e) by reference to the established framework of IHL.[110] Accordingly, the rape or sexual enslavement of *any person* could be charged under Article 8(2)(e) – so long as the conduct satisfied the 'nexus requirement' for war crimes, meaning it took place in the context of and was associated with an armed conflict.[111] As a final point, the Chamber referred to the 'recognised principle that one cannot benefit from one's own unlawful conduct.' Hence an armed

104 ICC-01/04-02/06-1278, 14 April 2016, [95].

105 Ibid., [96].

106 ICC-01/04-02/06-309, 9 June 2014, [17]. The Chamber identified this test by examining Common Article 3, which protects 'persons taking no active part in the hostilities', along with Article 4 of Additional Protocol II, which states that people who are not taking a direct' part in hostilities must be treated 'humanely', and must never be subjected to 'outrages upon personal dignity' including rape.

107 Ibid., [79].

108 Ibid., [80].

109 ICC-01/04-02/06-1707, 4 January 2017, [40]–[44].

110 Ibid., [45]–[53].

111 Ibid., [52].

group cannot recruit children in breach of IHL, and then claim that, *as a result of that breach,* the subsequent sexual abuse of those children is not a war crime.[112]

The Appeals Chamber agreed. It affirmed that the Rome Statute imposes no 'status requirements' on victims of the war crimes of rape and sexual slavery.[113] Moreover, the broader framework of IHL 'does not contain a general rule that categorically excludes members of an armed group from protection against crimes committed by members of the same armed group.'[114] Indeed, the grave breach provisions of the first and second 1949 Geneva Conventions do not only protect persons belonging to 'enemy' armed forces; they also protect wounded, sick and/or shipwrecked members of a party's *own* group.[115] The Appeals Chamber echoed the point that to qualify as a war crime, the 'nexus' between the alleged act of sexual violence and the conflict must be proven. It indicated that application of that 'nexus' test would prevent 'any undue expansion of the reach of the law of war crimes.'[116] The Appeals Chamber's reasoning did not distinguish based on age, suggesting that sexual abuse of *adult* soldiers by their fellow soldiers could likewise be prosecuted as a war crime in the ICC.

### *5.3.2 Gender-based Persecution*

In the ICC's practice so far, the crime against humanity of persecution has been used to prosecute sexual violence as often as the crime against humanity of rape (see Figure 5.3). Examples include the *Ongwen, Mudacumura, Muthaura et al., Gaddafi, Al-Senussi,* and *Al-Tuhamy* cases (in which the Prosecutor charged persecution on 'political' grounds); the *Ntaganda, Ahmad Harun & Ali Kushayb,* and *Hussein* cases (in which the Prosecutor charged persecution on 'ethnic' grounds); the *Gbagbo & Blé Goudé* and *Gbagbo* cases (in which the Prosecutor charged persecution on 'political, national, ethnic or religious' grounds), the *Mbarushimana* case (in which the Prosecutor initially charged persecution on 'gender' grounds, then changed this to 'political' grounds); and the *Al Hassan* case (in which the Prosecutor has brought one charge of persecution on

112 Ibid., [53].
113 ICC-01/04-02/06-1962, 15 June 2017, [46]–[51].
114 Ibid., [63].
115 Ibid., [59].
116 Ibid., [68].

'religious' grounds and another of persecution on 'gender' grounds). The incorporation of sexual violence into the crime of persecution is positive. It shows that as well as being an attack against individual victims, sexual violence can be used to degrade and devastate a group. Yet it is troubling that of the grounds of persecution that have been charged, gender has so seldom been used. In fact, as of 17 July 2018, the crime of gender-based persecution has *never* been charged at the confirmation stage. This finding raises questions, given the nature of alleged persecutory acts.

An example can be seen in the *Gbagbo & Blé Goudé* case, in which the Prosecutor alleged that pro-Gbagbo forces raped 38 women and girls during Côte d'Ivoire's 2010–2011 post-election crisis. As well as charging this sexual violence as rape, the Prosecutor charged it as persecution on 'political, national, ethnic or religious' grounds, without adding gender as an intersecting ground.[117] Further examples can be seen in the *Ahmad Harun & Ali Kushayb* and *Hussein* cases, both from the situation in Darfur, in which the persecution charge was based, *inter alia,* on evidence of rapes committed against women and girls. The OTP and the Pre-Trial Chamber described these rapes as persecution 'of the primarily Fur population' in Darfur – terms that focused exclusively on the victims' ethnicity.[118] Yet as Valerie Oosterveld has observed, the alleged facts on their face constitute persecution on intersecting ethnic *and* gender grounds.[119] The same critique can be made in relation to the counts relating to the massacre, detention and assault of Fur men, which are charged as murder, attacks against the civilian population, torture, deprivation of liberty, and persecution by reason for the victims' Fur ethnicity.[120]

There are several factors that may explain why gender-based persecution has so seldom been charged in the ICC's early cases. One possible reason is that, because gender-based persecution is often part of a broader campaign of ethnic or political persecution, prosecutors may at first have chosen to focus only on that 'main' ground of persecution to simplify the case, particularly if they are not tactically trying to raise the profile of gender-based persecution and establish legal precedents on that crime.

[117] ICC-02/11-01/11-656-Red, 12 June 2014, [272].

[118] ICC-02/05-56, 25 February 2007, Count 10 and [211]–[212]; Count 39 and [22]–[247]; ICC-02/05-237-Red, 24 January 2012, Counts 9 and 31; ICC-02/05-01/07-1-CORR), 27 April 2007, Counts 10, 21 and 39; ICC-02/05-01/12-2, 1 March 2012, 6–7.

[119] V. Oosterveld, 'Prosecuting Gender-Based Persecution as an International Crime' in A. de Brouwer et al. (eds), *Sexual Violence as an International Crime: Interdisciplinary Approaches* (Intersentia, 2013) 57, 60, 71.

[120] E.g. ICC-02/05-56, 25 February 2007, Counts 21-35 paired with [223]–[230].

A second likely reason is a lack of familiarity with the concept of gender within the Court. This term does not have an equivalent in all languages, it is not used in many domestic jurisdictions, and until the Rome Statute was adopted, it was not used in international criminal law either. As such, many experienced lawyers in the OTP may lack confidence in interpreting and applying the term 'gender', or may consider it a synonym for 'sex'. Prosecutors may also anticipate that this concept will be poorly understood by judges, particularly because the Rome Statute's definition of 'gender' is deliberately vague, as explained in Chapter 3. Thus, prosecutors may make a strategic decision to use a more well-known ground of persecution to avoid time-consuming argument about the meaning of the term 'gender' at trial.[121] In institutionalist theory, this risk-averse approach is known as 'path dependency'. Explaining how 'path dependency' works, Paul Pierson has argued that even in new institutions, actors 'do not inherit a blank slate that they can remake at will ... Instead, actors find that the dead weight of previous institutional choices seriously limits their room to maneuver'.[122]

An institutional approach also suggests that when assessing the evidence, prosecutors may not always *consider* the possibility of bringing charges of persecution on gender grounds. Institutionalists argue that in newly created institutions, old paradigms often continue to operate and to constrain the way that individuals approach their work, notwithstanding advances in the formal rules. For example, Fiona Mackay has argued: 'new institutions are inevitably informed by "legacies of the past." These include material legacies and existing patterns of power distribution but also cognitive and normative legacies – "frames of mind" and "habits of the heart"'.[123] From this perspective, it is relevant that historically speaking, gender has not been viewed as a relevant category of victimisation in international criminal law, whereas victimisation on the basis of race, religion, politics, nationality and ethnicity has long been considered relevant (as demonstrated by the crime of genocide, the crime of apartheid, and by previous definitions of persecution). This cognitive framework is likely to have carried over to the ICC, such that when prosecutors have

[121] For a similar analysis, see Oosterveld, 'Prosecuting Gender-Based Persecution as an International Crime', see n. 119, 70.

[122] P. Pierson, 'The Limits of Design: Explaining Institutional Origins and Design' (2000) 13(4) *Governance* 475, 493.

[123] F. Mackay, 'Nested Newness, Institutional Innovation, and the Gendered Limits of Change' (2014) 10(4) *Politics & Gender* 549, 552.

thought about group-based victimisation, the notion of gender-based targeting has not always come to mind.

A fourth likely reason is a lack of familiarity with the concept of 'intersectionality'. As explained in Chapter 1, this term originated in feminist scholarship in the late 1980s which argued that women of colour tend not to experience gender-based discrimination in isolation; rather, they face with discrimination on multiple, intersecting grounds. The concept of intersectionality is critical to understanding how gender-based persecution works in times of war or political crisis. In such situations, gender-based persecution usually intersects persecution on other grounds. For example, feminist scholars have argued that during the conflict in the former Yugoslavia, many women were subjected to sexual violence because of their gender *and* ethnicity.[124] Similarly, during the Rwandan genocide, many women who were Tutsi or married to Tutsi men targeted for sexual violence because of their gender *and* their ethnic connections.[125] Because the ICTY and ICTR Statutes did not recognise gender as a ground of persecution, sexual violence was not charged in those tribunals as persecution on intersecting gender and ethnic grounds. In a similar vein, the ICC is yet to see any charges of persecution on intersecting grounds, suggesting that prosecutors are either unfamiliar with this concept, or have not been prepared to invest the time explaining this concept to the judges.

A final likely reason is that gender-based violence is so ubiquitous that its gendered basis becomes invisible. In particular, sexual violence against women and girls is so common in war and peace alike that it comes to be seen as unremarkable, inevitable even, and not an issue requiring analysis in sociological terms.[126] Hence, a priority for early feminist scholarship in

[124] E.g. R. Copelon, 'Surfacing Gender: Re-Engraving Crimes against Women in Humanitarian Law' (1994) 5 *Hastings Women's Law Journal* 243.

[125] E.g. D. Buss, 'The Curious Visibility of Wartime Rape: Gender and Ethnicity in International Criminal Law' (2007) 25 *Windsor Yearbook of Access to Justice* 3; D. Buss, 'Sexual Violence, Ethnicity, and Intersectionality in International Criminal Law' in E. Grabham et al. (eds), *Intersectionality and Beyond* (Routledge, 2009) 105; C. Mibenge, *Sex and International Tribunals: The Erasure of Gender from the War Narrative* (University of Pennsylvania Press, 2013).

[126] E.g. C. Bunch, 'Women's Rights as Human Rights: Toward a Re-Vision of Human Rights' (1990) 12(4) *Human Rights Quarterly* 486, 491; M. Urban-Walker, 'Gender and Violence in Focus: A Background for Gender Justice in Reparations' in R. Rubio Marín (ed.), *The Gender of Reparations: Unsettling Sexual Hierarchies while Redressing Human Rights Violations* (Cambridge University Press, 2009) 1, 26–27; S. Chesterman, 'Never Again... and Again: Law, Order, and the Gender of War Crimes in Bosnia and Beyond' (1997) 22 *Yale Journal of International Law* 299, 342.

international criminal law was to recast sexual violence against women and girls as *gender-based* violence, as explained in Chapter 3.[127] If investigators and prosecutors are unfamiliar with this feminist interpretation of sexual violence against women and girls, they have not thought to charge this violence as gender-based persecution. Moreover, because *perpetrators* of such violence may not recognise their own actions as gender-based violence, they are unlikely to make explicit statements to that effect – statements that can later be used as evidence of a discriminatory intent. This does not mean that proving such an intent will be impossible. However, it means that the intent may need to be inferred from circumstantial evidence, including evidence that the victims of a crime were primarily or exclusively members of one gender group. If prosecutors are not used to drawing such inferences to prove the intent for persecution, this may contribute to a reluctance to charge persecution on gender grounds.

Most likely, all of these factors have contributed to the under-use of the crime of gender-based persecution in the ICC. However, in recent years, the OTP has begun to break with this pattern. In her request to open an investigation into the situation in Afghanistan, Prosecutor Bensouda has argued that the murder of female politicians and intimidation of female students by the Taliban amounts to persecution on gender grounds.[128] In its ongoing preliminary examination in Nigeria, the OTP is considering charging the abduction of female schoolgirls and use of female suicide bombers by Boko Haram as persecution on gender grounds.[129] And in the *Al Hassan case,* the most recent case initiated in the Mali situation, the arrest warrant includes a charge of persecution on gender grounds based on the sexual and non-sexual oppression of women and girls by Islamist militants who occupied Timbuktu between 2012 and 2013.[130]

Al-Hassan was transferred to the ICC on 31 March 2018, and the confirmation hearing is scheduled to start on 6 May 2019. If the charge of persecution on gender grounds is included in the DCC, or possibly, a combined charge of persecution on intersecting gender *and* religious

[127] E.g. Copelon, see n. 124; C. Niarchos, 'Women, War, and Rape: Challenges Facing the International Tribunal for the Former Yugoslavia' (1995) 17(4) *Human Rights Quarterly* 629; R. Chowdhury, 'Kadic v. Karadzic: Rape as a Crime against Women as a Class' (2002) 20(1) *Law & Inequality: A Journal of Theory and Practice* 91.

[128] ICC-02/17-7-Red, 20 November 2017, [115]–[121].

[129] ICC OTP, 'Report on Preliminary Examination Activities 2016' (14 November 2016), [293].

[130] ICC-01/12-01/18-1-Red, 20 March 2018, [162]–[174].

and/or political grounds, the Court may at last start to engage in detail with the gender dimensions of this crime. The OTP, which has invested much time in training its staff in gender analysis and has now benefited from the expertise of three Gender Advisors, will have a lead role to play in this process.

### *5.3.3 Forced Pregnancy*

The inclusion of this crime in the Rome Statute was highly controversial, as detailed in Chapter 3. The result was a very narrow definition, which states:

> 'Forced pregnancy' means the unlawful confinement of a woman forcibly made pregnant, with the intent of affecting the ethnic composition of any population or carrying out other grave violations of international law.[131]

The first case to include charges of forced pregnancy is the *Ongwen* case, concerning crimes allegedly committed by the LRA in Uganda. In the pre-trial proceedings, there was some debate about the 'special intent' requirement, i.e. the requirement that the perpetrator either intended to 'affect the ethnic composition of any population' or to 'carry out other grave violations of international law'. The OTP argued that the 'special intent' relates to the act of *unlawful confinement*, not the prior act of forced impregnation.[132] Applying this definition to the case at hand, it alleged that Ongwen had committed forced pregnancy by unlawfully confining several women who had been forcibly made pregnant (by him), with a view to continuing to use these women as 'wives', and to rape, enslave, sexually enslave and torture them – all of which are 'grave violations of international law'.[133] The Defence contended that the 'special intent' relates instead to the act of forcibly impregnating the woman, and that the Prosecution had not proved that intent in the case at hand.[134] The Pre-Trial Chamber accepted the OTP's interpretation of the crime, stating:

> The crime of forced pregnancy does not depend on the perpetrator's involvement in the woman's conception; it is only required that the perpetrator knows that the woman is pregnant and that she has been made pregnant forcibly. It is apparent that the essence of the crime of forced

[131] RS, Art. 7(2)(f).
[132] Cited in ICC-02/04-01/15-422-Red, 23 March 2016, [98].
[133] Ibid., [101].
[134] Ibid.

> pregnancy is in unlawfully placing the victim in a position in which she cannot choose whether to continue the pregnancy. By the same token, it is not necessary to prove that the perpetrator has a special intent with respect to the outcome of the pregnancy, or that the pregnancy of the woman is in any way causally linked to her confinement. While the first alternative of the special intent requirement (intent of 'affecting the ethnic composition of any population') would typically include such component, the second alternative (intent of 'carrying out other grave violations of international law') does not call for any such restrictive interpretation.[135]

This interpretation is progressive. It foregrounds the notion of reproductive autonomy, that is, the right to make decisions about one's own reproductive choices. It also enables the crime to be charged in a broad range of circumstances, even if there is no intent to degrade or diminish the national, ethnic, racial or religious group to which the victim 'belongs.'[136] Moreover, there is no need to show that the perpetrator was involved in woman's impregnation, or that she was confined for reasons related to her reproductive capacity. It will suffice that rather than being in a position to decide how to proceed with a pregnancy that was initiated forcibly, she is unlawfully confined for the purposes of committing any grave violation of international law.

### 5.3.4 *Imposition of 'Forced Marriage'*

The term 'forced marriage' is not used in any instrument of international criminal law. However, in the last decade, this term has been used in the ICC, Special Court for Sierra Leone (SCSL) and Extraordinary Chambers in the Courts of Cambodia (ECCC) to describe forced sexual and domestic relationships between two people – one male and female – that are generally not legal marriages under local law, but are nonetheless described as 'marriages' by the perpetrators and sometimes, the victims.[137] In most of these cases, the victims have been civilian women and girls, who were abducted by armed groups and told that they were the 'wife' of a particular man in that group, which meant cooking and cleaning for him,

[135] Ibid., [99]–[100] (emphasis added).

[136] R Grey, 'The ICC's first "forced pregnancy" case in historical perspective' (2017) 15(5) *Journal of International Criminal Justice* 905–930.

[137] E.g. *Ongwen*, ICC-02/04-01/15-422-Red, 23 March 2016, [93]; *Al Hassan*, ICC-01/12-01/18-35-Red2-tENG, 22 May 2018, [82]–[85]. See also Appeal Judgment, *Brima et al.* ('AFRC case') (SCSL-2004-16-A), 22 February 2008, [190]–[196]; Closing Order, *Nuon et al.* ('Case 002') (002/19-09-2007-ECCC OCIJ), 15 September 2010, [842]–[861], [1442]–[1447].

submitting to his sexual demands, and not having sex with anyone else.[138] In all cases, the imposition of the so-called 'marriage' has violated international human rights law, which requires that 'no marriage shall be entered into without the free and full consent of the intending spouses'.'[139]

Describing these relationships as 'forced *marriages*' is problematic.[140] This term privileges the perpetrator's view of the relationship, although the victim may not share that view. For example, in *Ongwen,* one of the alleged victims of this crime told the Court that she did not regard Ongwen as her husband.[141] Second, the term asserts that the relationship, while not a legal marriage, is nonetheless 'marriage-like'. This analogy that only works if 'marriage' is understood to mean a pairing of one man and one woman, the latter of whom is responsible for the couple's domestic chores. There is no reason why that specific version of marriage, which is only one of many versions recognised around the world, should be regarded as the universal idea of 'marriage' to which the relevant forced relationships are compared. The terms 'forced conjugal unions / associations / relationships', which have also been used in the ICC, SCSL and ECCC, are equally problematic.[142] As Oosterveld has pointed out, the word 'conjugal' is simply a synonym for 'marriage'; it does not avoid the 'marriage' analogy.[143] A generic term such as 'forced domestic relationship' would therefore be more appropriate, but I use the term 'forced marriage' here for consistency with the case law.

[138] E.g. ICC-02/04-01/15-375-AnxA-Red, 22 December 2015, [130]; ICC-02/04-01/15-533, 6 September 2016, [506]–[501]. See also Request for Leave to Amend the Indictment: Annex 2, Investigator's Statement, *Brima et al.* (SCSL-04-16-PT), 9 February 2004.

[139] *International Covenant on Civil and Political Rights,* 16 December 1966, 999 UNTS 171 (entered into force 23 March 1976), Art. 23(3). See also: *International Covenant on Economic, Social and Cultural Rights,* 16 December 1966, 933 UNTS 3 (entered into force 3 January 1976), Art. 10(1); *Convention on the Elimination of All Forms of Discrimination Against Women,* 18 December 1979, 1249 UNTS 13 (entered into force 3 September 1981), Art. 16(b).

[140] R. Grey, *Forced Marriage: A World of Challenges for International Criminal Law'* (University of Oslo, 6 June 2018).

[141] ICC-02/04-01/15-T-8-Red-ENG, 15 September 2009, 47(5–8).

[142] E.g. (ICC-02/04-01/15-422-Red, 23 March 2016, [93]. See also: Appeal Judgment, *Brima et al.* (SCSL-2004-16-A), 22 February 2008, [191]–[192]; Judgment, *Taylor* (SCSL-03-01-T), 18 May 2018, [425]; Closing Order, *Nuon et al. ('Case 002')* (002/19-09-2007-ECCC-OCIJ), 15 September 2010, [1443].

[143] V. Oosterveld, 'Forced Marriage during Conflict and Mass Atrocity' in F. Ní Aoláin et al. (eds), *The Oxford Handbook of Gender and Conflict* (Oxford University Press, 2018) 241, 245.

In the international jurisprudence, and in the academic literature, there has been much debate about how the conduct associated with 'forced marriage' should be charged.[144] Specifically, the question is how to charge *the acts undertaken or threats made* to force the victim into the 'forced marriage'.[145] The first case to face this question was the SCSL's *AFRC* case, in which the Prosecutor sought leave to add an extra charge to the indictment – which already included charges of rape and sexual slavery – namely, 'the crime against humanity of "other inhumane acts (forced marriages)"'.[146] The Trial Chamber allowed that extra charge, but at the end of the trial, the Majority held that the relevant conduct was captured by the charge of sexual slavery, and could therefore not be charged as an '*other* inhumane act'.[147] In a dissenting opinion, Judge Doherty accepted the 'forced marriage' charge.[148] The matter was resolved in February 2008, when the SCSL Appeals Chamber held that the imposition of 'forced marriages' during Sierra Leone's civil war was a *different* but *comparably grave* crime to sexual slavery, and could therefore be charged using the crime against humanity of 'other inhumane acts'.[149]

Seven months later, in the *Katanga & Ngudjolo* case, the ICC Pre-Trial Chamber took a different approach. In that case, the conduct of abducting civilian women and forcing them to become 'wives' of particular soldiers was charged as sexual slavery under Article 7(1)(g) of the Rome Statute, not as 'other inhumane acts' under Article 7(1)(k).[150] Without contemplating alternative charging strategies, the Pre-Trial Chamber confirmed the sexual slavery charges, reasoning that sexual slavery 'encompasses situations where women and girls are forced into "marriage", domestic servitude or other forced labour involving compulsory sexual activity, including rape, by their captors.'[151] In the ICC's

[144] E.g. P.V. Sellers, 'Wartime Female Slavery: Enslavement?' (2011) 44 *Cornell International Law Journal* 118; J. Gong-Gershowitz, 'Forced Marriage: A "New" Crime Against Humanity?' (2009) 8(1) *Northwestern Journal of International Human Rights* 53; N. Jain, 'Forced Marriage as a Crime against Humanity: Problems of Definition and Prosecution' (2008) 6(5) *Journal of International Criminal Justice* 1013.

[145] E.g. ICC-02/04-01/15-422-Red, 23 March 2016, [91]. See also Appeal Judgment, *Brima et al.* (SCSL-2004-16-A), 22 February 2008, [195].

[146] Decision on Prosecution Request for Leave to Amend the Indictment, *Brima et al.* (SCSL-04-16-PT), 6 May 2004, [10(a)].

[147] Judgment, *Brima et al.* (SCSL-2004-16-T), 21 June 2007, [713].

[148] Ibid. (Doherty).

[149] Appeal Judgment, *Brima et al.* (SCSL-2004-16-A), 22 February 2008, [181]–[203].

[150] ICC-01/04-01/07-649-AnxlA, 26 June 2008, [89], Counts 6 and 7.

[151] ICC-01/04-01/07-717, 14 October 2008, [431].

*Ongwen* case, the OTP changed tack. Rather than using the crime against humanity of sexual slavery to charge the conduct of compelling civilian women and girls into 'forced marriages' with particular LRA soldiers, the OTP charged this conduct as 'other inhumane acts'.[152] This crime is found in Article 7(1)(k) of the Rome Statute, which describes the crime against humanity of:

> Other inhumane acts of a similar character intentionally causing great suffering, or serious injury to body or to mental or physical health.

In support of this charge, the OTP argued that the crime of sexual slavery did not capture the experience of women and girls who were assigned as 'wives' to specific LRA soldiers for two reasons: first, because 'forced marriage is not predominantly a sexual crime … unlike sexual slavery the perpetrator of forced marriage demands conjugal and domestic duties of the victim quite separate from any sexual acts'; and second, because 'victims of forced marriage suffer separate and additional harm to those victims of the crime of sexual slavery', including a violation of 'the right to marry by consent and establish a family as a result of that union' and experiencing a 'lasting social stigma'.[153]

The Defence sought to have this charge struck out. Citing the *Katanga & Ngudjolo* confirmation decision, it argued that the act of forcing women into the role of a 'wife' could not constitute an '*other* inhumane act' because the conduct is already covered by a crime expressly enumerated in Article 7, namely, sexual slavery.[154] Notwithstanding the fact that the victims' counsel had supported the charge of 'forced marriage',[155] the Defence also claimed that this charge would be injurious to the victims because it would 'continue to hold the women involved in invisible chains where they and others in the community perceive them as married'.[156]

The Pre-Trial Chamber rejected the arguments of the Defence. It held that 'forced marriage may, in the abstract, qualify as "other inhumane acts" under article 7 of the [Rome] Statute rather than being subsumed by

[152] ICC-02/04-01/15-375-AnxA-Red, 22 December 2015, Count 61; ICC-02/04-01/15-533, 6 September 2016, Counts 50 and 61.
[153] ICC-02/04-01/15-T-20-Red-ENG, 21 January 2016, 31(22)–32(21).
[154] ICC-02/04-01/15-404-Red3, 25 May 2016, [128]–[130].
[155] ICC-02/04-01/15-403, 18 January 2016, [55].
[156] ICC-02/04-01/15-T-23-Red-ENG, 26 January 2016, 17(3–10).

the crime of sexual slavery',[157] noting that this position was consistent with the jurisprudence of the SCSL and ECCC.[158] The Chamber continued:

> The central element of forced marriage is the imposition of 'marriage' on the victim, i.e. the imposition, regardless of the will of the victim, of duties that are associated with marriage, as well as of a social status of the perpetrator's 'wife'. The fact that such 'marriage' is illegal and not recognised by, in this case, Uganda, is irrelevant. What matters is that the so-called 'marriage' is factually imposed on the victim, with the consequent social stigma.[159]

The Defence sought leave to appeal, arguing that the Pre-Trial Chamber had 'created a new element for a non-existent crime, to wit, exclusivity in the alleged conjugal unions'. In the view of the Defence, this display of 'judicial activism' undermined Ongwen's fair trial rights, 'since he is being charged with crimes that are not even enshrined in the Statute'.[160] The Chamber disagreed. It pointed out that Ongwen had been charged with an existing crime, namely, the crime against humanity of 'other inhumane acts'.[161] It remains to be seen whether this argument will be accepted by *Ongwen* Trial Chamber and if need be, by the Appeals Chamber.

In March 2018, in the *Al Hassan* case, the OTP again charged the imposition of 'forced marriage' as an 'other inhumane act'. The Pre-Trial Chamber included this charge on the arrest warrant.[162] The relationships in this case, are similar to those charged as 'forced marriages' in *Ongwen,* insofar as the victims are civilian women who were allegedly forced into sexual and domestic relationships with specific male combatants. However, unlike in *Ongwen,* these women were not removed from their communities; rather, the perpetrators allegedly forced the victims into 'marriages' locally, as a way to integrate themselves into the population of Timbuktu.[163]

Is this development in the ICC's jurisprudence positive? For many commentators, it is. For example, in the view of Women's Initiatives for Gender Justice, 'the recognition of forced marriage as a distinct crime

[157] ICC-02/04-01/15-422-Red, 23 March 2016, [91].
[158] Ibid., [89]–[90].
[159] Ibid., [93].
[160] ICC-02/04-01/15-423, 29 March 2016, [42].
[161] ICC-02/04-01/15-428, 29 April 2016, [36].
[162] ICC-01/12-01/18-2-tENG, 27 March 2018, [12].
[163] ICC-01/12-01/18-1-Red, 20 March 2018, [48], [124].

from sexual slavery under "other inhumane acts" allows prosecutors to recognise the victims of these crimes and the particular social stigmatisation they face.'[164] Several people interviewed for this book took a similar view. For example, Paolina Massidda, Principal Counsel of the OPCV, and also a victims' counsel in the *Ongwen* case, described the Prosecutor's decision to charge 'forced marriage' as an 'other inhumane act' as 'really important' and a 'very good improvement'.[165] In a similar vein, an OTP interviewee argued that the crime of 'forced marriage' captures a form of wrongdoing that is not specified in any other crime enumerated in the Statute, namely 'the imposition, regardless of the will of the victim, of duties that are associated with marriage, as well as of a social status of the perpetrator's "wife"'.[166] The interviewee observed that this crime overlaps with some other crimes charged in the *Ongwen* case, such as rape. However, they made the point that there is no jury in the ICC: rather, the facts and law are adjudicated by professional judges. As such, there isn't the same pressure to streamline charges and simplify the case as would apply to a common law jury trial.[167]

By contrast, Marie O'Leary of the Office of Public Counsel for Defence expressed misgivings about this direction in the ICC's jurisprudence. She explained,

> From a Defence perspective, it is of benefit for defendants to know what the crimes are before this Court. For example, forced marriage was identified in case law under 'other inhumane acts', but wasn't specifically noticed as a crime that could be prosecuted by the ICC in the core texts. To have bright lines from the ICC about what is ok and what is necessary to respect *nullum crimen sine lege* [the principle that crimes should be defined clearly and not retrospectively]. Such notice is not only a right, but can also reduce litigation.[168]

I also have some misgivings about this development, but not because of concerns about the principle of *nullum crimen sine lege*. In my view, that principle is not offended by applying the crime of 'other inhumane acts' to new facts: this crime is by definition open-ended. Rather, my misgiving is that one of the main rationales for distinguishing between sexual

[164] Women's Initiatives for Gender Justice, 'Statement on the Surrender of Al Hassan to the ICC and Charges of Forced Marriage' (3 April 2018).

[165] Interview, 15 June 2017.

[166] See ICC-02/04-01/15-422-Red, 23 March 2016, [93].

[167] Interview I, ICC OTP, 2017.

[168] Interview, 17 July 2018.

slavery and 'forced marriage' has been that the latter offence is 'not predominantly a sexual crime.'[169] Yet sexual slavery is not 'predominantly a sexual crime' either; in the ICC's legal framework, it is defined as enslavement (i.e. exercising rights of ownership over a person or subjecting them to a similar deprivation of liberty) coupled with at least one forced sexual act.[170] There is no requirement that the sexual violation eclipses any other aspect of the enslavement. This suggests that the conduct could equally be charged as enslavement or (if sexual violence occurred) as sexual slavery. Any specific harms associated with being known as the perpetrator's 'wife' (or 'husband') could be addressed at sentencing,[171] just as any specific harms suffered by victims who are used as the shared sexual slaves of a group of perpetrators (e.g. increased risk of HIV) could be addressed at that time. From this perspective, while the ICC's recognition of a separate crime of 'forced marriage' is not negative, I am not certain that it has been necessary.

What is most positive about the ICC's nascent 'forced marriage' jurisprudence, I suggest, is that it does not include some of the more dubious values judgments made by the SCSL. One such statement can be found in the SCSL's *Taylor* case, in which the Trial Chamber declared: 'what happened to the girls and women abducted in Sierra Leone and forced into this conjugal association was not marriage in the universally understood sense of a consensual and sacrosanct union'.[172] This generalisation was not supported by legal authority or evidence. It was also false: for countless people, marriage is not 'sacrosanct'; it is simply practical. Indeed for many women and girls, marriage is the only viable path to economic security and social inclusion and is entered for that reason alone.[173] Moreover, consensual marriage is hardly a 'universal' practice, as demonstrated by the continued practice of forced marriage in many parts of the world.[174] It is positive

[169] ICC-02/04-01/15-533, 6 September 2015, [5010], citing Appeal Judgment, *Brima et al.* (SCSL-2004-16-A), 22 February 2008, [195].

[170] EoC, Art. 7(1)(g)-1.

[171] For a supporting view, see Gong-Gershowitz, see n. 144.

[172] Trial Judgment, *Taylor* (SCSL-01-01-T), 18 May 2012, [427].

[173] J. Bruce, 'Economics before Romance: How Marriage Differs in Poor Countries' on *Think Big* (31 August 2018); Human Rights Watch, '"This Old Man Can Feed Us, You Will Marry Him" Child and Forced Marriage in South Sudan' (2013).

[174] E.g. CEDAW Committee, 'Concluding Observations on the Combined Third to Fifth Periodic Reports of Malaysia, UN Doc. CEDAW/C/MYS/CO/3-5' (9 March 2018) [25]; CEDAW Committee, 'Concluding Observations on the Fifth Periodic Report of Turkmenistan, UN Doc. CEDAW/C/TKM/CO/5' (23 July 2018), [20(a)].

to see that, thus far, the ICC has not repeated such baseless assertions about how marriage is 'universally' viewed and esteemed.

Nor has the ICC followed the SCSL's lead in making sweeping claims about the difference between 'forced marriages' to members of armed groups and traditional 'arranged marriage' practices. Both types of marriages were discussed in the SCSL's *AFRC* case, in which one trial judge and the full Appeals Chamber asserted that whereas some traditional arranged marriages in Sierra Leone violated international human rights law, the 'forced marriages' to rebel soldiers were 'clearly criminal in nature'.[175] This assertion was unnecessary, as there were no charges relating to arranged marriages in the case. Moreover, it implied that even if an arranged marriage violates international human rights law and causes serious harm – which some do – the fact that the marriage aligns with tradition precludes it from also being 'criminal'. That is an alarming implication, and could be interpreted as meaning that 'traditional' gender-based violence is necessarily less serious, or less 'criminal', than gender-based violence that disrupts the *status quo*. It is positive that thus far, no such argument has been endorsed by the ICC – especially given that an exception based on 'tradition' was rejected during the drafting of the ICC Elements of Crimes.[176]

### 5.3.5 'Other Sexual Violence'

The jurisprudence on the newly codified crime of 'sexual violence' has been quite problematic.[177] This crime is enumerated in Article 7(1)(g) of the Rome Statute, which refers to the crime against humanity of: 'rape, sexual slavery, enforced prostitution, forced pregnancy, enforced sterilization, or *any other form of sexual violence of comparable gravity*'. Article 8(2)(b)(xxi) describes those same acts plus 'any other form of sexual violence also constituting a grave breach of the Geneva Conventions' as war crimes in an international armed conflict, and Article 8(2)(e)(vi) lists the same acts plus 'any other form of sexual violence also constituting a serious violation of article 3 common to the four Geneva Conventions' as war crimes in a non-international armed conflict.

The first attempt to use this crime was in the *Bemba* case, in which the arrest warrant request included charges of 'sexual violence' based on evidence that female MLC fighters forced civilian men in the CAR

175 Appeal Judgment, *Brima et al.* (SCSL-2004-16-A), 22 February 2008, [194].

176 See Chapter 3, §3.2.2.

177 R. Grey, 'Conflicting Interpretations of "Sexual Violence" in the International Criminal Court' (2014) 29(81) *Australian Feminist Studies* 273.

to undress and/or have sexual intercourse with the perpetrator. The Pre-Trial Chamber dismissed those charges. In relation to the charge of 'sexual violence' as a war crime, it found that the relevant conduct was already captured by the charge of outrages on personal dignity. For the charge of 'sexual violence' as a war crime, it found that the alleged acts of forced nudity were not sufficiently grave to be prosecuted as 'sexual violence' under Article 7(1)(g), and ignored the allegation of forced intercourse altogether. This interpretation of Article 7(1)(g) was at odds with the drafting history of the Rome Statute and Elements of Crimes, which shows that the drafters intended the reference to 'sexual violence' to cover forced nudity.[178] It was also at odds with jurisprudence from the ICTY and ICTR, in which forced nudity was prosecuted using the war crime of 'outrages on personal dignity', the crime against humanity of 'other inhumane acts', and the crime of genocide through causing 'causing serious bodily or mental harm', all of which are very grave crimes.[179]

The next attempt was in the *Muthaura et al.* case, in which the Prosecutor used this crime to charge the mutilation & severance of men's genitals during Kenya's post-election violence. The charge was rejected by a differently constituted Pre-Trial Chamber to the one in *Bemba* (although comprising two of the same three judges). This time, the issue was not the gravity of the alleged crimes, but their character. The first signs of trouble showed at the summons stage, when the Pre-Trial Chamber declined to include the charge of 'sexual violence' because in its view, the alleged acts were not 'sexual' in nature. Once again, this interpretation was inconsistent with the drafting history of the Statute, which indicates that that the drafters regarded genital mutilation as 'sexual violence'.[180] Women's Initiatives for Gender Justice described the Chamber's rejection of the 'sexual violence' charge as a 'worrying move', and criticised the Prosecution for 'merely stating that the acts were of a sexual nature, without elaborating on this point'.[181]

[178] V. Oosterveld, 'Gender-Sensitive Justice and the International Criminal Tribunal for Rwanda: Lessons Learned for the International Criminal Court' (2005) 12(1) *New England Journal of International and Comparative Law* 119, 124.

[179] Judgment, *Akayesu* (ICTR-96-4-T), 2 September 1998, [688]; [731]–[734]; Judgment, *Kunarac et al.* (IT-96-23-T & IT-96-23/1-T), 22 February 2001, [766]–[774], [782]; Appeal Judgment, *Kunarac et al.* (IT-96-23 & IT-96-23/1-A), 12 June 2002, [166].

[180] Oosterveld, 'Gender-Sensitive Justice', see n. 178, 124; E. La Haye, 'Article 8(2)(b)(Xxii)' in R.S. Lee (ed.), *The International Criminal Court: Elements of Crimes and Rules of Procedure and Evidence* (Transnational Publishers, 2001) 184, 198.

[181] Women's Initiatives for Gender Justice, 'Legal Eye on the ICC' (July 2011).

Seemingly taking on that criticism, the OTP advanced arguments about the 'sexual' nature of the acts at the confirming hearing. It argued: 'men who were castrated were deprived of their manhood and debased in front of their families … these weren't just attacks on men's sexual organs as such but were intended as attacks on men's identities as men within their society and were designed to destroy their masculinity.'[182] This discussion of the impact on the victims' 'manhood' and their 'identities as men within their society' explained how the acts related to the Rome Statute's definition of 'gender'.[183] However, the OTP did not make separate arguments to show that the acts were 'sexual' in nature, which as its *Gender Policy* acknowledges, is not true of *every* gender-based crime.[184] The Pre-Trial Chamber was not persuaded by the OTP's arguments. It declined to confirm the charge of 'sexual violence', stating:

> Not every act of violence which targets parts of the body commonly associated with sexuality should be considered an act of sexual violence … the determination of whether an act is of a sexual nature is inherently a question of fact. The Chamber finds that the evidence placed before it does not establish the sexual nature of the acts of forcible circumcision and penile amputation visited upon Luo men. Instead, it appears from the evidence that the acts were motivated by ethnic prejudice and intended to demonstrate cultural superiority of one tribe over the other.[185]

Once the case was before the Trial Chamber, Prosecutor Bensouda asked the Chamber to give notice that the acts of genital mutilation might be re-characterised as 'other forms of sexual violence'.[186] In support of this request, the OTP cited numerous judicial decisions and works of highly qualified publicists in which genital mutilation was described as 'sexual violence',[187] and argued:

> The harm caused by the amputation or disfigurement of one's sexual organs is not merely physical; it also attacks the victim's sexuality. This is particularly true in patriarchal societies, where an assault on a man's sexual organs also constitutes an assault on his masculinity and identity

[182] ICC-01/09-02/11-T-5-Red-ENG, 22 September 2011, 84(12–13); 88(12–15).

[183] See RS, Art. 7(3).

[184] As the Policy states, 'Gender-based crimes *are not always manifested as a form of sexual violence*. They may include non-sexual attacks on women and girls, and men and boys, because of their gender'. ICC OTP, 'Policy Paper on Sexual and Gender-Based Crimes' (June 2014), 3 (emphasis added).

[185] ICC-01/09-02/11-382-Red, 23 January 2012, [265]–[266].

[186] ICC-01/09-02/11-445, 3 July 2012, [13]–[14]; Regulations of the Court, Reg. 55.

[187] Ibid., [20]–[21].

> within society. It is simply impossible to divorce the physical harm caused by forcible circumcision and penile amputation from the harm caused to the victim's sexuality. It is this latter form of harm – to the victim's sexuality – that is inherently 'of a sexual nature'.[188]

The victims' counsel agreed that these acts should be characterised as 'sexual violence'. He argued that by denying the sexual nature of these acts, the Pre-Trial Chamber had 'relied on an outdated conceptualization of sexual violence; namely, that such are purely about sex and not about the complex power dynamics at play.'[189] He explained that his clients wanted the acts of genital mutilation to be charged as 'sexual violence' because these acts had affected them 'physically and psychologically, including on their ability to have sexual intercourse' as well as their 'sense of manhood'.[190] He concluded: 'the victims maintain that an indicium of the sexual nature of the crimes of forced circumcision and penile amputation is the *effect that the crime has had on the sexual lives of the victims* in question and the *purpose behind why the crime was committed*, as well as the element of force.'[191] The Trial Chamber never addressed these arguments, because the charges were withdrawn before a decision on the possible recharacterisation of the facts was rendered.

Thus, in both the *Bemba* and the *Muthaura et al.* case, the charges of 'sexual violence' ran aground at the pre-trial stage. Hayes has described those pre-trial decisions as among 'the most retrograde developments at the ICC to date'.[192] Chappell has also criticised these decisions, particularly the decision on genital mutilation, which she calls 'the most egregious misrecognition of male sexual violence at the ICC'.[193] These critiques are justified: as argued previously, the Chamber's interpretation of the Statute was unduly restrictive and poorly reasoned. However, in both cases, some criticism of the OTP is warranted too. In *Bemba,* the OTP did not seek leave to appeal the decision in which 'sexual violence' charge was dismissed, nor did it re-introduce the charge at the confirmation stage. In *Muthaura et al.,* the OTP presented its strongest argument about the sexual character of genital mutilation at trial, i.e. after the charges had been confirmed.

[188] Ibid., [19].
[189] ICC-01/09-02/11-458, 24 July 2012, [12].
[190] Ibid., [14].
[191] Ibid., [15] (emphasis added).
[192] Hayes, see n. 9, 43.
[193] Chappell, *The Politics of Gender Justice*, see n. 20, 123.

Charges of 'sexual violence' were also included on the arrest warrants for Laurent Gbagbo, Simone Gbagbo and Charles Blé Goudé, all from the situation in Côte d'Ivoire. However, the public court records do not reveal the facts relevant to those charges, and the Prosecution later omitted this charge at the confirmation stage. Thus, those cases did not advance the jurisprudence on this crime.

In this tangle of case law, one positive development has been the Appeals Chamber's finding that when 'sexual violence' is charged as a war crime, there is no need to show that the acts amount to a grave violation of the Geneva Conventions or a serious violation of Common Article 3. It will suffice that the violence is of *comparable gravity* to those breaches.[194] This finding, which accords with the drafting history of the Elements of Crimes,[195] is significant. It means that the war crime of sexual violence can be charged even if the victim is not a 'protected person' under the Geneva Conventions at the time that the sexual act took place.

## 5.4 Trial Narratives

Having now examined charging strategies, charging outcomes and legal precedents, the chapter concludes with some reflections on trial narratives. In particular, it considers whether the ICC has been effective at overcoming two critiques that feminist scholars have made of previous international criminal tribunals: that they failed to acknowledge the significance of gender norms and hierarchies; and that they reinforced gender stereotypes (see Chapter 3)

### *5.4.1 Surfacing Gender*

As well as strengthening accountability for crimes under international law, there is a value to international criminal tribunals exposing and condemning the bigotry and violent ideology that often underpins mass crimes. Reflecting on this point in the so-called '*Medical case*', one of the cases tried in post-World War II Germany under Control Council Law 10, US Prosecutor Telford Taylor stated:

> It is our deep obligation to all peoples of the world to show *why and how* these things happened. It is incumbent upon us to set forth with conspicuous clarity the ideas and motives which moved these defendants to treat

[194] ICC-01/04-02/06-1962, 15 June 2017, [49].
[195] La Haye, see n. 180, 198.

> their fellow men as less than beasts. The perverse thoughts and distorted concepts which brought about these savageries are not dead. They cannot be killed by force of arms.... They must be cut out and exposed.[196]

As detailed in Chapter 3, from the 1990s onwards, feminist legal scholars have argued that as part of this history-making and norm-setting function, international criminal tribunals should acknowledge and de-legitimise sexist and/or misogynistic ideologies that contribute to violence in times of war and peace alike.[197] To some extent, the OTP has heeded this call. In particular, in several trials, it has articulated the links between gender and sexual violence. For instance, in his opening statements in the *Katanga & Ngudjolo* case, the Prosecutor argued that women who were raped or sexually enslaved in connection to the Bogoro attack 'were victimised on the basis of their gender. They were attacked in particular because they were women.[198] In his opening statements in the *Bemba* case, the Prosecutor argued that the 'massive rapes' during the conflict in the CAR 'were not just sexually motivated; as *gender crimes*, they were crimes of domination and humiliation directed against women, but also directed against men with authority', noting that 'women were raped systematically to assert dominance and to shatter resistance. Men were raped in public to destroy their authority, their capacity to lead.'[199] And in his opening statements in the *Muthaura et al.* trial, the Prosecutor said:

> The Prosecution wishes to highlight the gender dimension of this disaster. Sexual violence is aimed at creating a specific impact by destroying both individuals and an entire community's social structure. In committing rape and mutilation of genital organs, individuals are assaulted and wounded in ways that are socially gendered, in their identities as women and men as such, and in the social roles that they occupy, identify with, and anticipate filling as gendered members of their communities. Women who were gang-raped were violated, humiliated, desecrated so as to lower their status and deprive them of their dignity and equality as human beings and, for some of them, to reduce their value as wives or potential wives. Men who were castrated were deprived of their manhood and debased in front of their families.[200]

[196] Cited in Niarchos, see n. 127, 652.

[197] E.g. Copelon, see n. 124; Niarchos, see n. 127; Buss, 'Curious Visibility', see n. 125; Mibenge, see n. 125.

[198] ICC-01/04-01/07-T-80-ENG, 24 November 2009, 25(24–25).

[199] ICC-01/05-01/08-T-32-ENG, 22 November 2010, 10(14–19) (emphasis added).

[200] ICC-01/09-02/11-T-5-Red-ENG, 22 September 2011, 84(1–13).

These statements are important to situating the crimes in their political and ideological context, of which beliefs about gender, and associated power inequalities between men and women, are a part. They therefore go some way towards 'gendering' trial narratives, although as noted in §5.4.2.3, the narrative is only partially gendered if only the *victims'* sex and gender identity is discussed.

However, in other cases, ideas about gender have not been identified as relevant of the commission of the crimes. For example, the concept of gender was not discussed in the OTP's opening statements in *Lubanga,*[201] nor in its opening statements in the three cases currently at trial, namely *Ntaganda,*[202] *Ongwen,*[203] and *Gbagbo & Blé Goudé.*[204] It is unclear why the reference to gender norms has not been standardised in opening statements; this seems like another manifestation of the historic tendency not to see gender as a relevant category of victimisation.[205] The public attention to opening statements suggests that this would be an opportune point in the proceedings to institutionalise a practice of presenting a gender analysis where relevant—the more culturally specific, the better.

### 5.4.2 *Challenging Gender Stereotypes*

#### 5.4.2.1 Women and Girls

In law and the humanities, feminist scholars often seek to challenge prevailing stereotypes of women as perpetual victims, particularly of sexual violence crimes. The reasons for challenging this stereotype are many. For starters, it is inaccurate: women and girls are rarely passive victims; even in extraordinarily violent circumstances, they often exercise some degree of agency with a view to self-protection, resistance, and survival.[206] Second, the perception of women as the weaker sex is open to manipulation: the need to protect one's 'own' women from attack, or to 'liberate' the women

[201] ICC-01/04-01/06-T-107-ENG, 26 January 2009, 4(10)–36(4).

[202] ICC-01/04-02/06-T-23-ENG, 2 September 2015, 11(8)–66(15).

[203] ICC-02/04-01/15-T-26-ENG, 6 December 2016, 22(18)–89(4); ICC-02/04-01/15-T-27-ENG, 7 December 2016, 3(1)–51(14).

[204] ICC-02/11-01/15-T-9-ENG, 28 January 2016, 39(24)–79(4); ICC-02/11-01/15-T-10-ENG, 29 January 2016, 1(20)–40(16).

[205] Chapter 3, §3.1.6.

[206] E.g. E. Baines, *Buried in the Heart Women, Complex Victimhood and the War in Northern Uganda* (Cambridge University Press, 2017); M. Denov, *Child Soldiers: Sierra Leone's Revolutionary United Front* (McGill University Press, 2010) 132–133.

from another state, is often put forward as a justification for war.[207] Third, it is simplistic: it reduces women to one aspect of their experience, while deflecting attention from the many other ways that women are affected by, and complicit in, war.[208] In addition, it deflects attention away from the vulnerabilities of men and boys. As argued by Nivedita Menon,

> The dominant perception that it is only women who are perpetually violable and in danger of rape. This silence around male rape magnifies the shame and trauma of the raped man, reduced and feminized by the act; and simultaneously produces only women as eternally rapeable.[209]

To overcome this narrow and condescending perception of women's nature, it is necessary to recognise that women and girls can be victims, but they are also survivors, resisters, aggressors, protectors. Often, a single woman or girl embodies all of these identities. As Elizabeth Schneider has so eloquently argued:

> Women's victimization and agency are each understood to exist as the absence of the other … Feminist work should reject these extremes and should instead explore the interrelationship between, and simultaneity of, oppression and resistance. … This means that we reject simple dichotomies, give up either/ors … If we examine both of these dimensions simultaneously, our work will be more meaningful, and will be more grounded in, and more reflective of, the experiences of women's lives.[210]

To its credit, the ICC has made some useful contributions in this respect. Far from being presented as one-dimensional figures, women and girls are represented in ICC cases in many different roles. Certainly, one way that women and girls are represented is ICC cases is as victims of crimes. Indeed, this is true of all ICC cases except the two concerning the attack on the peacekeeping base in Darfur, which appear not to have caused any female casualties.[211] Very often, these crimes include rape and other

[207] H. Charlesworth and C. Chinkin, *The Boundaries of International Law: A Feminist Analysis* (Manchester University Press, 2000) 254–255.

[208] J. Gardam, 'A New Frontline for Feminism and International Humanitarian Law' in M. Davies and V. Munro (eds), *The Ashgate Research Companion to Feminist Legal Theory* (Ashgate, 2013) 217.

[209] N. Menon, *Seeing Like a Feminist* (Zubaan/Penguin Books, 2012) 140.

[210] E. Schneider, 'Feminism and the False Dichotomy of Victimization and Agency' (1993) 38 *New York Law School Law Review* 387, 396–399.

[211] The ICC court records and African Union report do not disclose the sex of all victims of this attack. However, it appears that none were female; they are all described in male or gender-neutral terms. See, e.g. ICC-02/05-02/09-91-Red, 24 September 2009, African Union, 'Investigation Report on the Attack on MGS Haskanita on 29/30 Sep 07 by Armed Faction to the Darfur Conflict' (9 October 2007).

forms of sexual violence. However, they also include crimes that are not gender-based (e.g. murder, looting, forced displacement, being forced to carry heavy goods, recruitment and use as 'child soldiers'). Since early on, the OTP has made a point of noting that female experiences of victimhood are not limited to sexual violence. This practice goes back to the *Lubanga* trial, in which Prosecutor Moreno-Ocampo used his opening statements to highlight the multiple roles played by female 'child soldiers' in the UPC. Echoing the report filed two years earlier by the UN Special Representative for Children and Armed Conflict, Radhika Coomaraswamy, the Prosecutor stated:

> Girl soldiers, some aged 12 years, were used as cooks and fighters, cleaners and spies, scouts and sexual slaves. One minute they will carry a gun, the next minute they will serve meals to the commanders, the next minute the commanders will rape them.[212]

Often, women and girls are also presented in ICC cases as circumscribed actors. This term comes from Mark Drumbl's work on 'child soldiers', in which he argues that a 'circumscribed actor' has the ability to act or not to act, however, this capacity for action is 'delimited, bounded, and confined.'[213] Of course, this conception of agency is true of all people, to varying degrees. The point is that, in numerous ICC cases, women and girls are shown to retain some margin of agency *even when they are the victims of crimes*. For instance, in the *Ongwen* case, one woman testified that she refused Ongwen's sexual advances for a week, despite receiving numerous beatings for doing so, before she yielded.[214] Another woman testified that that she refused to go to Ongwen's tent the first time that he sent his escorts to collect her, and she submitted only after they returned and physically took her to Ongwen, who held her down and raped her. In her words, 'he violated my rights. I was young and there was absolutely nothing that I could say about it.'[215] In his opening statements at trial, Senior Trial Lawyer Ben Gumpert, referred to these acts of defiance by the women, in addition to describing the violence inflicted upon them.[216]

[212] ICC-01/04-01/06-T-107-ENG, 26 January 2009, 4(19)–5(3); 11(25)–12(3). See also ICC-01/04-01/06-1229-AnxA, 18 March 2008, [22].

[213] M. Drumbl, *Reimagining Child Soldiers in International Law and Policy* (Oxford University Press, 2012) 17.

[214] ICC-02/04-01/15-T-8-Red-ENG, 15 September 2015, 38(17)–40(19).

[215] ICC-02/04-01/15-T-13-Red-ENG, 9 November 2015, 17(13)–18(9).

[216] ICC-02/04-01/15-T-27-ENG, 7 December 2016, 15(21)–16(8); 17(15–21).

Another example can be been in the *Ntaganda* case, in which a victim participant explained that when several soldiers tried to take her baby and told her to lie down, she resisted, but then they smashed her in the face with their rifle-butts and raped her.[217] A third example can be seen in the *Bemba* case, in which one victim participant's testimony of rape began as follows:

> Two of the soldiers came towards me. I was wondering whether my life was coming to an end this way, and how my children were going to fare. Then one of them asked me to take off my clothes, and *I refused to do so.* Then he took two bottles and broke them before me in order to frighten me and, yes, I was indeed frightened. *I tried to fight him off,* and then one of them kicked me in the - kicked me, kicked my feet, and then I fell to the ground....[218]

Increasingly in ICC cases, women and girls are also presented as rights bearers. For example, in the *Ongwen* case the OTP has argued that the crime of 'forced marriage' violates the 'right to consensually marry and establish a family',[219] and that crime of forced pregnancy is a violation of 'reproductive autonomy'.[220] More recently, in the *Al Hassan* case, the OTP has argued that women and girls who were forced out of public life, forced into 'marriages', and sexually abused by Islamist militants in Timbuktu were deprived of their right to physical integrity,[221] their right against discrimination the basis of sex,[222] and their right to freedom of association and assembly,[223] among others.

Fourth, the court records contain countless examples of women and girls contributing labour to armed groups. This labour, much of which is forced, includes fetching water and firewood, preparing meals, nursing wounded soldiers, birthing and raising the next generation of fighters, carrying heavy loads, and carrying infants when the group is on the move or under attack. It also includes combat roles. For example, in the *Lubanga, Ntaganda, Ongwen, Katanga, Ngudjolo* and *Bemba* cases, Prosecution witnesses referred to women and girls as fighters in the

[217] ICC-01/04-02/06-T-202-Red-ENG, 11 April 2017, 18(5–9); 21(4–6).
[218] ICC-01/05-01/08-T-220-ENG, 1 May 2012, 29(21)–30(22) (ellipses omitted and emphasis added).
[219] ICC-02/04-01/15-533, 6 September 2016, [511].
[220] Ibid., [512].
[221] ICC-01/12-01/18-1-Red, 20 March 2018, [137].
[222] Ibid., [142].
[223] Ibid., [143].

relevant armed groups. However, this evidence is not always reflected in court records. For example, in the *Bemba* case, although the OTP noted that the MLC included some women,[224] and that women formed part of the MLC contingent that went to the CAR in 2002–2003,[225] both the OTP and the Trial Chamber described that contingent as 1,500–2,000 'men'.[226]

Fifth, ICC cases show that women and girls are capable of violence. The tendency to see violence as incompatible with being 'womanly' is well documented.[227] However, that tendency reveals more about narrow conceptions of 'womanhood' than it does about the reality of women's lives. For example, in the *Katanga & Ngudjolo* trial, a defence witness stated that during the attack on Bogoro, 'even women had machetes, and they started cutting down people'.[228] In the *Bemba* case, a prosecution witnesses described seeing a female MLC soldier rob a civilian woman, threaten to rape with an iron bar, and encourage her male colleagues to rape themselves.[229] In the *Ongwen* case, one of Ongwen's alleged 'wives' alleged that a more senior 'wife' (who is also a Prosecution witness in the case) used to beat her when she was slow in doing her household chores,[230] several of his alleged 'wives' testified that they personally beat people to death after being ordered to do so,[231] and another female witness described being raped with an object and stomped on by a female LRA fighter at Odek camp.[232]

Sixth, women appear in ICC cases as political actors. For example, one of the four main attacks charged in the *Gbagbo and Blé Goudé* case concerned a political demonstration organised by women's rights groups in Côte d'Ivoire, at which several women were allegedly killed after

[224] ICC-01/05-01/08-950-Red-AnxA, 13 October 2010, [29].

[225] E.g. ICC-01/05-01/08-29-Red, 27 May 2008, [6(c)(v)]; ICC-01/05-01/08-3079-Corr-Red, 22 April 2016, [202]–[205].

[226] E.g. ICC-01/05-01/08-3079-Corr-Red, 22 April 2016, 4; ICC-01/05-01/08-T-32-ENG, 22 November 2010, 11(4); ICC-01/05-01/08-3343, 21 March 2016, [410].

[227] H. Durham and K. O'Byrne, 'The Dialogue of Difference: Gender Perspectives on International Humanitarian Law' (2010) 92(877) *International Review of the Red Cross* 31, 40–41; C. Gentry and L. Sjoberg, *Mothers, Monsters, Whores: Women's Violence in Global Politics* (Zed Books, 2015); N. Hodgson, 'Gender Justice or Gendered Justice? Female Defendants in International Criminal' (2017) 25(3) *Feminist Legal Studies* 337.

[228] ICC-01/04-01/07-T-256-Red2-ENG, 9 May 2011, 39(16–17).

[229] ICC-01/05-01/08-3079-Corr-Red, 22 April 2016, [203]; ICC-01/05-01/08-3343, 21 March 2016, [522]–[523].

[230] ICC-02/04-01/15-T-27-ENG, 7 December 2016, 24(5–9).

[231] ICC-02/04-01/15-T-27-ENG, 7 December 2016, 18(23)–19(2); 31(14–18).

[232] ICC-02/04-01/15-375-AnxC-Red, 15 February 2016 (confidential version filed on 21 December 2015), [251].

pro-Gbabgo forces opened fire. Sometimes, women also appear in ICC cases as political leaders, although, mirroring the under-representation of women in senior political and military roles generally, this does not happen often. Exceptions include Côte d'Ivoire's former first Lady, Simone Gbagbo, who is charged for her role in planning attacks by pro-Gbabgo forces following the 2010 presidential election. Another is the late Alice Lakwena, a relative of Joseph Kony's, who has been identified as the leader of the political and religious movement out of which Kony's own rebel group, the LRA, emerged.[233]

#### 5.4.2.2 Men and Boys

As with women and girls, men and boys appear in many different roles in cases before the ICC. They are often identified as victims of crimes, including sexual and gender-based crimes. There is a reason to think that going forward, sexual violence against men and boys will feature more prominently in ICC investigations and, where there is evidence, in prosecutions also. This issue was mentioned by every OTP official interviewed for this book, as noted in Chapter 2. Moreover, the Prosecutor's current Gender Advisor, Patricia Sellers, has identified this issue as a concern. In our 2018 interview, she explained:

> Among the biggest things that I'd like to bring to the Office is integrating this discussion of male sexual violence and female sexual violence so that we understand the nature of the entirety of sexual violence. Just to understand the nature of sexual violence against females but not males is to miss something again.[234]

In addition, men and boys are widely recognised as political and military actors: in ICC cases, the majority of political dissidents, and of fighting forces, tend to be men. In addition, often men and boys are very often recognised as the physical perpetrators of crimes. In particular, for sexual violence crimes, almost all perpetrators have been described as men and boys, usually members of armed groups, who often sexually assault the same victim in succession (i.e. gang-rape). Occasionally, female victims have recalled that in the group of men who assaulted them, there was one man who refused to join his peers.[235] However, men have mostly been described as acting in concert, with no objectors in the group.

[233] ICC-02/04-01/15-375-AnxC-Red, 15 February 2016, [14]–[15].
[234] Interview, February 2018.
[235] E.g. ICC-01/04-02/06-T-202-Red-ENG, 11 April 2017, 25(18–19); ICC-01/05-01/08-T-220-ENG, 1 May 2012, 30(21–22).

Finally, it should be noted that all but one of the ICC accused are men. We often hear that the accused are all African (which is also true), but the gender pattern is rarely commented on. Yet this pattern is significant also: it reflects the reality that men dominate the most senior positions in political and military affairs, and that those with the power to prevent or control armed forces, and to curb violence committed by those forces, are overwhelmingly male.

#### 5.4.2.3 Information Gaps

It is common in international courts and tribunals for prosecutors and judges to identify the victims of crimes by their sex, without doing the same for the perpetrators. This is an old pattern, dating back to the trial in the International Military Tribunal in Nuremberg after World War II. In that trial, the French prosecutor led to evidence that while held captive by the Gestapo in Clermont-Ferrand, 'some women were stripped naked and beaten before they were raped',[236] that in Saint-Jean-de-Maurienne, a 21-year-old woman 'was raped by a German soldier of Russian origin',[237] and that in Saint-Donat, '54 women or young girls from 13 to 50 years of age were raped by the maddened [German] soldiers'.[238]

This pattern has carried into the ICC, including in opening statements at trial, which are often attended by media, and are a key opportunity for the Prosecution, Defence and victims' counsel to frame their case. For example, in his opening statements in the *Lubanga* trial, Prosecutor Moreno-Ocmapo stated: 'girl soldiers were the daily victims of rape by the commanders ... One minute they will carry a gun, the next minute they will serve meals to the commanders, the next minute the commanders will rape them.'[239] Similarly, in his opening statements in the *Bemba* trial, the Prosecutor stated: 'groups of three or four soldiers invaded houses one-by-one; they stole all the possessions that could be carried off and raped the women, girls and elders... Women were raped systematically to assert dominance and to shatter resistance. Men were raped in public to destroy their authority, their capacity to lead.'[240] Likewise, in her opening

[236] Trial of the Major War Criminals Before the International Military Tribunal, Nuremberg, 14 November 1945–1 October 1946 ('Blue Series') (William s Hein & Co, 1951) Vol. IV, 25 January 1946, 178.

[237] Ibid., 31 January 1946, 404.

[238] Ibid., 405.

[239] ICC-01/04-01/06-T-107-ENG, 26 January 2009, 11(24)–12(3).

[240] ICC-01/05-01/08-T-32-ENG, 22 November 2010, 9(25)–10(19).

statements in the *Gbagbo & Blé Goudé* trial, Prosecutor Bensouda referred to a female witness who was 'gang raped at the prefecture of the police by armed gendarmes', noting that 'the other women detained with her were also repeatedly gang raped.'[241]

The same pattern can be detected in court documents, which have been scrutinised and re-drafted by numerous people before being filed or published. For example, in the *Katanga* case, the Prosecutor brought charges of rape, sexual slavery and outrages on personal dignity against 'civilian female residents or civilian women' by persons of an unknown sex.[242] The DCC explained:

> Women, who were captured at Bogoro and spared because they hid their ethnicity, were raped, sexually enslaved or humiliated. Threatened with death by the combatants, one woman was stripped and forced to parade half naked in front of them. Others were raped and forcibly taken to military camps. Once there, they were sometimes given as a 'wife' to their captors or kept in the camp's prison, which was a hole dug in the ground. The women detained in these prisons were repeatedly raped by soldiers and commanders alike and also by soldiers who were punished and sent to prison.[243]

The Pre-Trial Chamber confirmed these charges, against without disclosing the sex of the perpetrators.[244] Likewise, the Trial Chamber referred numerous times to women being raped, sexually enslaved and forced to do household chores for combatants of an unknown sex,[245] with the exception of a few paragraphs which noted, in passing, that the perpetrators of these crimes were men.[246]

This vague language, which I acknowledge is used in this book on occasion, is problematic for two reasons. First, identifying females but not males by their sex reinforces a view that being male is to be neutral, whereas there is something non-standard about being female.[247] Second, the Court's ability to shed light on the nature of gender-based violence is impaired if its analysis only considers the sex and/or socially

[241] ICC-02/11-01/15-T-9-ENG, 28 January 2016, 47(4–7).
[242] ICC-01/04-01/07-649-Anx1A, 26 June 2008, Counts 6–10.
[243] Ibid., [89].
[244] ICC-01/04-01/07-717, [247]–[354].
[245] ICC-01/04-01/07-3436-tENG, 7 March 2014, [200]–[201], [719], [959], [989]–[991], [998], [999], [1021]–[1023], [1663].
[246] Ibid., [992], [993], [997].
[247] See S. de Beauvoir, *The Second Sex (1949)* (Vintage, 2011) 5–6.

constructed gender of the victims. It is surely not irrelevant if particular crimes are carried out by and large by males, as a close reading of transcripts indicates is true for sexual violence crimes. In the interests of presenting a comprehensive and accurate history of period of national and international significance, patterns in the sex of perpetrators should be clearly acknowledged, just as patterns in the sex of the victims already are.

## 5.5 Conclusion

Despite the Rome Statute enumerating a wider range of gender-based crimes than any prior instrument of international criminal law, accountability for gender-based crimes appears not to have been a high priority in the early years. These early experiences suggest that the perceptions and attitudes that contributed to impunity for gender-based crimes under international criminal law in the past have continued, to some extent, in this new court. This observation is sobering, as is the fact that by 17 July 2018, the OTP is yet to secure any convictions for gender-based crimes.[248]

Yet if one takes a broader view of the ICC's goals, and its potential contribution to the fight against gender-based crimes, the practice thus far offers much to celebrate. Gender-based crimes now comprise almost half of all charges that have been brought before the ICC to date. These charges are not limited to the rape of women and girls: they *include* that crime (it would be a travesty if they did not), but they also include many other sexual and non-sexual gender-based crimes against women, girls, boys and men. Moreover, despite some serious losses and missed opportunities, outcomes for gender-based crimes are improving. Since 2014, all charges of gender-based crimes have been confirmed, which bodes well for ongoing and future cases.

It is not surprising that in the ICC, it has taken time for the OTP to develop the skills to investigate and prosecute gender-based crimes, and to overcome centuries of received wisdom about whose experiences of violence should be addressed as a priority. As Chappell has observed, 'undermining gender legacies is a long-term task.'[249] Similarly, in our 2018 interview, Sellers stated: 'I think ideas really take time to incubate

[248] This remains true as of 1 February 2019.

[249] Chappell, 'The Politics of Gender Justice,' see n. 20, 199.

and then to be applied and then to become conventional wisdom.'[250] Moreover, when evaluating the ICC's evolving practice on prosecuting gender-based crimes, it must be remembered that this is still a fairly new court. Although the Rome Statute was adopted on 17 July 1998, it did not enter into force until 1 July 2002, and the ICC's first investigation did not start until June 2004. In the intervening years, the OTP has conducted investigations in nine situations, each of which presents its own logistical challenges and requires staff to understand a new conflict situation, to meet new linguistic challenges, to build relationships with the affected communities, and to navigate relationships with one or more additional states. This is a different enterprise to the tasks of an ad hoc international criminal tribunal, and no doubt makes prosecuting all crimes – including gender-based crimes – particularly difficult. The OTP's early gains and losses must be viewed in that context.

In addition to making advances in its charging strategies, the ICC has started to produce some fairly gender-sensitive historical accounts of recent and ongoing armed conflicts. That is, the concept of gender is starting to 'surface' in ICC cases. The inclusion of charges of gender-based persecution in the *Al Hassan* case, and in the Prosecutor's request to open an investigation in Afghanistan, are concrete signs of progress on this front. In addition, the ICC court records tend not to reinforce narrow and potentially damaging gender stereotypes. To the contrary, those seeking to better understand the breadth of people's experiences in conflict situations, male and female, the ICC offers rich source material.

Above all, when it has come to developing the international jurisprudence on gender-based crimes, the OTP and the ICC as a whole have already excelled. Recent examples include the *Ntaganda* case, in which the Appeals Chamber has affirmed that the sexual abuse of 'child soldiers' by their commanders can be prosecuted as a war crime in the ICC, and the *Ongwen* case, which includes the ICC's first charges of forced pregnancy and 'forced marriage'. In our 2018 interview, Patricia Sellers highlighted this precedent-setting function as one of the strengths of the OTP's practice in prosecuting gender-based crimes to date. She explained:

> I think there's a great sense that we want to do something, we will do something, we are doing something. I think people are very proud of *Ongwen*, and *Ntaganda* has been a real booster, it's kind of like the

[250] Interview, February 2018.

> ICC's version of the *Tadić* appeals decision [the decision rendered on 2 October 1995, which was a breakthrough decision on the jurisdiction of the ICTY].[251]

Building on that momentum, the final chapter of the book identifies some areas where the ICC's jurisprudence on gender-based crimes can potentially expand in the years ahead.

[251] Interview, February 2018, citing: Decision on the Defence Motion for Interlocutory Appeal on Jurisdiction, *Tadić* (IT-94-1), 2 October 1995 (in that decision, the ICTY Appeals Chamber found that the ICTY was lawfully established by the UN Security Council, and that the Tribunal had jurisdiction to prosecute crimes committed in international *and* non-international armed conflicts).

# 6

# Looking Forward

The Rome Statute's twentieth anniversary is not only a time to review past progress and challenges. It is also an opportunity to reflect on the International Criminal Court's (ICC's) *future:* to think broadly about how the Court can stay relevant and responsive in the years ahead. In that spirit, this final chapter offers my thoughts about how the ICC's practice in prosecuting gender-based crimes could evolve, within the confines of the existing law. Guided by those principles, it then reflects on how the Court's jurisprudence might move forward in four important areas: (1) the crime against humanity of persecution; (2) the use of 'child soldiers'; (3) the protection of cultural heritage; and (4) the newly-codified crime of 'other forms of sexual violence'.

## 6.1 Interpretive Principles

As an international treaty, the Rome Statute must be interpreted by reference to certain rules. Very briefly, its terms must be given their ordinary meaning, in light of their context, object and purpose, and one can also look to the negotiating history if needed to make sense of ambiguous terms.[1] However, there is an emerging literature on how this *particular* treaty should be interpreted, given its specific aims and its peculiar blend of international criminal law, international humanitarian law, international human rights law and public international law.[2]

[1] *Vienna Convention on the Law of Treaties*, 23 May 1969, 1155 UNTS 331 (entered into force 27 January 1980), Art. 31 and 32.

[2] E.g. L. Sadat and J. Jolley, 'Seven Canons of ICC Treaty Interpretation' (Washington University in St. Louis Legal Studies Research Paper 13-11-06, 15 November 2013); L. Grover, *Interpreting Crimes in the Rome Statute of the International Criminal Court* (Cambridge University Press, 2014).

That literature recognises the importance of the principle of *nullum crimen sine lege* to the ICC. Meaning 'no crime without law', *nullum crimen sine lege* is a check on judicial power: it precludes courts from convicting people for crimes that were not defined clearly and specifically at the time of commission. This principle is enshrined in Article 22 of the Rome Statute, which also specifies that 'the definition of a crime shall be strictly construed and shall not be extended by analogy.'[3] The *nullum crimen* principle is central to fair trial rights, and is therefore protected by Article 21(3), which states that in the ICC, all sources of law must be interpreted and applied in a manner 'consistent with internationally recognized human rights.'[4] In my ICC interviews, this provision was emphasised by both speakers from the Office of Public Counsel for the Defence.

Among other things, Article 21(3) also compels the ICC to interpret the Rome Statute without discrimination on the basis of sex (in line with 'internationally recognized human rights') and without 'adverse distinction' on gender grounds. As observed by Patricia Sellers, Gender Advisor to the ICC Prosecutor, this means that the Chambers, Office of the Prosecutor (OTP) and all organs of the Court 'must share the responsibility to vigilantly gauge whether adverse gender discrimination results from the application or interpretation of substantive or procedural international law.'[5] The concept of 'feminist jurisprudence', as developed by feminist scholars, shines a light on what this approach to legal interpretation can mean.

Unlike methods of legal interpretation that purport to be neutral, feminist jurisprudence is a self-consciously subjective approach. It is challenge to the masculinist jurisprudence that has long been the norm in this field. Its basic aim is to 'theoris[e] about law from the perspective of constituencies of law which have traditionally been excluded.'[6] This does not mean ignoring legal authorities – instead, it means thinking about whether purportedly neutral provisions might be discriminatory in their effect; understanding factual allegations in the context of broader power relations; and seeking to improve the circumstances of

[3] RS, Art. 22(2).

[4] RS, Art. 21(3); ICCPR, Art. 15(1). See also M. Shahabuddeen, 'Does the Principle of Legality Stand in the Way of Progressive Development of Law?' (2004) 2(4) *Journal of International Criminal Justice* 1007; B. Van Schaack, 'Crimen Sine Lege: Judicial Lawmaking at the Intersection of Law and Morals' (2008) 87 *Georgetown Law Journal* 119.

[5] P.V. Sellers, 'Gender Strategy Is Not Luxury for International Courts' (2009) 17(2) *American University Journal of Gender, Social Policy & the Law* 301, 315.

[6] H. Barnett, *Introduction to Feminist Jurisprudence* (Cavendish Publishing, 1998) 13.

marginalised groups through the application of the law.[7] Drawing on the concept of 'intersectionality', I would emphasise that a 'feminist jurisprudence' does not only mean thinking about the experiences of 'women' generically but also means thinking about gender, race, class and other variables that shape a person's life.[8] Guided by these principles, and with a view to building on the successes in the ICC's practice so far, the following section identifies opportunities to further develop the ICC's jurisprudence on gender-based crimes.

## 6.2 Opportunities

### *6.2.1 Persecution*

As a means of prosecuting gender-based violence, the crime against humanity of 'persecution' has enormous potential. As with all crimes against humanity enumerated in the Rome Statute, this crime can apply in times of war *and* peace, so long as the persecutory acts are part of a 'widespread or systematic attack against a civilian population'. The crime is defined in Article 7(1)(h) of the Statute, which refers to:

> Persecution against any identifiable group or collectivity on political, racial, national, ethnic, cultural, religious, gender as defined in paragraph 3, or other grounds that are universally recognized as impermissible under international law, in connection with any act referred to in this paragraph or any crime within the jurisdiction of the Court.

Under Article 7(2)(g), the term 'persecution' is defined to mean:

> The intentional and severe deprivation of fundamental rights contrary to international law by reason of the identity of the group or collectivity.

#### 6.2.1.1 Persecution Due to Membership of a Gender Group

When thinking through the relevance of this crime from a feminist perspective, the concept of persecution on the grounds of 'gender' is a strong place to start. Reflecting on this point in our 2017 interview, Fabricio Guariglia, head of the OTP's Prosecution Division, stated: 'one thing that we're interested in exploring more and more is persecution on gender grounds, for instance. So, targeting women for their gender, persecution of certain forms of sexual identity.'[9] When contemplating

[7] Ibid., 8.

[8] K. Crenshaw, 'Demarginalizing the Intersection of Race and Sex' (1989) 140 *University of Chicago Legal Forum* 139.

[9] Interview, June 2017.

the crime of persecution on gender grounds, attention must be paid to Article 7(3) of the Statute, which states:

> For the purpose of this Statute, it is understood that the term 'gender' refers to the two sexes, male and female, within the context of society. The term 'gender' does not indicate any meaning different from the above.

Persecution on the grounds of 'gender', as defined in Article 7(3), clearly captures acts aimed at severely depriving a group people of their rights under international law due to their status as male or female in their social setting. The OTP's most recent case (*Al Hassan)*, which concerns the actions of Islamist militants in Mali, includes a charge of gender-based persecution of this nature.[10] The jurisprudence that this charge generates can potentially pave the way for the prosecution of similar arbitrary interference with the rights of people due to their membership of a male or female gender group. To take a present example, the so-called Islamic State has reportedly forbade many people from leaving home, forced them to wear clothing which impedes their ability to work, and authorised their enslavement and sexual abuse, on the basis that these people are female and, in its view, women exist to do men's bidding and they belong in the home.[11] If proven, that conduct would on its face amount to the intentional and severe deprivation of numerous rights enshrined the International Covenant on Civil and Political Rights (ICCPR) such as the right to liberty, the right to freedom of movement, and the right against torture or to cruel, inhuman or degrading treatment or punishment.[12]

#### 6.2.1.2 Persecution of Sexual Orientation Minorities

The ICC's practice in prosecuting persecution can also evolve by addressing acts targeted at people who are (or are perceived as) lesbian, gay, bisexual, or otherwise not-heterosexual.[13] Again, this argument is timely in the

[10] See Chapter 4, §4.8.2.

[11] L. Davis, 'Reimagining Justice for Gender Crimes at the Margins: New Legal Strategies for Prosecuting' (2018) 24(3) *William & Mary Journal of Women and the Law* 513; CUNY Law School, MADRE, and Organization of Women's Freedom in Iraq, 'Communication to the ICC Prosecutor Pursuant to Article 15 of the Rome Statute Requesting a Preliminary Examination into the Situation of: Gender-Based Persecution and Torture as Crimes Against Humanity and War Crimes Committed by the Islamic State of Iraq and the Levant (ISIL) in Iraq' (8 November 2017).

[12] ICCPR, Art. 7, 9(1), 12(1).

[13] For present purposes I will focus on persecution on the basis of sexual orientation, although these arguments could readily be transposed to other LGBTIQ people.

context of the Islamic State's reported murder and torture of people it regards as homosexual – sometimes based on nothing more than the content of the victim's social media, the shape of their trousers, or the style of their hair.[14] Yet this is not a 'new' issue: persecution on the grounds of sexual orientation has been known to international criminal law since the International Criminal Tribunal in Nuremberg.[15] In the intervening decades, the political will to address this issue has not been strong: persecution on the basis of sexual orientation has not been expressly criminalised any international instrument, and as detailed in Chapter 3, and the prospect that it *might* be criminalised in the Rome Statute was terrifying for some states and NGOs.[16]

However, despite their protestations, this bloc did not succeed in precluding the ICC from prosecuting the persecution of sexual orientation minorities. Depriving a person of fundamental rights because their sexual/romantic partners are (in the perpetrator's view) inappropriate for someone of their sex would fall squarely within the ICC's definition of persecution on 'gender' grounds, where it occurs in connection with another crime within the jurisdiction of the Court. Importantly, this interpretation does not assert that the persecution of sexual orientation minorities is *like* persecution on gender grounds, and therefore, could be prosecuted under Article 7(2)(g) (indeed, that argument would be invalid, because Article 22 prohibits the extension of a crime by analogy). Rather, the argument is that the persecution of sexual orientation minorities *is* gender-based persecution, because at its core, this violence is aimed at punishing, intimidating or degrading the victim due for non-adherence to gender norms for a person of their sex.[17]

Having said that, due to the constraints of the statutory definition of 'gender', it is also worth considering other relevant grounds of persecution.

[14] Davis, see n. 11; CUNY Law School, MADRE, and Organization of Women's Freedom in Iraq, see n. 11.

[15] Chapter 3, §3.1.6.

[16] Chapter 3, §3.2.1.

[17] For supporting views, see B. Bedont, 'Gender Specific Provisions in the Statute of the International Criminal Court' in F. Lattanzi and W. Schabas (eds), *Essays on the Rome Statute of the International Criminal Court* (Il Sirente, 1999) 183, 188; R. Copelon, 'Gender Crimes as War Crimes: Integrating Crimes against Women into International Criminal Law' (2000) 46 *McGill Law Journal* 217, 237; Davis, see n. 11, 540–542; V. Oosterveld, 'The Definition of Gender in the Rome Statute of the International Criminal Court: A Step Forward or Back for International Criminal Justice?' (2005) 18 *Harvard Human Rights Journal* 55, 76–68.

For example, if faced with a Bench that is hostile to the previous argument, the OTP could consider charging violence directed at homosexual people as persecution on 'cultural' grounds. This term, which is not constrained by statutory definition or case law, seems a logical fit for queer communities that have different courtship rituals, different artistic traditions and/or different notions of kinship than the heterosexual mainstream.

The OTP may also use the residual category of 'other grounds that are universally recognized as impermissible under international law', interpreted in light of Article 21(3) of the Rome Statute (which requires the ICC to interpret and apply the law in accordance with 'internationally recognized human rights'). In the two decades since the Statute was adopted, numerous UN treaty bodies and regional human rights courts have recognised a right against discrimination on the basis of sexual orientation. Some of these decisions were issued before the Rome Statute entered force. For example, in 1999, the Human Rights Committee held that discrimination on the basis of sexual orientation is a form of 'sex'-based discrimination under Articles 2(1) and 26 of ICCPR.[18] That same year, the European Court of Human Rights held that discrimination on the basis of sexual orientation falls foul of Article 14 of the European Convention on Human Rights, which does not refer expressly to sexual orientation, but provides a non-exhaustive list of grounds.[19] Decisions to this effect have continued to be rendered in the intervening years.[20] While not binding on the ICC, these human rights precedents make it difficult for the Defence to be shielded by the principle of *nullum crimen sine lege*, or to argue that the accused could not have known that the crime of persecution on 'other grounds that are universally recognized as impermissible under international law' included persecution on the basis of sexual orientation at the time of the relevant conduct.

In most cases, the persecutory acts could also be prosecuted without recourse to the crime of persecution: the OTP could charge the conduct as murder or torture, for example. In short, when it comes to violence directed at sexual orientation minorities, the Rome Statute provides plenty of pathways. So long as the evidence is solid, the charges should succeed.

[18] Views, *Toonen v. Australia*, Human Rights Council, 31 March 1994, [8.7].

[19] Judgment, *Salgueiro da Silva Mouta v. Portugal*, ECtHR, 21 December 1999, [28].

[20] E.g. Views, *X v. Colombia*, Human Rights Committee, 30 March 2007, [7.2]; Judgment, *Atala Riffo and daughters v. Chile*, IACtHR, 24 February 2012, [83]–[93]; Judgment, *Vejdeland and others v. Sweden*, ECtHR, 9 February 2012, [55].

#### 6.2.1.3 Persecution on Intersecting Grounds

Finally, to make full use of the 'persecution' crime, ICC cases should recognise persecution on intersecting grounds. This would be an asset for gender-based persecution, because in conflict settings, gender-based persecution often intersects with persecution on other grounds, such as, ethnicity, religion and/or perceived political affiliation.[21] By the time of the Rome Statute's twentieth anniversary, no 'intersecting' persecution charges have been laid. However, there are signs that this might soon change. The concept of 'intersectionality' is referenced in the OTP's 2014 *Gender Policy*,[22] and its relevance is understood by the current Gender Advisor, Patricia Sellers. When I raised the possibility of charging persecution on intersecting grounds in our 2018 interview, Sellers replied:

> I think that's just the natural evolution not only of a gender analysis, but I think it's what the true facts are going to bring forward… we've gotten to a stage where that should become part of a norm… we're looking at that person in a more integrated way. So, it will sound almost like an old-fashioned judgment if we only look at one aspect of it. I think we're beyond that now.[23]

### *6.2.2 Use of 'Child Soldiers'*

As alleged in numerous ICC cases, 'child soldiers' in armed groups are often abused in gendered ways alongside their militarised roles. Girls are allegedly raped and forced to perform domestic labour; boys are allegedly forced or instructed (in highly coercive circumstances) to commit sexual violence crimes against others. The first ICC case to address this issue was the *Lubanga* case, in which the OTP argued that the alleged sexual abuse of female 'child soldiers' in the *Union des Patriotes Congolais* (UPC)

[21] R. Copelon, 'Surfacing Gender: Re-Engraving Crimes against Women in Humanitarian Law' (1994) 5 *Hastings Women's Law Journal* 243; D. Buss, 'The Curious Visibility of Wartime Rape: Gender and Ethnicity in International Criminal Law' (2007) 25 *Windsor Yearbook of Access to Justice* 3; D. Buss, 'Sexual Violence, Ethnicity, and Intersectionality in International Criminal Law' in E. Grabham et al. (eds), *Intersectionality and Beyond* (Routledge, 2009) 105; C. Mibenge, *Sex and International Tribunals: The Erasure of Gender from the War Narrative* (University of Pennsylvania Press, 2013); V. Oosterveld, 'Prosecuting Gender-Based Persecution as an International Crime' in A. de Brouwer et al. (eds), *Sexual Violence as an International Crime: Interdisciplinary Approaches* (Intersentia, 2013) 57.

[22] ICC OTP, 'Policy Paper on Sexual and Gender-Based Crimes' (June 2014), [27].

[23] Interview, February 2018.

was captured by the crime of 'using children under fifteen to participate actively in hostilities'. This approach did not succeed – but not because the Trial Chamber rejected this interpretation on the crime. Rather, the Majority of the Trial Chamber declined to rule on this interpretation of the crime because the allegations of sexual violence had been made too late, and in a dissenting opinion, Judge Odio Benito accepted the Prosecutor's interpretation of the crime.[24]

In the *Ntaganda* case, the OTP has broken new ground by charging the alleged sexual abuse of UPC 'child soldiers' using the war crimes of rape and sexual slavery.[25] However, beginning at the pre-trial stage, the OTP has also advanced a gender-sensitive interpretation of the war crime of 'using child soldiers to participate actively in hostilities' in this case. Specifically, it has argued that female 'child soldiers' were used for gathering intelligence, which involved entering the camps of enemy soldiers in civilian clothing, having sex with those soldiers, and returning to the UPC with information on the number of troops and the type of weapons they possessed.[26] This charging strategy is progressive and inclusive: it allows the OTP to prosecute the alleged sexual violence allegedly perpetrated against 'child soldiers' by members of their own group, while also showing that the use of children to gather intelligence can involve sexual and gender-based violence.

The *Lubanga* Appeals Chamber judgment, rendered on 1 December 2014, potentially opens up further opportunities for a gender-sensitive interpretation of the war crime of 'using children to participate actively in hostilities'. The Appeals Chamber held that in order to determine if child was a victim of that crime, one need not ask if he or she was exposed to danger as a potential target, but must instead 'analyse the link between the activity for which the child is used and the combat in which the armed force or group of the perpetrator is engaged'.[27] The Appeals Chamber did not list all of the activities that would satisfy this definition, arguing that a closed list would be short-sighted in view of the 'unforeseeable scenarios presented by the rapidly changing face of warfare in the modern world'.[28] However, it held that in deciding whether a given activity constitutes

[24] See Chapter 4.

[25] See Chapter 5, §5.3.1.

[26] ICC-01/04-02/06-503, 9 March 2015, [396]; ICC-01/04-02/06-T-23-ENG, 2 September 2015, 62(3–7).

[27] ICC-01/04-01/06-3121-Red, 1 December 2014, [335].

[28] Ibid., [335].

'active participation in hostilities', the ICC would be guided by the ICRC commentary on the 1977 Additional Protocols and the 1998 Draft ICC Statute. Those instruments indicate that military groups must not use children for 'gathering and transmission of military information', 'transportation of arms and munitions', 'provision of supplies', 'transmitting orders', 'transporting ammunition and foodstuffs', or 'acts of sabotage'.[29]

The Appeals Chamber's interpretation of the crime could enable the prosecution of gendered abuses of 'child soldiers', if there is a close link between the sexual abuse and the group's participation in hostilities in a particular case.[30] For example, the sexual abuse of 'child soldiers' by their commanders could be regarded as 'combat-related' – and therefore within the scope of the crime – in groups where girls are 'given' to other fighters to reward or incentivise military prowess. Examples of this reward mentality can be seen in Myriam Denov's study from Sierra Leone,[31] and more recently, in the ICC's *Ongwen* case, in which the OTP has argued that 'having wives was considered by LRA fighters to be a symbol of rank, seniority, or privilege.'[32] In addition, charges of 'using children to participate actively in hostilities' could potentially incorporate evidence that the child has been used to prepare meals, fetch water, and collect firewood – tasks that seem frequently to fall to female children in armed groups. It makes sense to view these activities as 'combat-related' if they literally fuel

[29] Ibid., [335]. The 1998 Draft ICC Statute also states that: 'The words "using" and "participate" have been adopted in order to cover both direct participation in combat and also active participation in military activities linked to combat such as scouting, spying, sabotage and the use of children as decoys, couriers or at military checkpoints. It would not cover activities clearly unrelated to the hostilities such as food deliveries to an airbase of the use of domestic staff in an officer's married accommodation. However, use of children in a direct support function such as acting as bearers to take supplies to the front line, or activities at the front line itself, would be included within the terminology'. 'Report of the Preparatory Committee on the Establishment of an International Criminal Court: Addendum 1, UN Doc. A/CONF.183/2/Add.1 ("1998 Draft ICC Statute")' (14 April 1998), n. 12.

[30] R. Grey, 'Interpreting International Crimes from a "Female Perspective": Opportunities and Challenges for the International Criminal Court' (2017) 17(2) *International Criminal Law Review* 325, 341–349. For another feminist perspective on the interpretation of this crime, see Y. Brunger et al., 'Prosecutor v. Thomas Lubanga Dyilo: International Criminal Court' in L. Hodson and T. Lavers (eds), *Feminist Judgments in International Law* (Hart Publishing, forthcoming).

[31] M. Denov, *Child Soldiers: Sierra Leone's Revolutionary United Front* (McGill University Press, 2010) 132. See also D. Mazurana and S. McKay, 'Child Soldiers: What about the Girls?' (2001) 57(5) *Bulletin of the Atomic Scientists* 30, 33.

[32] ICC-02/04-01/15-375-AnxC-Red, 15 February 2016, [431].

the fighting forces, as was apparently true in Sierra Leone.[33] Compared to being used as a sexual slave or being forced into battle, this forced domestic labour may not seem as significant. However, it seems that many children, particularly girls, are used in *all* of these ways: in the kitchen, in the bedroom, and on the battlefield. In such cases, excluding forced domestic labour from the charge would seem to devalue the importance of a type of work performed primarily by women and girls, and would not address all aspects of the child's abuse.

### 6.2.3 *Cultural Heritage*

On its face, the notion of protecting cultural heritage seems non-discriminatory. The goal is to preserve property which is of significant cultural or historic value to 'humanity' at large. However, recent scholarship suggests that efforts to protect cultural heritage often begin with, and reinforce, a biased idea about *which* buildings, artworks, artefacts, etc., are deemed worthy of preserving. For example, Jo Littler argues that 'the groups who got to define "the Heritage" – and in a related sense, who possessed heritage – were mainly upper or upper middle-class white people, particularly men.'[34] Adding a gender perspective to this critique, Laurajane Smith, argues that the designation of particular items as cultural heritage 'is too often "masculine", and tells a predominantly male-centred story, promoting a masculine, and in particular elite-Anglo-masculine, vision of the past and present.'[35] In Smith's view, 'sites and places of significance to women's history and experience are neglected in registers of conserved or preserved heritage.'[36]

The ICC's *Al Mahdi* case, which focused on the destruction of cultural heritage in Timbuktu, did not replicate those problems. This case did not focus on sites frequented by white, male, elites. Rather, it focused on sites of importance to Muslim people, especially West-African Muslims, sites that were cherished and maintained by women and men.[37] To continue to promote an inclusive idea of cultural heritage, and to help rectify the

[33] Denov, see n. 31, 108–109.

[34] J Littler, 'Heritage and "Race"' in P. Howard and B. Graham (eds), *The Ashgate Research Companion to Heritage and Identity* (Ashgate, 2008) 89, 91.

[35] L. Smith, 'Heritage, Gender and Identity' in B. Graham and P. Howard (eds), *The Ashgate Research Companion to Heritage and Identity* (Ashgate, 2008) 159, 159.

[36] Ibid., 162.

[37] See Chapter 4, §4.8.1.

male-bias of past approaches to this topic, it is important that the OTP pays close attention to the destruction of property of central importance to women's lives. This would include buildings and artworks that celebrates female historical figures, or which are used for women's-only rituals, or which give particular meaning to women's lives.

The destruction of such property could be charged using the crime for which Al Mahdi was convicted, namely the war crime of 'intentionally directing attacks against buildings dedicated to religion, education, art, science or charitable purposes, historic monuments, hospitals and places where the sick and wounded are collected, provided they are not military objectives.' But an ICC Prosecutor may also want to prosecute the destruction of *intangible* cultural property, such as poems, folklore, or skills that have been passed down through the generations.[38] Potentially, the destruction of this property could be charged using the war crime of outages on personal dignity, or the war crime of cruel treatment, or as part of a persecution charge.

### 6.2.4 *Sexual Violence*

The Rome Statute is the first instrument of international criminal law to include a general 'sexual violence' crime. Specifically, the Statute defines the crime against humanity of 'rape, sexual slavery, enforced prostitution, forced pregnancy, enforced sterilization, or *any other form of sexual violence of comparable gravity*'.[39] There is an analogous war crime of 'other forms of sexual violence' as well.[40] The Elements of Crimes states that to prove this crime, the Prosecutor must show that:

> The perpetrator committed an *act of a sexual nature* against one or more persons or caused such person or persons to engage in an act of a sexual nature by force, or by threat of force or coercion ... or by taking advantage of a coercive environment or such person's or persons' incapacity to give genuine consent.[41]

This general crime of 'sexual violence' is extremely valuable. It could potentially be used to prosecute all manner of acts that are not otherwise expressly enumerated in the Rome Statute, including: forcing a victim to

[38] J. Blake, 'Human Rights Dimensions of Gender and Intangible Cultural Heritage' (2015) 24(2) *Human Rights Defender* 5.

[39] RS, Art. 7(1)(g)-6.

[40] RS, Art. 8(2)(b)(xxi)-6 and 8(2)(e)(vi)-6.

[41] EoC, Art. 7(1)(g)-1, 8(2)(b)(xxi)-6 and 8(2)(e)(vi)-6.

undress; subjecting the victim to sexualised insults; mutilating the victims' sexual organs; forcing the victim to engage in non-penetrative acts with themselves or other people (including the perpetrator); and forcing the victim to rape a third party, among others. The OTP has recognised the potentially broad use of this crime. For example, in its ongoing preliminary examination in relation to crimes allegedly committed by UK forces in Iraq, the OTP is contemplating using the residual crime of 'sexual violence' in relation to acts allegedly committed against men in detention facilities, including:

> Inflicting physical injuries to the genitalia of detainees, enforced masturbation, provocative physical touching of detainees' genital and anal area, and touching detainees' body with perpetrators' sexual organs. In addition, detainees were forcibly maintained in a state of forced nudity, compelled to perform physical exercises naked, repeatedly exposed to genitalia and pornography, and photographed whilst naked.[42]

However, as detailed in Chapter 5, efforts to charge this crime in ICC cases have been unsuccessful so far. The conduct has been deemed not sufficiently 'grave' (as with the forced nudity in *Bemba*), or not 'sexual' in nature (as with the genital mutilation in *Muthaura et al.*).[43] There is a need for the ICC to develop clear jurisprudence on this crime. In particular, there is a need for judges to determine a viable and culturally sensitive method for determining: (a) the gravity of the alleged acts; and (b) whether the acts can be described as 'sexual'. These are subjective questions, which must ultimately be answered by the Bench. However, so that judges are not limited to assessing the evidence through their own cultural and personal lens, it is vital that they have access to alternative perspectives from the OTP, Defence, victims' counsel, and expert witnesses or *amici curiae*. This information will equip the Court to understand how the violence was intended by the perpetrator, how it was interpreted by the victim and their community, and how (if at all) the crime has affected the victim's sexual confidence, sexual identity, sexual health, and/or ability engage in sexual activity.

In developing such a definition, the ICC may look to the negotiating history of the Rome Statute, which indicates that this general 'sexual violence' crime was included to cover 'acts such as forced nudity and sexual

[42] E.g. ICC OTP, 'Report on Preliminary Examination Activities 2016' (14 November 2016), [94].

[43] Chapter 5, §5.3.5.

mutilation, or any other similarly degrading acts.'[44] It may also consider the drafting history of the Elements of Crimes, which shows that the definition was drafted to cover two situations: (a) the situation where the perpetrator commits sexual acts against the victims; and (b) the situation where the victim is forced or coerced to perform sexual acts. The latter was included in the elements to also include forced nudity.[45]

The ICC may also make reference to jurisprudence of other international criminal tribunals, which is not binding in the ICC, but is frequently cited in the Court as persuasive precedent. For example, in the *Kvočka et al.* case, the ICTY Trial Chamber proclaimed that in addition to the specific acts of listed in Article 7(1)(g) of the Rome Statute (i.e. rape, sexual slavery, enforced prostitution, forced pregnancy and enforced sterilisation), 'sexual violence would also include such crimes as sexual mutilation, forced marriage, and forced abortion.'[46] Another example can be seen in the *Akayesu* case, in which the ICTR Trial Chamber held that:

> Sexual violence is not limited to physical invasion of the human body and may include acts which do not involve penetration or even physical contact. The incident described by Witness KK in which the Accused ordered the Interahamwe to undress a student and force her to do gymnastics naked in the public courtyard of the bureau communal, in front of a crowd, constitutes sexual violence.[47]

Guidance may be sought from definitions of sexual violence put forward by experts, which again are not binding in the ICC, but may assist the judges to think through the possibilities. For example, in 1998, the UN Special Rapporteur on the Situation of Systematic Rape, Sexual Slavery and Slavery-like Practices during Armed Conflict defined 'sexual violence' as:

> Any violence physical or psychological, carried out through sexual means or by targeting sexuality. Sexual violence covers both physical and psychological attacks directed at a person's sexual characteristics, such as forcing a person to strip naked in public, mutilating a person's genitals,

[44] V. Oosterveld, 'Gender-Sensitive Justice and the International Criminal Tribunal for Rwanda: Lessons Learned for the International Criminal Court' (2005) 12(1) *New England Journal of International and Comparative Law* 119, 124.

[45] K. Dörmann, *Elements of War Crimes under the Rome Statute of the International Criminal Court Sources and Commentary* (Cambridge University Press, 2003), 331.

[46] Judgment, *Kvočka et al.* (IT-98-30/1), 2 November 2011, n. 343.

[47] Judgment, *Akayesu* (ICTR-96-4-T), 2 September 1998, [688].

> or slicing off a woman's breasts. Sexual violence also characterizes situations in which two victims are forced to perform sexual acts on one another or to harm one another in a sexual manner. Such crimes are often intended to inflict severe humiliation on the victims and when others are forced to watch acts of sexual violence, it is often intended to intimidate the larger community.[48]

Yet it would be remiss to only consult these judicial or expert opinions, which are not necessarily representative of concepts of sexual violence worldwide. To be truly inclusive and culturally appropriate, the Court must also avail itself to non-expert, local perspectives on this issue. Already, civil society is taking action to assist the ICC in this regard. In 2017, following a discussion in The Hague among NGOs, the author, and gender expert Niamh Hayes, a survey has gone out to global civil society to develop a shared understanding of this crime. This survey was launched in September 2018 by Women's Initiatives, which explained:

> We seek to develop a civil society definition, in the form of a non-exhaustive list of acts that could be considered an 'act of a sexual nature' to assist defence counsel, prosecutors, victims and perpetrators to better understand what crimes which include an 'act of a sexual nature' could entail. Importantly, such a definition would consider acts that may be intended as sexual by perpetrators, and/or perceived as such by victims in specific cultural environments.[49]

The interpretative statement that comes out of this process will better enable the ICC to appreciate how differently the concepts of sex and sexuality are interpreted around the world.[50]

## 6.3 Conclusion

For its first decade of practice, the ICC did not significantly advance the international jurisprudence on gender-based crimes. However, from 2014 onward, the OTP has put forward increasingly bold and gender-sensitive interpretations of Rome Statute crimes, some of which have been accepted by the judges.[51]

[48] 'Contemporary Forms of Slavery: Systematic Rape, Sexual Slavery and Slavery-like Practices during Armed Conflict (E/CN.4/Sub.2/1998/13)' (22 June 1998), [21]–[22].

[49] Women's Initiatives for Gender Justice, 'Developing a Working Definition of "an Act of Sexual Violence"' (18 September 2018): https://4genderjustice.org/developing-a-working-definition-of-an-act-of-sexual-violence/.

[50] See M. Handl, 'Blogpost: Calling it what it is: It is time to define "sexual violence"' (13 December 2018): 4genderjustice.org/calling-it-what-it-is-it-is-time-to-define-sexual-violence/.

[51] See Chapter 5, §5.3.

Building on that trend, and picking up on ideas raised in my interviews and in feminist scholarship on international criminal law, this chapter has identified opportunities to further develop the ICC's jurisprudence on gender-based crimes in the years ahead. It has articulated some broad principles that may guide the ICC in developing a jurisprudence that is both fair and gender-sensitive, and has sketched out how these principles might be applied in relation to four issues of pressing concern to the ICC: persecution on the grounds of gender and/or sexual orientation; the use of 'child soldiers'; the protection of cultural heritage; and the prosecution of sexual violence. Underpinning this legal analysis is an understanding that decisions made by the ICC do not only function as roadmaps for this institution: they also function as persuasive precedents for many international, regional and domestic courts with jurisdiction to prosecute war crimes, crimes against humanity, and genocide.

A challenge, as the ICC moves forward, will be to develop a jurisprudence which responds to the causes and consequences of gender-based violence in places throughout the world. This includes the African countries discussed in this book, as well as other countries relevant to situations under investigation or preliminary examination, including Afghanistan, Burundi, Colombia, Georgia, Guinea, Iraq, Myanmar, Nigeria, Palestine, the Philippines, Ukraine, and Venezuela. Reflecting on this point in our interview, Melinda Reed observed:

> As cases before the Court arise from countries outside of Africa, understanding the context in which the crimes are committed will be critical. If the Court is going to truly be the international criminal court, covering the world, it needs to know that sexual and gender based crimes are going to look very, very different in different places and that a real gendered analysis of all international crimes will require adequate resources and expertise. They need to make sure that they're able to properly assess these crimes in the context in which they're occurring.[52]

Seeing not only *that* gender operates in all conflicts of relevance to the ICC, but also how it operates *differently* across all of these conflicts, will be a difficult feat. It requires a gender-sensitive OTP, judges with expertise in gender analysis, and input from NGOs, experts and victimised communities with local knowledge of what it means to be male, female, both, or neither within the context of the relevant society. The more this can be done, the better equipped the ICC will be to investigate, prosecute and adjudicate gender-based crimes.

[52] Interview, July 2018 (ellipses omitted).

APPENDIX

# Modes of Liability (MoL) at Confirmation Stage

| Count | Crime Charged | MoL Charged | Article | MoL Confirmed | Article |
|---|---|---|---|---|---|
| ***Prosecutor v. Lubanga*** | | | | | |
| 1 | War crime: Conscripting children into armed group | 'Direct co-perpetration' | 25(3)(a) | 'Direct co-perpetration' | 25(3)(a) |
| 2 | War crime: Enlisting children into armed group | As above | As above | As above | As above |
| 3 | War crime: Using children to participate actively in hostilities | As above | As above | As above | As above |
| ***Prosecutor v. Ntaganda*** | | | | | |
| 1 | Crime against humanity: Murder and attempted murder[*] | 'Direct perpetration'; or<br>'Indirect co-perpetration'; or<br>'Ordering/inducing'; or<br>'Contributing'; or<br>'Command responsibility' | 25(3)(a); or<br>25(3)(a); or<br>25(3)(b); or<br>25(3)(d)(i)/(ii); or<br>28(a) | 'Direct perpetration'; or<br>'Indirect co-perpetration'; or<br>'Ordering/inducing'; or<br>'Contributing'; or<br>'Command responsibility' | 25(3)(a); or<br>25(3)(a); or<br>25(3)(b); or<br>25(3)(d)(i)/(ii); or<br>28(a) |
| 2 | War crime: Murder and attempted murder[*] | As above | As above | As above | As above |
| 3 | War crime: Attacking civilian population | As above | As above | As above | As above |
| 4 | Crime against humanity: Rape (of 'civilians') | 'Indirect co-perpetration'; or<br>'Ordering/inducing'; or<br>'Contributing'; or<br>'Command responsibility' | 25(3)(a); or<br>25(3)(b); or<br>25(3)(d)(i)/(ii); or<br>28(a) | 'Indirect co-perpetration'; or<br>'Ordering/inducing'; or<br>'Contributing'; or<br>'Command responsibility' | 25(3)(a); or<br>25(3)(b); or<br>25(3)(d)(i)/(ii); or<br>28(a) |
| 5 | War crime: Rape (of 'civilians') | As above | As above | As above | As above |

| | | | | | |
|---|---|---|---|---|---|
| 6 | Crime against humanity: Rape (of 'child soldiers') | 'Indirect co-perpetration'; or<br>'Contributing'; or<br>'Command responsibility' | 25(3)(a); or<br>25(3)(d)(i)/(ii); or<br>28(a) | 'Indirect co-perpetration'; or<br>'Contributing'; or<br>'Command responsibility' | 25(3)(a); or<br>25(3)(d)(i)/(ii); or<br>28(a) |
| 7 | Crime against humanity: Sexual slavery (of 'civilians') | 'Indirect co-perpetration'; or<br>'Ordering/inducing'; or<br>'Contributing'; or<br>'Command responsibility' | 25(3)(a); or<br>25(3)(b); or<br>25(3)(d)(i)/(ii); or<br>28(a) | 'Indirect co-perpetration'; or<br>'Ordering/inducing'; or<br>'Contributing'; or<br>'Command responsibility' | 25(3)(a); or<br>25(3)(b); or<br>25(3)(d)(i)/(ii); or<br>28(a) |
| 8 | War crime: Sexual slavery (of 'civilians') | As above | As above | As above | As above |
| 9 | War crime: Sexual slavery (of 'child soldiers') | 'Indirect co-perpetration'; or<br>'Contributing'; or<br>'Command responsibility' | 25(3)(a); or<br>25(3)(d)(i)/(ii); or<br>28(a) | 'Indirect co-perpetration'; or<br>'Contributing'; or<br>'Command responsibility' | 25(3)(a); or<br>25(3)(d)(i)/(ii); or<br>28(a) |
| 10 | Crime against humanity: Persecution ('ethnic' grounds) | 'Direct perpetration'; or<br>'Indirect co-perpetration'; or<br>'Ordering/inducing'; or<br>'Contributing'; or<br>'Command responsibility' | 25(3)(a); or<br>25(3)(a); or<br>25(3)(b); or<br>25(3)(d)(i)/(ii); or<br>28(a) | 'Direct perpetration'; or<br>'Indirect co-perpetration'; or<br>'Ordering/inducing'; or<br>'Contributing'; or<br>'Command responsibility' | 25(3)(a); or<br>25(3)(a); or<br>25(3)(b); or<br>25(3)(d)(i)/(ii); or<br>28(a) |
| 11 | War crime: Pillage | As above | As above | As above | As above |
| 12 | Crime against humanity: Forcible transfer | 'Indirect co-perpetration'; or<br>'Ordering/inducing'; or<br>'Contributing'; or<br>'Command responsibility' | 25(3)(a); or<br>25(3)(b); or<br>25(3)(d)(i)/(ii); or<br>28(a) | 'Indirect co-perpetration'; or<br>'Ordering/inducing'; or<br>'Contributing'; or<br>'Command responsibility' | 25(3)(a); or<br>25(3)(b); or<br>25(3)(d)(i)/(ii); or<br>28(a) |
| 13 | War crime: Displacement of civilians | As above | As above | As above | As above |

| | | | | | |
|---|---|---|---|---|---|
| 14 | War crime: Conscripting children into armed group | 'Indirect co-perpetration'; or<br>'Contributing'; or<br>'Command responsibility' | 25(3)(a); or<br>25(3)(d)(i)/(ii); or<br>28(a) | 'Indirect co-perpetration'; or<br>'Contributing'; or<br>'Command responsibility' | 25(3)(a); or<br>25(3)(d)(i)/(ii); or<br>28(a) |
| 15 | War crime: Enlisting children into armed group | 'Direct perpetration'; or<br>'Indirect co-perpetration'; or<br>'Contributing'; or<br>'Command responsibility' | 25(3)(a); or<br>25(3)(a); or<br>25(3)(d)(i)/(ii); or<br>28(a) | 'Direct perpetration'; or<br>'Indirect co-perpetration'; or<br>'Contributing'; or<br>'Command responsibility' | 25(3)(a); or<br>25(3)(a); or<br>25(3)(d)(i)/(ii); or<br>28(a) |
| 16 | War crime: Using children to participate actively in hostilities | 'Direct perpetration'; or<br>'Indirect co-perpetration'; or<br>'Ordering/inducing'; or<br>'Contributing'; or<br>'Command responsibility' | 25(3)(a); or<br>25(3)(a); or<br>25(3)(b); or<br>25(3)(d)(i)/(ii); or<br>28(a) | 'Direct perpetration'; or<br>'Indirect co-perpetration'; or<br>'Ordering/inducing'; or<br>'Contributing'; or<br>'Command responsibility' | 25(3)(a); or<br>25(3)(a); or<br>25(3)(b); or<br>25(3)(d)(i)/(ii); or<br>28(a) |
| 17 | War crime: Attacking protected objects | As above | As above | As above | As above |
| 18 | War crime: Destruction of property | Indirect co-perpetration'; or<br>'Contributing'; or<br>'Command responsibility' | 25(3)(a); or<br>25(3)(d)(i)/(ii); or<br>28(a) | 'Indirect co-perpetration'; or<br>'Contributing'; or<br>'Command responsibility' | 25(3)(a); or<br>25(3)(d)(i)/(ii); or<br>28(a) |
| ***Prosecutor v. Ngudjolo*** | | | | | |
| 1 | Crime against humanity: Murder | 'Direct co-perpetration'; or<br>'Ordering' | 25(3)(a)<br>25(3)(b) | 'Indirect co-perpetration' | 25(3)(a) |
| 2 | War crime: Murder / Wilful killing | As above | As above | As above | As above |
| 3 | Crime against humanity: Other inhumane acts | As above | As above | Not confirmed | Not confirmed |

| | | | | | |
|---|---|---|---|---|---|
| 4 | War crime: Cruel treatment / Inhuman treatment | As above | As above | As above | As above |
| 5 | War Crime: Using children to participate actively in hostilities | As above | As above | 'Direct co-perpetration' | 25(3)(a) |
| 6 | Crime against humanity: Sexual slavery | As above | As above | 'Indirect co-perpetration' | 25(3)(a) |
| 7 | War crime: Sexual slavery | As above | As above | As above | As above |
| 8 | Crime against humanity: Rape | As above | As above | As above | As above |
| 9 | War crime: Rape | As above | As above | As above | As above |
| 10 | War crime: Outrages on personal dignity | As above | As above | Not confirmed | Not confirmed |
| 11 | War crime: Attacking civilian population | As above | As above | 'Indirect co-perpetration' | 25(3)(a) |
| 12 | War crime: Pillage | As above | As above | As above | As above |
| 13 | War crime: Destruction of property | As above | As above | As above | As above |
| ***Prosecutor v. Katanga*** | | | | | |
| 1 | Crime against humanity: Murder | 'Direct co-perpetration'; or 'Ordering' | 25(3)(a) 25(3)(b) | 'Indirect co-perpetration' | 25(3)(a) |
| 2 | War crime: Murder / Wilful killing | As above | As above | As above | As above |
| 3 | Crime against humanity: Other inhumane acts | As above | As above | Not confirmed | Not confirmed |

| | | | | | |
|---|---|---|---|---|---|
| 4 | War crime: Cruel treatment / Inhuman treatment | As above | As above | As above | As above |
| 5 | War Crime: Using children to participate actively in hostilities | As above | As above | 'Direct co-perpetration' | 25(3)(a) |
| 6 | Crime against humanity: Sexual slavery | As above | As above | 'Indirect co-perpetration' | 25(3)(a) |
| 7 | War crime: Sexual slavery | As above | As above | As above | As above |
| 8 | Crime against humanity: Rape | As above | As above | As above | As above |
| 9 | War crime: Rape | As above | As above | As above | As above |
| 10 | War crime: Outrages on personal dignity | As above | As above | Not confirmed | Not confirmed |
| 11 | War crime: Attacking civilian population | As above | As above | 'Indirect co-perpetration' | 25(3)(a) |
| 12 | War crime: Pillage | As above | As above | As above | As above |
| 13 | War crime: Destruction of property | As above | As above | As above | As above |
| ***Prosecutor v. Mbarushimana*** | | | | | |
| 1 | War crime: Attacking civilian population | 'Contributing' | 25(3)(d) | Not confirmed | Not confirmed |
| 2 | Crime against humanity: Murder | As above | As above | As above | As above |
| 3 | War crime: Murder | As above | As above | As above | As above |
| 4 | War crime: Mutilation | As above | As above | As above | As above |

| | | | | | |
|---|---|---|---|---|---|
| 5 | Crime against humanity: Other inhumane acts | As above | As above | As above | As above |
| 6 | War crime: Cruel treatment | As above | As above | As above | As above |
| 7 | Crime against humanity: Rape | As above | As above | As above | As above |
| 8 | War crime: Rape | As above | As above | As above | As above |
| 9 | Crime against humanity: Torture | As above | As above | As above | As above |
| 10 | War crime: Torture | As above | As above | As above | As above |
| 11 | War crime: Destruction of property | As above | As above | As above | As above |
| 12 | War crime: Pillage | As above | As above | As above | As above |
| 13 | Crime against humanity: Persecution ('political' grounds) | As above | As above | As above | As above |
| ***Prosecutor v. Ongwen*** | | | | | |
| 1 | War crime: Attacking civilian population | 'Indirect co-perpetration'; or 'Aiding/abetting/assisting'; or 'Contributing'; or 'Command responsibility' | 25(3)(a); or 25(3)(c); or 25(3)(d)(i)/(ii); or 28(a) | 'Indirect co-perpetration'; or 'Aiding or abetting'; or 'Contributing'; or 'Command responsibility' | 25(3)(a); or 25(3)(c); or 25(3)(d)(i)/(ii); or 28(a) |
| 2 | Crime against humanity: Murder | As above | As above | As above | As above |
| 3 | War crime: Murder | As above | As above | As above | As above |
| 4 | Crime against humanity: Torture | As above | As above | As above | As above |
| 5 | War crime: Torture | As above | As above | As above | As above |
| 6 | War crime: Cruel treatment | As above | As above | As above | As above |

| | | | | | |
|---|---|---|---|---|---|
| 7 | Crime against humanity: Other inhumane acts | As above | As above | As above | As above |
| 8 | Crime against humanity: Enslavement | 'Indirect co-perpetration;' or<br>'Ordering'; or<br>'Aiding/abetting/assisting'; or<br>'Contributing'; or<br>'Command responsibility' | 25(3)(a); or<br>25(3)(b); or<br>25(3)(c); or<br>25(3)(d)(i)/(ii); or<br>28(a) | 'Indirect co-perpetration;' or<br>'Ordering'; or<br>'Aiding or abetting'; or<br>'Contributing'; or<br>'Command responsibility' | 25(3)(a); or<br>25(3)(b); or<br>25(3)(c); or<br>25(3)(d)(i)/(ii); or<br>28(a) |
| 9 | War crime: Pillage | As above | As above | As above | As above |
| 10 | Crime against humanity: Persecution | 'Indirect co-perpetration'; or<br>'Ordering'; or<br>'Contributing'; or<br>'Command responsibility' | 25(3)(a); or<br>25(3)(b); or<br>25(3)(d)(i)/(ii); or<br>28(a) | 'Indirect co-perpetration'; or<br>'Ordering'; or<br>'Contributing'; or<br>'Command responsibility' | 25(3)(a); or<br>25(3)(b); or<br>25(3)(d)(i)/(ii); or<br>28(a) |
| 11 | War crime: Attacking civilian population | As above | As above | As above | As above |
| 12 | Crime against humanity: Murder | As above | As above | As above | As above |
| 13 | War crime: Murder | As above | As above | As above | As above |
| 14 | Crime against humanity: Attempted murder* | As above | As above | As above | As above |
| 15 | War crime: Attempted murder* | As above | As above | As above | As above |
| 16 | Crime against humanity: Torture | As above | As above | As above | As above |
| 17 | War crime: Torture | As above | As above | As above | As above |
| 18 | Crime against humanity: Other inhumane acts | As above | As above | As above | As above |

| | | | | | |
|---|---|---|---|---|---|
| 19 | War crime: Cruel treatment | As above | As above | As above | As above |
| 20 | Crime against humanity: Enslavement | As above | As above | As above | As above |
| 21 | War crime: Pillage | As above | As above | As above | As above |
| 22 | War crime: Outrages on personal dignity | As above | As above | As above | As above |
| 23 | Crime against humanity: Persecution | As above | As above | As above | As above |
| 24 | War crime: Attacking civilian population | As above | As above | As above | As above |
| 25 | Crime against humanity: Murder | As above | As above | As above | As above |
| 26 | War crime: Murder | As above | As above | As above | As above |
| 27 | Crime against humanity: Attempted murder[*] | As above | As above | As above | As above |
| 28 | War crime: Attempted murder[*] | As above | As above | As above | As above |
| 29 | Crime against humanity: Torture | As above | As above | As above | As above |
| 30 | War crime: Torture | As above | As above | As above | As above |
| 31 | Crime against humanity: Other inhumane acts | As above | As above | As above | As above |
| 32 | War crime: Cruel treatment | As above | As above | As above | As above |
| 33 | Crime against humanity: Enslavement | As above | As above | As above | As above |
| 34 | War crime: Pillage | As above | As above | As above | As above |

| | | | | | |
|---|---|---|---|---|---|
| 35 | War crime: Destruction of property | As above | As above | As above | As above |
| 36 | Crime against humanity: Persecution | As above | As above | As above | As above |
| 37 | War crime: Attacking civilian population | As above | As above | As above | As above |
| 38 | Crime against humanity: Murder | As above | As above | As above | As above |
| 39 | War crime: Murder | As above | As above | As above | As above |
| 40 | Crime against humanity: Attempted murder* | As above | As above | As above | As above |
| 41 | War crime: Attempted murder* | As above | As above | As above | As above |
| 42 | Crime against humanity: Torture | As above | As above | As above | As above |
| 43 | War crime: Torture | As above | As above | As above | As above |
| 44 | Crime against humanity: Other inhumane acts | As above | As above | As above | As above |
| 45 | War crime: Cruel treatment | As above | As above | As above | As above |
| 46 | Crime against humanity: Enslavement | As above | As above | As above | As above |
| 47 | War crime: Pillage | As above | As above | As above | As above |
| 48 | War crime: Destruction of property | As above | As above | As above | As above |
| 49 | Crime against humanity: Persecution | As above | As above | As above | As above |

| | | | | | |
|---|---|---|---|---|---|
| 50 | Crime against humanity: Other inhumane acts ('forced marriage') | 'Direct perpetration' | 25(3)(a) | 'Direct perpetration' | 25(3)(a) |
| 51 | Crime against humanity: Torture | As above | As above | As above | As above |
| 52 | War crime: Torture | As above | As above | As above | As above |
| 53 | Crime against humanity: Rape | As above | As above | As above | As above |
| 54 | War crime: Rape | As above | As above | As above | As above |
| 55 | Crime against humanity: Sexual slavery | As above | As above | As above | As above |
| 56 | War crime: Sexual slavery | As above | As above | As above | As above |
| 57 | Crime against humanity: Enslavement | As above | As above | As above | As above |
| 58 | Crime against humanity: Forced pregnancy | As above | As above | As above | As above |
| 59 | War crime: Forced pregnancy | As above | As above | As above | As above |
| 60 | War crime: Outrages on personal dignity | As above | As above | As above | As above |
| 61 | Crime against humanity: Other inhumane acts ('forced marriage') | 'Indirect co-perpetration'; or 'Ordering'; or 'Contributing'; or 'Command responsibility' | 25(3)(a); or 25(3)(b); or 25(3)(d)(i)/(ii); or 28(a) | 'Indirect co-perpetration'; or 'Ordering'; or 'Contributing'; or 'Command responsibility' | 25(3)(a); or 25(3)(b); or 25(3)(d)(i)/(ii); or 28(a) |
| 62 | Crime against humanity: Torture | As above | As above | As above | As above |
| 63 | War crime: Torture | As above | As above | As above | As above |

| | | | | | |
|---|---|---|---|---|---|
| 64 | Crime against humanity: Rape | As above | As above | As above | As above |
| 65 | War crime: Rape | As above | As above | As above | As above |
| 66 | Crime against humanity: Sexual slavery | As above | As above | As above | As above |
| 67 | War crime: Sexual slavery | As above | As above | As above | As above |
| 68 | Crime against humanity: Enslavement | As above | As above | As above | As above |
| 69 | War crime: Conscripting children into armed group | As above | As above | As above | As above |
| 70 | War crime: Using children to participate actively in hostilities | As above | As above | As above | As above |
| ***Prosecutor v. Abu Garda*** | | | | | |
| 1 | War crime: Murder or attempted murder* | 'Direct co-perpetration' or 'Indirect co-perpetration' | 25(3)(a) | Not confirmed | Not confirmed |
| 2 | War crime: Attacking peacekeepers | As above | As above | As above | As above |
| 3 | War crime: Pillage | As above | As above | As above | As above |
| ***Prosecutor v. Banda & Jerbo*** | | | | | |
| 1 | War crime: Murder or attempted murder* | 'Direct co-perpetration' or 'Indirect co-perpetration' | 25(3)(a) | 'Direct co-perpetration' | 25(3)(a) |
| 2 | War crime: Attacking peacekeepers | As above | As above | As above | As above |
| 3 | War crime: Pillage | As above | As above | As above | As above |

| | | | | | |
|---|---|---|---|---|---|
| ***Prosecutor v. Bemba*** | | | | | |
| 1 | Crime against humanity: Rape | 'Indirect co-perpetrator'; or 'Command responsibility' | 25(3)(a); or 28(a) or (b) | 'Command responsibility' | 28(a) |
| 2 | War crime: Rape | As above | As above | As above | As above |
| 3 | Crime against humanity: Torture | As above | As above | Not confirmed | Not confirmed |
| 4 | War crime: Torture | As above | As above | As above | As above |
| 5 | War crime: Outages on personal dignity | As above | As above | As above | As above |
| 6 | War crime: Murder | As above | As above | 'Command responsibility' | 28(a) |
| 7 | Crime against humanity: Murder | As above | As above | As above | As above |
| 8 | War crime: pillage | As above | As above | As above | As above |
| ***Prosecutor v. Muthaura et al.*** | | | | | |
| 1 | Crime against humanity: Murder (Muthaura & Kenyatta) | 'Indirect co-perpetration' | 25(3)(a) | 'Indirect co-perpetration' | 25(3)(a) |
| 2 | Crime against humanity: Murder (Ali) | 'Contributing' | 25(3)(d) | Not confirmed | Not confirmed |
| 3 | Crime against humanity: Deportation or forcible transfer (Muthaura & Kenyatta) | 'Indirect co-perpetration' | 25(3)(a) | 'Indirect co-perpetration' | 25(3)(a) |
| 4 | Crime against humanity: Deportation or forcible transfer (Ali) | 'Contributing' | 25(3)(d) | Not confirmed | Not confirmed |

| | | | | | |
|---|---|---|---|---|---|
| 5 | Crime against humanity: Rape and other forms of sexual violence (Muthaura & Kenyatta) | 'Indirect co-perpetration' | 25(3)(a) | 'Indirect co-perpetration' (for rape only) | 25(3)(a) |
| 6 | Crime against humanity: Rape and other forms of sexual violence (Ali) | 'Contributing' | 25(3)(d) | Not confirmed | Not confirmed |
| 7 | Crime against humanity: Other inhumane acts (Muthaura & Kenyatta) | 'Indirect co-perpetration' | 25(3)(a) | 'Indirect co-perpetration' | 25(3)(a) |
| 8 | Crime against humanity: Other inhumane acts (Ali) | 'Contributing' | 25(3)(d) | Not confirmed | Not confirmed |
| 9 | Crime against humanity: Persecution ('political' grounds) (Muthaura & Kenyatta) | 'Indirect co-perpetration' | 25(3)(a) | 'Indirect co-perpetration' | 25(3)(a) |
| 10 | Crime against humanity: Persecution ('political' grounds) (Ali) | 'Contributing' | 25(3)(d) | Not confirmed | Not confirmed |
| ***Prosecutor v. Ruto et al.*** | | | | | |
| 1 | Crime against humanity: Murder (Ruto & Kosgey) | 'Indirect co-perpetration' | 25(3)(a) | 'Indirect co-perpetration' (for Ruto only) | 25(3)(a) |
| 2 | Crime against humanity: Murder (Sang) | 'Contributing' | 25(3)(d) | 'Contributing' | 25(3)(d) |

| | | | | | |
|---|---|---|---|---|---|
| 3 | Crime against humanity: Deportation or forcible transfer (Ruto & Kosgey) | 'Indirect co-perpetration' | 25(3)(a) | 'Indirect co-perpetration' (for Ruto only) | 25(3)(a) |
| 4 | Crime against humanity: Deportation or forcible transfer (Sang) | 'Contributing' | 25(3)(d) | 'Contributing' | 25(3)(d) |
| 5 | Crime against humanity: Persecution ('political' grounds) (Ruto & Kosgey) | 'Indirect co-perpetration' | 25(3)(a) | 'Indirect co-perpetration' (for Ruto only) | 25(3)(a) |
| 6 | Crime against humanity: Persecution ('political' grounds) (Sang) | 'Contributing' | 25(3)(d) | 'Contributing' | 25(3)(d) |
| ***Prosecutor v. (Laurent) Gbagbo*** | | | | | |
| 1 | Crime against humanity: Murder | 'Indirect co-perpetration'; or 'Ordering etc'; or 'Contributing'; or 'Command responsibility' | 25(3)(a); or 25(3)(b); or 25(3)(d) or 28(a) or (b) | 'Indirect co-perpetration'; or 'Ordering etc'; or 'Contributing' | 25(3)(a); or 25(3)(b); or 25(3)(d) |
| 2 | Crime against humanity: Rape | As above | As above | As above | As above |
| 3 | Crime against humanity: Other inhumane acts or attempted murder' | As above | As above | As above | As above |
| 4 | Crime against humanity: Persecution ('political, national, ethnic and religious' grounds) | As above | As above | As above | As above |

| | | | | | |
|---|---|---|---|---|---|
| ***Prosecutor v. Blé Goudé*** | | | | | |
| 1 | Crime against humanity: Murder | 'Indirect co-perpetration'; or<br>'Ordering etc'; or<br>'Aiding etc'; or<br>'Contributing' | 25(3)(a); or<br>25(3)(b); or<br>25(3)(c); or<br>25(3)(d) | 'Indirect co-perpetration'; or<br>'Ordering etc'; or<br>'Aiding etc'; or<br>'Contributing' | 25(3)(a); or<br>25(3)(b); or<br>25(3)(c); or<br>25(3)(d) |
| 2 | Crime against humanity: Rape | As above | As above | As above | As above |
| 3 | Crime against humanity: Other inhumane acts or attempted murder* | As above | As above | As above | As above |
| 4 | Crime against humanity: Persecution ('political, national, ethnic and religious' grounds) | As above | As above | As above | As above |
| ***Prosecutor v. Al Mahdi*** | | | | | |
| 1 | War crime: Attacking protected objects | 'Direct perpetration'; or<br>'Direct co-perpetration'; or<br>'Soliciting/inducing'; or<br>'Aiding/abetting/assisting' or<br>'Contributing' | 25(3)(a); or<br>25(3)(a); or<br>25(3)(b); or<br>25(3)(c); or<br>25(3)(d) | 'Direct perpetration'; or<br>'Direct co-perpetration'; or<br>'Soliciting/inducing'; or<br>'Aiding/abetting/assisting' or<br>'Contributing' | 25(3)(a); or<br>25(3)(a); or<br>25(3)(b); or<br>25(3)(c); or<br>25(3)(d) |

* For attempted murder, the modes of liability specified above are applied in conjunction with Art. 25(3)(f).

# BIBLIOGRAPHY

Aboa, A., '*Ivory Coast's Simone Gbagbo Leaves Detention after Amnesty*' (Reuters, 8 August 2018).

Ackerly, B. and J. True, *Doing Feminist Research in Political and Social Science* (Palgrave Macmillan, 2010).

African Union, 'Investigation Report on the Attack on MGS Haskanita on 29/30 Sep 07 by Armed Faction to the Darfur Conflict' (9 October 2007): www.africa-confidential.com/uploads/documents/AU_Haskanita_report.pdf.

African Union (Assembly), 'Decision on the Implementation of the Decisions of the International Criminal Court, EX.CL/639(XVIII)' (30 January 2011): au.int/sites/default/files/decisions/9645-assembly_en_30_31_january_2011_auc_assembly_africa.pdf.

'Decision on Africa's Relationship with the International Criminal Court, Ext/Assembly/AU/Dec.1(Oct.2013)' (13 October 2013).

Agirre Aranburu, X., 'Sexual Violence beyond Reasonable Doubt: Using Pattern Evidence and Analysis for International Cases' (2000) 23(3) *Leiden Journal of International Law* 609.

Al Jazeera, 'ICC Judges Summon Ocampo Six' (9 March 2011).

'Explainer: Tuareg-Led Rebellion in North Mali' (4 April 2012).

Amann, D., 'In Bemba and Beyond, Crimes Adjudged to Commit Themselves' on *EJIL Talk!* (13 June 2018): www.ejiltalk.org/in-bemba-and-beyond-crimes-adjudged-to-commit-themselves/.

'Amicus Brief Respecting Amendment of the Indictment and Supplementation of the Evidence to Ensure the Prosecution of Rape and Other Sexual Violence within the Competence of the Tribunal' (27 May 1997): www1.essex.ac.uk/armedcon/story_id/000053.pdf.

Amnesty International, 'Democratic Republic of Congo: Mass Rape – Time for Remedies' (25 October 2004).

'Central African Republic: Five Months of War against Women' (10 November 2004).

'The Bemba Appeals Judgment Warrants Better Investigations and Fair Trials – Not Efforts to Discredit the Decision' on *Human Rights in International Justice* (19 June 2018): https://hrij.amnesty.nl/bemba-verdict-warrants-better-investigations-and-fair-trials/.

Apreotesei, A., 'The International Criminal Court: First Cases and Situations' (2008) 5(1) *Eyes on the ICC* 1.

Arendt, H., *Eichmann in Jerusalem: A Report on the Banality of Evil* (Viking, 1963).

Askin, K., *War Crimes against Women: Prosecution in International War Crimes Tribunals* (Martinus Nijhoff, 1997).

'Sexual Violence in Decisions and Indictments of the Yugoslav and Rwandan Tribunals: Current Status' (1999) 93(1) *American Journal of International Law* 97.

'Prosecuting Wartime Rape and Other Gender Related Crimes: Extraordinary Advances, Enduring Obstacles' (2003) 21(2) *Berkeley Journal of International Law* 288.

'A Treatment of Sexual Violence in Armed Conflicts: A Historical Perspective and The Way Forward' in A. de Brouwer et al. (eds), *Sexual Violence as an International Crime: Interdisciplinary Approaches* (Intersentia, 2013) 19.

'Katanga Judgment Underlines Need for Stronger ICC Focus on Sexual Violence' on *Open Society Foundations* (11 March 2014): www.opensocietyfoundations.org/voices/katanga-judgment-underlines-need-stronger-icc-focus-sexual-violence.

'Assembly of States Parties to the Rome Statute of the International Criminal Court: First Session, Official Records, ICC-ASP/1/3' (3 September 2002): documents-dds-ny.un.org/doc/UNDOC/GEN/N02/603/35/PDF/N0260335.pdf?OpenElement.

Avocats Sans Frontières et al., 'DR Congo: ICC Charges Raise Concern' (31 July 2006): www.hrw.org/news/2006/07/31/dr-congo-icc-charges-raise-concern.

Baines, E., *Buried in the Heart Women, Complex Victimhood and the War in Northern Uganda* (Cambridge University Press, 2017).

Barnett, H., *Introduction to Feminist Jurisprudence* (Cavendish Publishing, 1998).

Barsony, R., *Sexual Violence and the Triumph of Justice* (ICTY, 2012).

Bartlett, K., 'Feminist Legal Methods' (1989) 103(4) *Harvard Law Review* 829.

Bassiouni, M., *Crimes against Humanity* (Cambridge University Press, 2011).

BBC News, 'China Defends Visit by Sudan President Omar Al-Bashir' (21 June 2011).

'Uhuru Kenyatta Denounces ICC as Kenya Charges Dropped' (5 December 2014).

'Osaka Cuts San Francisco Ties Over "Comfort Women" Statue' (4 October 2018).

de Beauvoir, S., *The Second Sex (1949)* (Vintage, 2011, translated by C. Borde and S. Malovany-Chevallier).

Bedont, B. and K. Hall-Martinez, 'Ending Impunity for Gender Crimes Under the International Criminal Court' (1999) 6(1) *Brown Journal of World Affairs* 65.

Bedont, B, 'Gender Specific Provisions in the Statute of the International Criminal Court' in F Lattanzi and W Schabas (eds), *Essays on the Rome Statute of the International Criminal Court* (Il Sirente, 1999) 183.

Bedont, B. and D. Matas, 'Negotiating for an International Criminal Court' (1999) 14(5) *Peace Magazine* 21.

Benedetti, F. and J. Washburn, 'Drafting the International Criminal Court Treaty: Two Years to Rome and an Afterword on the Rome Diplomatic Conference' (1999) 5(1) *Global Governance* 1.

Bensouda, F., 'Statement' (at the Ceremony for the solemn undertaking of the Prosecutor of the International Criminal Court, The Hague, 15 June 2012).

'Gender Justice and the ICC' (2014) 16(4) *International Feminist Journal of Politics* 538.

Bjørkhaug, I. and M. Bøås, 'Men, Women and Gender-Based Violence in North Kivu, DRC' (Fafo, 2014).

Blake, J. 'Intangible Cultural Heritage' in UNESCO, *Gender Equality: Heritage and Creativity* (UNESCO, 2014) 48.

'Human Rights Dimensions of Gender and Intangible Cultural Heritage' (2015) 24(2) *Human Rights Defender* 5.

Boister, N. and R. Cryer, *Documents on the Tokyo International Military Tribunal: Charter, Indictment and Judgments* (Oxford University Press, 2008).

Boot, M., 'Article 7(1)(G)' in O. Triffterer (ed.), *Commentary on the Rome Statute of the International Criminal Court* (Nomos Verlagsgesellschaft, 1999) 139.

Bosson, J. et al., 'Precarious Manhood and Displays of Physical Aggression' (2009) 35(5) *Personality and Social Psychology Bulletin* 623.

Brady, H., 'The Power of Precedents: Using the Case Law of the Ad Hoc International Criminal Tribunals and Hybrid Courts in Adjudicating Sexual and Gender-Based Crimes at the ICC' (2012) 18(2) *Australian Journal of Human Rights* 75.

Brammertz, S. and M. Jarvis (eds), *Prosecuting Conflict-Related Sexual Violence in the ICTY* (Oxford University Press, 2016).

Brownmiller, S., *Against Our Will: Men, Women and Rape* (Simon & Schuster, 1975).

Bruce, J., 'Economics before Romance: How Marriage Differs in Poor Countries' on *Think Big* (31 August 2018).

Brunger, Y., 'ICC's Bemba Ruling Is a Landmark, but Falls Short of a Big Leap' on *The Conversation* (25 March 2016): http://theconversation.com/iccs-bemba-ruling-is-a-landmark-but-falls-short-of-a-big-leap-56687.

Brunger, Y. et al., 'Prosecutor v Thomas Lubanga Dyilo: International Criminal Court' in L. Hodson and T. Lavers (eds), *Feminist Judgments in International Law* (Hart Publishing, forthcoming).

Bunch, C., 'Women's Rights as Human Rights: Toward a Re-Vision of Human Rights' (1990) 12(4) *Human Rights Quarterly* 486.

Bureleigh, M. and W. Wipperman, *The Racial State: Germany 1933–1945* (Cambridge University Press, 1991).

Burke-White, W., 'A Wife Accused of War Crimes: The Unprecedented Case of Simone Gbagbo' (The Atlantic, 3 December 2012).

Buss, D., 'The Curious Visibility of Wartime Rape: Gender and Ethnicity in International Criminal Law' (2007) 25 *Windsor Yearbook of Access to Justice* 3.

'Sexual Violence, Ethnicity, and Intersectionality in International Criminal Law' in E Grabham et al. (eds), *Intersectionality and Beyond* (Routledge, 2009) 105.

'Knowing Women: Translating Patriarchy in International Criminal Law' (2014) 23(1) *Social & Legal Studies* 73.

Butler, J., 'Performative Acts and Gender Constitution: Essay in Phenomenology and Feminist Theory' (1988) 40(4) *Theatre Journal* 519.

*Gender Trouble* (Routledge, 1990).

Byrnes, A., 'Women, Feminism, and International Human Rights Law: Methodological Myopia, Fundamental Flaws or Meaningful Marginalisation?' (1989) 12 *Australian Year Book of International Law* 205.

Byron, C. and D. Turns, 'The Preparatory Commission for the International Criminal Court' (2001) 50(2) *International and Comparative Law Quarterly* 420.

Carpenter, C., '"Women and Children First": Gender, Norms, and Humanitarian Evacuation in the Balkans 1991–95' (2003) 57(4) *International Organization* 661.

*Forgetting Children Born of War: Setting the Human Rights Agenda in Bosnia and Beyond* (Columbia University Press, 2010).

Carroll, A. and L. Mendos, 'State Sponsored Homophobia 2017: A World Survey of Sexual Orientation Laws' (International Lesbian, Gay, Bisexual, Trans and Intersex Association, 2017).

Cassese, A., 'On the Current Trends towards Criminal Prosecution and Punishment of Breaches of International Humanitarian Law' (1998) 9(1) *European Journal of International Law* 2.

CEDAW Committee, 'Concluding Observations on the Combined Third to Fifth Periodic Reports of Malaysia, UN Doc. CEDAW/C/MYS/CO/3-5' (9 March 2018).

'Concluding Observations on the Fifth Periodic Report of Turkmenistan, UN Doc. CEDAW/C/TKM/CO/5' (23 July 2018).

Chang, I., *The Rape of Nanking: The Forgotten Holocaust of World War II* (Penguin Books, 1997).

Chappell, L., 'Women's Rights and Religious Opposition: The Politics of Gender at the International Criminal Court' in Y. Abu-Laban (ed.), *Gendering the Nation State: Canadian Comparative Perspectives* (University of British Columbia Press, 2008) 139.

Chappell, L. and G. Waylen, 'Gender and The Hidden Life of Institutions' (2013) 91(3) *Public Administration* 599.

Chappell, L., 'Conflicting Institutions and the Search for Gender Justice at the International Criminal Court' (2014) 67(1) *Political Research Quarterly* 183.

Chappell, L., A. Durbach and E. Odio Benito, 'Judge Odio Benito: A View of Gender Justice from the Bench' (2014) 16(4) *International Feminist Journal of Politics* 648.

Chappell, L., *The Politics of Gender Justice at the International Criminal Court: Legacies and Legitimacy* (Oxford University Press, 2016).

'The Gender Injustice Cascade: "Transformative" Reparations for Victims of Sexual and Gender-Based Crimes in the Lubanga Case at the International Criminal Court' (2017) 21(9) *International Journal of Human Rights* 1223.

Charlesworth, H., C. Chinkin and S. Wright, 'Feminist Approaches to International Law' (1991) 85(4) *American Journal of International Law* 613.

Charlesworth, H., 'Feminist Methods in International Law' (1999) 93(2) *American Journal of International Law* 379.

Charlesworth, H. and C. Chinkin, *The Boundaries of International Law: A Feminist Analysis* (Manchester University Press, 2000).

Charlesworth, H., 'International Law: A Discipline of Crisis' (2002) 65(3) *Modern Law Review* 377.

'The Hidden Gender of International Law' (2002) 16(1) *Temple International and Comparative Law Journal* 93.

Chesterman, S., 'Never Again… and Again: Law, Order, and the Gender of War Crimes in Bosnia and Beyond' (1997) 22 *Yale Journal of International Law* 299.

Chowdhury Fink, N. and A. Davidian, 'Complementarity and Convergence?: Women, Peace and Security and Counterterrorism' in F. Ní Aoláin et al. (eds), *The Oxford Handbook of Gender and Conflict* (Oxford University Press, 2018) 158.

Chowdhury, R., 'Kadic v. Karadzic: Rape as a Crime against Women as a Class' (2002) 20(1) *Law & Inequality: A Journal of Theory and Practice* 91.

Cockburn, C., 'The Continuum of Violence: A Gender Perspective on War and Peace' in W. Giles and J. Hyndman (eds), *Sites of Violence: Gender and Conflict Zones* (University of California Press, 2004) 24.

Cohen, D., A. Green and E. Wood, 'Wartime Sexual Violence: Misconceptions, Implications, and Ways Forward' (United States Institute of Peace, February 2013).

Combahee River Collective, '1977 Combahee River Collective Statement' in B. Smith (ed.), *Home Girls: A Black Feminist Anthology* (Kitchen Table Press, 1983) 264.

'Comments by Colombia on Document PCNICC/1999/WGEC/RT.6, PCNICC/1999/WGEC/DP.30' (10 November 1999): www.legal-tools.org/doc/e01ec9/pdf/.

Commission of Inquiry into Post-Election Violence, 'Final Report' (16 October 2008): http://reliefweb.int/sites/reliefweb.int/files/resources/15A00F569813F4D549257607001F459D-Full_Report.pdf.

Commission on the Responsibility of the Authors of the War and on Enforcement of Penalties, 'Report Presented to the Preliminary Peace Conference, 29 March 1919' (1920) 14(1) *American Journal of International Law* 95.

'Contemporary Forms of Slavery: Systematic Rape, Sexual Slavery and Slavery-like Practices during Armed Conflict (E/CN.4/Sub.2/1998/13)' (22 June 1998): www.refworld.org/docid/3b00f44114.html.

Connell, R., *Masculinities* (Allen & Unwin, 2000).

'On Hegemonic Masculinity and Violence: Response to Jefferson and Hall' (2002) 6(6) *Theoretical Criminology* 89.

Connell, R. and J. Messerschmidt, 'Hegemonic Masculinity: Rethinking the Concept' (2005) 19(6) *Gender & Society* 829.

Connell, R. and R. Pearce, *Gender in World Perspectives* (Polity Press, 3rd edn, 2015).

Cook, R., 'Human Rights and Reproductive Self-Determination' (1995) 44(4) *American University Law Review* 975.

Copelon, R., 'Surfacing Gender: Re-Engraving Crimes against Women in Humanitarian Law' (1994) 5 *Hastings Women's Law Journal* 243.

'Gender Crimes as War Crimes: Integrating Crimes against Women into International Criminal Law' (2000) 46 *McGill Law Journal* 217.

Cossman, B., 'Gender Performance, Sexual Subjects and International Law' (2002) 15(2) *Canadian Journal of Law & Jurisprudence* 281.

Cottier, M. and S. Mzee, 'Paragraph 2(b)(Xxii)' in O. Triffterer and K. Amobs (eds), *The Rome Statute of the International Criminal Court: A Commentary* (C.H. Beck, Hart, Nomos, 3rd edn, 2016) 477.

Cowan, S., '"What a Long and Strange Trip It's Been": Feminist and Queer Travels with Sex, Gender, and Sexuality' in M. Davies and V. Munro (eds) (*The Ashgate Research Companion to Feminist Legal Theory*, 2016) 105.

Crenshaw, K., 'Demarginalizing the Intersection of Race and Sex' (1989) 140 *University of Chicago Legal Forum* 139.

'Crimes against Humanity: Texts and Titles of the Draft Preamble, the Draft Articles and the Draft Annex Provisionally Adopted by the Drafting Committee on First Reading, UN Doc A/CN.4/L.892' (26 May 2017).

Cryer, R. et al., *An Introduction to International Criminal Law and Procedure* (Cambridge University Press, 3rd edn, 2014).

CUNY Law School, MADRE, and Organization of Women's Freedom in Iraq, 'Communication to the ICC Prosecutor Pursuant to Article 15 of the Rome Statute Requesting a Preliminary Examination into the Situation of: Gender-Based Persecution and Torture as Crimes against Humanity and War Crimes Committed by the Islamic State of Iraq and the Levant (ISIL) in Iraq' (8 November 2017).

D'Aoust, M., 'Sexual and Gender-Based Violence in International Criminal Law: A Feminist Assessment of the Bemba Case' (2017) 17(1) *International Criminal Law Review* 208.

Davies, S. and J. True, 'The Pandemic of Conflict-Related Sexual Violence and the Political Economy of Gender Inequality' in A. Powell, N. Henry and A. Flynn (eds), *Rape Justice Beyond the Criminal Law* (Palgrave Macmillan, 2015) 160.

De Brouwer, A., *Supranational Criminal Prosecution of Sexual Violence: The ICC and the Practice of the ICTY and ICTR* (Intersentia, 2005).

De la Cruz, J., *Answer by the Poet to the Most Illustrious Sister Filotea de La Cruz (1691)* (2008).

De Londras, F., 'Prosecuting Sexual Violence in the Ad Hoc International Criminal Tribunals for Rwanda and the Former Yugoslavia' in M. Albertson Fineman (ed.), *Transcending the Boundaries of Law: Generations of Feminism and Legal Theory* (Routledge, 2011) 290.

De Vos, C., 'Investigating from Afar: The ICC's Evidence Problem' (2013) 26(4) *Leiden Journal of International Law* 1009.

De Vos, D., 'A Day to Remember: Ongwen's Trial Starts on 6 December' on *Int Law Grrls* (5 December 2016): https://ilg2.org/2016/12/05/a-day-to-remember-ongwens-trial-starts-on-6-december/.

*Complementarity's Gender Justice Prospects and Limitations: Examining Normative Interactions between the Rome Statute and National Accountability Processes for Sexual Violence Crimes in Colombia and the Democratic Republic of Congo* (PhD Thesis, European University Institute, 2017).

'Decisions Taken by the Preparatory Committee at Its Session Held from 1 to 12 December 1997, UN Doc. A/AC.249/1997/L.9/Rev.1' (18 December 1997).

'Decisions Taken by the Preparatory Committee at Its Session Held from 11 to 21 February 1997, UN Doc. A/AC.249/1997/L.5' (12 March 1997).

deGuzman, M., 'An Expressive Rationale for the Thematic Prosecution of Sex Crimes' in M. Bergsmo (ed.), *Thematic Prosecution of International Sex Crimes* (Torkal Opsahl Academic EPublisher, 2012) 11.

Denov, M., *Child Soldiers: Sierra Leone's Revolutionary United Front* (McGill University Press, 2010).

'Discriminatory Laws and Practices and Acts of Violence against Individuals Based on Their Sexual Orientation and Gender Identity: Report of the United Nations High Commissioner for Human Rights, UN Doc. A/HRC/19/41' (17 November 2011).

'Discriminatory Laws and Practices and Acts of Violence against Individuals Based on Their Sexual Orientation and Gender Identity: Report of the United Nations High Commissioner for Human Rights, UN Doc. A/HRC/29/23' (4 May 2015).

'Discussion Paper: Delegation of Bosnia and Herzegovina' (14 April 1998): www.legal-tools.org/doc/dd58b8/pdf/.

Dolan, C., 'Victims Who Are Men' in F. Ní Aoláin et al. (eds), *The Oxford Handbook of Gender and Conflict* (Oxford University Press, 2018) 86.

Dolgopol, U. and S. Paranjape, 'Comfort Women: An Unfinished Ordeal: Report of a Mission' (International Commission of Jurists, 1994).

Dolgopol, U., 'The Tokyo Women's Tribunal' in A. Byrnes and G. Simm (eds), *People's Tribunals and International Law* (Cambridge University Press, 2018) 84.

Dörmann, K., *Elements of War Crimes under the Rome Statute of the International Criminal Court Sources and Commentary* (Cambridge University Press, 2003).

Douglas, H. et al., 'Reflections on Rewriting the Law' in H. Douglas et al. (eds), *Australian Feminist Judgments* (Hart, 2014).

Douglas, L., *The Memory of Judgment: Making Law and History in the Trials of the Holocaust* (Yale University Press, 2001).

Drumbl, M., *Atrocity, Punishment, and International Law* (Cambridge University Press, 2007).

*Reimagining Child Soldiers in International Law and Policy* (Oxford University Press, 2012).

'Victims Who Victimise' (2016) 4(2) *London Review of International Law* 217.

Dunne, D. and H. Durham, 'The Prosecution of Crimes against Civilians' in F. Fitzpatrick, T. McCormack and N. Morris (eds), *Australia's War Crimes Trials 1945–51* (Brill/Nijhoff, 2016) 196.

Durbach, A. and L. Chappell, 'Leaving Behind the Age of Impunity: Victims of Gender Violence and the Promise of Reparations' (2014) 16(4) *International Feminist Journal of Politics* 543.

Durham, H. and K. O'Byrne, 'The Dialogue of Difference: Gender Perspectives on International Humanitarian Law' (2010) 92(877) *International Review of the Red Cross* 31.

Elander, M., 'The Victim's Address: Expressivism and the Victim at the Extraordinary Chambers in the Courts of Cambodia' (2013) 7 *International Journal of Transitional Justice* 95.

Elbert, T. et al., 'Sexual and Gender-Based Violence in the Kivu Provinces of the Democratic Republic of Congo: Insights from Former Combatants' (World Bank, September 2013).

Engle, K., 'Feminism and Its (Dis)Contents: Criminalizing Wartime Rape in Bosnia and Herzegovina' (2005) 99(4) *American Journal of International Law* 778.

Eriksson Baaz, M. and M. Stern, 'The Complexity of Violence: A Critical Analysis of Sexual Violence in the Democratic Republic of Congo' (SIDA/Nordiska Afrikainstitutet, 2010).

'Knowing Masculinities in Armed Conflict?: Reflections from Research in the Democratic Republic of Congo' in F. Ní Aoláin et al. (eds), *The Oxford Handbook of Gender and Conflict* (Oxford University Press, 2018) 533.

Facio, A., 'All Roads Lead to Rome, But Some Are Bumpier than Others' in S. Pickering and C. Lambert (eds), *Global Issues: Women and Justice* (Sydney Institute for Criminology, 2004) 308.

Fahey, D., 'Ituri: Gold, Land, and Ethnicity in North-Eastern Congo' (Rift Valley Institute & Usalama Project, 2013).

FIDH, 'Crimes de Guerre En République Centrafricaine: "Quand Les Éléphants Se Battent, c'est l'herbe Qui Souffre"' translated by Women's Initiatives for Gender Justice (FIDH, 13 February 2003).

'Mali: The Hearing of Al Mahdi before the ICC Is a Victory, but Charges Must Be Expanded' (30 September 2015).

'Final Report of the Commission of Experts Established Pursuant to Security Council Resolution 780 (1992), UN Doc. S/1994/674 (Annex 1)' (27 May 1994).

Fisk, R., 'Bosnia War Crimes: "The Rapes Went on Day and Night"' (Independent, 8 February 1993).

Franklin, J., *George Washington Williams* (University of Chicago Press, 1985).

Fus, T., 'Criminalizing Marital Rape' (2006) 39 *Vanderbilt Journal of Transnational Law* 481.

Gaggioli, G., 'Sexual Violence in Armed Conflicts?' (2014) 96(984) *International Review of the Red Cross* 503.

Gänsler, K., 'Life in Timbuktu after the Islamists' (DW) 8 May 2013.

Gardam, J., 'A Feminist Analysis of Certain Aspects of International Humanitarian Law' (1989) 12 *Australian Yearbook of International Law* 265.

'A New Frontline for Feminism and International Humanitarian Law' in M. Davies and V. Munro (eds), *The Ashgate Research Companion to Feminist Legal Theory* (Ashgate, 2013) 217.

Gentry, C. and L. Sjoberg, *Mothers, Monsters, Whores: Women's Violence in Global Politics* (Zed Books, 2015).

Gillet, M., 'Has the Pre-Trial Chamber Jeopardized the Gbagbo Trial at the International Criminal Court' on *Beyond The Hague* (29 December 2014): https://beyondthehague.com/2014/12/29/has-the-pre-trial-chamber-jeopardized-the-gbagbo-trial-at-the-international-criminal-court/.

Glasius, M., *The International Criminal Court: A Global Civil Society Achievement* (Routledge, 2006).

Glassborrow, K., 'ICC Investigative Strategy Under Fire' (Institute for War and Peace Reporting, 27 October 2008).

Gong-Gershowitz, J., 'Forced Marriage: A "New" Crime against Humanity?' (2009) 8(1) *Northwestern Journal of International Human Rights* 53.

Goshko, J., 'U.N. Chief Fires Top Officials of Rwanda War Crimes Tribunal' (*Washington Post*, 27 February 1997).

de Gouges, O., *Declaration of the Rights of Woman and of the Female Citizen* (1791).

Graditzky, T., 'War Crimes Issues Before the Rome Diplomatic Conference on the Establishment of an International Criminal Court' in O. Bekou and R. Cryer (eds), *The International Criminal Court* (Ashgate, 2004) 199.

Green, J. et al., 'Affecting the Rules for the Prosecution of Rape and Other Gender-Based Violence Before the International Criminal Tribunal for the Former Yugoslavia: A Feminist Proposal and Critique' (1994) 5(2) *Hastings Women's Law Journal* 171.

Grewal, K., 'Rape in Conflict, Rape in Peace: Questioning the Revolutionary Potential of International Criminal Justice for Women's Human Rights' (2010) 33 *Australian Feminist Law Journal* 57.

Grey, R. and L. Chappell, 'Simone Gbagbo & the International Criminal Court: The Unsettling Spectre of the Female War Criminal' on *Int Law Grrls* (26 November 2012): www.intlawgrrls.com/2012/11/simone-gbagbo-international-criminal.html.

'"Gender Just Judging" in International Criminal Courts: New Directions for Research' in S. Harris-Rimmer and K. Ogg (eds), *Research Handbook on The Future of Feminist Engagement with International Law* (Edward Elgar, forthcoming).

Grey, R. and L. Shepherd, '"Stop Rape Now?" Masculinity, Responsibility, and Conflict-Related Sexual Violence' (2013) 16(1) *Men and Masculinities* 115.

Grey, R., 'Conflicting Interpretations of "Sexual Violence" in the International Criminal Court' (2014) 29(81) *Australian Feminist Studies* 273.

'The ICC's First "Forced Pregnancy" Case in Historical Perspective' (2017) 15(5) *Journal of International Criminal Justice* 905.

'Interpreting International Crimes from a "Female Perspective": Opportunities and Challenges for the International Criminal Court' (2017) 17(2) *International Criminal Law Review* 325.

'Forced Marriage: A World of Challenges for International Criminal Law' (University of Oslo, 6 June 2018).

Grey, R. and S. Wharton, 'Lifting the Curtain: Opening a Preliminary Examination at the International Criminal Court' (2018) 16(3) *Journal of International Criminal Justice* 593.

Grover, L., *Interpreting Crimes in the Rome Statute of the International Criminal Court* (Cambridge University Press, 2014).

Hall, C., 'The Fifth Session of the UN Preparatory Committee on the Establishment of an International Criminal Court' (1998) 92(2) *American Journal of International Law* 331.

Hallward-Driemeier, M. and T. Hasan, 'Empowering Women: Legal Rights and Economic Opportunities in Africa' (Agence Française de Développement and World Bank, 2013).

Harbour, G., 'International Concern Regarding Conflict-Related Sexual Violence in the Lead-up to the ICTY's Establishment' in S. Brammertz and M. Jarvis (eds), *Prosecuting Conflict-related Sexual Violence at the ICTY* (Oxford University Press, 2016) 19.

Hayes, N., 'Sisyphus Wept: Prosecuting Sexual Violence at the International Criminal Court' in W. Schabas, Y. McDermott and N. Hayes (eds), *The Ashgate Research Companion to International Criminal Law* (Ashgate, 2013) 7.

'La Lutte Continue: Investigating and Prosecuting Sexual Violence at the ICC' in C. Stahn (ed.), *The Law and Practice of the International Criminal Court* (Oxford University Press, 2015) 801.

'The Bemba Trial Judgment: A Memorable Day for the Prosecution of Sexual Violence by the ICC' on *PhD Studies in Human Rights* (21 March 2016): http://humanrightsdoctorate.blogspot.com/2016/03/hayes-bemba-trial-judgement-memorable.html.

von Hebel, H. and D. Robinson, 'Crimes within the Jurisdiction of the Court' in R.S. Lee (ed.), *The International Criminal Court: The Making of the Rome Statute* (Kluwer Law International, 1999) 79.

Heger, H., *The Men with the Pink Triangle* (Merlin-Verlag, 1972).

Heinze, A., 'Some Reflections on the Bemba Appeals Chamber Judgment' on *Opinio Juris* (18 June 2018): http://opiniojuris.org/2018/06/18/some-reflections-on-the-bemba-appeals-chamber-judgment/.

Heller, K., 'Stick to Hit the Accused With': The Legal Recharacterization of Facts under Regulation 55' in C. Stahn (ed.), *The Law and Practice of the International Criminal Court* (Oxford University Press, 2015) 981.

Henry, N., 'Silence as Collective Memory: Sexual Violence and the Tokyo Trial' in Y. Tanaka, T. McCormack and G. Simpson (eds), *Beyond Victor's Justice? The Tokyo War Crimes Trial Revisited* (Brill/Nijhoff, 2010) 263.

'The Fixation on Wartime Rape: Feminist Critique and International Criminal Law' (2014) 23(1) *Social & Legal Studies* 93.

Ho, J. and B. Simmons, 'Can the International Criminal Court Deter Atrocity?' (2016) 70(3) *International Organization* 443.

Hochschild, A., *King Leopold's Ghost* (Houghton Mifflin, 1999).

Hodgson, N., 'Gender Justice or Gendered Justice? Female Defendants in International Criminal' (2017) 25(3) *Feminist Legal Studies* 337.

hooks, b., *Ain't I a Woman?: Black Women and Feminism* (South End Press, 1981).

Human Rights Watch, 'Stolen Children: Abduction and Recruitment in Northern Uganda' (March 2003).

'Abducted and Abused: Renewed Conflict in Northern Uganda' (July 2003).

'World Report 2004' (2004).

'The Prosecution of Sexual Violence in the Congo War' (March 2005).

'Seeking Justice: The Prosecution of Sexual Violence in the Congo War' (March 2005).

'Ballots to Bullets: Organized Political Violence and Kenya's Crisis of Governance' (March 2008).

'DR Congo: Suspected War Criminal Wanted' (29 August 2008).

'"You Will Be Punished": Attacks on Civilians in Eastern Congo' (December 2009).

'Unfinished Business: Closing Gaps in the Selection of ICC Cases' (September 2011).

'World Report 2012: Events of 2011' (2012).

'World Report 2013: Events of 2012' (2013).

'"This Old Man Can Feed Us, You Will Marry Him" Child and Forced Marriage in South Sudan' (2013).

'World Report 2014: Events of 2013' (2014).

ICC, 'Pre-Trial Practice Manual' (September 2015).

'The Prosecutor v. Joseph Kony and Vincent Otti (ICC-PIDS-CIS-UGA-001-006/18_Eng)' (April 2018): www.icc-cpi.int/CaseInformationSheets/KonyEtAlEng.pdf.

'Press Release: Al Hassan Ag Abdoul Aziz Ag Mohamed Ag Mahmoud Makes First Appearance before the ICC' (4 April 2018).

'Statement of the President of the Court in Relation to the Case of Mr Jean-Pierre Bemba Gombo' (14 June 2018).

'ICC Trial Chamber VI to Deliberate on the Case against Bosco Ntaganda' (30 August 2018).

ICC OTP, 'The Office of the Prosecutor of the International Criminal Court Opens Its First Investigation' (23 June 2004).

'The Prosecutor of the ICC Opens Investigation in Darfur' (6 June 2005).

'Report on the Activities Performed during the First Three Years (June 2003–June 2006)' (12 September 2006).

'Prosecutor Opens Investigation in the Central African Republic' (22 May 2007).

'ICC Prosecutor to Open an Investigation in Libya' (2 March 2011).

'Statement of the International Criminal Court Prosecutor, Luis Moreno-Ocampo, on Decision by Pre-Trial Chamber I to Issue Three Warrants of Arrest for Muammar Gaddafi, Saif Al-Islam Gaddafi and Abdulla [Sic] Al-Senussi' (28 June 2011).

'Situation in Mali Article 53(1) Report' (16 January 2013).

'ICC Prosecutor Opens Investigation into War Crimes in Mali: "The Legal Requirements Have Been Met. We Will Investigate"' (16 January 2013).

'Strategic Plan June 2012–2015' (11 October 2013).

'Draft Policy Paper on Sexual and Gender Based Crimes' (February 2014).

'Policy Paper on Sexual and Gender-Based Crimes' (June 2014).

'Statement of the Prosecutor of the International Criminal Court, Fatou Bensouda, on Germain Katanga's Notice of Discontinuance of His Appeal against His Judgment of Conviction' (25 June 2014).

'Statement of the Prosecutor of the International Criminal Court, Fatou Bensouda, on Opening a Second Investigation in the Central African Republic' (24 September 2014).

'Statement of the Prosecutor of the International Criminal Court, Fatou Bensouda, on the Withdrawal of Charges against Mr. Uhuru Muigai Kenyatta' (5 December 2014).

'Strategic Plan 2016–2018' (16 November 2015).

'Report on Preliminary Examination Activities 2016' (14 November 2016).

'Statement of ICC Prosecutor, Fatou Bensouda, on International Day for the Elimination of Violence against Women' (25 November 2017).

'Report on Preliminary Examination Activities 2017' (4 December 2017).

'Twenty-Sixth Report of the Prosecutor of the International Criminal Court to the UN Security Council Pursuant to UNSCR 1593 (2005)' (17 December 2017).

'Statement of ICC Prosecutor, Fatou Bensouda, on the Recent Judgment of the ICC Appeals Chamber Acquitting Mr Jean-Pierre Bemba Gombo' (13 June 2018).

'Twenty-Seventh Report of the Prosecutor of the International Criminal Court to the United Nations Security Council Pursuant to UNSCR 1593 (2005)' (20 June 2018).

'ICC: Promise of Justice or Threat of Tyranny?' (The Interim: Canada's Life and Family Newspaper, 12 August 1998).

ICTR OTP, 'Best Practices Manual for the Investigation and Prosecution of Sexual Violence Crimes in Post-Conflict Regions: Lessons Learned from the Office of the Prosecutor for the International Criminal Tribunal for Rwanda' (30 January 2014).

ICTY, 'Sexual Violence: In Numbers' (undated): www.icty.org/en/features/crimes-sexual-violence/in-numbers.

Inder, B., 'A Critique of the Katanga Judgment' (at the Global Summit to End Sexual Violence in Conflict, London, 11 June 2014): www.iccwomen.org/documents/Global-Summit-Speech.pdf.

International Crisis Group, 'Kenya in Crisis: Africa Report No. 137' (21 February 2008).

International Law Commission, 'Draft Statute for an International Criminal Court with Commentaries ('1994 Draft ICC Statute')' (22 July 1994).

'Draft Code of Crimes against the Peace and Security of Mankind, UN Doc. A/CN.4/L.532 + Corr.1–3' ('1996 Draft Code of Crimes') (17 July 1996).

'International Military Tribunal: Judgment and Sentence, October 1, 1946' (1947) 41 *American Journal of International Law* 172.

Irwin, R., 'Interview with Fatou Bensouda, ICC Deputy Prosecutor' on *International Justice Monitor* (31 July 2009): www.ijmonitor.org/2009/07/interview-with-fatou-bensouda-icc-deputy-prosecutor.

Irving, E., 'And So It Begins… Social Media Evidence In An ICC Arrest Warrant' on *Opinio Juris* (17 August 2017): http://opiniojuris.org/2017/08/17/and-so-it-begins-social-media-evidence-in-an-icc-arrest-warrant/.

'Ivory Coast Court Sentences Wife of Ex-President to 20 Years in Prison' (*The Guardian*, 10 March 2015).

'Ivory Coast's Former First Lady Simone Gbagbo Acquitted of War Crimes' (*The Guardian*, 29 March 2017).

Jain, N., 'Forced Marriage as a Crime against Humanity: Problems of Definition and Prosecution' (2008) 6(5) *Journal of International Criminal Justice* 1013.

Jarvis, M. and E. Martin Saldago, 'Future Challenges to Prosecuting Sexual Violence Under International Law: Insights from ICTY Practice' in A. de Brouwer et al. (eds), *Sexual Violence as an International Crime: Interdisciplinary Approaches* (Intersentia, 2013) 101.

Jarvis, M. and N. Nabti, 'Policies and Institutional Strategies for Successful Sexual Violence Prosecutions' in S. Brammertz and M. Jarvis (eds), *Prosecuting Conflict-related Sexual Violence at the ICTY* (Oxford University Press, 2016) 73.

Jarvis, M., 'Overview: The Challenge of Accountability for Conflict-Related Sexual Violence Crimes' in S. Brammertz and M. Jarvis (eds), *Prosecuting Conflict-related Sexual Violence at the ICTY* (Oxford University Press, 2016) 1.

Jarvis, M. and K. Vigneswaran, 'Challenges to Successful Outcomes in Sexual Violence Cases' in S. Brammertz and M. Jarvis (eds), *Prosecuting Conflict-related Sexual Violence at the ICTY* (Oxford University Press, 2016) 33.

Johnson, K. et al., 'Association of Sexual Violence and Human Rights Violations With Physical and Mental Health in Territories of the Eastern Democratic Republic of the Congo' (2010) 204(5) *Journal of the American Medical Association* 553.

Kambale, P., 'A Story of Missed Opportunitie' in C. De Vos, S. Kendall and C. Stahn (eds), *The Politics and Practice of International Criminal Court Interventions* (Cambridge University Press, 2015) 171.

Kapur, A., 'Complementarity as a Catalyst for Gender Justice in National Prosecutions' in F. Ní Aoláin et al. (eds), *The Oxford Handbook of Gender and Conflict* (Oxford University Press, 2018) 226.

Kapur, R., 'Gender, Sovereignty and the Rise of a Sexual Security Regime in International Law and Postcolonial India' (2013) 14(2) *Melbourne Journal of International Law* 317.

Kendall, S. and S. Nouwen, 'Representational Practices at the International Criminal Court: The Gap between Juridified and Abstract Victimhood' (2013) 24/2013 University of Cambridge Faculty of Law Research Paper.

Kesic, V., 'A Response to Catharine MacKinnon's Article "Turning Rape Into Pornography: Postmodern Genocide"' (1994) 5(2) *Hastings Women's Law Journal* 267.

Kirk MacDonald, G., 'Crimes of Sexual Violence: The Experience of the International Criminal Tribunal' (2010) 39 *Columbia Journal of Transnational Law* 1.

Kirsch, P. and J.T. Holmes, 'The Birth of the International Criminal Court: The 1998 Rome Conference' in O. Bekou and R. Cryer (eds), *The International Criminal Court* (Ashgate Publishing, 2004) 3.

Kotiswaran, P., 'Feminist Approaches to Criminal Law' in M. Dubber and T. Hörnle (eds), *The Oxford Handbook of Criminal Law* (Oxford University Press, 2014) 59.

Krook, M. and F. Mackay (eds), *Gender, Politics and Institutions: Towards a Feminist Institutionalism* (Palgrave Macmillan, 2010).

Kuo, P., 'Prosecuting Crimes of Sexual Violence in an International Tribunal' (2002) 34(3) *Case Western Reserve Journal of International Law* 305.

Kwamboka, E., 'Sigh of Relief for Ocampo Six' (*The Standard*, 11 May 2011).

La Haye, E, 'Article 8(2)(b)(Xxii)' in R.S. Lee (ed.), *The International Criminal Court: Elements of Crimes and Rules of Procedure and Evidence* (Transnational Publishers, 2001) 184.

Lehr-Lehnardt, R, 'One Small Step for Women: Female-Friendly Provisions in the Rome Statute of the International Criminal Court' (2002) 16(2) *Brigham Young University Journal of Public Law* 317.

'Letter Dated 23 March 2011 from the Permanent Representative of Kenya to the United Nations Addressed to the President of the Security Council Request of Kenya for Deferral under Article 16 of the Rome Statute of the International Criminal Court, UN Doc. S/2011/201' (29 March 2011).

Lewis, D., 'Unrecognized Victims: Sexual Violence against Men in Conflict Settings Under International Law' (2009) 27(1) *Wisconsin International Law Journal* 1.

Lifesite, 'About Lifesite' (undated): www.lifesitenews.com/about.

'International Criminal Court Strips Family Protection' (17 December 1999): www.lifesitenews.com/news/international-criminal-court-strips-family-protection.

Littler, J., 'Heritage and "Race"' in P. Howard and B. Graham (eds), *The Ashgate Research Companion to Heritage and Identity* (Ashgate, 2008) 89.

Lixinski, L. and S. Williams, 'The ICC's Al-Mahdi Ruling Protects Cultural Heritage, but Didn't Go Far Enough' on *The Conversation* (18 October 2016): https://theconversation.com/the-iccs-al-mahdi-ruling-protects-cultural-heritage-but-didnt-go-far-enough-67071.

Lorde, A., 'The Master's Tools Will Never Dismantle The Master's House' in C. Moraga and G. Anzaldúa (eds), *This Bridge Called My Back: Writings by Radical Women of Color* (Kitchen Table Press, 1981) 94.

Lowndes, V. and M. Roberts, *Why Institutions Matter: The New Institutionalism in Political Science* (Palgrave Macmillan, 2013).

Luping, D., 'Investigation and Prosecution of Sexual and Gender-Based Crimes Before the International Criminal Court' (2009) 17(2) *American University Journal of Gender, Social Policy and the Law* 433.

Lydon, G., 'Inventions and Reinventions of Sharia in African History and the Recent Experiences of Nigeria, Somalia and Mali' (2018) 40(1) *Ufahamu: A Journal of African Studies* 67.

Mackay, F., M. Kenny and L. Chappell, 'New Institutionalism Through a Gender Lens: Towards a Feminist Institutionalism?' (2010) 31(5) *International Political Science Review* 573.

Mackay, F., 'Nested Newness, Institutional Innovation, and the Gendered Limits of Change' (2014) 10(4) *Politics & Gender* 549.

MacKinnon, C., *Sexual Harassment of Working Women: A Case of Sex Discrimination* (Yale University Press, 1979).

*Feminism Unmodified: Discourses on Life and Law* (Harvard University Press, 1987).

'Women's September 11th: Rethinking the International Law of Conflict' (2006) 47(1) *Harvard International Law Journal* 1.

'Creating International Law: Gender as Leading Edge' (2013) 36(1) *Harvard Journal of Law & Gender* 105.

Maclean, R., 'Ivory Coast President Pardons 800 People Including Ex-First Lady' (*The Guardian*, 7 August 2018).

'Make Way for Justice #4' (Trial International, 2018).

Maliti, T., 'The Ongwen Trial: The Prosecution's Case in Numbers' on *International Justice Monitor* (6 June 2018): www.ijmonitor.org/2018/06/the-ongwen-trial-the-prosecutions-case-in-numbers/.

'Manoba and Cox: There Is a Conspiracy of Silence About Male Victims of Sex Crimes' on *International Justice Monitor* (14 September 2018): www.ijmonitor.org/2018/09/manoba-and-cox-there-is-a-conspiracy-of-silence-about-male-victims-of-sex-crimes/.

Mandal, S., 'The Impossibility of Marital Rape: Contestations Around Marriage, Sex, Violence and the Law in Contemporary India' (2014) 29(1) *Australian Feminist Studies* 255.

Manji, A. and D. Buss (eds), *International Law: Modern Feminist Approaches* (Hart, 2005).

Marcus, M., 'Investigation of Crimes of Sexual and Gender-Based Violence under International Criminal Law' in A. de Brouwer et al. (eds), *Sexual Violence as an International Crime: Interdisciplinary Approaches* (Intersentia, 2013) 211.

Mazurana, D. and S. McKay, 'Child Soldiers: What about the Girls?' (2001) 57(5) *Bulletin of the Atomic Scientists* 30.

McCarthy, C., *Reparation and Victim Support in the International Criminal Court* (Cambridge University Press, 2012).

McLeod, L. et al., 'Gendering Processes of Institutional Design: Activists at the Negotiating Table' (2014) 16(2) *International Feminist Journal of Politics* 54.

Meger, S., 'Rape of the Congo: Understanding Sexual Violence in the Conflict in the Democratic Republic of Congo' (2010) 28(2) *Journal of Contemporary African Studies* 119.

Menon, N., *Seeing Like a Feminist* (Zubaan/Penguin Books, 2012).

Mertus, J., 'Shouting from the Bottom of the Well' 6(1) *International Feminist Journal of Politics* 110.

Mibenge, C., *Sex and International Tribunals: The Erasure of Gender from the War Narrative* (University of Pennsylvania Press, 2013).

Mischkowski, G. and G. Mlinarevic, '*The Trouble with Rape Trials: Views of Witnesses, Prosecutors and Judges on Prosecuting Sexualised Violence during the War in the Former Yogoslavia [sic]*' (Medica Mondiale, 2009).

Mohanty, C., 'Under Western Eyes: Feminist Scholarship and Colonial Discourses' (1984) 12(3) *Boundary 2* 333.

Morgan, J. and R. Graycar, *The Hidden Gender of Law* (Federation Press, 2002).

Natale, K. 'I Could Feel My Soul Flying Away From My Body: A Study on Gender-Based Violence During Democratic Kampuchea in Battambang and Svay Rieng Provinces' (Cambodian Defenders Project, November 2011).

Ngozi Adichie, C., *We Should All Be Feminists* (Vintage, 2014).

Ní Aoláin, F., D. Haynes and N. Cahn, 'International and Local Criminal Accountability for Gendered Violence' in F Ní Aoláin, D. Haynes and N Cahn (eds), *On The Frontlines: Gender, War and the Post-Conflict Process* (Oxford University Press, 2011) 153.

Ní Aoláin, F. et al., 'Introduction' in F. Ní Aoláin et al. (eds), *The Oxford Handbook of Gender and Conflict* (Oxford University Press, 2017) xxxv.

Niarchos, C., 'Women, War, and Rape: Challenges Facing the International Tribunal for the Former Yugoslavia' (1995) 17(4) *Human Rights Quarterly* 629.

Nickson, R. and J. Braithwaite, 'Deeper, Broader, Longer Transitional Justice' (2014) 11(4) *European Journal of Criminology* 445.

Nouwen, S. and W. Werner, 'Doing Justice to the Political: The International Criminal Court in Uganda and Sudan' (2010) 21(4) *European Journal of International Law* 941, 251.

Nowrojee, B., '*Shattered Lives: Sexual Violence During the Rwandan Genocide and Its Aftermath*' (Human Rights Watch/FIDH, 1996).

'"*Your Justice Is Too Slow" Will the ICTR Fail Rwanda's Rape Victims?*' (UN Research Institute for Social Development, 2005).

Nyambura, Z., 'In Kenya, Politics Split on Ethnic Divide' (DW, 26 October 2017): www.dw.com/en/in-kenya-politics-split-on-ethnic-divide/a-37442394?.

O'Donohue, J., R. Grey and L. Krasny, 'Evidence of Sexual Violence against Men and Boys Rejected in the Ongwen Case' on *Human Rights in International Justice* (10 April 2018): https://hrij.amnesty.nl/evidence-sexual-violence-men-boys-rejected-ongwen/.

*Official Records: United Nations Diplomatic Conference of Plenipotentiaries on the Establishment of an International Criminal Court, Rome, 15 June–17 July 1998, Vol. II ('Rome Conference Official Records, Vol II').*

Oosterveld, V., 'Gender and the Charles Taylor Case at the Special Court for Sierra Leone' (7–33) 19(1) *William & Mary Journal of Women and the Law* 2012.

'The Making of a Gender-Sensitive International Criminal Court' (1999) 1(1) *International Law Forum du Droit International* 38.

'The Elements of Genocide' in R.S. Lee (ed.), *The International Criminal Court: Elements of Crimes and Rules of Procedure and Evidence* (Transnational Publishers, 2001) 41.

'The Definition of Gender in the Rome Statute of the International Criminal Court: A Step Forward or Back for International Criminal Justice?' (2005) 18 *Harvard Human Rights Journal* 55.

'Gender-Sensitive Justice and the International Criminal Tribunal for Rwanda: Lessons Learned for the International Criminal Court' (2005) 12(1) *New England Journal of International and Comparative Law* 119.

'Prosecuting Gender-Based Persecution as an International Crime' in A. de Brouwer et al. (eds), *Sexual Violence as an International Crime: Interdisciplinary Approaches* (Intersentia, 2013) 57.

'Evaluating the Special Court for Sierra Leone's Gender Jurisprudence' in C. Jalloh (ed.), *The Sierra Leone Special Court and its Legacy: the impact for Africa and International Criminal Law* (Cambridge University Press, 2014) 234.

'Sexual Violence Directed against Men and Boys in Armed Conflict or Mass Atrocity' (2014) 10 *Journal of International Law and International Relations* 107.

Oosterveld, V. and P.V. Sellers, 'Issues of Sexual and Gender-Based Violence at the ECCC' in S. Meisenberg and I. Stegmiller (eds), *The Extraordinary Chambers in the Courts of Cambodia: Assessing Their Contribution to International Criminal Law* (Springer, 2016) 321.

Oosterveld, V., 'The ICC Policy Paper on Sexual and Gender-Based Crimes: A Crucial Step for International Criminal Law' (2018) 24(3) *William & Mary Journal of Women and the Law* 443.

'Forced Marriage during Conflict and Mass Atrocity' in F. Ní Aoláin et al. (eds), *The Oxford Handbook of Gender and Conflict* (Oxford University Press, 2018) 241.

'Constructive Ambiguity and the Meaning of "Gender" for the International Criminal Court" 16(4) *International Feminist Journal of Politics* 563.

O'Smith, K., 'Prosecutor v. Lubanga: How the International Criminal Court Failed the Women and Girls of the Congo' (2013) 54(2) *Howard Law Journal* 467.

Ostrom, E., 'Institutional Rational Choice' in P. Sabatier (ed.), *Theories of the Policy Process* (Westview Press, 1999) 21.

Otto, D., 'Feminist Approaches to International Law' in A. Orford and F. Hoffmann (eds), *The Oxford Handbook of the Theory of International Law* (Oxford University Press, 2016) 489.

Palmer, E. and S. Williams, 'A "Shift in Attitude"? Institutional Change and Sexual and Gender-Based Crimes at the Extraordinary Chambers in the Courts of Cambodia' (2017) 19(1) *International Feminist Journal of Politics* 22.

Pena, M. and G. Carayon, 'Is the ICC Making the Most of Victim Participation' (2013) 7(3) *International Journal of Transitional Justice* 518.

Pierson, P., 'The Limits of Design: Explaining Institutional Origins and Design' (2000) 13(4) *Governance* 475.

Plesch, D., S. SáCouto and C. Lasco, 'The Relevance of the United Nations War Crimes Commission to the Prosecution of Sexual and Gender-Based Crimes Today' (2014) 25(1) *Criminal Law Forum* 349.

Powderly, J. and N. Hayes, 'The Bemba Appeal: A Fragmented Appeals Chamber Destablises the Law and Practice of the ICC' on *PhD Studies in Human Rights* (26 June 2018): http://humanrightsdoctorate.blogspot.com/2018/06/the-bemba-appeal-fragmented-appeals.html.

'Proceedings of the Preparatory Commission at Its First, Second and Third Sessions (16–26 February, 26 July-13 August and 29 November-17 December 1999): Annex III: Elements of Crimes, UN Doc. PCNICC/1999/L.5/Rev.1/Add.2' (22 December 1999).

'Proceedings of the Preparatory Commission at Its First Session (16–26 February 1999): Annex III, PCNICC/1999/L.3/Rev.1' (2 March 1999).

'Proposal by the Holy See, UN Doc A/AC.249/1998/DP.13' (1 April 1998).

'Proposal Submitted by Bahrain, Iraq, Kuwait, Lebanon, the Libyan Arab Jamahiriya, Oman, Qatar, Saudi Arabia, the Sudan, the Syrian Arab Republic and United Arab Emirates Concerning the Elements of Crimes against Humanity, PCNICC/1999/WGEC/DP.39' (3 December 1999).

Ramji-Nogales, J., 'Designing Bespoke Transitional Justice: A Pluralist Process Approach' (2010) 32(1) *Michigan Journal of International Law* 1.

Refugee Law Project, 'Comments on the ICC Draft Policy Paper on Sexual and Gender Based Crimes' (23 February 2014).

'Report of the Detailed Findings of the Commission of Inquiry on Human Rights in the Democratic People's Republic of Korea, UN Doc. A/HRC/25/CRP.1' (7 February 2014).

'Report of the High Commissioner under Human Rights Council Resolution S-15/1, UN Doc. A/HRC/17/45' (7 June 2011).

'Report of the International Commission of Inquiry on Darfur to the United Nations Secretary-General Pursuant to Security Council Resolution 1564 (2004) of 18 September 2004, UN Doc S/2005/60' (1 February 2005).

'Report of the International Commission of Inquiry on Libya, UN Doc. A/HRC/19/68' (2 March 2012).

'Report of the Mission to Rwanda on the Issues of Violence against Women in Situations of Armed Conflict, E/CN.4/1998/54/Add.1' (4 February 1998).

'Report of the Office of Internal Oversight Services on the Audit and Investigation of the International Criminal Tribunal for Rwanda, A/51/789' (6 February 1997).

'Report of the Preparatory Commission for the International Criminal Court: Addendum Part II Finalized Draft Text of the Elements of Crimes, PCNICC/2000/1/Add.2 ('Draft ICC Elements of Crimes')' (2 November 2000).

'Report of the Preparatory Committee on the Establishment of an International Criminal Court: Addendum 1 (Draft Statute of the International Criminal Court), UN Doc. A/CONF.183/2/Add.' (14 April 1998).

'Report of the Preparatory Committee on the Establishment of an International Criminal Court: Addendum 1, UN Doc. A/CONF.183/2/Add.1 ('1998 Draft ICC Statute')' (14 April 1998).

'Report of the Preparatory Committee on the Establishment of an International Criminal Court: Volume I, UN Doc. A/51/22' (13 September 1996).

'Report of the Secretary-General on the Situation in Mali, UN Doc. S/2012/894' (28 November 2012).

'Report on the Mission to the Democratic People's Republic of Korea, the Republic of Korea and Japan on the Issue of Military Sexual Slavery in Wartime, UN Doc. E/CN.4/1996/53/Add.1' (4 January 1996).

'Report on the Situation of Human Rights in Rwanda Submitted by Mr. René Degni-Ségui, Special Rapporteur of the Commission on Human Rights, under Paragraph 20 of Resolution S-3/1 of 25 May 1994, UN Doc. E/CN.4/1996/68' (29 January 1996).

'Report on the Situation of Human Rights in the Territory of the Former Yugoslavia Submitted by Mr. Tadeusz Mazowiecki, Special Rapporteur of the Commission on Human Rights, Pursuant to Commission Resolution 1992/S-1/1 of 14 August 1992, UN Doc. E/CN.4/1993/50' (10 February 1993).

Réseau des Femmes pour un Développement Associatif, Réseau des Femmes pour la Défense des Droits et la Paix, International Alert, 'Women's Bodies as a Battleground: Sexual Violence against Women and Girls During the War in the Democratic Republic of Congo South Kivu (1996–2003)' (2005).

'Resolution of the Assembly of States Parties on the Proposed Programme Budget for 2018, ICC-ASP/16/Res.1' (14 December 2017).

Rich, A. et al., 'Compulsory Heterosexuality and Lesbian Experiences' in *Powers of Desire: The Politics of Sexuality* (Virago, 1983) 177.

Rigney, S., '"The Words Don't Fit You": Recharacterisation of the Charges, Trial Fairness, and Katanga' (2014) 15(2) *Melbourne Journal of International Law* 515.

Ringin, A., 'Women and Girls Must Not Be Excluded from Reparation in the Al Mahdi Case' on *Human Rights in International Justice* (2 October 2017): https://hrij.amnesty.nl/gender-justice-reparation-al-mahdi/.

Robinson, D., 'Defining "Crimes against Humanity" at the Rome Conference' (1999) 93(1) *American Journal of International Law* 43.

Ross, T., 'A Woman's Fury Holds Lifetimes of Wisdom' (at the TED Conference, April 2018): www.ted.com/talks/tracee_ellis_ross_a_woman_s_fury_holds_lifetimes_of_wisdom.

Ruff-O'Herne, J., 'Fifty Years of Silence: Cry of the Raped' in H. Durham and T. Gurd (eds), *Listening to the Silences: Women and War* (Martinus Nijhoff, 2005) 3.

Ruse, A., 'Catholic, Muslim Nations Unite against "Enforced Pregnancy" and "Gender Justice"' on *C-Fam* (10 June 1998): https://c-fam.org/friday_fax/catholic-muslim-nations-unite-against-enforced-pregnancy-and-gender-justice/.

'Feminists Refuse to Define Their "Gender Agenda" for the International Criminal Court' on *C-Fam* (26 June 1998): https://c-fam.org/feminists-refuse-to-define-their-gender-agenda-for-the-international-criminal-court/.

'Protection for Families Dropped From New International Criminal Court' on *C-Fam* (17 December 1999): https://c-fam.org/friday_fax/protection-for-families-dropped-from-new-international-criminal-court/.

SáCouto, S. and K. Cleary, 'The Importance of Effective Investigation of Sexual Violence and Gender Based Crimes at the International Criminal Court' (2009) 17(2) *American University Journal of Gender, Social Policy & the Law* 337.

SáCouto, S., 'Victim Participation at the International Criminal Court and the Extraordinary Chambers in the Courts of Cambodia: A Feminist Project' 18(2) *Michigan Journal of Gender and Law* 297.

'The Impact of the Appeals Chamber Decision in Bemba: Impunity for Sexual and Gender-Based Crimes?' on *International Justice Monitor* (22 June 2018): www.ijmonitor.org/2018/06/the-impact-of-the-appeals-chamber-decision-in-bemba-impunity-for-sexual-and-gender-based-crime.

Sadat, L., 'Fiddling While Rome Burns? The Appeals Chamber's Curious Decision in Prosecutor v. Jean-Pierre Bemba Gombo' on *EJIL Talk!* (12 June 2018): www.ejiltalk.org/fiddling-while-rome-burns-the-appeals-chambers-curious-decision-in-prosecutor-v-jean-pierre-bemba-gombo/.

Sadat, L. and J. Jolley, 'Seven Canons of ICC Treaty Interpretation' (Washington University in St. Louis Legal Studies Research Paper 13-11-06, 15 November 2013).

Sajor, I., 'Challenging International Law: The Quest for Justice of the Former 'Comfort Women' in S. Pickering and C. Lambert (eds), *Global Issues: Women and Justice* (Sydney Institute for Criminology, 2004) 288.

Scheffer, D., *All The Missing Souls: A Personal History of the War Crimes Tribunals* (Princeton University Press, 2012).

Schiff, B., *Building the International Criminal Court* (Cambridge University Press, 2008).

Schneider, E.., 'Feminism and the False Dichotomy of Victimization and Agency' (1993) 38 *New York Law School Law Review* 387.

Seifert, R., 'War and Rape: A Preliminary Analysis' in A. Stiglmayer (ed.), *Mass Rape: The War against Women in Bosnia-Herzegovina* (University of Nebraska Press, 1994) 54.

Sellers, P.V., 'The Context of Sexual Violence: Sexual Violence as Violations of International Humanitarian Law' in G. Kirk MacDonald and O. Swaak-Goldman (eds), *Substantive and Procedural Aspects of International Criminal Law* (Kluwer Law International, 2000) vol 1, 263.

'Wartime Female Slavery: Enslavement?' (2011) 44 *Cornell International Law Journal* 118.

'Genocide Gendered: The Srebrenica Cases' (at the 9th Annual International Humanitarian Law Dialogs, Chautauqua Institution, 31 August 2015).

'Ntaganda: Re-Alignment of a Paradigm' (International Institute of Humanitarian Law, 2018): www.iihl.org/wp-content/uploads/2018/03/Ntaganda-V.pdf.

'Gender Strategy Is Not Luxury for International Courts' (2009) 17(2) *American University Journal of Gender, Social Policy & the Law* 301.

'Senior Lord's Resistance Army Commander Surrenders to US Troops' (8 January 2015).

Shahabuddeen, M., 'Does the Principle of Legality Stand in the Way of Progressive Development of Law?' (2004) 2(4) *Journal of International Criminal Justice* 1007.

Shepherd, L., 'Sex or Gender? Bodies in Global Politics and Why Gender Matter' in L. Shepherd (ed.), *Gender matters in global politics: a feminist introduction to international relations* (Routledge, 2nd edn, 2015) 24.

Simpson, G., *Law, War & Crime: War Crimes Trials and the Reinvention of International Law* (Polity Press, 2007).

Sivakumaran, S., 'Sexual Violence against Men in Armed Conflict' (2007) 18(2) *European Journal of International Law* 253.

'Lost in Translation: UN Responses to Sexual Violence against Men and Boys in Situations of Armed Conflict' (2010) 92(877) *International Review of the Red Cross* 259.

Sloane, R., 'The Expressive Capacity of International Punishment' (2007) 43(1) *Stanford Journal of International Law* 39–94.

Smith, L, 'Heritage, Gender and Identity' in B. Graham and P. Howard (eds), *The Ashgate Research Companion to Heritage and Identity* (Ashgate, 2008) 159.

Smith-van Lin, L., 'Victims' Participation at the International Criminal Court: Benefit or Burden' in W. Schabas, Y. McDermott and N. Hayes (eds), *The Ashgate Research Companion to International Criminal Law* (Ashgate, 2013) 181.

Solnit, R., *The Mother of All Questions: Future Feminisms* (Granta, 2017).

Song, S., 'From Punishment to Prevention Reflections on the Future of International Criminal Justice' (at the 'Justice for All' Conference, University of New South Wales, 14 February 2012).

Spees, P., 'Women's Advocacy in the Creation of the International Criminal Court: Changing the Landscapes of Justice and Power' (2003) 28(4) *Signs* 1233.

Steains, C., 'Gender Issues' in R.S. Lee (ed.), *The International Criminal Court: The Making of the Rome Statute* (Kluwer Law International, 1999) 357.

'Summary of the Proceedings of the Preparatory Committee during the Period 25 March-12 April 1996, UN Doc. A/AC.249/1' (7 May 1996).

Tanaka, Y., *Hidden Horrors: Japanese War Crimes in World War II* (Rowman & Littlefield, 2nd edn, 2018).

Tenove, C., 'International Justice for Victims? Assessing the International Criminal Court from Victims' Perspectives in Kenya and Uganda' (Africa Initiative Research Papers, September 2013).

Thurston, A. and A. Lebovich, 'A Handbook on Mali's 2012–2013 Crisis' (Institute for the Study of Islamic Thought in Africa, 2 September 2013).

Trahan, J., 'Bemba Acquittal Rests on Erroneous Application of Appellate Review Standard' on *Opinio Juris* (25 June 2018): http://opiniojuris.org/2018/06/25/bemba-acquittal-rests-on-erroneous-application-of-appellate-review-standard.

*Trial of the Major War Criminals Before the International Military Tribunal, Nuremberg, 14 November 1945–1 October 1946* ('Blue Series') (William S. Hein & Co., 1951).

UN Audiovisual Library of International Law, 'Statute of the Special Court for Sierra Leone: Procedural History' (undated): http://legal.un.org/avl/pdf/ha/scsl/scsl_e.pdf.

UN Organization Mission in the Democratic Republic of the Congo, 'Special Report on the Events in Ituri, January 2002–December 2003, UN DOC. s/2004/573' (16 July 2004).

UN Security Council, 'Press Release: Security Council Resolution Seeking Deferral of Kenyan Leaders' Trial Fails to Win Adoption' (15 November 2013): www.un.org/press/en/2013/sc11176.doc.htm.

UNESCO, 'Overview' in UNESCO, *Gender Equality: Heritage and Creativity* (UNESCO, 2014) 32.

UNESCO, 'Director-General Praises the People of Timbuktu for the Reconstruction of the City's Mausoleums' (19 July 2015).

Urban-Walker, M., 'Gender and Violence in Focus: A Background for Gender Justice in Reparations' in R. Rubio Marín (ed.), *The Gender of Reparations: Unsettling Sexual Hierarchies while Redressing Human Rights Violations* (Cambridge University Press, 2009) 1.

Van den Wyngaert, C., 'Victims before International Criminal Courts: Some Views and Concerns of an ICC Trial Judge' (2011) 44(1) *Case Western Review of International Law* 475.

Van Schaak, B., '*Engendering Genocide: The Akayesu Case Before the International Criminal Tribunal for Rwanda*' (Santa Clara Law School Digital Commons, 2008).

'Crimen Sine Lege: Judicial Lawmaking at the Intersection of Law and Morals' (2008) 87 *Georgetown Law Journal* 119.

'Obstacles on the Road to Gender Justice: The International Criminal Tribunal for Rwanda as Object Lesson' (2009) 17(2) *American University Journal of Gender, Social Policy & the Law* 362.

Van Woudenberg, A., '*Democratic Republic of Congo: On the Brink*' (*Human Rights Watch*, 1 August 2006).

Vandello, J. et al., 'Precarious Manhood' (2008) 95(6) *Journal of Personality and Social Psychology* 1325.

Vasisliev, S., 'Victim Participation Revisited: What the ICC Is Learning About Itself' in C. Stahn (ed.), *The Law and Practice of the International Criminal Court* (Oxford University Press, 2015) 1133.

Verini, J., '*The Prosecutor and the President*' (*New York Times*, 22 June 2016).

Verrall, S., 'The Picture of Sexual Violence in the Former Yugoslavia Conflicts as Reflected in ICTY Judgments' in S. Brammertz and M. Jarvis (eds), *Prosecuting Conflict-Related Sexual Violence at the ICTY* (Oxford University Press, 2016) 299.

Vigneswaran, K., 'Charging and Outcomes in ICTY Cases Involving Sexual Violence' in *Prosecuting Conflict-Related Sexual Violence at the ICTY* (Oxford University Press, 2016) 429.

Whiting, A., 'Appeals Judges Turn the ICC on Its Head with Bemba Decision' on *Just Security* (14 June 2018): www.justsecurity.org/57760/appeals-judges-turn-icc-head-bemba-decision/.

Wollstonecraft, M., *A Vindication of the Rights of Woman* (1792).

Women's Caucus for Gender Justice, 'About the Women's Caucus' (undated): www.iccwomen.org/wigjdraft1/Archives/oldWCGJ/aboutcaucus.html.

'Recommendations and Commentary For December 1997 PrepCom On The Establishment of An International Criminal Court' (1 December 1997): www.iccnow.org/documents/5PrepComRecommWomensC.pdf.

'Justice for Women: The Crime of Forced Pregnancy' (26 June 1998) (on file).

'Gender Justice and the ICC' (at the United Nations Diplomatic Conference of Plenipotentiaries on the Establishment of an International Criminal Court, Rome, 15 July 1998) (on file).

'ICC: Urgent Action Alert' (1 December 1999): www.jca.apc.org/fem/news/women2000/128.html.

'Recommendations and Commentary for the Elements of Crimes and Rules of Procedure and Evidence, Submitted to the Preparatory Commission for the International Criminal Court' (12 June 2000): www.iccnow.org/documents/WCGJElementsofCrimeMay2000.pdf.

'Clarification of Term "Gender"' (undated): www.iccwomen.org/wigjdraft1/Archives/oldWCGJ/resources/gender.html.

Women's Initiatives for Gender Justice, 'Public Redacted Version of Confidential Letter to ICC Prosecutor' (16 August 2006): www.iccwomen.org/news/docs/Prosecutor_Letter_August_2006_Redacted.pdf.

'Making a Statement' (2008).

'Gender Report Card 2010' (2010).

'Legal Eye on the ICC' (July 2011).

'Reflection: Gender Issues and Child Soldiers - the Case of Prosecutor v Thomas Lubanga Dyilo' (25 August 2011).

'Legal Eye on the ICC' (May 2012).

'Gender Report Card 2013' (March 2014).

'Appeals Withdrawn by Prosecution and Defence: The Prosecutor vs. Germain Katanga' (26 June 2014).

'Statement on the Surrender of Al Hassan to the ICC and Charges of Forced Marriage' (3 April 2018).

'Developing a Working Definition of "an Act of Sexual Violence"' (18 September 2018): https://4genderjustice.org/developing-a-working-definition-of-an-act-of-sexual-violence/.

Women's International War Crimes Tribunal For the Trial of Japan's Military Sexual Slavery, 'Judgment, The Prosecutors and the Peoples of the Asia-Pacific Region v. Hirohito Emperor Showa et al.' (4 December 2001).

Yates, P., *The Reckoning: The Battle for the International Criminal Court* (Skylight Pictures, 2009).

# INDEX

## Books in the Series

143 *Prosecuting Sexual and Gender-Based Crimes at the International Criminal Court: Practice, Progress and Potential*
Rosemary Grey

142 *Narratives of Hunger in International Law: Feeding the World in Times of Climate Change*
Anne Saab

141 *Sovereignty in China: A Genealogy of a Concept Since 1840*
Adele Carrai

140 *Narratives of Hunger: Climate-Ready Seeds and International Law*
Anne Saab

139 *Victim Reparation under the Ius Post Bellum: An Historical and Normative Perspective*
Shavana Musa

138 *The Analogy between States and International Organizations*
Fernando Lusa Bordin

137 *The Process of International Legal Reproduction: Inequality, Historiography, Resistance*
Rose Parfitt

136 *State Responsibility for Breaches of Investment Contracts*
Jean Ho

135 *Coalitions of the Willing and International Law: The Interplay between Formality and Informality*
Alejandro Rodiles

134 *Self-Determination in Disputed Colonial Territories*
Jamie Trinidad

133 *International Law as a Belief System*
Jean d'Aspremont

132 *Legal Consequences of Peremptory Norms in International Law*
Daniel Costelloe

131 *Third-Party Countermeasures in International Law*
Martin Dawidowicz

130 *Justification and Excuse in International Law: Concept and Theory of General Defences*
Federica Paddeu

129 *Exclusion from Public Space: A Comparative Constitutional Analysis*
Daniel Moeckli

128 *Provisional Measures before International Courts and Tribunals*
Cameron A. Miles

127 *Humanity at Sea: Maritime Migration and the Foundations of International Law*
Itamar Mann

126 *Beyond Human Rights: The Legal Status of the Individual in International Law*
Anne Peters

125 *The Doctrine of Odious Debt in International Law: A Restatement*
Jeff King

124 *Static and Evolutive Treaty Interpretation: A Functional Reconstruction*
Christian Djeffal

123 *Civil Liability in Europe for Terrorism-Related Risk*
Lucas Bergkamp, Michael Faure, Monika Hinteregger and Niels Philipsen

122 *Proportionality and Deference in Investor-State Arbitration: Balancing Investment Protection and Regulatory Autonomy*
Caroline Henckels

121 *International Law and Governance of Natural Resources in Conflict and Post-Conflict Situations*
Daniëlla Dam-de Jong

120 *Proof of Causation in Tort Law*
Sandy Steel

119 *The Formation and Identification of Rules of Customary International Law in International Investment Law*
Patrick Dumberry

118 *Religious Hatred and International Law: The Prohibition of Incitement to Violence or Discrimination*
Jeroen Temperman

117 *Taking Economic, Social and Cultural Rights Seriously in International Criminal Law*
Evelyne Schmid

116 *Climate Change Litigation: Regulatory Pathways to Cleaner Energy*
Jacqueline Peel and Hari M. Osofsky

115 *Mestizo International Law: A Global Intellectual History 1842–1933*
Arnulf Becker Lorca

114 *Sugar and the Making of International Trade Law*
Michael Fakhri

113 *Strategically Created Treaty Conflicts and the Politics of International Law*
Surabhi Ranganathan

112 *Investment Treaty Arbitration As Public International Law: Procedural Aspects and Implications*
Eric De Brabandere

111 *The New Entrants Problem in International Fisheries Law*
Andrew Serdy

110 *Substantive Protection under Investment Treaties: A Legal and Economic Analysis*
Jonathan Bonnitcha

109 *Popular Governance of Post-Conflict Reconstruction: The Role of International Law*
Matthew Saul

108 *Evolution of International Environmental Regimes: The Case of Climate Change*
Simone Schiele

107 *Judges, Law and War: The Judicial Development of International Humanitarian Law*
Shane Darcy

106 *Religious Offence and Human Rights: The Implications of Defamation of Religions*
Lorenz Langer

105 *Forum Shopping in International Adjudication: The Role of Preliminary Objections*
Luiz Eduardo Salles

104 *Domestic Politics and International Human Rights Tribunals: The Problem of Compliance*
Courtney Hillebrecht

103 *International Law and the Arctic*
Michael Byers

102 *Cooperation in the Law of Transboundary Water Resources*
Christina Leb

101 *Underwater Cultural Heritage and International Law*
Sarah Dromgoole

100 *State Responsibility: The General Part*
James Crawford

99 *The Origins of International Investment Law: Empire, Environment and the Safeguarding of Capital*
Kate Miles

98 *The Crime of Aggression under the Rome Statute of the International Criminal Court*
Carrie McDougall

97 *'Crimes against Peace' and International Law*
Kirsten Sellars

96 *Non-Legality in International Law: Unruly Law*
Fleur Johns

95 *Armed Conflict and Displacement: The Protection of Refugees and Displaced Persons under International Humanitarian Law*
Mélanie Jacques

94 *Foreign Investment and the Environment in International Law*
Jorge E. Viñuales

93 *The Human Rights Treaty Obligations of Peacekeepers*
Kjetil Mujezinović Larsen

92 *Cyber Warfare and the Laws of War*
Heather Harrison Dinniss

91 *The Right to Reparation in International Law for Victims of Armed Conflict*
Christine Evans

90 *Global Public Interest in International Investment Law*
Andreas Kulick

89 *State Immunity in International Law*
Xiaodong Yang

88 *Reparations and Victim Support in the International Criminal Court*
Conor McCarthy

87 *Reducing Genocide to Law: Definition, Meaning, and the Ultimate Crime*
Payam Akhavan

86 *Decolonising International Law: Development, Economic Growth and the Politics of Universality*
Sundhya Pahuja

85 *Complicity and the Law of State Responsibility*
Helmut Philipp Aust

84 *State Control over Private Military and Security Companies in Armed Conflict*
Hannah Tonkin

83 *'Fair and Equitable Treatment' in International Investment Law*
Roland Kläger

82 *The UN and Human Rights: Who Guards the Guardians?*
Guglielmo Verdirame

81 *Sovereign Defaults before International Courts and Tribunals*
Michael Waibel

80 *Making the Law of the Sea: A Study in the Development of International Law*
James Harrison

79 *Science and the Precautionary Principle in International Courts and Tribunals: Expert Evidence, Burden of Proof and Finality*
Caroline E. Foster

78 *Transition from Illegal Regimes in International Law*
Yaël Ronen

77 *Access to Asylum: International Refugee Law and the Globalisation of Migration Control*
Thomas Gammeltoft-Hansen

76 *Trading Fish, Saving Fish: The Interaction between Regimes in International Law*
Margaret A. Young

75 *The Individual in the International Legal System: Continuity and Change in International Law*
Kate Parlett

74 *'Armed Attack' and Article 51 of the UN Charter: Evolutions in Customary Law and Practice*
Tom Ruys

73 *Theatre of the Rule of Law: Transnational Legal Intervention in Theory and Practice*
Stephen Humphreys

72 *Science and Risk Regulation in International Law*
Jacqueline Peel

71 *The Participation of States in International Organisations: The Role of Human Rights and Democracy*
Alison Duxbury

70 *Legal Personality in International Law*
Roland Portmann

69 *Vicarious Liability in Tort: A Comparative Perspective*
Paula Giliker

68 *The Public International Law Theory of Hans Kelsen: Believing in Universal Law*
Jochen von Bernstorff

67 *Legitimacy and Legality in International Law: An Interactional Account*
Jutta Brunnée and Stephen J. Toope

66 *The Concept of Non-International Armed Conflict in International Humanitarian Law*
Anthony Cullen

65 *The Principle of Legality in International and Comparative Criminal Law*
Kenneth S. Gallant

64 *The Challenge of Child Labour in International Law*
Franziska Humbert

63 *Shipping Interdiction and the Law of the Sea*
Douglas Guilfoyle

62 *International Courts and Environmental Protection*
Tim Stephens

61 *Legal Principles in WTO Disputes*
Andrew D. Mitchell

60 *War Crimes in Internal Armed Conflicts*
Eve La Haye

59 *Humanitarian Occupation*
Gregory H. Fox

58 *The International Law of Environmental Impact Assessment: Process, Substance and Integration*
Neil Craik

57 *The Law and Practice of International Territorial Administration: Versailles to Iraq and Beyond*
Carsten Stahn

56 *United Nations Sanctions and the Rule of Law*
Jeremy Matam Farrall

55 *National Law in WTO Law: Effectiveness and Good Governance in the World Trading System*
Sharif Bhuiyan

54 *Cultural Products and the World Trade Organization*
Tania Voon

53 *The Threat of Force in International Law*
Nikolas Stürchler

52 *Indigenous Rights and United Nations Standards: Self-Determination, Culture and Land*
Alexandra Xanthaki

51 *International Refugee Law and Socio-Economic Rights: Refuge from Deprivation*
Michelle Foster

50 *The Protection of Cultural Property in Armed Conflict*
Roger O'Keefe

49 *Interpretation and Revision of International Boundary Decisions*
Kaiyan Homi Kaikobad

48 *Multinationals and Corporate Social Responsibility: Limitations and Opportunities in International Law*
Jennifer A. Zerk

47 *Judiciaries within Europe: A Comparative Review*
John Bell

46 *Law in Times of Crisis: Emergency Powers in Theory and Practice*
Oren Gross and Fionnuala Ní Aoláin

45 *Vessel-Source Marine Pollution: The Law and Politics of International Regulation*
Alan Khee-Jin Tan

44 *Enforcing Obligations Erga Omnes in International Law*
Christian J. Tams

43 *Non-Governmental Organisations in International Law*
Anna-Karin Lindblom

42 *Democracy, Minorities and International Law*
Steven Wheatley

41 *Prosecuting International Crimes: Selectivity and the International Criminal Law Regime*
Robert Cryer

40 *Compensation for Personal Injury in English, German and Italian Law: A Comparative Outline*
Basil Markesinis, Michael Coester, Guido Alpa and Augustus Ullstein

39 *Dispute Settlement in the UN Convention on the Law of the Sea*
Natalie Klein

38 *The International Protection of Internally Displaced Persons*
Catherine Phuong

37 *Imperialism, Sovereignty and the Making of International Law*
Antony Anghie

35 *Necessity, Proportionality and the Use of Force by States*
Judith Gardam

18 *International Commercial Arbitration and African States: Practice, Participation and Institutional Development*
Amazu A. Asouzu

17 *The Enforceability of Promises in European Contract Law*
James Gordley

16 *International Law in Antiquity*
David J. Bederman

15 *Money Laundering: A New International Law Enforcement Model*
Guy Stessens

14 *Good Faith in European Contract Law*
Reinhard Zimmermann and Simon Whittaker

13 *On Civil Procedure*
J. A. Jolowicz

12 *Trusts: A Comparative Study*
Maurizio Lupoi and Simon Dix

11 *The Right to Property in Commonwealth Constitutions*
Tom Allen

10 *International Organizations before National Courts*
August Reinisch

9 *The Changing International Law of High Seas Fisheries*
Francisco Orrego Vicuña

8 *Trade and the Environment: A Comparative Study of EC and US Law*
Damien Geradin

7 *Unjust Enrichment: A Study of Private Law and Public Values*
Hanoch Dagan

6 *Religious Liberty and International Law in Europe*
Malcolm D. Evans

5 *Ethics and Authority in International Law*
Alfred P. Rubin

4 *Sovereignty over Natural Resources: Balancing Rights and Duties*
Nico Schrijver

3 *The Polar Regions and the Development of International Law*
Donald R. Rothwell

2 *Fragmentation and the International Relations of Micro-States: Self-Determination and Statehood*
Jorri C. Duursma

1 *Principles of the Institutional Law of International Organizations*
C. F. Amerasinghe

Printed in the USA
CPSIA information can be obtained
at www.ICGtesting.com
LVHW020717130924
790781LV00009B/42